Cambridge Commemorated

SOUVENT ME SOUVIENT

The motto of the Beaufort family over the doorway to
the Master's Lodge, Christ's College

Cambridge Commemorated

AN ANTHOLOGY OF UNIVERSITY LIFE

COLLECTED AND EDITED
BY
LAURENCE & HELEN FOWLER

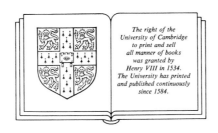

The right of the
University of Cambridge
to print and sell
all manner of books
was granted by
Henry VIII in 1534.
The University has printed
and published continuously
since 1584.

CAMBRIDGE UNIVERSITY PRESS

CAMBRIDGE

LONDON   NEW YORK   NEW ROCHELLE

MELBOURNE   SYDNEY

Published by the Press Syndicate of the University of Cambridge
The Pitt Building, Trumpington Street, Cambridge CB2 1RP
32 East 57th Street, New York, NY 10022, USA
296 Beaconsfield Parade, Middle Park, Melbourne 3206, Australia

First published 1984

Printed in Great Britain by the University Press, Cambridge

Library of Congress catalogue card number: 83–14254

British Library cataloguing in publication data
Cambridge commemorated.
1. University of Cambridge – History
I. Fowler, Laurence   II. Fowler, Helen
378.426′59   LF 108
ISBN 0 521 25743 3

The title of this book is taken from a recital of readings and music in March 1980 given by Dame Peggy Ashcroft, Dr. George Rylands and Mr. Martin Best for the benefit of Newnham College. The recital inspired the late Sir Geoffrey de Freitas to want to make it possible for a more substantial anthology to be compiled. His generous contribution towards the editorial costs has ensured that the royalties will go to the Newnham College Development Fund. *Et ille commemoretur.*

Contents

Illustrations

Sources

The editors and publisher gratefully acknowledge the permission of the following to reproduce their illustrations in this book: the Syndics of the Cambridge University Library: 1, 10, 11, 20, 23, 24, 28, 31, 35, 36 and the illustrations on pages 182, 220, 225, and 247; the Provost and Scholars of King's College: 21; Dr. George Rylands: 39 and 40; the Principal and Fellows of Newnham College: 27; the Principal and Fellows of Girton College: 32; Mr. E. K. Frankl: 3, 43, 44 and 46; the City Surveyor, the Guildhall, Cambridge: 41; the Fitzwilliam Museum: 19; the Cambridgeshire Collection, Cambridgeshire Libraries: 7, 8, 12, 13, 14, 16, 18, 22, 25, 26, 33 and 34; the Department of Physics, University of Cambridge: 30; Mr. George Kennethson: 45; Mr. John Stewart: 47; Chatto and Windus Limited, London: 38; Mrs. Sophie Gurney: the woodcuts by Gwen Raverat on pages 3, 17, 28, 36 and 83; Mr. David Gentleman: 9a and 9b; *Country Life*, 37; Mr. A. C. Barrington-Brown: 42; Mr. Martin Walters: frontispiece and 5; Mr. F. A. Reeve: 29. Illustrations 2, 4, 6 and 15 are reproduced from R. Willis and J. W. Clark, *The Architectural History of the University of Cambridge*, 1886.

Foreword by H.R.H. The Duke of Edinburgh, Chancellor of the University of Cambridge

Universities become known to the public for their institutions and for the works of their scholars and teachers; but unless some internal drama or scandal reaches the newspapers, what goes on behind the scenes, as it were, appears to go unrecorded. Yet, as this delightful collection makes plain, a wealth of material has accumulated over the ages about every mundane detail of life in the rather unusual community of Cambridge University. Helen and Laurence Fowler have dipped into this fund and produced an anthology which will be certain to give pleasure, instruction and amusement to many generations of Cambridge people.

By a fortunate coincidence the printing and publishing of this book by the Press of Cambridge University appropriately commemorates the granting of its Royal Charter 450 years ago.

1983   PHILIP

Preface

The editors hope that their pleasure in composing this anthology will be shared by those who read it. Ours has been the delight of exploration, of reading and sifting through material relevant to our object: which was to reflect the life and work of the University through the ages, to give an insight into the Cambridge mind and its particular flavour. In trying to achieve this we set ourselves certain limits, restricting ourselves mostly to published works and when quoting Cambridge-nurtured writers using only relevant material. No doubt we shall disappoint people who have their favourite stories and passages; we apologise to them; in the end it becomes a personal choice.

We have had the benefit of much help and advice and are grateful to Mrs. Jean Floud and Dr. George Rylands, in different ways the originators of this book, to Dr. Sutherland particularly and to other fellows of Newnham, to Mrs. Cecil Robertson who did much valuable spade work for us, to the archivists and staff of the Rare Books Room and the 'Cam' collection in the University Library, and to many other friends who have made suggestions and comments.

Like all writers of books about Cambridge we also owe a debt to its historians and antiquarians led, we think, by Charles Henry Cooper, whose *Annals of Cambridge* is a supreme source book (used, we regret to have discovered, without acknowledgement by many writers). J. E. B. Mayor, himself an invaluable source, dedicated a book to Cooper in 1856, with the following words: 'your labours, the labours of a townsman working in the spirit, with the materials, and upon the lives, of gownsmen of old – of Fuller, and Strype, and Baker – appear to me a happy sign of . . . the much needed union of Learning and Working'. To these names we could add Dyer, Heywood, Willis, Clark, Mullinger, Venn and Winstanley and all the others whose material we have used.

The reader may wonder why the book refuses, as if wilfully, to follow a strict date order. The reason is that the themes and patterns which emerged did not permit a strait-jacket treatment: each age has its contradictions, its traditionalists, its rebels and pioneers. The book almost demanded to be constructed like a patchwork, with recurring patterns in an overall design.

LAURENCE AND HELEN FOWLER

Note on the texts

Most old texts have been left in their original spelling, though we have occasionally altered this where it might not be understood. The idiosyncratic shorthand used by many diarists and letter-writers has been left, to stamp their prose; but printing conventions have invariably been modernised: no 'ye' or long 's' to create an archaic effect. Like John Worthington, in his edition of Joseph Mede's *Works*, we have tried to avoid making 'an astonishing clatter with many words of a strange sound and of an unknown sense to some in the Auditory'.

The beginnings: dreaming chroniclers and sundry facts

In the past, several pro-Cambridge historians claimed that the University's history went way back before the thirteenth century.

Camboritum or . . . Cambericus, was a Roman colony and mentioned in the best Copies among the 28 cities of Britain and (that) the Roman Colonies had their Schools of Learning, wherein the several Professors of Arts and Sciences did instruct both the Roman and British youth.

(James Brome, *Travels over England,*
Scotland and Wales, 1694)

Cambridge was the ancient Camboritum of the Romans. If our *dreaming chroniclers* may be believed, the university was first founded by Cantaber, a Spaniard bred at Athens, 375 years before the commencement of the Christian era.

(Joseph Wilson, *Memorabilia Cantabrigiae,*
1803)

The poet John Lydgate, a Suffolk man, but not so far as is known a Cambridge one, agreed with them:

> Divers Schollers by diligent labour
> Made their resorte of great affection
> To that stooddie great plentie there cam downe
> To gather fruites of wysdome and science
> And sondrie flowers of sugred eloquence.
> And as it is put eke in memorie,
> Howe Julius Cesar entring this region
> On Casybellan after his victorye
> Tooke with him clarkes of famouse renowne
> Fro Cambridg and ledd theim to rome towne,
> Thus by processe remembred here to forne
> Cambridg was founded longe or Chryst was borne.

'Dreaming chroniclers' *apart, little is really known about the origins of the University. We know that in 1209 there was an influx of students from Oxford because of disturbances there with the townspeople, but whether they came to Cambridge by chance or whether they chose it because there was already some teaching going on, is not known. Some returned to Oxford, some went to Northampton and elsewhere. We do know that in 1225 Cambridge had a Chancellor and that in 1233 Pope Gregory II granted the University certain legal privileges. In 1229 King Henry III offered asylum to scholars from Paris and some of them came to Cambridge. If new at the beginning of the century, the University grew speedily, for by 1303 the University was publishing its own Statutes:*

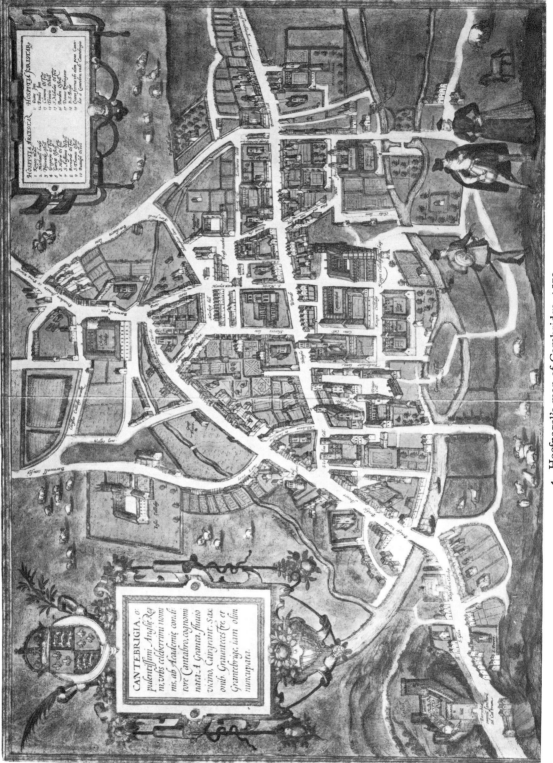

1. Hocfnagel's map of Cambridge, 1572

By the authority of the whole University of Cambridge, both regents and non-regents, it is ordained that in making statutes, which concern the common advantages of the aforesaid University, that alone shall be accounted a statute which shall have been enacted, by decree, with the consent of the greater and more discreet part of the aforesaid regents, and with the consent of the non-regents . . . given at Cambridge in the church of the blessed Mary, on the 15th of the Kalends of April A.D. 1303.

(*Early University and College Statutes, in the English Language*, collected by James Heywood, 1855)

In the year 1318 Pope John XXII confirmed that Cambridge was indeed a 'studium generale', that is, that it had acquired the standing of a university. In fact, King Edward II had himself sought such confirmation as he had sent his 'King's Scholars' to Cambridge and in 1317 had founded King's Hall for

Cows by the river (woodcut by Gwen Raverat)

scholars from his household. But in spite of continuing royal support, the University had to fight on at least two fronts for its survival, one of which was against excessive ecclesiastical control. There was also the fight against the townspeople of Cambridge who not unnaturally were unwilling to take a subservient role; the rumblings of this lasted well into the eighteenth if not the twentieth century.

In 1231 Henry III stepped in on over-charging:

The king to the mayor and bailiffs of Cambridge, greeting.

You are aware that a multitude of scholars from divers parts, as well from this side the sea as from overseas, meets at our town of Cambridge for study, which we hold a very gratifying and desirable thing, since no small benefit and glory accrues therefrom to our whole realm; and you, among whom these students personally live, ought especially to be pleased and delighted at it.

We have heard, however, that in letting your houses you make such heavy charges to the scholars living among you, that unless you conduct yourselves with more restraint and moderation towards them in this matter, they will be driven by your exactions to leave your town and, abandoning their studies, leave our country, which we by no means desire.

And therefore we command and firmly enjoin you that in letting the aforesaid houses you follow University custom and allow the said houses to be valued by two masters and two good and lawful men of your town assigned for the purpose, and allow them to be let according to their valuation, so conducting yourselves in this matter that no complaint may reach us through your doing otherwise, which may compel us to interfere.

(*English Historical Documents*, vol. IV, ed. A. R. Myers, 1969)

Thomas Fuller, at Queens' in the early 1620s, Cambridge's first great historian, puts forward another reason for trouble:

A crew of pretenders to scholarship (as long as there are diamonds there will be counterfeit) did much mischief at this time (1231) in the University. These lived under no discipline, having no tutor (saving him who teacheth all mischief) and when they went to act any villany, then they would be *scholars*, to sin with the more secrecy and less suspicion. When cited to answer for their wickedness, in the Chancellor's court, then they would be *no-scholars*, and exempt themselves from his jurisdiction ... Civil students suffered much *by* and more *for* these incorrigible rake-hells, especially from such mouths who are excellent at an uncharitable synecdoche, to call all after a part, and to condemn the whole University for a handful of hang-byes, such as were never matriculated members therein.

(*The History of the University from the Conquest to 1634*, 1840)

In 1270, King Henry III, accompanied by his son Prince Edward, later Edward I, visited Cambridge. The Prince undertook to be a mediator and the following agreement was made:

1. That there should be annually chosen ... of any county of England five

scholars of the more discreet there abiding, and three of Scotland, and two of Wales, and three of Ireland; and also ten burgesses (namely seven of the city and three of the suburbs) all of whom ... should severally take their corporal oaths to keep the peace and tranquillity of the University, and to cause the same to be kept by others.

2. That if any wicked or rebellious scholars or laymen should be found ... the scholars should as much as became their clerical orders assist the burgesses in apprehending them.

(George Dyer, *Privileges of the University*, 1824)

In 1275 proctors were appointed:

At a congregation of all Masters ... and Bachelors of the University, in St. Mary's Church, on the feast of St. Withburga, John Hooke, the chancellor, being present, a statute for the peace and tranquillity of the University was made by unanimous assent to the following effect: –

1. That the rectors [i.e. proctors] might suspend the transgressors of the statutes relating to their offices.

2. That the fixing the times and mode of reading and disputing, of celebrating exequies, of incepting, and of observing feasts, should pertain to the rectors.

3. That the rectors might punish those who transgressed, as also bedells disobeying their commands.

(Charles Henry Cooper, *Annals of Cambridge*, 1842. Hereafter 'Cooper')

In 1371 there was bad behaviour:

About this time certain scholars or clerks were indicted for breaking open doors, entering the townsmen's houses, and beating the owners, &c. in the night-time. It was also presented that when the mayor sent his bailiffs with others towards Trumpington Ford to capture certain malefactors and thieves, a little before midnight came John Rector of the church of Elsing, Robert Ravendale, and Richard Crowland, armed, together with the aforesaid scholars, who assaulted, beat, and ill-treated the bailiffs, so that they scarcely escaped with their lives. Walter Fridaye of Multon, Robert Ravendale, Richard Crowland, and others, were also indicted for having, at midnight, at Trumpington Ford, feloniously stolen four-score yards of netting, with the fowl therein being ...

And in 1381 retribution:

On Saturday the 15th of June, the bailiffs and commonalty, by the advice and consent of the mayor, met together and went to Shingay Hospital, and to the house of Thomas Haselden, where they joined certain traitors of the county, with whom they returned to Cambridge, and then went with the mayor to the Tolbooth, where they elected one James de Grancestre for their commander ...

About ten o'clock at night they reassembled in the Tolbooth, where they made a proclamation that every man should go and destroy the house of William Wigmore bedell of the University, and that if any man should meet or find him he should cut off his head. They thereupon proceeded to Wigmore's house,

which they destroyed, and carried away his goods and chattels. They afterwards
went to Corpus Christi college, where they broke open the apartments of the
schollars, and took away or destroyed all the books, charters, writings and effects
belonging to the society. At St. Mary's church they broke open the common
chest of the University, and burnt and destroyed the bulls, charters, and muni-
ments therein, and at the Friary of the Carmelites they seized another chest
belonging to the University.

On the following day, the burgesses and commonalty assembled in great routs,
and perambulated out of the town to the traitors of the county, whom they
brought to the town, and then the mayor, bailiffs, burgesses, and commonalty
. . . compelled the masters and scholars, by menace of death, to deliver up their
charters and letters patent, and publicly burnt the statutes, ordinances, and
other evidences of the University in the market-place, amidst the rejoicing of
the populace. An old woman named Margaret Starre, gathering the ashes of the
burning documents, scattered them to the winds and exclaimed, 'Away with the
learning of the clerks, away with it!' . . . on Monday the 17th of June, proclamation was made by virtue of the King's letters, prohibiting any persons upon pain
of death to make congregations, conventicles, or affrays. The mayor, bailiffs,
burgesses, and commonalty, in defiance of this proclamation, gathered to them
a great number of rebels in the meadow called Grenecroft (Midsummer
Common), and thence with one accord they repaired to the Priory of Barnwell,
where, in a warlike manner, they broke down the Prior's close, cut and carried
away a great number of trees, 'and there made other great affrays'.

On news of these disturbances being brought to Henry le Spencer, the warlike
Bishop of Norwich, at his manor-house of Burley, near Oakham, in Rutland-
shire, he marched thence with not above eight lances and a few archers to
Cambridge where he attacked the rebels, killed some, and imprisoned others.

(Cooper)

As a direct result of this uprising, King Richard II granted a Charter to the
University which contained the following provisions:

That the Chancellor of the University and his successors and their viceregents,
wholly and solely, for ever, in the town of Cambridge, and the suburbs of the
same, should have the custody of the assize of bread, wine, and beer, and the
punishment of the same with the fines, amerciaments, and profits thence arising.

That they should also have the custody of the assize and assay, and the oversight of measures and weights in the town and suburbs . . .

That the Chancellor and his successors, or their viceregents, should for ever,
wholly and solely, have power to inquire and take conusance of forestallers and
regrators, and of putrid, corrupt, and unfit flesh and fish, in the town and
suburbs . . .

That the Chancellor and his successors, and their viceregents, should have and
exercise the assize, assay, oversight, correction, punishment, chastisement,
power, and government aforesaid, as fully and freely and in the same manner
and places forever as the mayor, bailiffs, aldermen, and burgesses of the town,
theretofore had and exercised the same.

That the mayor, bailiffs, aldermen, or men of the town, should not interfere in the premises, but should therein humbly aid and attend the Chancellor, his viceregent, or commissary.

(Dyer, Privileges)

In 1418 the mayor of Cambridge petitioned the King's council. One of the complaints was:

That on the vigil of St. James the Apostle, many scholars . . . armed in a warlike manner, caused great terror to the mayor, by lying in wait to kill him and his officers, if they on that night had issued out of their houses; and that when they perceived they could not effect their malicious purpose, they affixed on the mayor's gate a certain schedule, to his great scandal, and so that the mayor and burgesses dared not to preserve the peace.

The 'schedule' was, in part, as follows:

> Looke out here Maire with thie pilled pate,
> And see wich a scrowe, is set on thie gate;
> Warning thee of hard happes,
> For and it lukke thou shalt have swappes;
> Therefor I rede keepe the at home;
> For thou shalt abey for that is done;
> Or els kest on a coate of mayle;
> Truste well thereto withouten faile. etc.

The answer of the University was:

As to the schedule, &c. they denied knowing anything thereof. That at the time in question, Fyshwicke was at York, and Markaunte in London, and that it was notorious that at that time, many laymen were every night in the streets armed for jetting, whilst all the scholars were in their houses.

(Cooper)

The most spirited account of town and gown comes from the 'Reeve's Tale' in the 'Canterbury Tales':

> At Trumpyngtoun, nat fer from Cantebrigge,
> Ther gooth a brook, and over that a brigge,
> Upon the whiche brook ther stant a melle;
> And this is verray sooth that I yow telle:
> A millere was ther dwellynge many a day.
> As any pecok he was proud and gay . . .
> Greet sokene hath this millere, out of doute,
> With whete and malt of al the land aboute;
> And nameliche ther was a greet collegge
> Men clepen the Soler Halle at Cantebregge;
> Ther was hir whete and eek hir malt ygrounde.
> And on a day it happed, in a stounde,
> Sik lay the maunciple on a maladye;
> Men wenden wisly that he sholde dye.

[7]

For which this millere stal bothe mele and corn
An hundred tyme moore than biforn;
For therbiforn he stal but curteisly,
But now he was a theef outrageously,
For which the wardeyn chidde and made fare.
But thereof sette the millere nat a tare;
He craketh boost, and swoor it was nat so.
    Thanne were ther yonge povre scolers two,
That dwelten in this halle, of which I seye.
Testif they were, and lusty for to pleye,
And, oonly for hire myrthe and revelrye,
Upon the wardeyn bisily they crye
To yeve hem leve but a litel stounde,
To goon to mille and seen hir corn ygrounde;
And hardily they dorste leye hir nekke
The millere sholde not stele hem half a pekke
Of corn by sleighte, ne by force hem reve;
And at the laste the wardeyn yaf hem leve.
John highte that oon, and Aleyn highte that oother;
Of o toun were they born, that highte Strother,
Fer in the north, I kan nat telle where . . .

Despite their vigilance, the miller tricks them out of some corn by setting their horse loose on the fen. They chase after it, as it is their warden's palfrey:

    Thise sely clerkes rennen up and doun
With 'Keep! keep! stand! stand! jossa, warderere,
Ga whistle thou, and I shal kepe hym heere!'
But shortly, til that it was verray nyght,
They koude nat, though they dide al hir myght,
Hir capul cacche, he ran alwey so faste,
Til in a dych they caughte hym atte laste.
    Wery and weet, as beest is in the reyn,
Comth sely John, and with him comth Aleyn.
'Allas,' quod John, 'the day that I was born!
Now are we dryve til hethyng and til scorn.
Oure corn is stoln, men wil us fooles calle,
Bathe the wardeyn and oure felawes alle,
And namely the millere, weylaway!'

In the end these 'children', as the miller calls them, have the better of him – and of his wife and daughter.

The University had to fight for its independence from ecclesiastical control, first from the Bishop of Ely, then from 'higher authorities' and it was not until 1430 that Pope Martin V, by what is known as the 'Barnwell Process', gave the University its ecclesiastical independence. Despite these victories, the University remained very much a clerical body: heads of houses and fellows moved easily between livings and bishoprics well into the nineteenth century.

From very early days there were many religious houses in Cambridge. The Priory at Barnwell was founded in 1112 and St. Rhadegund's Nunnery in 1133. There were Dominicans on the site of Emmanuel, Franciscans where Sidney Sussex now is, Augustine Friars on Peas Hill, Carmelites where St. Catharine's is, and White Canons near Peterhouse. Fuller writes in his 'History':

These Friars living in these convents were capable of degrees, and kept their Acts, as other University-men. Yet were they gremials [resident members of the University] and not-gremials, who sometimes would so stand on the tiptoes of their privileges, that they endeavoured to be higher than other students: so that oftentimes they and the scholars could not set their horses in one stable, or rather their books on one shelf.

In the late thirteenth century most members of the University lived in hostels. Fuller, writing in 1630, gives a list, including these:

St. Edward's-Hostel, against Little St. Mary's, where lately a victualling-house, called the Chopping-Knife.

God's-House, taken down by king Henry VI, but not in that sacrilegious sense wherein the Psalmist complains: 'They have taken the houses of God into their possession', . . . for when he took this into King's-College, in lieu thereof he founded another.

God's-House, now parcel of Christ's College.

Jesus'-Hostel . . . and

St. John's-Hostel; for it is a pity to part them which stood close together (as John usually lay in Jesus's bosom) . . . and now both compounded into Peter-House.

St. Nicholas-Hostel, over against Christ's-College, where now a private house, with the public name of the Brazen George. The scholars hereof, as eminent for hard studying, so infamous for their brawlings by night.

Ovings'-Inn, the buildings under which the kennel betwixt Caius and Trinity-College emptieth itself.

Pythagoras's-House, beyond the bridge . . . It now belongeth to Merton-College in Oxford.

St. Thomas's-Hostel, where now the orchard of the Master of Pembroke-Hall, and where the neighbouring Leas retain their name; formerly the *campus martius* of the scholars here exercising themselves, sometimes too violently; lately disused, either because young scholars now have less valour, or more civility.

He continues:

In these Hostels Scholars were more conveniently accommodated than in townsmen's houses, wherein anciently they lived; both because here they were united under one head; and because they were either rent-free, or paid it by agreement to a chief of their own Society . . . but these Hostels decayed by degrees, when endowed Colleges began to appear.

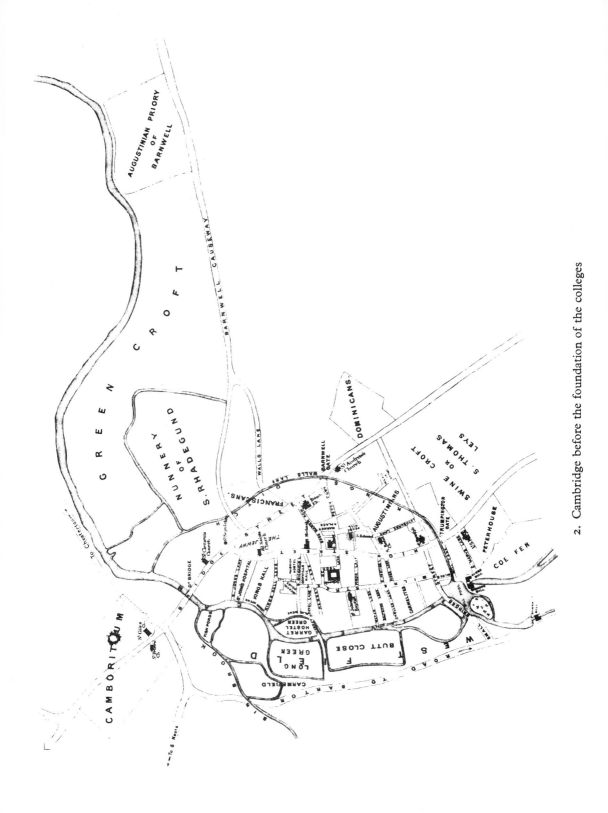

2. Cambridge before the foundation of the colleges

The early part of the fourteenth century saw the establishment in the University of a collegiate system. Between 1284 and 1352 nine colleges were founded and by the end of the sixteenth century there is this account, drawn up for Sir Robert Cecil, the Chancellor:

THE UNIVERSITY is a Society of Studentes in all and every of the liberal Artes and Sciences, incorporated by the name of the Chancellor, Masters and Scolers.

The frame of this little Commonwelthe or Body standeth not upon the union of Families &c. but upon the Union of a feawe Societies, devoted as it were unto the Study of learning and knowledge, for the better service of the Church and Commonwelthe.

Of this sort there are at this day Sixteene, called by the name of Colledges or Halls.

Houses, halls and colleges founded from 1284 to 1596

St. Peter's College (later Peterhouse)	1284
Michaelhouse[a]	1324
University Hall[b]	1326
King's Hall[a]	1337
Clare House or Hall[b]	1338
Pembroke Hall (later Pembroke College)	1347
Gonville Hall[c]	1348
Trinity Hall	1350
Corpus Christi College[d]	1352
Buckingham College[e]	1428
King's College	1441
God's House[f]	1448
Queens' College	1448
St. Catharine's College or Hall	1473
Jesus College	1496
Christ's College	1505
St. John's College	1511
Magdalene College	1542
Trinity College	1546
Emmanuel College	1584
Sidney Sussex College	1596

[a] Refounded as Trinity College
[b] Refounded as Clare College
[c] Refounded as Gonville and Caius College in 1557
[d] For nearly 500 years known as Benet College: 'another working-day name' according to Fuller, *History*.
[e] Refounded as Magdalene College
[f] Refounded as Christ's College

STATUTES

Early Statutes for colleges, originally modelled on those for Merton College, Oxford (1264), reflect the ideals and intentions of their founders for the life of learning to be pursued in them. Their prohibitions tell us much about medieval young men.

Peterhouse (1338)

Every one on his first entrance as fellow, shall upon his admission before the college, make bodily oath that he will steadfastly observe all the following articles. In the first place – that he will conduct himself honorably among the fellows of the house, and also in the University, and that in the faculty to which he may happen to belong he will studiously attend the lectures and disputations held in the schools and in the house, and that he will always appear in the University dressed in the proper robes of a scholar . . . upon his admission he shall swear that within three months from the time of his admission he will possess a surplice for the performance of divine service. Also, that he will bestow upon the community of the said house, within the same prescribed time, a mazer cup and a silver spoon, of such quality as may best beseem him, according to the judgment of the majority of the fellows of the house . . .

We enact and moreover ordain, that the persons to be henceforth admitted into our aforesaid house as perpetual scholars, for the purpose of applying themselves to the study of letters, shall be bound to devote themselves to the study of arts, Aristotle, canon law, or theology; in such wise, however, that the greater part do diligently apply themselves to the study of the liberal arts until, having, in the judgment of the master and of the fellows, or at least of the major and sounder part of them, made laudable progress and being competently instructed in the said knowledge, they shall be in a fitting state to betake themselves to the study of theology; but that two, and not more (at the same time), shall be free to study in canon and civil law, and one in medicine, those, in fact, who may be determined upon by the discretion of the master and scholars, or the majority of them, under the obligation of their oath, as the more suitable and apt for these studies, to whom a dispensation shall be granted by the master, in virtue of this ordinance, as far as shall appear expedient to him, and for such time as his judgment shall fix.

In order that the scholars may exercise themselves in their magistral and scholastic acts, we enact and moreover ordain, that on two days of the week the scholars shall dispute together in the time allotted for reading (*tempore legibili*), as far as the faculties may unanimously accord among themselves, viz. on Wednesdays in logic and physical sciences (*naturalibus*), and on Fridays (when the number of doctors and bachelors of divinity may be sufficiently augmented so to do) in theology, according as shall be determined and ordained (as mentioned above) by the aforesaid deans, unless indeed the scholars be prevented by any legitimate impediment from carrying on their disputations on the said days; and that they shall act in such sort in their disputations, that none shall dispute with impetuosity and clamour, but in a civil and honest manner; that none shall interrupt another while declaiming, either in argument or reply, but listen to

3. Peterhouse: The Hall, thirteenth century

him with diligence; that all contumelious, quarrelsome, and indecorous words, which, as is frequently the case, only generate hatred and discord, shall be interdicted among them. But if the contrary be attempted by any one, he shall be gently reprehended by the aforesaid deans . . .

The master, and all and each of the scholars of our house, shall adopt the clerical dress and tonsure, as becomes the condition of each, and wear it conformably in every respect, as far as they conveniently can, and not allow their beard or their hair to grow contrary to canonical prohibition, nor wear rings upon their fingers for their own vain glory and boasting . . .

We forbid moreover the above mentioned scholars to pass the night out of our aforesaid house, in the town, or to wander about at undue hours, either by night or day, beyond their place of habitation; and should they happen to be walking about, for the sake of exercise, or for any other reasonable cause, more especially after the hour of vespers, let them return at a seasonable time and at the proper hour . . .

If any female of their relations or any other honest female should desire to hold counsel, conversation, or discourse with them, for any honorable and lawful reasons, the interview shall take place in the hall or some other respectable place . . . The scholars vestments, to be cleansed by means of laundresses, shall be carried to them to be cleansed by one of the sworn attendants of the said house whenever it may be necessary, and afterwards be brought back again, when cleansed, by him or some other, unless perchance they may have a male washer. But if the scholars stand in need of having their heads washed or their beards shaved, that the master shall provide a person for that purpose, the porter if possible, or some other servant of the house, who may be both willing and able to perform both offices . . . It is better certainly that all these matters be performed by males, than that by the coming in of women (as has been seen) any thing should by any means happen to the scandal of the whole house.

(Heywood, *Early Statutes*)

Statutes of other colleges follow similar lines, though often with their own particular slant.

Trinity Hall (1352)

A fellow must qualify for a doctorate in law within three years, or sooner if the majority judge him fit to attempt it, and he will receive a prize of 100 shillings if successful. He must then proceed to the doctor's degree without much delay and act as a regent in the university (i.e. lecturing and teaching) for at least one year, and may so continue for a further year if needed by the College.

(Charles Crawley, *Trinity Hall: 1350–1975*, 1976)

King's (1443)

Chapter 18. Of not lingering in the hall . . . when the seniors . . . have had their drink in hall at the hour of curfew, they shall go to their studies or other places, and the juniors shall not be permitted to make any delay, except on the principal feasts, and on greater double feasts, or when the deliberations of the College necessitate, or other important business affecting the College is to be transacted in the hall, or when for the reverence of God, or his Mother or any other saint, a fire in winter is lit in the hall for the fellows. Then after dinner or supper the scholars and fellows shall be allowed to stay in the hall for recreation by singing and other honourable pastimes, and to enjoy soberly poetry, chronicles of kings, the wonders of the world, and other things suitable for the clerical estate . . .

All fellows and scholars are forbidden to wear red and green shoes, or secular ornaments or fancy hoods, either inside or outside the university, or swords or long knives, or any other weapons, offensive or defensive, or girdles and belts adorned with gold and silver, within the said King's College, either inside or outside the university and town of Cambridge, either publicly or secretly, unless they are given special permission by the provost, vice-provost, deans, and bursars. All the scholars and fellows are moreover forbidden to let their hair or beard grow; they must wear the crown and tonsure appropriate to their order, rank, and station, appropriately, honestly, and in due fashion, as they should . . .

Chapter 25. That no scholar or fellow, chaplain or clerk or other officer, may keep dogs, birds hawks, etc. or throw, play or shoot, within or outside the college, to the injury of the same King's College.

Since it is not fitting for the poor, especially those living on alms, to give the children's bread to the dogs to eat . . . we order . . . that no scholar, fellow, chaplain, or clerk, or other servant of King's College shall keep or have dogs, hunting or fishing nets, ferrets, hawks, or falcons, or indulge in hunting or fishing, nor keep in King's College any monkey, bear, fox, stag, hind, doe, or badger, or any other wild animal or strange bird . . . Moreover, all games of dice, hazard, or ball, and all other harmful disorderly, unlawful, and dishonest games are forbidden, especially games which might cause the loss of money, property, or goods of any servant within our King's College, or indeed anywhere within our aforesaid university . . . The fellows and scholars aforesaid are expressly forbidden to throw or shoot stones, balls, wood, earth, or arrows, or anything else, or to play any games . . . within the aforesaid King's College, or its close or garden, whereby the church, hall, houses, or other buildings of the said college should be damaged in their window glass, walls, roofs, coverings, or anywhere else within or without.

(English Historical Documents, ed. Myers)

Many colleges had precise rules about which part of the country their fellows and scholars should come from.

Christ's (1506)

Fellows: We appoint that those are always to be preferred at every election, provided that in all other respects they are equal, who are dependent upon the poorest people for assistance and who are most needy; for which reason, as well as for other motives, we have decreed that those counties whose names follow below shall be preferred to the rest: the Counties of Northumberland, Durham, Westmoreland, Cumberland, York, Richmond, Lancaster, Derby and Nottingham; from which nine counties we desire that there shall always be six Fellow Scholars in the said College; Provided nevertheless that there shall never be more than one from any one of the aforesaid Counties at one time. Richmond, with its neighbourhood ... we wish to be accepted as a separate county from the county of York ...

Scholars: ... from which nine counties we will that there shall always be 23 Pupil Scholars.

(H. Rackham, *Early Statutes of Christ's College*, 1927)

Benefactors and the growth of the 'little Commonwealth' of colleges

I could wish that I had some fine sindon of oratory to enrappe their memoryes; some flowers of commendation to make them a garland; and some boxe of sweet spikenard to perfume theyr names. I will only deale with them as they (in the Acts) did with Dorcas, when she was dead, to move affection: show you the garments and coates which they have made to cloath poore schollars: yet with some fringe and lace of commendation.

(Part of sermon preached in Christ's, July 1623. H. Rackham, *Christ's College in Former Days*, 1939)

Colleges seem immediately to have flourished, thanks to their original endowments which were soon increased by successive benefactions, large and small.

Pembroke (1347)

Mary de Saint Paul daughter to Guido Castillion Earl of Saint Paul in France, third wife to Audomare de Valentia, Earl of Pembroke, maid, wife, and widow all in a day (her husband being unhappily slain at a tilting at her nuptials) sequestered herself on that sad accident from all worldly delights, bequeathed her soul to God, and her estate to pious uses, amongst which this a principal, that she founded in Cambridge, the college of Mary de Valentia, commonly called Pembroke Hall ...

The aforesaid Mary de Valentia founded also Denny Abbey nigh Cambridge, richly endowed, and filled it with nuns, whom she removed from Water-Beach. She enjoined also her fellows of Pembroke Hall, to visit those nuns, and give them ghostly counsel on just occasion; who may be presumed (having not only a fair invitation, but full injunction) that they were not wanting both in their courteous and conscientious addresses unto them.

(Fuller, *History*)

Queens'

Sir Thomas Smith, 1577, by will, gave to this college all his Latin and Greek books, with a great globe of his own making, and a rent charge of 12*l* 7*s* 4*d*

Clare Bridge (woodcut by Gwen Raverat)

payable out of the manor of Overston, in Northamptonshire. The following was to be the disposition of this sum: 4*l* was to be paid for a lecture in Arithmetic; 3*l* for a lecture in Geometry, 4*l* 7*s* 4*d* for two scholarships; directing that the preference in the choice of these scholars should be given to his own relations, or to the scholars of Walden School. The remaining 20*s* was devoted to a yearly commemoration.

(Rudolph Ackermann, History of the
University of Cambridge, 1815)

Trinity Hall

Dr. Hervey (1562) (Sometime Mr. of this college)

To Robert Hervey His Nephew The Angel in Newmarket, on condition that he deliver to Trinity Hall between the 1st Day of May and the last Day of August yearly 3 loads of Charcoal at 13 sacks the Load, every Sack to contain five Bushels at the Least, to be spent nightly in the Comon Parlour, or other Common-place as the Mr. shall think fit, beginning on the Feast of All Saints, at two Bushels pr night 'till they are spent.

(Warren's Book, ed. A. A. W. Dale, 1911)

Caius (1586/7)

Joyce Frankland left money to Gonville and Caius College for scholars and for a fellow to be known as her Chaplain. Dr. Nowell, Dean of St. Paul's, relates the story:

One Mrs. Frankland, late of Herts, widowe, having one only sonne, who youthfully venturing to ride upon an unbroken young horse, was throwne down and slaine. Whereuppon the mother fell into sorrowes uncomfortable . . . And I founde her cryenge, or rather howlinge continually, 'Oh my sonne! my sonne!' And when I could, by no comfortable words stay her from that cry and tearinge of her haire; God, I thinke, put me in minde at the last to say: 'Comfort yourselfe good Mrs. Frankland, and I will tell you how you shall have twenty good sonnes to comfort you in these your sorrowes which you take for this sonne.' To the which words only she gave care, and lookinge up, asked, 'How can that be?' 'And I sayd unto her, You are a widowe, rich and now childlesse, and there be in both universities so many pore towarde youthes that lack exhibition, for whom if you would founde certain fellowships and schollerships, to be bestowed uppon studious younge men, who should be called Mrs. Frankland's schollers, they would be in love towardes you as deare children, and will most hartely pray to God for you duringe your life; and they and their successors after them, being still Mrs. Frankland's schollers, will honour your memory for ever and ever.'

(John Venn, Caius College, 1901)

St. Catharine's (1514)

Lady Elizabeth Barnadiston left money to the College:

to receive and to dwell with in the said Hall or College such a child or scholar, conveniently learned in grammar, as the said Dame Elizabeth during her life shall present . . . which child and scholar and his successors shall be accounted, reckoned and named the butler, or else my Lady Barnadiston's child, and shall always be attendant to minister and serve all things necessary concerning the buttery to Fellows, suggeraunts, and strangers being within the said College. To the which child and his successors for ever the said Master and his successors shall at his first coming assign and appoint an honest chamber . . . and also pay and yield weekly for ever to him and his successors meat and drink to the clear value of six pence a week, and also money once in the year for ever six shillings and eightpence for and towards his linen . . . For the which the said child . . . shall daily for ever say the psalm of Miserere with De Profundis and the collect of Fidelium for the souls above rehearsed.

(Henry Philpott, Documents relating to St. Catharine's College, 1861)

Lady Margaret, Countess of Richmond and Derby, and mother of King Henry VII, founded both Christ's and St. John's Colleges. (She is always known in Cambridge as 'The Lady Margaret'.)

One may probably conjecture, that a main motive, which drew King Henry this year (1506) to Cambridge, was with his presence to grace his mother's foundation of Christ's College, now newly laid . . . in a place where God's House formerly stood, founded by king Henry VI. This king had an intention . . . to advance the Scholars of this foundation to the full number of sixty, though (a great fall) never more than four lived there, for lack of maintenance. Now the lady Margaret . . . (heir to all king Henry's godly intentions) only altered the name from God's House to Christ's College, and made up the number . . .

Once the lady Margaret came to Christ's College, to behold it when partly built; and, looking out of a window, saw the dean call a faulty Scholar to correction; to whom she said, Lente, lente! 'Gently, gently', as accounting it better to mitigate his punishment than to procure his pardon: mercy and justice making the best medley to offenders.*

(Fuller, History)

* This I heard in a Clerum, from Dr. Collings.

It was John Fisher who persuaded the Lady Margaret to found Christ's and who, as her executor, saw that her intention to found St. John's was carried out.

This John, being nowe come to Cambridge, was there committed to the government of *maister* william Melton, a reverend priest and grave Devine; then *maister* of the College called Michael howse . . . he fell to more profitable learnings, and, leaving all his former studie, betooke himself to the high and heavenly philosophie, in which, accordinge to the order of schollers, he kept his disputacion with great laude and commendacion, so that in short space he grew to such profoundnes, that he was easily accounted the flower of all the universitie, and at his dewe time proceeded to the dignitie of Bachelor, and after, Doctor of devinity, which, with no small praise, he achieved in the yere of Christ 1502.

At length his name grewe so famous, that, passinge the bondes of the universitie, it spread over all the Realme, in so much as the noble and vertuous ladie Margaret, Countesse of Richmond and Darbie, mother to the wise and sage prince king Henrie the vii[th], hearinge of his great vertue and learninge, ceased not till she had procured him out of the universitie to her service . . .

(Life of Fisher, ed. Ronald Bayne, 1921)

He was Chancellor in 1501, again in 1504 and elected for life in 1514. He was beheaded in 1535 for 'denying the King's supremacy'.

Henry VIII was indeed now supreme, having repudiated the Pope's authority. He dissolved the monasteries and divided up their estates, all with the consent of Parliament. In 1544 there was even an Act passed for the dissolution of colleges and this caused great consternation in Oxford and Cambridge. Fortunately the University had friends at Court; John Cheke was tutor to the Prince of Wales and Thomas Smith clerk to Queen Katherine Parr. A letter was sent to the Queen and her reply gave cause for hope:

Your letters I have received presented on your behalf by Mr. Doctor Smythe your discreet and learned advocate . . .

I (according to your desires) have attempted my lord the King's Majesty, for the establishment of your livelihood and possessions: in which, notwithstanding his Majesty's property and interest, through the consent of the high court of parliament, his Highness being such a patron to good learning, doth tender you so much, that he will rather advance learning and erect new occasion thereof than to confound those your ancient and godly institutions, so that learning may hereafter justly ascribe her very original whole conservation and sure stay to our Sovereign Lord . . . Scribbled with the hand of her that prayeth to the Lord and immortal God to send you all prosperous success in godly learning and knowledge.

(W. W. Rouse Ball, Cambridge Papers, 1918)

Meanwhile the King had demanded an investigation into the finances of the colleges and Matthew Parker, the Vice-Chancellor, caused a detailed report to be drawn up. He himself presented a summary of it to the King at Hampton Court and wrote an account of what happened:

In the end, the said commissioners resorted up to Hampton Court to present to the King a brief summary written in a fair sheet of vellum . . . describing the revenues, the reprises, the allowances, and number and stipend of every college. Which book the King diligently perused; and in a certain admiration said to certain of his lords which stood by, that he thought he had not in his realm so many persons so honestly maintained in living by so little land and rent.

Not only was disaster averted, but in 1546 the King used the Act to dissolve the two colleges Michael-house and King's Hall and build on their sites and that of Phisick Hostel a new college:

consisting of one master and sixty fellows and scholars, to be called 'TRYNITIE COLLEGE, within the Towne and Universitie of Cambrydge, of Kynge Henry the Eights Fundacion'.

(Cooper)

Once persuaded, Henry VIII was a powerful advocate:

whereas we had a regard only to pull down sin by defacing the monasteries, you have a desire also to overthrow all goodness by subversion of colleges. I tell you, sirs, that I judge no land in England better bestowed than that which is given to our universities, for by their maintenance our realm shall be well governed when we be dead and rotten ...

as was the Duke of Somerset, Lord Protector and Chancellor of the University:

If learning decay, which of wild men maketh civil; of blockish and rash persons, wise and goodly counsellors; and of evil men, good and godly Christians; what shall we look for else but barbarism and tumult? For when the lands of colleges be gone, it shall be hard to say whose staff shall stand next the door.

(Both quoted in William Harrison,
Description of England, 1577)

Matthew Parker, Master of Corpus Christi from 1544 to 1553 (later to be Archbishop of Canterbury) was also a Benefactor, giving his college books and the University a street:

When the Abbeys and Religious Houses were dissolved, and the Books that were contained in the Libraries thereunto belonging, underwent the same fate, being embezzled, and sold away to Tradesmen for little or nothing; then did our *Parker* and some other Lovers of antient Learning procure, both of their Money and their Freinds, what Books so ever they could. He was therefore a mighty Collector of Books, to preserve, as much as could be, the antient Monuments of the learned men of our Nation from perishing, and for that purpose he did employ divers Men proper for such an end, to search all *England* over, and *Wales* (and *Scotland* and *Ireland* too), for Books of all sorts, more modern as well as antient; and to buy them up for his use; giving them Commission and Authority, under his own Hand, for doing the same.

(John Strype, *Life of Archbishop Parker*,
1711)

TRACING THE CAMBRIDGE SCENE

By 1500 there were a dozen colleges, most of which were situated between the High street and the river. In thinking of these early foundations we must not envisage the trim lay-out of the present-day 'Backs' along the Cam, but a belt of commercial quarters, of sheds and warehouses as well as colleges, along narrow lanes leading to hithes at the river-side on the margins of alluvial marshes; their names, Cornhythe, Flaxhythe, Salthythe, tell their own story of the unloading of traffic that had come from King's Lynn. Today, the river flows along a straightened channel through made-up ground converted into college lawns and gardens, but small ditches and trenches still hint at an older state of affairs.

(H. C. Darby, *Medieval Cambridgeshire*, 1977)

Various glorious enterprises of greater or lesser degree were embarked on.

King Henry VI could not attend the laying of the foundation stone of King's College Chapel.

Forasmuch as we have founded first to the worship of God, of our Lady Seint Mary & St. Nicholas, on whose day we were brought first into the world . . . our College of the same . . . We have ordered the first Stoon of our Chappell there to be layd . . . on Michaelmas day next coming . . . At the which we had disposed us to be there in our owne person. Nevertheless for the aier and the Pestilence that hath long regned in our said Universite, we come not there at this time, but send thiddre our Cousin the Marquesse of Suffolk.

(Cooper)

but in his will he left full instructions for the building:

And as touching the dimensions of the church of my said college of our Lady and St. Nicholas at Cambrige, I have devised and apointed that the same church shall containe 288 feete of assise in length, without any yles, and all of the wideness of 40 feete, and the length of the same church from the west end to the altare at the quier doore, shall containe 120 feete, and from the provosts stall unto the greece called Gradus Chori 90 feete, for 36 stalles on either side of the same quire, answering to 70 fellowes and ten priests conducts, which must be *de prima forma*. And from the said stalles unto the est end of the said church 72 feete of assize: also a reredos bearing the roodclofte departing the quier and the body of the church, containing in length 40 feete, and in breadth 14 feete; the walles of the same church to be in height 90 feete, imbattelled, vawted, and chare roffed, sufficiently butteraced, and every butterace fined with finials etc.

Expansion of buildings meant endless negotiation by colleges, with other colleges, townsfolk, hostels and friaries, some amicable, some fractious.

Town Council to King's College, 9 January 1445

Hit is to be remembred that wher hit lyked the Kyng our sovereign lord to send his gracious letters to his Meir and Bailifs of his towne of Cambrigge be wich he desired certen comyn groundes and lanes . . . to the use of his Colege of oure lady and Sent Nicholas in Cambrig' aforeseid for wich comyn groundes and lanes the kyng willed by his seid letters the seid Meir should be recompensed so thei shuld not be hurt; of wich comyn groundes and lanes . . . is specially desired a comyn lane called Pyrion lane.

(R. Willis and J. W. Clark, *Architectural History of the University of Cambridge*, 1886. Hereafter 'W. & C.')

In the year 1494 an end was put to a suit that had been depending for some time between Trinity Hall & King's College before the Vice-chancell^r concerning the drain or water-course, running from King's College under Trinity Hall. The matter was put to a Reference, & 'twas agreed, that King's College should keep the Drain Clean &c, and that Trinity Hall shou'd suffer the water to pass under the college.

(*Warren's Book*, ed. Dale)

And we also by these presents do testifie that when we shalbe required thereunto we shall depart from the seid house and ground and give place unto them.

(W. & C.)

In 1516 the Johnians were keeping up:

Indenture between Master and Thomas Loveday of Sudbury in the County of Suffolk carpenter:

He shall make and cause to be made all the Staulls within the Qwier . . . that is to say, 24 Staulls on eyther syde of the said Qwier; the Desks wyth the Bakke halfe, wyth Creests over the Seats and Staulls, as in the southe parte of the Qwyer in Jhesus College in Cambr., or better in every poynt; and the Seats thereof shall be made after and accordyng to the seats within the Qwyer of Pembroke Hall in Cambr. aforesaid, or larger and better in every poynte . . .and also shall make 3 payr of broad Gates, whereof oon shall be mete and convenient for the Tower Gatte . . . and the oder Gate shall be mete and convenient for the Gate next unto the Kynges Hall . . . and the thyrd Gate shall be mete and convenient for the gat at the water syde . . . and which gate shall be made also with a wykket of good and able Oke and waynescott, better than any Gats be wythin ony College in Cambr.

Much money was spent on paint:

Christ's: painting of woodwork and images 1510/11

Item to Paule Smyth for certen coloures as in white led red led generall mastyke vernysch yelowe moty orpment roch vermylyon vergres Bisse oyle coperose white vitriall wex Ceruse Synoper red okyr yelowe oker Inde ffyne gold iiij C di'.

Furnishings and accoutrements were also organised:

Inventory from King's   3 July 1451   The Provost's Lodge

The Parlour
   hanged with reed worsted, late bought, and j banker for the same (old): j cupbord cuvered with old tapstre work: j chere of turned werk: j table with a paire trestles: iij stoles: j fire forke of yren broken
The chambre over the Parlour
   hanged with blewe worsted; j bed hanged with blewe bokeram and a feble coveryng therto of blewe worsted, and j bed running upon wheles under the other grete bed . . .
The Provost chambre
   hanged with reed worsted; an hanged bed of the same; j forme; j joyned stole; j litel folding trestel for a table standyng by the chymney to fore where the Provost sitteth.

Sir John Cheke to his friend Mr. Peter Osborne

O what pleasure is it to lacke pleasures, and how honorable is it to fli from honors throws. Among other lacks I lack painted bucrum to lai betweyne bokes and

[23]

bordes in mi studi, which I now have trimd. I have nede of xxx yardes. Chuse you the color. I prai yow bi me a reme of paper at London. Fare ye wel . . . From Cambridge the xxx of Mai 1549, 3 E. 6.

Yr^s known

(*Letters of Eminent Literary Men*, ed. Henry Ellis, 1843)

Items were bought for the common good:

Trinity College (1560)

In the Hall:

Item A mappe of thole world sett in a Frame
Item a joynid Chare for the maister
Item a Payr of Stockes above the screne

(W. & C.)

and gardens were begun:

Queens' College

Order dated 1532

That whereas the president of this College hath before this tyme no garden appointid severalli for hymself, nether for frute, nor to walk in . . . Now . . . the said President shall have, enjoy, and take from hensforth the Garden or Orchard over against the College brode gaates with all the frutes growing within the same to his own propir use . . . the said President from hensforthe, shall have no parte nor divident of suche frutes as growithe within the Colleges grett orchard.

Teste Simone Heynes

As time went on, niceties were taken care of:

Register of Christ's College

It is agreed betwixte the m^r and the fellowes that they shall every one of them have ij table napkins bought by the Colledge of this condition that every fellowe at his departure shall deliver unto the master ij whole table napkins for the use of his successoure . . . Also it is agreed that if either fellowe or pensioner do wipe his hande or fingers of the table clothe he shall pay for every time j^d to the use of the commins.

the 24 daye of October 1575

Noblemen bought expensive items for their rooms. In 1577 at Trinity:

THE PARCELLS which my Lord of Essex bought at his entrance in his chamber at Cambridge.
Imprimis, twenty yards of new grene brode sayes, lvj*s*.
Item, the frame of the South Window in the first Chamber, vj*s*. 4*d*.
Item, for more glasse in the same, iiij*s*.

Item, for 40 foote of quarters under the hangings, ij*s*.
Item, two casements with hingells in the south wyndow, ij*s* vj*d*
Item, new hangings in the study of painted cloth, xvj*s* viij*d*
Item, for paintinge both Chamber and study overhead, v*s*
Item, a conveyance to the bedchamber out of the study, ij*s* vj*d*
Item, a place makinge for the trindle bed to drawe through the waule, xvj*d*
Item, little irons to hould open the casements with, viij*d*
Item, my part of the dore betwixt Mr. Forcett and me, iij*s* vj*d*
Item, a crest at the chimnay, 4*d*
Item, for a footestoole at the window, 4*d*
Item, for two shelves mo in the frame of the study, xij*d*.

(Cooper)

More money was spent on gardens:

Queens' College (1575)

March   Item, to Robert Geordenor carpenter and vij of his men for xj dayes woorke setting uppe the frame of the vine in the fellowes garden, xxviij*s* vj*d*.
Item, to Thomas Thatcher and his man for iij dayes woorke in framing the stones to sett the vyne's frame on and making holes in the wall for the same, v*s* iiij*d*.
Item, payed for 3500 privie and one thousand of hunnysucles for the iland and other places of the colledge, ix*s* x*d*.

(W. & C.)

An uneasy truce was observed between town and gown. For its part, the town tried to impose cleanliness; there was an annual proclamation from 1445:

WE COMAUNDEN on the Kynges halve of Engelond, and on the Maires and Bayles of this Town of Cambrygge, that alle maner of men that have leyd ony Muk or Fylthe in the market, or in any other Stretys or Lanes within this town, and enspecial in the Kynges dych, that they do voyde hyt awey within Alhalew-day next comyng upon the peyne conteyned in the Statute of Cambrig, that is to say, eche man that is founde gylty to pay to the Kyng xx*l*.
    AND ALSO, that ne maner of man lets his swyn gon abroad on the pavement, from sevene on the clokk in the mornyng tyl syxe at aftyr noon, opon peyne for to paye to the Mayr and Bayles for iche foot a peny, as often as they ben founden in defaute.

(Cooper)

Colleges and their members were not exempt from the town's bye-laws nor were their habits cleaner than those of ordinary citizens. The following were pre-sented at the Law Hundred of the town in 1502:

For having the pavement before their tenements broken and ruinous. William Tomlyn master or keeper of St. John's House, and the masters of Katherine hall and Corpus Christi College, were amongst the parties presented upon this account.
    For having gutters running down from their houses to the King's highway; amongst the parties presented on this account, were the master and fellows of Powles In and the President of Michaelhouse.

4. Queens' College and its gardens, 1688

For making seges or privies overhanging the common river and the King's ditch. The master or keeper of Buckingham College, the master or keeper of Clement Hostel, and the keeper of Trinity Hall were amongst the persons presented on this account.

The filthy state of the King's ditch is a recurring theme: as late as 1574, Dr. Perne, the Vice-Chancellor, complains to Lord Burghley the Chancellor:

Allthough we must confesse that our synnes is the principall cause of this and of all other plages sent by Allmightie God, Yet the secondarie cause and meanes is that God did use to bringe the same, so far fourth as I do understand, is not the corruption of the ayer as the Phisitians saieth at this tyme, but partlie by the apparell of one that cam from London to Midsomer fayer and dyed of the plage in Barnwell, where the plage hath been and is now most vehement. The other cause as I conjecture, is the corruption of the King's dytch the which goeth thorough Cambridge, and especially in those places where there is most infection the which I will procure, so sone as we shall have any hard frost, to be clensed.

(Cooper)

College buildings aroused complaints

In 1446, the burgesses complained that houses were standing empty and that craftsmen were leaving because sites acquired for King's College and for students' lodgings were exempted from taxation, thus burdening the rest of the town.

(Darby, *Medieval Cambridgeshire*)

and there were grievances about lane enclosures etc. For example in 1549:

Item, we fynde that Trinitie college hath inclosed a common lane, which was a common course both for cart, horse, and man, leading to the ryver, unto a common grene, and no recompense made therefore.

Item, we fynde that the seyde College dothe commonlye use to laye ther mucke and meanor on ther backe syde upon the foreseyde common grene, wher thei wyll suffer no man ells to do the lyke, and have builded a common Jakes apon part of the same.

Item, we fynde that the Kynges College hath taken in and inclosed Saynt Austen's lane, leadinge from the high streets unto the waterside, withowte recompense.

Item, we fynde that the Queens College have taken in a pece of common ground commonlye called Goslinge grene withowte recompense.

(Cooper)

No one was exempt from the citizen's important task of road mending:

26 May 1570:

It was adjudged and decreed by Mr. Dr. Mey, V. Chancellor ... that no inhabitant within the town of Cambridge, being either Scholer or Scholer's servant, can or may be privileg'd by that title from the common days works of mending the high ways; but that all & singular shall either work or find sufficient

[27]

Silver Street Bridge (woodcut by Gwen Raverat)

labourers upon the paine limited in the Statute, except he be a labourer & so
accounted.
(Dyer, Privileges)

Football could raise tempers (1579):

James Bates, of Chesterton . . . sworne, saith:

That upon Tewsdaye, being Shrovetewsdaye was twoe yeare, some of the
townesmen and youth of Chesterton mynding to playe at the foteball, and
looking for schollers, procured staves and other weapons to be sett in the church
porche of Chesterton; and afterward, when they were hotte in playe, sodenlye
one cryed, Staves! and incontinently some ran forth with the staves, and so fell
upon the schollers, and did beate divers of them; and some runnyng awaye, they
did folowe, and caused to swymme over the water. And longe Johan, servaunt to
Mr. Brakyn, did folowe one Edward Wylton, scholler of Clarehall, with a
javelyn; and if this deponent had not rescued hym, he beleaveth he would have
runne the said Wylton thorough, for so the said Johan said he would doe. Item,
he saith that Tho. Parys, his constable, was one of the players at the foteball at
that tyme.

Also at Chesterton there was trouble over bear-baiting (1581):

Upon a complaynt of the resorting to a beare bayting at Chesterton . . . Tho.
Nevile, proctour of th'universitie of Cambridg, accompanied with Henry Farr,
tasker, Jo. Hutchinson, Samuell Farr, and a bedell, sent by Mr. Vice-chancelour
to inhibite a bearbayting at Chesterton; and finding the beare at the stake, where
he had bene bayted in the sermon tyme, betwene one and twoe of the clocke in
the afternone . . . the proctour asking the bearward by what authoritie he bayted
his beare there, etc., made answer, that he was the lord Vaux his man . . . and
when John Standish, the bedyll, went to apprehende the said bearward, Richard
Parys said to the bearward, Doe not goe with him; for if thow do, thow art a
fowle; and long Johan said to the bearward, Thow shalt not goe; and then the
said long Johan went between the bedell and the bearward; and then the
multitude thrust upon the bedell, and crowded hym to the beare, and shouted,
Goe not, Goe not . . . and so after conveyed the bearward awaye . . . Item, this
said Richard Parys, the constables brother, bragged and said, that if evensong
were done, when the schollers were gone, they would go into a yarde, and bayte
in despight of theim.
(James Heywood and Thomas Wright,
Cambridge University Transactions during
the Puritan Controversies of the Sixteenth and
Seventeenth Centuries, 1854)

Much was forbidden to both senior and junior members of the University. In
1561, Queen Elizabeth banned women from colleges:

Understanding of late, that within certain . . . Houses as well the chief Governors, as the Prebendaries, Students & Members thereof being married, do keep
particular Households, with their Wives, Children & Nurses, whereof no small
Offense groweth to the Intent of the Founders, & to the quiet & orderly Profession of Study & Learning . . . Her Majesty therefore . . . expressly willeth and
commandeth that no Manner of Person, being either the Head or Member of

[29]

any College . . . within this Realm, shall have or be permitted to have within the Precinct of any such College, his Wife or other Woman to abide & dwell in the same.

9th August third year of our Reign

at about the same time the Bishop of Ely wrote to Archbishop Parker:

Truly methinketh it very reasonable that places of students should be in all quietness among themselves and not troubled with any families of women or babes.

(Dyer, *Privileges*)

Stone bows were banned in 1577:

Whereas of late great destruction of dove-houses hath fortuned, by the lewde and wilful wantonness of some persons using stone-boes, and much pewter vessell hath been consumed and molten for the mayntenance of pellets, and great hurt done in Glasse of Churches, Chapels and College Halls . . . YT IS AND WAS ORDERED, DEFYNED AND DECREED . . . that no scholar . . . shall shoute or use any stone-boe.

and football outside college precincts. The Vice-Chancellor in 1580 decreed:

that no scholar of what degree or condition soever he were, should at any place or at any time hereafter, play at the foot-ball, but only within the precincts of their several colleges, not permitting any stranger or scholars of other colleges or houses to play with them or in their company, and in no place else . . .

Item, the little green lying between the river and Trinity college, is allowed unto and for the only company of the said Trinity college for that pastime.

Dress was a constant concern of the authorities, with sometimes proctors and regents setting a bad example. Heads of houses to the Chancellor, Lord Burghley in 1572:

As touching the statute for apparell none in all the University do more offend against that statute than the two proctors, who should give best ensample, and these otheir two Regents Nicholls and Browne, withe a fewe more of their adherents, whoe doe not only go verye disorderlie in Cambridge, waring for the most part their hates and continually verye unsemly ruffes at their handes, and great Galligaskens and Barreld hooese stuffed with horse Tayles, with skabilon-ions and knitt netherstockes to fine for schollers; but also most disguysedlie theie goo abroade wearinge such Apparell, even at this time in London.

Gowns were the answer:

ORDERS OF APPARELL for Schollars of the Universitie of Cambridge, Anno 1585.

FIRST, that no Graduate remayninge within any Colledge, Hostell, or Hall, or clayminge to enjoye the priviledge of a Scholler, doe weare any stuffe in the outward part of his gowne, but woollen cloth of blacke, puke, London Browne,

or other sad color: And the gowne to be made with a standing coller, as the use hath bene, and not falling: And the hood that is worne with the same gowne, to be of the same or like cloth and color that the gowne is of. And that none as is aforesaid, doe weare for the upper apparell of his bodye, in the daye tyme out of his colledg, hostell, hall, or habitation, and precinctes of the same, in any common streete of the Towne, that is to say, in the high streets from the greate bridge, as it leadeth right to Christes Colledge, in the streete called the High Ward streete from St. John's Colledge as it leadeth right to Pembroke Hall and Peter House, in anye of the Markett places, in the streete called the Peticurie, or in the Court or Quadrant of any other Colledge then that where he remayneth, or within the common schooles, or at any disputation or any common lecture, or at any Sermon or common prayers, or being called and coming to the Vice-chancellor or Proctors, any other than the saied gowne and hood or tippett . . .
ALSO, that everie graduate wearing the above gowne and gaberdyne within the Universitie or Towne, out of his chamber or lodging, doe weare withall in the daye tyme a square cap and none other: no hatt to be worne except for infirmities sake, with a kerchiffe about his head, or in going to and fro the Feeldes, or in the streete or open ayre when it shall happen to rayne hayle or snowe . . .
ALSO, that no Graduat remayning within any Colledge . . . doe weare within the Universitie nor without the same . . . any stuffe in upon or about his doublett, coates, Jerkyn, jackett, cassock or hose, of velvett or silke, or of any stuffe as is forbidden by her Majesties said proclamation and lawes. Nor any other stuffe not so forbidden that shal be embrodred, powdred, pynked, or welted, savinge at the handes, verge, showlder, or coller: or gathered, plated, garded, hacked, raced, laced, or cutt, saving the cutt of the welt and button holes, nor of any other redde, grene, and suche other like colour . . .

(Cooper)

In spite of regulations, there was a great deal of enjoyment of different kinds to be had. A homesick wandering Scots scholar, John Mair, took up residence in God's House in the late fifteenth century:

When I was a student at Cambridge I have spent the greatest part of the night during the great feasts without sleep so that I might listen to the melody of the bells. The University stands on a river, and on that account the sound is sweeter from the undulations of water.

(Rackham, *Christ's College in Former Days*)

Roger Ascham thinks longingly of a scholar's life in a letter to Sir William Cecil:

March 1553

I having now som experience of liffe led at home and abrode, and knowing what I can do most fitlie, and how I would live most gladly, do wel perceyve their is no such quietnesse in England, nor pleasure in strange contres, as even in S. Jons Colledg to kepe company with the Bible, Plato, Aristotle, Demosthenes, and Tullie.

(*Letters of Eminent Literary Men*, ed. Ellis)

Simple pleasures were remembered later in life by Henry Peacham who was a sizar at Trinity in 1572:

Yes, sir, I dare say you and I were first acquainted in Cambridge (the world is altered), it is a good while, I was laid hold on in an evening by our Vice-master D.R. for whistling in the Court; and I told him (and told him truely) I could never whistle in all my life; you made answere, No sir, it was not hee; for could he have whistled, his father would never have sent him to Cambridge, hee would have made a plough boy of mee . . .

Let me remember you likewise (said I) of another merrie accident when wee were boys, and Sophisters in the schooles, when you and two more of your acquaintances, went one frostie morning to eate Black-puddings to break-fast, and wanting a penny of the reckoning to pay for an odde pudding (having no more money amongst you all three) you ventur'd on it, and spet out a single penny that was buried in the Puddings end; so that by wonderfull fortune, the pudding payd for itselfe; and after you declaim'd upon, Audaces Fortune juvat.

(*Coach and Sedan,* 1636)

and lively times described in a letter by William Soone to George Braunius in Cologne in 1575:

The common dress of all is a sacred cap; (I call it sacred because worn by priests); a gown reaching down to their heels, of the same form as that of priests. None of them live out of their colleges in the townsmen's houses; they are perpetually quarrelling and fighting with them; and this is more remarkable in the mock fights which they practise in the streets in summer with shields and clubs. They go out in the night to show their valour, armed with monstrous great clubs furnished with a cross piece of iron to keep off the blows, and frequently beat the watch. When they walk the streets they take the wall, not only of the inhabitants, but even of strangers, unless persons of rank. Hence the proverb that a Royston horse, and a Cambridge Master of Arts, are a couple of creatures that will give way to nobody . . . In standing for degrees, the North-country and South-country men have warm contests with each other.

(Cooper)

Undergraduates came up at a very tender age sometimes and often distinguished themselves:

The Reverend John Dod . . . born 1549 at Shotlidge; near Malpas, in Cheshire . . . when he was about 14 years old, was disposed of to Jesus College, Cambridge, where he was chosen first scholar, and afterwards fellow in that college, where he remained near 16 years.

(*Memorials of the Reverend John Dod,* MA, 1875)

Of William Bedell, born 1571, his son writes:

In the eleventh year of his age he was sent to Cambridge, and after strict trial admitted into Emmanuel college, and not long after his admission chosen scholar of that house. The first four years (as himself was wont to say) he lost, only keeping pace with the rest of his years . . . But after, he fell to his study in so good earnest, that he got the start of the rest and the regents of the college thought fit to choose him fellow before or as soon as ever he was of age sufficient by their statutes to be capable of a fellowship.

('Life of William Bedell, by his son', in J. E. B. Mayor, *Cambridge in the Seventeenth Century*, 1855–77)

Dr. John Dee, the astrologer, was only 15 when he came up:

ANNO 1542 I was (in November) sent by my father, Rowland Dee, to the Universitie of Cambridge, there to begin with logick, and so to proceede in the learning of good artes and sciences . . .

In the yeares 1543, 1544, 1545, I was so vehemently bent to studie, that for those yeares I did inviolably keepe this order; only to sleepe four houres every night; to allow to meate and drink (and some refreshing after) two hours every day; and of the other eighteen houres all (except the tyme of going to and being at divine service) was spent in my studies and learning.

After I was Batchellor of Art, I went beyond the seas (anno 1547 in May) to speake and conferr with some learned men, and chiefly mathematicians . . . and after some months . . . I returned home, and brought with me the first astrono-mer's staff of brass . . .

I was out of St. John's Colledge chosen to be Fellow of Trinity Colledge, at the first erection thereof by King Henry the Eight . . . Hereupon I did sett forth (and it was seene of the University) a Greeke comedy of Aristophanes . . . with the performance of the *Scarabeus* his flying up to Jupiter's pallace, with a man and his basket of victuals on her back: whereat was great wondring, and many vaine reports spread abroad of the meanes how that was effected.

(*Autobiographical Tracts*, ed. James Crossley, 1851)

Scholars lived austere lives:

There be dyvers ther which rise daily betwixte foure and fyve of the clocke in the mornynge, and from five untyll syxe of the clock, use commen prayer with an exortacyon of gods worde in a common chappell, and from syxe unto ten of the clocke use ever eyther private studye or commune lectures. At ten of the clocke they go to dynner, where as they be contente wyth a penye piece of biefe amongst iiii, havynge a few porage made of the brothe of the same biefe, wyth salte and otemel, and nothynge elles.

After this slender dynner they be either teachynge or learnynge untyll v of the clocke in the evening, when as they have a supper not much better than theyr dynner. Immediatelye after the whyche, they go eyther to reasonyng in prob-lemes or unto some other studye, untyl it be nine or tenne of the clocke, and there beyng without fyre, are fayne to walk or runne up and downe halfe an houre, to gette a heate on theyr fete whan they go to bed.

(Thomas Lever, sermon preached at Paul's Cross, 1550, from Cooper)

[33]

and worked hard:

(1549) . . . yet was not knowledge fullie confirmed in hir Monarchie amongst us, till that most famous and fortunate Nurse of all learning, Saint *Johns* in *Cambridge*, that at that time was an universitie within it selfe; shining so farre above all other Houses, Halls, and Hospitalls whatsoever, that no Colledge in the Towne, was able to compare with the Tythe of her students; having (as I have hearde grave men of credite report) more candles light in it, everie Winter Morning before fowre of the clocke, than the fowre of clocke bell gave stroakes.

> (Thomas Nashe: 'To the Gentlemen
> Students of Both Universities', prefixed to
> Robert Greene's *Menaphon*, 1589)

and with pleasure:
Francis Beaumont writes to Thomas Speght, editor of Chaucer's Works, in
1598 (both were at Peterhouse):

And here I cannot forget to remember unto you those auncient learned men of our time in Cambridge whose diligence in reading of his [Chaucer's] works themselves, and commanding them to others of the younger sorte, did first bring you and mee in love with him: and one of them at that time was and now is as you knowe one of the rarest schollers of the worlde . . . From Leicester, the last of June 1597. [The 'rare scholar' might have been Whitgift.]

> (H. P. Stokes, *The Cambridge Scene*, 1921)

There was much music, both for pleasure and study:

I must say this much of him [Doctor Still, his former tutor at Christ's, later Master of St. John's, then of Trinity]; his breeding was from his childhood in good litterature, and partly in musique, which was counted in those days a preparation to divinitie, neither could any be admitted to *primam tonsuram*, except he could first . . . reade well, to conster well, and to sing well; in which last he hath good judgement, and I have heard good music of voyses in his house.

> (Sir John Harington, *Nugae Antiquae*,
> ed. Thomas Park, 1804)

Extract from Corpus Christi Statutes, 1580:

All which said schollers shall and must at the time of their election be so entred into the skill of song as that they shall at the first sight solf and singe plainesong.

> (Quoted in John Bakeless, *The Tragical*
> *History of Christopher Marlowe*, 1942)

Teaching was mostly centred on colleges but a course of university lectures in
Divinity was established by the Lady Margaret in 1503:

Lady Margaret's Lecturer to read . . . such Books as the Vicechancellor & Doctors shall judge fittest, either from 7 to 8 in the Morning, or any other Hour at the Discretion of the Vicechancellor.

To read every accustomed Day in Term, except in Lent, & in the Long Vacation, to the 8th of Septemb. unless excused by the Vicechancellor for Infirmity or other just Cause.

Not to omitt his Lectures above 4 Daies in a Term, but upon just & reasonable Cause known and approved by the Vicechan. & the major Part of the Doctors in Divinity, & with Leave of the Vicechancellor . . .

To swear at his Admission to observe these Orders: & to have for his Salary £13 06s 08d yearly of the Abbot of Westm.

(Dyer, Privileges)

Disputation was both a method of instruction and a process of 'continuous assessment'; it eventually became a formal oral examination, not dispensed with until finally superceded by written examinations in the nineteenth century:

In primis, the Questionists shall gyve the Bedels warnynge upon Le Daye, that they may proclayme before thordynarie Readers in the common schooles thentrynge of their Questions at the accustomed Hower, which is IX of the clocke, at the which tyme the Bedells or one of them shall go to the Colledge, Howse, Hall or Hostell where the sayd Questionists be, & at their entryng into the sayd Howse & shall call & gyve warninge in the middest of the Courte with thees words, Alons, Alons, goe, Masters, goe, goe, and then to toll, or cause to be tolled the Bell of the Howse to gather the Masters, Bachilers, Schoolers and Questionists together, and all the Companye in their Habitts and Hoodds being assembled, the Bedells shall go before the Junior Questionite, & so all the Rest in their order shall follow bareheaded, then the Father, & after all the Graduate & company of the sayd Howse unto the Common Schooles in dew order . . .

Then there follows the Tripos examination, with buns and beer in the interval:

All the Determiners dothe sytte in the New Chappel within the schooles from one of the Clocke untyll fyve, upon the Mondaye, Twesdaye, Wensdaye, & Thursdaye in the weeke before Shrove Sondaye, abyding there examynation of so many masters as wyll repayre for that cause thether; & from three to 4 all they have a Potation of Figgs, Reasons, & Almons, Bonnes & Beer, at the charge of the says Determiners, whereat all the Bedells maye be present daylye: & upon the Thursdaye they be onlye examined in Songe & wrytynge.

(George Peacock, Observations on Statutes
of the University, 1841)

Protestants – the New Learning, Elizabethans and Puritans

Erasmus was in Cambridge from 1511 to 1514. In his 'History' Fuller writes:

having his abode in Queens' College, where a study on the top of the south-west tower in the old court still retaineth his name . . . Queens' College accounteth it no small credit thereunto that Erasmus (who no doubt might have picked and

Trinity Bridge (woodcut by Gwen Raverat)

chose what house he pleased) preferred this for the place of his study for some years in Cambridge. Either invited thither with the fame of the learning and love of his friend Bishop Fisher . . . or allured with the situation of this college so near the river (as Rotterdam his native place to the sea) with pleasant walks thereabouts.

Things did not go particularly well for him from the start:

Queens' College   Aug 25 1511

The beer in this place doesn't suit me at all and the wines aren't quite satisfactory either. If you are in a position to arrange for a cask of Greek wine, the best obtainable, to be shipped to me here, you will have done what will make your friend perfectly happy. (But I'd like it to be quite *dry* wine.)

To Ammonio   Cambridge   November 27   1511

I'm sending you the *Icaromenippus* for you to copy out, if you can do this without boredom or inconvenience, or else ask More to give it to his brother for copying. Reason: I'm preparing some morsels in readiness for January 1, though (unless I'm mistaken) it will be futile. And here in Cambridge – what a University! No one can be found who will write even moderately well at any price.

The explanation of his aversion to the local beer and wine and his tetchiness in general may be explained by the next extract:

To Ammonio   Cambridge   December 9   1511

On Conception Day I was brought painfully to bed, whereupon I was delivered of several large rocks. Please include this kind of stone among the pebbles you use for working out the calculus of my 'happiness!'

A problem solved:

To Colet   Cambridge   July 11   1513

Your protégé – yes, he is yours indeed – Thomas Lupset is helping me and delighting me greatly with his company every day, and with the assistance he's giving me in the revision of these texts. And I return aid for aid: which is something I'd do more liberally if his studies allowed the time, for I shouldn't like to take a young man away from those. Believe me, nothing on earth outdoes him in affection for yourself.

To Thomas More   Cambridge   July   1513

Lupset thinks that with our help he has been reborn and quite returned from hell. But the Masters are trying every trick to drag the youth back to their treadmill; for that very day he tore up his books of (scholastic) sophistry and bought Greek ones instead!

In 1514, in a letter from the Netherlands, he gives a famous reference to Cambridge:

In this place are colleges in which there's so much religion and so marked a sobriety in living that you'd despise every form of religious regime in comparison, if you saw it.

In 1516 he is told in a letter from an old pupil:

Here at Cambridge, men are devoting themselves ardently to Greek literature. They profoundly wish you would come; such persons hold in great favour this newly published work of yours upon the New Testament: great gods, how clever it is, how clearly reasoned, and to all men of sound judgement how pleasing and how indispensable!

(D. F. S. Thompson and H. C. Porter, *Erasmus and Cambridge*, 1963)

Erasmus opened the door to a new wind, with the smell of Protestantism in it, which blew through libraries, chapels, studies and meeting places. The King's divorce, to which Cambridge lent its assent finally in 1530, opened that door wider still.

The revolutionary aspect of Erasmus's 'Novum Instrumentum', published in 1516, lay in its commentary, with textual and historical criticism applied for the first time to the 'divine page'. Thomas Bilney, who was a Fellow of Trinity Hall in 1524, describes its impact on him:

After this the Scriptures began to be more pleasant unto me than the honey or the honey-comb; wherein I learned, that all my travails, all my fasting and watching, all the redemption of masses and pardons . . . these, I say, I learned to be nothing else but even . . . a hasty and swift running out of the right way . . .

(John Foxe, *Actes and Monuments*, 1563)

Bilney converted Hugh Latimer, who came up to Clare College in 1506, became a Fellow, and then keeper of the books in the University Library. Latimer describes his conversion:

Here I have occasion to tell you a story which happened in Cambridge. Master Bilney, or rather Saint Bilney, that suffered death for God's word sake; the same Bilney was the instrument whereby God called me to knowledge; for I may thank him, next to God, for that knowledge that I have in the word of God. For I was as obstinate a papist as any was in England . . . from that time forward I began to smell the word of God, and forsook the school-doctors and such fooleries.

(*Sermons*, 1844)

Thomas Bilney was an austere man:

This godly man, being a bachelor of law, was but of little stature and very slender of body . . . He could abide no swearing or singing. Coming from the church where singing was, he would lament to his scholars the curiosity of their dainty singing . . . and when Dr. Thurlby, Bishop after, then scholar lying in the chamber underneath him, would play upon his recorder (as he would often do), he would resort strait to his prayer . . .

He made other converts, such as Robert Barnes, prior of the Augustines in Cambridge. Barnes declared himself in a sermon at St. Edward's Church:

For that sermon he was immediately accused of heresy by two fellows of the King's Hall. Then the godly learned in Christ both of Pembroke-hall, St. John's,

Peter-house, Queen's college, the King's college, Gunwell-hall, and Benet college, showed themselves, and flocked together in open sight, both in the schools, and at open sermons at St. Mary's, and at the Augustines, and at other disputations; and then they conferred continually together.

The house that they resorted most commonly unto, was the White Horse, which, for despite of them, to bring God's word into contempt, was called Germany. This house especially was chosen because many of them of St. John's, the King's college, and the Queen's college, came in on the back side.

(Foxe, *Acts and Monuments*)

Stories began to get about:

There is a collage in Cambridge called Gunwel Haule, of the foundation of a Bishop of Norwich. I hear no clerk that hath comen ought lately of that collage but saverith of the frying panne, tho he spek never so holely.

(Bishop Nix of Norwich to Archbishop Warham (1530), quoted in Venn, *Caius College*)

Even the pronunciation of Greek had a smack of the new ideas:

Mr. Cheke, being Greek Lecturer, had endeavoured some time before to make a reformation in the pronouncing of Latin, but especially Greek. For as Greek books were not long before brought into study and reading, not without opposition in the University, so the way of sounding the vowels and diphthongs and some consonants, was very odd and untoward . . . Cheke's pretence in reforming the sound of the Greek language was to vindicate truth. But this moved not the Chancellor . . . This popish Bishop cared not indeed to have truth too narrowly searched after.

(John Strype, *Ecclesiastical Memoirs*, 1721)

Amongst those who opposed Cheke was one Ratecliffe who 'went up to read somewhat, and having spoke a little, was so laughed at by the boys, so exploded and hissed, and so tossed in the crowd which came together in a great assembly to laugh rather than to hear, that his own friends were ashamed of him; and he himself repented him of his folly; though he had but little modesty and less brains'.

(Strype, *Life of Sir John Cheke*, 1705)

In 1535 there was royal assent to the new learning. The royal injunctions contained the following clauses:

That by a writing to be sealed with the common seal of the University, and subscribed with their hands, they should swear to the King's succession, and to obey the statutes of the realm made or to be made, for the extirpation of the papal usurpation, and for the assertion and confirmation of the King's jurisdiction, prerogative and preeminence.

That all students should be permitted to read the Scriptures privately, or to repair to public lectures upon them.

That as the whole realm, as well clergy as laity, had renounced the Pope's right, and acknowledged the King to be supreme head of the Church, no one should thereafter publicly read the Canon Law, nor should any degrees in that Law be conferred.

That students in arts should be instructed in the elements of logic, rhetoric, arithmetic, geography, music, and philosophy, and should read Aristotle, Rodolphus Agricola, Philip Melancthon, Trapezuntius, &c. and not the frivolous questions and obscure glosses of Scotus, Burleus, Anthony Trombet, Bricot, Bruliferius, &c.

(Cooper)

But there was still tension between adherents of the old and new faiths: there were stormy proceedings in the Senate House in 1539 at the election of a new Vice-Chancellor:

MR. CWNERFORTH dyde laye violent handes upon the sete wher I satt and Mr. Perne dyde pull me bakwarde by the hood soo that yf the chaire had not beyn upholden by certayn that stode bye thaye hade overthroyn hit ande me . . . and indede Swayn dyd reporte that yf Doctor Malet hade gone to the election upon Saturdaye he hade beyn servyde as I was and Stokes had beyn throwne down the steres theye had provyded wepyns and armur soo to do and had them redye ther then as este before.

(J. Lamb, *Original Documents from Corpus Christi College Library*, 1838)

There was an influx of foreign refugees under Cranmer's auspices, the chief amongst them being Bucer and Fagius, though they were not long in Cambridge. Fagius died in November 1549. Thomas Horton, Fellow of Pembroke and future Marian exile, comments:

Dr. Bucer cries incessantly, now in daily lectures, now in frequent sermons, that we should practise penitence, discard the depraved customs of hypocritical religion, correct the abuses of fasts, be more frequent in hearing and having sermons, and constrain ourselves by some sort of discipline. Many things of this kind he impresses on us even *ad nauseam*.

(H. C. Porter, *Reformation and Reaction in Tudor Cambridge*, 1958)

Bucer died in March 1551 and three thousand townsmen and gownsmen are said to have followed the coffin to Great St. Mary's.

On the death of King Edward VI Cambridge was the scene of much political activity. The Duke of Northumberland, Chancellor of the University, ran Lady Jane Grey, his niece, as a Protestant candidate; and Dr. Sands, the Vice-Chancellor, did not want to see the ardent Catholic, the Princess Mary, Edward's half-sister, on the throne. Foxe tells the story:

King Edward dead, the world being unworthy of him, the duke of Northumberland came down to Cambridge with an army of men, having commission to proclaim lady Jane queen . . . The duke sent for Dr. Sands, being vice-chancellor, for Dr. Parker, for Dr. Bill, and master Leaver, to sup with him . . . Dr. Sands, being vice-chancellor, was required to preach on the morrow . . .

The duke, with the rest of the nobility, required Dr. Sands to put his sermon in writing, and appointed master Leaver to go to London with it, and to put it in print . . . At the time appointed he made it ready, and master Leaver was ready booted to receive it at his hands, and carry it to London. As he was delivering of it, one of the beadles, named master Adams, came weeping to him, and prayed him to shift for himself, for the duke was retired, and queen Mary proclaimed.

Dr. Sands was not troubled therewith, but gave the sermon written to master Layfield . . . and he went to dinner to one master More's, a beadle, his great friend. At the dinner mistress More . . . drank unto him, saying: 'Master vice-chancellor, I drink unto you, for this is the last time I shall ever see you.' And so it was; for she was dead before Dr. Sands returned out of Germany. The duke that night retired to Cambridge, and sent for Dr. Sands to go with him to the market-place, to proclaim queen Mary. The duke cast up his cap with the others, and so laughed, that the tears ran down his cheeks for grief.

(*Acts and Monuments*)

Stow takes up the story:

The Duke . . . had letters from the counsell, by the handes of Richard Rose, herault . . . if the Duke of Northumberland do not submit himselfe to the Queenes highnesse, Queene Mary, he shall be accepted as a traytour . . .

The rumour of these letters was no sooner abroad, but every man departed. And shortly after, the Duke was arrested in the Kings Colledge by one master Slegge, Sergeant at armes.

(John Stow, *Chronicles of England*, 1580)

Foxe:

certain grooms of the stable were as busy with Dr. Sands, as if they would take him a prisoner. But sir John Gates, who lay then in Dr. Sands' house, sharply rebuked them, and drave them away. Dr. Sands, by the advice of sir John Gates, walked in the fields. In the mean time the university, contrary to all order, had met together in consultation and ordered that Dr. Mouse and Dr. Hatcher should repair to Dr. Sands' lodging, and fetched away the statute-book of the university, the keys and such other things that were in his keeping, and so they did: for Dr. Mouse, being an earnest protestant the day before, and one whom Dr. Sands had done much for, was now become a papist, and his great enemy. Certain of the university had appointed a congregation at afternoon. As the bell rang to it, Dr. Sands cometh out of the fields, and sending for the beadles, asketh what the matter meaneth, and requireth them to wait upon him to the schools, according to their duty. So they did. And as soon as Dr. Sands, the beadles going before him, came into the regent-house, and took his chair, one master Mitch, with a rabble of unlearned papists, went into a bye-school, and conspired together to pull him out of his chair.

Sands was eventually arrested, sent to the Marshalsea, remaining there for nine weeks before he was freed. A fresh warrant for his arrest was issued, but he escaped to Germany.

At the accession of Queen Mary thirteen Heads of Houses were removed. Dr. Gardiner, the new Chancellor, ensured that instead of the forty-two articles of religion a series of fifteen articles were drawn up and subscription to these articles was an indispensable condition for the resident electors and for admission to degrees. Some ninety members of colleges became exiles as a result, as Roger Ascham laments:

An. 1553 whan mo perfite scholers were dispersed from thence in one moneth, than many yeares can reare up againe . . . and therefore did som of them at Cambrige (whom I will not name openlie,) cause hedge priestes fette [fetched] oute of the contrie, to be made fellowes in the universitie: saying, in their talke privilie, and declaring by their deedes openlie, that he was, felow good enough for their tyme, if he could were a gowne and a tipet cumlie, and have hys crowne shorne faire and roundlie, and could turne his Portesse and pie readilie: whiche I speake not to reprove any order either of apparell, or other dewtie, that may be well and indifferentlie used, but to note the miserie of that time, whan the benefites provided for learning were so fowlie misused.

(The Scholemaster, 1570)

Two views:

Cambridge had the honour of educating those celebrated Protestant bishops whom Oxford had the honour of burning.

(Thomas Babington Macaulay, *Essay on Bacon*, 1837)

It is impossible . . . not to blame those of folly and madness, who by remaining, suffered themselves rather to be burnt alive than fly their country for a time, as their martyrdom was of no use to the cause, and they knew that Queen Mary's successor was a Protestant.

(Wilson, *Memorabilia Cantabrigiae*)

In 1555, Latimer, Ridley and Cranmer, examined at Oxford by a commission of divines from both Oxford and Cambridge Universities, were found guilty of heresy, and burnt at the stake in Oxford. Latimer and Ridley were burnt together. Latimer, according to Foxe, saying:

Be of good comfort, Master Ridley, and play the man. We shall this day light such a candle, by God's grace, in England, as I trust shall never be put out.

Ridley had already written a farewell letter to his College and University:

Now that I have taken my leave of my Countrimen and Kinsfolk, and the Lord doth lend me life and giveth me leisure, I wil bid my other good friends in God of other places also farewel. And whom first or before other than the University of Cambridge, where I have dwelt longer, found more faithful and hearty friends, received more benefits (the benefits of my natural parents only excepted) than ever I did in mine own native country wherein I was born.

Farewel therefore Cambridge, my loving mother and tender Nurse. If I should not acknowledge thy manifold benefits, yea, if I should not for thy benefits at the least love thee again, truly I were to be accounted too ungrate and unkind. What benefits hadst thou ever, that thou usest to give and bestow upon thy best beloved children, that thou thoughtest too good for me . . .

Farewel Pembroke Hall, of late mine own colledge my cure and my charge; what case thou art in now, God knoweth, I know not well. Thou wast ever named since I knew thee, (which is now a thirty years ago,) to be studious, well learned, and a good setter forth of Christ's Gospel, and of God's true word, so I found thee and blessed be God so I left thee indeed. Wo is me for thee mine own dear Colledge if ever thou suffer thyself by any means to be brought from that trade. In thy orchard (the walls, buts and trees, if they could speak would bear me witness) I learned without book almost all Pauls Epistles, yea, and I ween all the Canonical Epistles, save only the Apocalyps of which study although in time a great part did depart from me, yet the sweet smell thereof . . . I think I have felt in all my life time ever after.

Cranmer was a son of Cambridge.

Thomas Cranmer was outed of his fellowship in Jesus College for being married. His wife was kinswoman to the hostess at the Dolphin, which causing his frequent repair thither, gave the occasion to that impudent lie of ignorant papists, that he was an ostler. Indeed with his learned lectures, he rubbed the galled backs, and curried the lazy hides, of many an idle and ignorant friar, being now made divinity reader in Buckingham College. But soon after, his wife dying within the year, being a widower, he was re-elected into Jesus College.

(Fuller, *History*)

In 1556 Cardinal Pole sent Visitors to the University with a view to 'the more complete re-establishment of the Catholic religion'. John Mere, Esquire Bedell, kept a diary of the visit, which lasted from 11 January to 17 February:

XI Januar.

On munday a lyttle mysling but wetted lyttle. It. at vii the Vyc. [Vice-Chancellour] with all the hole universitie in habitibus met in St. Marys . . . from thence all wente to trinitie College and thuniversitie Crosse before them . . .

XII Januar.

On tuesday fayre and the Vyc. and senior Proct. went agayne to the Visitors to be further examyned at trinitie Coll. where they sate all this day; then they examyned the Junior Proc. & taxors and scrutators and spent all the day abowt them . . . at one the Heddes met in the scholes where and by whom it was concluded that for as myche as Bucer had byn an arche heretycke, teachynge by his life tyme many detestable heresies and errors, sute [suit] should be made unto the Visitors by the University that he might be taken upp and ordered, according to the law and lykwys P. Fagius.

IV Februr.

It. they sent for D. Sedgewycke Mrs. Parker, Godeshalf, and Rud to peruse the exhibited bookes, which were heretycall and which were otherwyse. It. Roger Briskoo browght in ii baskets full of Mr. Lakon's books, D. Yale also the commissary browght in moo books. It. they sente for the Vic. about iiii of the clock.

V Februar.

On Friday rayne. It. the visitors sitting all day as they have done these iii days in trinitie Coll. herde mass sayde in the chapell betwyxt vi and vii and shortly after the Mr. and seniors of the house there sate in oppositions of scholers and the rest of the Visitors sate in seryous matters all the forenoone . . . It. the Vic. &c. sate in commission at the hall cheffly between Wympole men and their parson. It. the Mr. of trinitie Coll. had a sore fytt and cryed owt I am deade, with lyke frontyke words abowt v of the clock. It. the visitors sente worde to the Vic. to wryte owt his sermon of late preeched in St. Mary's in laten. It. I browght in a baskett full of bookes from the Vic. and of myn owte. (owne ?)

VI Februar.

It. Grayne rose in the Market namely wheate. It. Mr. Stokes the orator supped with me. It. Mr. Lewen sente unto the visitors vi Couple conyes and a panier full of hennes and other wylde fowle.

(Lamb, *Original Documents*)

But the main business of 6 February was the burning of the books and the exhumed bodies of Bucer and Fagius:

Smith the Maior of the town which should be their executioner, commaunded certaine of his townsmen to wait upon him in harnesse, by whom the dead bodyes were garded, & being bound with ropes, and layd upon mens shoulders . . . were borne into the middes of the market sted with a great trayne of people following them . . . When they came thyther, the chestes were set up on end, wyth the dead bodyes in them, and fastened on both sides wyth stakes, and bound to the poste with a long yron chayne, as if they had bene alive. Fyre beinge forthwith put to, as soon as it began to flame rounde aboute, a greate sorte of books that were condemned wyth theym, were caste into the same.

(Cooper)

On the accession of Queen Elizabeth in 1559 many of the heads of houses were restored. Among them was Andrew Perne, Master of Peterhouse.

It is a coincidence worth noting, that Dr. Perne who was Vicechancellor when the bodies of Bucer and Fagius were burnt, again filled the office when they were restored to their honours.

(Cooper)

For such trimming he became unpopular. It is said that undergraduates invented a Latin word, perno, 'I turn, I rat, I change often'; and that the letters 'A.P.A.P.' on the weathercock of St. Peter's Church were said to mean, 'Andrew Perne a papist, or protestant or puritan'. Martin Marprelate called him Old Andrew Turncoat.

In 1564 the Queen paid a state visit, described by Matthew Stokys, Esquire Bedell and Registrary of the University:

At two a clock all the whole University, at the ringing of the University bell, assembled at King's College. And there, by the Chancellor, Vicechancellor,

Proctors, and Bedells, were set in order and straightly charged, every man to keep their place. And all other, not to mingle themselves with them.

First, at the corner of the Queen's College and Martin Gill's house, was set a great falling-gate, with a lock and staple. From that place, unto the King's College Church west door, stoode, upon both sides, one by one, all the University. From the gate stood the Scholars; then the Batchellors of Arts; then the Batchellors of Law; then the Master Regents; then the Non-regents and Batchellors of Divinity. Then, at last, the Doctors in their degree; and every one in habits and hoods. The last Doctor and the Vicechancellor stood upon the lowest greese of the west doore. And by him the three Bedells.

The whole lane, between the King's College and the Queen's College, was strawed with rushes, and flags hanging in divers places, with coverlets and boughes; and many verses fixed upon the wall.

Saint Austin's lane was boarded up, for the keeping of these ways, and for observing of order. And, that no person should stand there but Scholars, there were appointed eight men as tipt-staves. And the great south gate of the King's College was kept by the Queen's porters; who received such charge, that, after the Queen's train was entered, they should suffer none to come in.

All the Scholars had in commandment, at the Queens Majesties passing by them, to cry out 'Vivat Regina', lowly kneeling. And after that, quietly and orderly to depart home to their colleges; and, in no wise to come to the Court, the Disputations, or to the Plays. And if upon some just occasion, they were enforced to goe into the towne; that then they should go two and two; upon a great pain . . .

When her Majestie was about the middle of the Scholars or Sophisters, two appointed for the same, came forth and kneeled before her Grace; and kissing their papers exhibited the same unto her Majestie. Wherein were contained two orations gratulatory; the one in verse, the other prose. Which her Highness received, and gave them to one of the footmen. The like was observed and done by the Batchellours of Arts; and of two Masters of Arts. And so she was brought among the Doctors; where all the Lords and Ladies did forsake their horses; and her Majestie only remained on horseback.

She was dressed in a gown of black velvet pinked; a call upon her head, set with pearls and pretious stones; a hat that was spangled with gold, and a bush of feathers.

The Major of the Town, riding before her Majestie bareheaded, stayed himself at the Kings College south-gate; as acknowledging that he had no authority or jurisdiction in that place. Of this he was advertised the day before by Mr. Secretary.

When the Queens Majestie came to the west doore of the church, Sir William Cecyl kneeled downe and welcomed her Grace; shewing unto her the order of the doctors. And the Bedells, kneeling, kissed their staves, and so delivered them to Mr. Secretary; who likewise kissed the same, and so delivered them to the Queens hands; who could not well hold them all. And her Grace gently and merrily redelivered them, willing him and other magistrates of the University, to minister justice uprightly, as she trusted they did. Or she would take them into her own hands, and see to it. Adding, that, although the Chancellor did hault (for his leg was sore, as is before-mentioned); yet she trusted that Justice did not hault.

(Cooper)

Religious controversy continued. At King's in 1565 some fellows complained to the Visitor, the Bishop of Lincoln, about the Provost:

Item, that his ordinarie gests are the most suspected Papistes in all the countrie, as Mr. Bedill, Mr. Gardiner, and others, whiche weekely use to resort unto him.

Item, that about three yeres past he used Mr. Wullward verie extreemly (who was of late one of our societie, but now a fellow of Eaton colledg) bicause he refusid to exequute the service at the communion, with his face towards the East, and his back towards the congregacion, according to the manner of the masse.

Item, that he enterteyned Doctour Heskyns, the famouse Papist, being brought to his table at Cambridg in the darke, and conveyed away in the darke againe.

(J. Heywood and T. Wright, Ancient Laws
of the Fifteenth Century for King's College . . .
1850)

John Caius had the last years of his life made unhappy by squabbles about religion. He had been at Gonville Hall from 1529 to 1533 before studying medicine in Padua. On his return he became Queen Mary's physician. In 1558 he returned to Cambridge, first introducing to the University new and revolutionary ideas on medicine, and secondly re-founding his old college, giving it, as Fuller sums up:

(1) land to a great proportion, (2) good building, (3) *cordial* statutes, (4) a new name, (5) a coat of arms.

He became the first Master of the reconstituted college and was allowed to remain after the accession of Queen Elizabeth. But his mastership was a troubled one. The fellows complained about him to the Archbishop:

He mainteyneth wythin his colledge copes, vestments, albes, crosses, tapers . . . with all massinge abominations, and termeth them the colledge treasure. He hath erected and sett up of late a crucifix and other idoles with the image of a doctor kneeling before them.

Archbishop Parker tried to strike a balance: in the Master he finds:

overmoche rashness for expelling felowes so sodonly . . .

but:

Suerly the contemptuouse behaviour of these felowes hath moch provoked hym. The truth is I do rather beare with the oversight of the Master in respect of his good done, and like to be done in the College by him, than with the brag of a fond sort of troublouse factiouse bodyes. Founders and benefactors be very rare in these dayes . . . Scholars controversies be nowe many and troublouse, and their delite is to come before men of authoritye to shewe their witts . . . My olde experyence hath taught me to spye daye light at a smal hole.

The truth is both parties are not excusable from folye.

(Venn, Caius College)

The Mad Puritan

In the pure house of Immanuel
I had my education,
Where my friends surmise
I dazzled my eyes
With the light of revelation:
Boldly I preach,
Hate a cross, hate a surplice,
Mitres, copes, and rochets:
Come, hear me pray
Nine times a day,
And fill your heads with crochets.

(*Pierce's Collection of English Ballads*, quoted in E. S. Shuckburgh, *Emmanuel College*, 1904)

One of the first outward signs of Puritanism was an unwillingness to wear surplices. In 1565 some three hundred fellows and scholars of St. John's 'threw of their surplices with one consent'. The Chancellor wrote calmly but firmly:

I require yew . . . to recommend my most harty and earnest desire to every one of them . . . so they will persist in the observation of uniform order in these external things: which of themselves are of no other value, but to make a demonstration of obedience, and to render a testament of unity; and being broken and neglected, argue a manifest disobedience, and gyve occasion of no small offence to many good and godly men.

(Cooper)

Bartholomew Clarke, Ll.D. of King's College also took a sensible, if light-hearted, view in a letter to the Chancellor:

these contenders are surplice and hat fanatics and the contests mere trifles, matters of self-love and self-admiration . . . These men by their counsels so disturb all things that the time which was wont heretofore to be employed in good arts and sciences is now spent and consumed in trivial janglings . . . A sophister of one of our colleges recently came into the Choir, placed himself among the thickest of the rest of the company, all with their surplices on, but he alone without one. When the censor of the college called him and questioned him for this irregularity he answered modestly . . . that the true cause was that he had pawned his surplice to a cook with whom he had run into debt for his belly. I beseech you to remedy these gross follies . . . and put an end to these controversies, or rather dotages.

(Lamb, *Original Documents*)

Thomas Cartwright, first at Clare then at St. John's College, later Fellow of Trinity and in 1569 Lady Margaret Professor of Divinity, was less concerned with surplices than with the government of the Church itself: not to be by bishops but by ministers and the Presbytery of the Church. The Archbishop of York, Edmund Grindal, former Master of Pembroke, complained to the Chancellor:

The youth of the universitie ... doth frequente his lecture in a greate number and therefore in danger to be poysoned by hym with love of contention and lykynge of novelties and to become hereafter not only unprofitable but also hurtful to the Church.

(John Strype, History of Edmund Grindal,
1710)

In June 1570 at a stormy meeting of the Senate, the Vice-Chancellor refused to admit Cartwright to his doctor's degree. He wrote a dignified letter to the Chancellor:

In my lectures I have discussed nothing which does not arise naturally from the text ... I have, it is true, asserted that the English Church has deviated from the ancient and apostolic type, but I have done so in quiet and temperate language in which only ignorance or malignity could find occasion for offence.

(J. B. Mullinger, History of the University, 1884)

That same year John Whitgift, one of Cartwright's chief opponents, was made Vice-Chancellor. Backed up by other heads of houses, he deprived Cartwright of his professorship. A year later, as Master of Trinity, he wrote to Matthew Parker:

I have pronounced Mr. Cartwright to be no Fellow here, because contrary both to the express words of his oath, and a plain statute of the college, he hath continued here above his time not being a full minister. Which truly I did not know until now of late; for if I had known it before, I might have eased myself of much trouble, and the college of great contention. Hitherto (I thank God) it hath been as quiet a college as any was in all Cambridge. Now it is clean contrary marvellous contentious, which I can ascribe to no cause so much as to Mr. Cartwright's presence here.

Cartwright left Cambridge, but the battle of words continued. In 1583, the year in which he was made Archbishop of Canterbury, Whitgift wrote:

It hath been reported that I should repent me of my works against Mr. Cartwright, but I protest I do it not, nor never will, yet I love the man, and if he would return and live in the peace of the church, he should not find a better friend than myself.

(A. F. S. Pearson, Thomas Cartwright and Elibethan Puritanism, 1925)

Many years later he did return:

After long discontinuance Master *Cartwright* coming to *Cambridge,* was importuned to preach on a week day in *Saint Maries:* where there was a great Confluence of all sorts to hear him. Grave men ran like Boys in the Streets to get places in the Church. After Sermon he dined at Master *Chaddertons,* and many went to the House to see and hear him speak.

(Samuel Clarke, Lives of Thirty-Two English Divines, 1683)

In 1584, the University Press published a book by Walter Travers entitled 'Disciplina'. It was in favour of the Presbyterian form of Church government and Whitgift wrote at once to the Chancellor:

Ever since I heard that they had a Printer in Cambridge, I did greatly fear this and such like inconveniences would follow, neither do I think that it will so stay, for although Mr. Vice-Chancellor that now is, be a very careful man and in all respects greatly to be commended, yet it may fall out hereafter, that some such as shall succeed him will be not so well affected, not have such care for the public peace of the Church . . . I think it very convenient that the books should be burned, being very factious and full of untruths; and that (if printing do still there continue) sufficient bonds with sureties should be taken of the printer not to print any books, unless they be first allowed by lawful authority, for if restraint be made here and liberty granted there, what good can be done.

(John Strype, *The Life and Acts of Archbishop J. Whitgift*, 1718)

All copies which could be found were destroyed, but the right to print 'all kinds of books' at the Press was stoutly defended.

Emmanuel College, founded by Sir Walter Mildmay, was reputed to be a Puritan College:

Coming into court after he had founded his college, the queen told him, 'Sir Walter, I hear you have erected a Puritan foundation'. 'No, madam,' saith he, 'far be it from me to countenance anything contrary to your establishment laws, but I have set an acorn, which when it becomes an oak, God alone knows what will be the fruit thereof.'

(Fuller, *History*)

Samuel Ward was a convinced and enthusiastic Puritan in his young days at Christ's and Emmanuel, though later a pillar of the Established Church and Master of Sidney Sussex. He was even imprisoned by the Parliamentarians in 1643 and his last words were, 'God bless the King and my Lord Hopton.' As an undergraduate he kept a diary of his shortcomings:

May 13 1595   My little pity of the boy who was whipt in the hall.
June 22   . . . My immoderate dyet in eating chese, very hurtful for my body att 3 a clock . . .
June 24   My no care for Norton, thinking that I am as good as he, att what time he looked sourly att me, for that I had complayned to his tutor of him.
June 27   . . . My goyng to drink wyne, and that in the Taverne, befor I called upon God . . .
July 24   My over much myrth att bowling after supper.
Sept. 15   My *crapula* in eating peares in a morning and other things which might have diminished my health. As also my too much gluttony at dinner tyme. My unfitnes to do any thing after dinner . . .
Oct. 3   . . . My immoderate eating of walnutes and cheese after supper, wherby I did distemper my body . . .

Nov. 6 My dissembling with Mr. Bourn about his cittern. Also my prid in doyng things in geometry . . .

Feb. 1 1595/6 . . . Oh the greivous sinnes in T(rinity) Colledg. which had a woman which was (carried?) from chamber to chamber on the night tyme. My adulterous dream that night.

July 18 1596 Also my gluttony in eating plumes and raisins and drinking so much after supper . . .

July 22 . . . my grief for being excluded out of the orchard . . .

July 28 My over bold spech to Mr. Montagu of Mr. Bainbridge saying he was in his coler when he put us out of the archard. Also my anger at them who would not throw over our boule in the orchard. Also at Mr. Newhouse for throwing over the stick . . .

Aug. 8 . . . my longing after damsons when I made a vow not to eat in the orchard . . .

Aug. 14 My long sleping in the morning, and my negligence in making the Analysis of the Chapter.

(Two Elizabethan Puritan Diaries,
ed. M. M. Knappen, 1933)

Let Aubrey have the last word:

Lancelot Andrewes was a great long boy of 18 yeares old at least before he went to the university. He was a fellowe of Pembroke-hall . . .

The Puritan faction did begin to increase in those dayes, and especially at Emanuel College. That party had a great mind to drawe in this learned young man, whom if they could make theirs, they knew would be a great honour to them . . . They preached up very strict keeping and observing the Lord's day . . . Yet these hypocrites did bowle in a private green at their college every Sunday after sermon; and one of the college (a loving friend to Mr. L. Andrewes) to satisfie him one time lent him the key of a private back dore to the bowling green, on a Sunday evening, which he opening, discovered these zealous preachers, with their gownes off, earnest at play. But they were strangely surprised to see the entry of one that was not of *the brotherhood*.

('Brief Lives'. Lives of Eminent Persons,
ed. A. Powell, 1949)

It was during Queen Elizabeth's reign that the University, renowned for its churchmen, now appeared to nurture all manner of men, particularly poets, with interests remote from Church affairs.

Groatsworth of Wit bought with a Million of Repentance

For being at the Universitie of Cambridge, I light amongst wags as lewd as my selfe, with whom I consumed the flower of my youth.

(Robert Greene, 1592)

Gabriel Harvey, son of a master rope maker in Saffron Walden, came up to Christ's in 1566, then became a Fellow, first at Pembroke, then Trinity Hall. Friend of Spenser, enemy of Nashe and Greene, he was the touchy but articulate victim of other fellows of Pembroke. He wrote continually to the absentee that I wuld needs in all hast be a studdiing in Christmas, when other were a plaiing, and was then hottist at mi book when the rest were hardist at their cards. Here althouh there was little need of excuse, yit, to satisfie his mind and abate his heat, I said that I had veri urgent busines this last Christmas, more than everi man knew of, or els I had bene man like enouh to have dun as other did. He tould me again, na, I had dune so everi Christmas sins I cam to the house.

and preventing him from lecturing.

When Harvey had his chance to deliver a lecture, his demanding and importun-
ate father, on a visit to Cambridge, sent for him:

Uppon Mundai, the same dai that your wurship took your jurni towards Lundon, even immediatly before I should go to read the Grek lecture (for the whitch, as for mani things mo, I recount miself infinitely bownd unto you, and the rather, by caus it was frely offrid of yow, not ambitiusly souht of me) being inded fully purposid, and providid to read, my father sent for me of the sudden to go praesently to him to the Griffin. Whereuppon the bel being tould to the lecture, as I had willid the butler before, I cam by and by into the hall, and tould the schollars mi business was sutch that I could not in ani wise read that dai, willing them to provide themselvs of bookes against the next dai, and telling them what book I intended to read unto them. Al this while a fower or five of the fellows, and Gawber, clusterid togither about the hall dore, as if there had bene sum muster towards. And M. Osburn amongst the rest, as I hard sins, in the hearing of sum schollars, like a tall fellow stept forth, and avouchid manfully that if I wuld never so fain have red, I shuld not.

(Letter-Book, ed. E. J. L. Scott, 1884)

He was a man easy to mock:

So upon his first manumission in the mysterie of Logique, becaus he observed Ergo was the deadly clap of the peece, or driv'n home stab of the Syllogisme, hee accustomed to make it the Faburden to anie thing he spake; As if anie of his companions complained he was hungry, hee would straight conclude Ergo you must goe to dinner; or if the clocke had stroke or bell tould, Ergo you must goe to such a Lecture; or if anie stranger said he came to seeke such a one, and desir'd him he would shew him which was his chamber, he would forthwith come upon him with Ergo he must go up such a paire of staires; whereupon (for a great while) he was called nothing but Gabriell Ergo up and downe the colledge.

(Thomas Nashe, *Have With You to Saffron Walden*, 1596)

But Harvey's love for learning and for his college is apparent in his hopes at the
end of the letter to John Young:

I trust yit to see the dai, and I hope shortly, and I think by your means, as I said before, when we shal al go quietly and rowndly to our books, and so in time grow to that ripenes of learning, wisdum, and eloquens whitch thos our praede-cessors grew unto: that at length it mai pas for a gud consequent, he is a Pembrook Hal man, ergo a good schollar.

Not so much is known about Edmund Spenser at Cambridge. He came up in 1569. Aubrey writes:

Mr. Edmund Spencer was of Pembrooke-hall in Cambridge; he misst the fellowship there which bishop Andrewes gott. He was an acquaintance and frequenter of Sir Erasmus Dreyden. His mistris, Rosalind, was a kinswoman of Sir Erasmus' lady's. The chamber there at Sir Erasmus' is still called Mr. Spencer's chamber. Lately, at the College takeing-downe the wainscot of his chamber, they found an abundance of cards, with stanzas of the *Faerie Queen* written on them (from John Dreyden, esq., Poet Laureate.)

Mr. Beeston sayes he was a little man, wore short haire, little band and little cuffs.

(Brief Lives)

Spenser refers only once to 'my mother Cambridge' in his poetry.

There was an abundance of 'Wits' in Cambridge in the 1580s, with Nashe at St. John's, Greene at St. John's and Clare, Marlowe at Corpus Christi and Joseph Hall at Emmanuel.

Nashe could not resist mocking Gabriel Harvey:

Let him denie that there was a Shewe made at Clare-hall of him and his two Brothers, called,

Tarrarantantara turba tumultuoso Trigonum,
Tri-Harveyorum, Tri-harmonia.

Let him denie that there was another Shewe made of the little Minnow his Brother, *Dodrans Dicke*, at *Peter-house*, called,

Duns furens. Dick Harvey in a frensie.

Whereupon Dick came and broke the Colledge glasse windowes; and Doctor Perne (being then either for himselfe or Deputie Vice-chancellour) caused him to be fetcht in and set in the Stockes till the Shew was ended, and a great part of the night after.

(Nashe, Saffron Walden)

Elsewhere in the book he defended Perne:

he had his falls, yet the Universitye had not a more carefull Father this 100 yeare.

He claimed that Marlowe was on his side against Harvey:

of whom Kit Marlowe was wont to say that he was an asse, good for nothing but to preach of the Iron Age.

Christopher Marlowe possibly wrote his first play, Tamburlaine, while he was still at Corpus. He was given a dispensation to enable him to obtain a degree without fulfilling all the necessary residence; he had clearly done the state some service, probably as a foreign agent.

Acts of the Privy Council, 29 June 1587 (addressed to the University authorities):

Whereas it was reported that Christopher Morley [Marlowe] was determined to have gone beyond the seas to Reames, and there to remaine Their Lordships thought good to certefie that he had no such intent but that in all his accons [actions] he had behaved him selfe orderlie and discreetlie wherebie he had done her majestie good service, and deserved to be rewarded for his faithfull dealinge: Their Lordships' request was that the rumor thereof should be allaied by all possible meanes, and that he should be furthered in the degree he was to take this next Commencement: Because it was not her majestie's pleasure that anie emploied as he had been in matters touching the benefitt of his Countrie should be defamed by those that are ignorant in th'affaires he went about.

(Bakeless, *Tragical History*)

Thomas Tusser (1524?–80), farmer-poet, came back thankfully to his old college in later life, possibly as a singing-clerk:

Trinity Hall

From London hence, to Cambridge thence,
With thanks to thee, O Trinitee,
That to thy hall, so passing all,
     I got at last:
There joy I felt, there trim I dwelt,
There heaven from hell I shifted well,
With learned men, a number then,
     the time I past.

When gaines was gon, and yeres grew on,
And death did crie, from London flie
In Cambridge then, I found agen,
     a resting plot:
In Colledge best of all the rest,
With thanks to thee, O Trinitee,
Through thee and thine, for me and mine,
     some stay I got.

Francis Bacon came up to Trinity in April 1573 with his elder brother Antony. Francis was then only 12. There is some knowledge of their lives because Whitgift, then Master, kept a minute account of expenses: e.g.

5 of April 1573	Antony frances (*sic*)	bacon
for anthonie beeing syck		xij*s* vj*d*
oyle for frances neck		xij*d*
concerve of barberries		x*d*
2 tables for there studies		x*s*
for meate for frances beeing syck		iiij*s* iiij*d*
for dyeng frances stockings		xij*d*
a cubbert of waynscot		ij*s*

In 1574 the following entry:

from michel mas till the beginning of march there was no dayes recorded
bycause of the breaking up for the plage, by the whole consent of the seniors

then:

carriadge of a cloke bagg from london	xij*d*
for meat from the Dolphin whiles	
Anthonie was syck	xij*s* ij*d*
the potigaries byll as yt appeareth by	
the same by doctor hatchers consta	xv*s*
a mouse trap	iiij*d*

and in 1575:

for glacing fraunces chamber windowes	ij*s*
2 dosen sylk pontes for fraunces	xvj*d*

(from articles by S. R. Maitland in
British Magazine, vol. 33, 1848)

Bacon's 'potigary' was John Hatcher of St. John's, 2nd Regius Professor of Physick, Vice-Chancellor in 1580. He bought the site of the suppressed Austin Friary at the back of Corpus.

His house was on a palatial style, containing twenty-seven rooms, the largest of which was 70 yards long and 9 feet high. Other rooms were 55 yards and 23 yards round. The walls were hung with tapestry or coloured cloth. In his 'shop' were several pairs of scales, 2 cwt of lead, a pestle and mortar, and a settle. But elsewhere were 'two crystal stones', which recall the fact that Drs. Hatcher and Dee were contemporaries at St. John's. There were also 50 lbs of 'cipery' root valued at 26*s* 8*d* which was a remedy for dropsy. Also a marble stone to cast *manus Christi*, a kind of lozenge or cough drop.

He had 540 oz. of silver plate – much double gilt. Also a scarlet gown faced with red damask and lined with red baze, a silk grogram gown guarded with velvet and faced with coney, also velvet caps, both for night and day.

(Quoted in R. W. T. Gunther, *Early Science in Cambridge*, 1937)

In some colleges one of the chief amusements was putting on plays:

In the months of January, February and March, to beguile the long evenings, they amuse themselves with exhibiting public plays, which they perform with so much elegance, such graceful action, and such command of voice, countenance and gesture, that if Plautus, Terence, or Seneca were to come to life again, they would admire their own pieces.

(William Soone, quoted in Cooper)

College accounts have many entries:

1539/40	Christ's	8*s* 8*d* expendyde by the Lorde in Chrystymas for players garmentes
1552	Trinity	Mr. Rooke for his alowance beying lord in Christymas xl*s*
1552/3	Christ's	ii*d* for sedge whan the Christemas Lords came at candlemas to the college with shewes
1560/1	Queens'	for 30 Irone candlestickes for the stage 5*s*
		for a great nosell for the stage Lantehorne 8*d*
1578	St. John's	Richard III for paper to write out the bookes for the tragedy.

(G. C. Moore Smith, *College Plays*, 1923)

But plays often caused trouble:

1578/9	St. John's	for nettes to hang before the windowes of the Halle vi*s*
1582/3	Trinity	for lv foot of newe glasse in the hall after the playes, xxviiij*s*
1598/9		given to those that watched the glasse windowes on the Comodie night vi*s*

9 December 1579

The Vice-Chancellor, John Hatcher, writes:

Punter, late scholar of St. John's (who was one of the actors in Hymenaeus) uncased, as they call it, one of the stage-keepers of Caius colledge, pluckinge off his visor; and at the first playes . . . at Trinitie Colledge had violently pressed to come into the colledge, even against the wills of such Maysters of Arts as were there appointed to see good order kept, insomuch that he had almost set that house and St. John's together by the eares; and afterwards to revenge himself for the repulse there sustained had prively crept into Benet Colledge, & takinge upon him the habit of a stage keeper there, to the greate disturbaunce of the whole assembly, did assault one of Trinitie Colledge, whom also he afterwards challenged into the fields.

(Moore Smith, College Plays)

There was bad behaviour at King's College too, as a Statute dated 20 February 1606 indicates:

Whereas there was foul & great disorder committed at the time of a comedy in King's Colledge by most rude and barbarous throwing of many great stones at and thorough the hall windows, with great outcries and shouting by multitudes of Scholars and others, for the space of about two hours altogether; there being then assembled the said hall full, not only of the inferiour sort, but also of divers young noblemen, doctors, batchelors in divinity, and masters of arts, to their great offence, annoyance and disturbance; besides the breaking of many other windows . . . and a great post of timber violently pulled out of the ground . . . offenders shall be stay'd for one whole year for taking further degrees &c.

(Heywood and Wright, Cambridge
Transactions)

For two nights in February 1610/11 during the performance of a comedy in Trinity College Hall there was rioting at the Great Gate. The stage-keepers (stewards) were subsequently brought to the Vice-Chancellor's court by the fellows and scholars of St. John's. The Registrary, James Tabour, MA, of Corpus Christi, recorded the evidence.

Nicholas Aiger, BA, of St. John's: . . . a stage-keeper, who was in a carsey sute, did smyte with a lyte lynke [i.e. a lighted link] over Sir Elsborrogh his heade, and then Sir Elsborrogh houlding up his arm to hould of the torch dropping, that stage-keeper did hitt him a good blowe with his clubb upon his arme, and then Sir Oxley stept forward and helped to rescue Sir Elsborrogh, then other stage-keepers came to rescue that stage-keeper and . . .

Willyam Twelves, undergraduate, of Trinity: . . . was in the street when as Mr. Coote came out the colledge to the ende of Trinitye walk before the Sone gate (agaynst the church-gate of Alhallows), houlding his dagger by the poynte, did saye, 'Wher be these Jonians? Is ther none of the rougues will answer a man? Zounds, I will throwe my dagger amongst them' . . . Mr. Coote did not know that Mr. Vice Chancellor was ther, for that after, when Mr. Coote sawe Mr. Vice Chancellor come upp towards Trinitye Colledge, he Mr. Coote did put the dagger under his arme to hyde it . . .

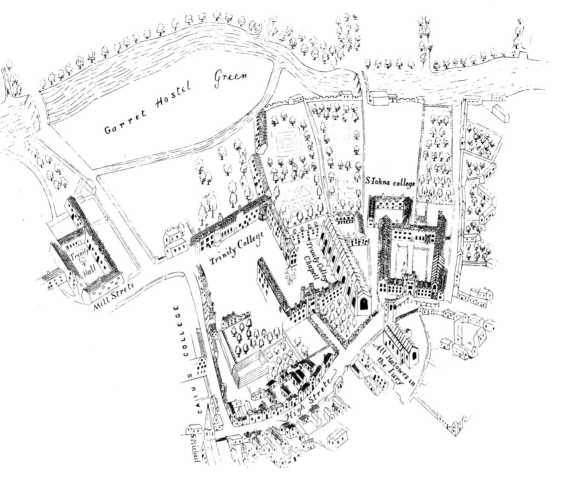

6. Trinity and St. John's Colleges, 1592

Tristram Otbey, undergraduate of St. John's: he sayeth he sawe Sir Osborne John's lynked without Trinitye Colledge gates, and did see a stage-keeper . . . synge him with a lyted torch on his hatt, and it went out with the stroke; and then he did see him smyte him agayne with lynk agayne lyted, and his clubb, soe violently that Sir Osborne reled agaynst the wall . . .

Isacke Wood, undergraduate of Christ's: he sayeth he was at Trynitye gates the night before the fyrst comedye began and befor St. John's men came out with clubbs, and he sayeth that he stoode under Trynitye Colledge garden wall which is Mr. Tompsons, and was smitted with a stone which came from Trynitye Colledge ward, but from what parte he doth not know; he also sayeth one Cally of Christ's Colledge was also smytten with a stone, but knoweth not from what place of Trynitye Colledge it came.

Jeffrey Allott, servant: sayeth the fyrst night of the Comedyes he was going after his master who went to the Comedye; and being mydwaye upp in Trynitye Colledge walke, a stagekeeper miscalled him, and strock at him with a clubb,

[57]

and beet him backe, and after yt standing by agynst Trynitye Chappell by Allhallows church wall, he had a great bricke batt which [he] did bring into the Court. [This bricke batt] was thrown out Trynitye Garden, and did hitt him upon the shoulder. He also did se manye stones thrown down from Trynitye Colledge Towre. This stone and the other were throwne after yt Mr. Vice-chancellor was gone in. He sayeth Sir Oxley and Sir Elborough had noe weapons when they wer smitten by stagekeepers.

Dr. Samuel Herne, DD of Trinity: he sayeth that about five of the clock the fyrst night Sir Elborough, [as he taketh his name to be], did come unto him, and shewe him a littell strooke which bled upon the backe of his hands, which he tould him the stagekeepers gave him, and this examinant tould him that yf he would shew him the partye that had hurt him he should have amenns made him; but then he, and one Sir Oxley who was also by, wer very unrulye, and pressed forward agaynst the stagekeepers, and would not by any good perswasion that he could use give back; wheruppon he this examinant willed the stage-keepers to give back even to the Colledge gates; and then presently the Clubbmen in great number followed and pressed after, and then presently one Mr. Johnson, President of St. Johns, did come to putt them back, and did box some, and perswade others to goe back, but they would in noe weas be perswaded, wheruppon he this examinant, seeing stones throwen out Mr. Thompson's garden, did bid them to leave throwing, which they presently did. The stones were thrown after that the Clubbmen came, and would not suffer the stagekeepers to keepe the walke, and cryed out 'Clubbs', 'Clubbs', and 'Brake downe there gates'; and the stones were thrown only to the corner of the walke to keepe the clubbmen off the walke.

(J. W. Clark, *Riot at the Great Gate of Trinity*, 1906)

Much depended on whether the attacks were premeditated:

Goodwyfe Feisbien on Weddensday att night, when stagekeepers were abroad, related unto her neighbours that foure Schollers, more or lesse, of Trinitye Colledge, coming into her shopp for Tobacco, att what tyme certaynly she knew not, spake ther of some provision of stones layd upp in the towers or gardens or therabout, and also of some buckets to be provyded to fetch water from the conduyte to powre downe upon St. Jhons menne from the towers.

George Ferne, scholar of Trinity: . . . on Thursday morning, being in moother Benn's house betwixt tenne and eleven of the clocke, reported thatt the foregoing night ther wer six boyes which carryed upp stones in ther hatts to maynteyne them that threw from the towres.

Nicholas Carr, undergraduate of St. John's: sayeth that his brother of Trinitye did bid him one Tuysdaye night, before the comedye, that he should not come to the comedye, for the stagekeepers wer Masters of Arts and none but Masters of Arts would be suffered to come in.

William Whaley, churchwarden of Trinity Church: that Sir Bickly Petri and he, being together at the Sune by the fyer, about a fortnight before the Comedye, a Scholler of Trynetye Colledge, whom he knoweth not, being ther, he did hear the sayd Scholer saye that yf the Sir Coupers came to Trynetye Colledge Comedyes he would not be in ther cases for c^{li}, they would be soe beaten they

[58]

would be neere spoyled, and 'You St John's men look to your selves, for we are provided thre score stronge for you.'

Sir Bickly sayeth that Winter of Trinitye Colledg said before the comedyes wer at the Sone that it wer best for Sir Couper of St. Johns to keep out the Comedyes.

There was some evidence of an attempt to bribe a witness:

John King, porter of Trinity: that on two or three dayes after that the comedyes at Trinitye Colledge were past, he was sent for unto Mr. Kemp's chamber at Trinitye Colledge, and being come thither Mr. Kempe did shutt his dore to and then shrewdlye examined him whither yt he came at the storr before the gates at the Comedyes, and who he knew ther, and such-like questions, and Mr. Kempe tould him he would give him an angell in silver or gould; but strove more to tell where they were, and what was done; but because he knew none, he tould him he could not saye anye thinge.

Punishments ranged from suspension of graduates, whipping of undergraduates, to payment for damage. A porter and four townsmen who were implicated in the fight were given short prison sentences followed by a period in the stocks.

There was trouble from long-haired undergraduates. In the yard of the Black Bear Inn on 28 May 1600, there was an interlude at which:

Dominus Pepper was seen with an improper habit, having deformed long locks of unseemly sight, and great breeches, undecent for a graduate or a scholar of orderly carriage; therefore, the said Pepper was commanded to appear presently, and procure his hair to be cut or prowled, and which being done, the said Pepper returning to the consistory was then suspended *ab omni gradu suscepto et suscipiendo*. (*Retrospective Review*, anon. 1825)

There was also trouble from over-sensitive ladies:

'The tragedy of Roxana' by William Alabaster

It was acted several times in Trinity College Hall, and so admirably and so pathetically, that a gentlewoman present thereat, upon hearing the last words, *sequar, sequar*, so hideously pronounced, fell distracted and never after recovered her senses.

Probably the most sophisticated of the anonymous undergraduate plays were the three 'Parnassus' plays performed at St. John's between 1598 and 1601. In them there are comments on contemporary poets,

> Marlowe was happy in his buskind muse,
> Alas unhappy in his life and end.
> Pitty it is that wit so ill should dwell,
> Wit lent from heaven, but vices sent from hell ...

parody,

> A gentle pen rides prickinge on the plaine,
> This paper plaine, to resolute my love ...

> Let scholars be as thrifty as they may
> They will be poor ere their last dying day;
> Learning and poverty will ever kiss . . .

Why, our emptie handed sattine sutes doe make more accounte of some foggie faulkner, than of a wittie scholler, had rather rewarde a man for setting of a hayre, than a man of wit for making of a poeme. Eache long eared ass rides on his trappinges and thinkes it sufficiente to give a scholler a majesticke nodd with his rude nodle . . . Why, woulde it not greeve a man of good spirit to see Hobson finde more money in the tayles of 12 Jades, than a scholler in 200 bookes?

and the contrast between poor parents and their graduate sons:

> Why ist not strange to see a ragged clarke,
> Some stamell* weaver or some butchers sonne,
> That scrubd a late within a sleeveles gowne,
> When the Commencement, like a morice dance
>   Hath put a bell or two about his legges,
> Created him a sweet cleane gentleman:
> How then he gins to follow fashions?
> He whose thin sire dwells in a smokye roufe,
> Must take Tobacco and must weare a locke.
> His thirsty Dad drinkes in a wooden bowle,
> But his sweet selfe is serv'd in silver plate.

> (*The Three Parnassus Plays,*
> ed. J. B. Leishman, 1949)

1603–1645

The proximity of Newmarket brought various royal visitors to Cambridge. James I first came in 1614.

In deference to his known dislike of tobacco it was ruled, according to a letter from John Chamberlain to Sir Dudley Carleton,

that no Graduate, Scholler, or Student of this Universitie presume to resort to any Inn, Taverne, Ale-howse, or Tobacco-shop, at any tyme dureing the abode of his Majestie here; nor doe presume to take tobacco in St. Marie's Church or in Trinity Colledge Hall upon payne of finall expellinge the Universitie . . . The King made his entry there the 7th of this present, with as much solemnity and concourse of gallants and great men, as the hard weather and extreme foul ways would permit. The Prince came along with him, but not the Queen, by reason (as it is said) that she was not invited: which error is rather imputed to their Chancellor, than to the scholars, that understand not these courses. Another defect was that there were no Ambassadors . . . The King and Prince lay at Trinity College where the plays were represented; and the hall so well ordered for room, that above 2000 persons were conveniently placed . . . The

* Rough woollen cloth.

divinity act was performed reasonably well, but not answerable to the expectation; the law and physic acts stark naught; but the philosophy act made amends, and indeed was very excellent.

(Cooper)

The 'philosophy act' took place in Great St. Mary's, with Matthew Wren of Pembroke as 'answerer' and John Preston of Emmanuel as first opponent. The subject was 'whether dogs can make syllogismes':

Preston said, 'An Enthimeme is a lawful and real Syllogisme, but Dogs can make them'. He instanced in an Hound who had the major Proposition in his mind, namely, '*The Hare is gone either this or that way;* smels out the minor with his Nose; namely, *She is not gon that way*, and follows the Conclusion, *Ergo this way with open* mouth.' . . . The instance suited with the Auditory, and was applauded, and put the Answerer to his distinctions, that Dogs might have *sagacity*, but not *sapience*, had much in their Mouthes, little in their Minds; that their lips were larger than their Understandings . . . Now the Moderator began to be afraid, and to think how troublesome a pack of Hounds, well followed and Applauded, at last might prove, and so came in into the Answerer's aid, and told the Opponent that his Dogs, he did believe, were very weary, and desired him to take them off, and start another Argument . . . Preston would not yield, but hallooed still and put them on . . . The King who in his conceit was all the time upon *New-Market Heath,* stood up and told the Moderator that he was not at all satisfied, since he had a hound at *Newmarket* which, having routed a hare and realising it needed help, set up a baying which called the rest of the pack. The King wanted to know how this could be contrived and carried on without the use and exercise of understanding . . . Whereupon Wren protested that *his Majesties Dogs were always to be excepted, who hunted not by Common Law, but by Prerogative* . . . The Moderator did acknowledge . . . that whereas in the morning the Reverend and Grave *Divines* could not make *Syllogisms*, the *Lawyers* could not, nor the *Physitians*, now ever Dog could, especially his Majesties.

(W. T. Costello, The Scholastic Curriculum,
1958)

The King called for a repeat performance of one of the plays, 'Ignoramus', in 1615. A surprise disputation was also held:

certain Jesuits or priests, being to be conveyed from London to Wisbich castle, were not suffered to come through Cambridge, but by the sheriff carried over the back side of the town to Cambridge castle, where they lodged one night, which the vice-chancellor did carefully and wisely to prevent the dangers which might have ensued if the younger sort of students had seen them . . . which also to prevent, the vice-chancellor attended their coming into the castle, and then sent back all such young students as he saw there. This they perceiving, offered a disputation to the vice-chancellor upon 3 questions . . . The vice-chancellor told them they were to make no abode there, neither had he the power from his majesty to give leave for a disputation, which might give them occasion to stay and cause a meeting of the students, and so left them; whereupon the Papists gloried as in the victory, that they offered to dispute, and the vice-chancellor did refuse it, and, that this might be better known, they writ divers copies of the questions, and fastened them to boughs; and the next morning, as they went to take boat for Wisbich, they threw them over Magdalen college walls, which were brought to the vice-chancellor; whereupon the vice-chancellor certified the king what they had done, so the king, about 8 days before his coming, notified that at his coming to Cambridge he would have a disputation there of those questions . . .

Upon Saturday, the 13 Maii, 1615, news was brought that his majesty would be at Cambridge that night, and that in the way he meant to hunt a buck; so at 2 of the clock the school bell and St. Mary's bells rung to call the universitie together.

(account by John Tabor, Registrary of the University, quoted in Cooper)

Disputations formed a predominant part of the still medievally slanted scholastic discipline, and those who took part often enjoyed the cut and thrust.

Simonds D'Ewes was an undergraduate at St. John's in 1618:

In the afternoon I went to the schooles and disputed extempore upon two senior sophisters the one of Trinitye the other of Christs, I my selfe being but a junior sophister; the first of them tooke my questions, but the other was brooken offe by the proctors comming, howsoever for my part I had very good successe in both.

Yesterdayes worke made mee skarce know my selfe to daye; yet did I to the uttermost restrain my approaching pride, wherefore noe sooner was dinner ended this Wednesday but I thought long to bee at the schooles to trye my fortunes once again, where I was soe intolerably pusseld by an excellent scholler much above mee in standing, both in giving mine and taking his questions, as I had good cause to pluck downe my plumes . . .

His other studies, despite his enthusiasm, seem to reflect a conservative curriculum:

I bought Aristotles and Golius politics because I had a desire to read them over and my Tutour was willing to helpe mee the best hee could in them. On Wednesdaye night wee had begunn Virgils first Eglog; but both Thursdaye night and this our progresse was hindred by divers occasions.

The day being passed over in my wonted affaires, of which I had at this time wonderfull varietye as Logicke, historye, physicks and ethicks beside my private meditations elaborate letters and other necessary exercises.

(from the diary of D'Ewes, quoted in *The Eagle*)

Milton later complained:

I think there never can be any place for these studies on Parnassus, unless perhaps some uncultivated nook at the foot of the hill, unlovely, rough and horrid with brambles and thorns, overgrown with thistles and thick nettles.

(from 'Oration in the Schools – Against Scholastic Philosophy' in J. S. Diekhoff, *Milton on Himself*, 1939)

Other undergraduates' studies do show a greater variety of interest and much dedication to work.

John Williams went to St. John's in 1598, aged 16 and was a fellow in 1603.
He later became Archbishop of York and Lord Keeper of the Great Seal:

From his Youth upward he never required more than three Hours sleep in Twentyfour, to keep him in perfect Health.

Greek and Hebrew he ply'd closely, as the best Introduction to Divinity; and in these he had the Assistance of the most Eminent Men at that Time in Cambridge. To master French, he found it a task of no great difficulty: He dipt into the Elements of Geometry; and found amidst his Bus'ness some leisure hours to soften his severer Studies with Musick, in which, both vocal and instrumental, he had attain'd to a competent skill.

(Ambrose Philips, *Life of John Williams,* 1700)

John Preston:

he was sent to Cambridge and admitted of King's College under the tuition of Mr. Busse, one of the Fellows, Anno Domini 1604.

Here he did as young schollars used to doe, that is applyed himself to the Genius of the College, and that was musique; and finding that the theory was shorte and soone atteyned, he made account the practice would also be so; and accordingly adventured upon the Lute, the hardest instrument; but heere he found though theory was shorte, art was long . . . and while his fingers were thus foundred on the Lute, it fell out that his Tutor Mr. Busse was chose Master of the Schole at Eaton, and so removed from the Colledge, about two yeares after he was admitted.

He moved to Queens' College:

His genius led him unto Naturall Philosophy, wch by that time was became his propp task . . . adoreth Aristotle as his tutelary saint, and had a happiness usually to enter when others stuck, and what was difficult to others he made little of.

No darke untrodden path in all his physicks and metaphysics but he was perfect in it; and so drowned and devoted was he, that he seldom or never could be seen abroad, to the wonder and amazement of his former brave companions, so that no time passed (without working) no, not that betweene the ringing and tolling of the Bell to meales . . . I have heard him say, that there was nothing that wer Scotus or Occham wrote, but he had weighed and examined; he delighted much to read them in the first and oldest editions that could be got; I have still a Scotus, in a very old print and a paper not inferior to parchment, that hath his hand and notes upon it throughout; yet he continued longer in Aquinas, whose summes he would sometimes read as the Barber cut his haire, and when any fell upon the place he read, he would not lay downe his booke, but blow it off . . .

Mr. Preston in his youth would not sleep, but let the bed clothes hang downe so as to awaken him.

(Thomas Ball, *Life of Doctor Preston,* ed. E. W. Harcourt, 1885)

Some were lucky in their teachers.

Joseph Mede is described, probably by John Worthington:

After he had by daily Lectures well grounded his Pupills in Humanity, Logick and Philosophy, and by frequent converse understood to what Studies their Parts might be most profitably applied, he gave them his Advice accordingly. And when they were able to goe alone he chose rather to set every one his daily Task, than constantly to confine himself and them to precise hours for Lectures. In the Evening they all came to his Chamber to satisfy him that they had perform'd the Task he had set them. The first question which he us'd then to propound to every one in his order was ... What Doubts have you met in your studies today? (For he supposed that To doubt nothing and To understand nothing were verifiable alike.)

('Life of Joseph Mede', in Mede's *Works*, 1645)

The great mathematician William Oughtred came up to King's in 1592 and was later rector of Albury, where he was constantly visited by students:

generally reputed the greatest Mathematician of his age and country ... He was the first that gave a turn for mathematical studies in the University of Cambridge ... his very study seems to have had a good effect on his health, as the Mathematics was not only recreation to him, but Epicurism. He was sprightly and active at about eighty years of age; and died in an ecstacy of joy, upon hearing of the Restoration of Charles II.

(Wilson, *Memorabilia Cantabrigiae*)

John Aubrey records other contemporary Cambridge mathematicians:

Mr. Edward Wright: he was of Caius College in Cambridge. He published his book intituled *Certain Errors of Navigation Corrected* in 1610. It is dedicated to the high and mighty Henry, prince of Wales, etc.

He was one of the best mathematicians of his time; and the *then* new way of sayling, which yet goes by the name of 'sayling by Mr. Mercator's chart', was purely his invention, as plainely doeth and may appear in his learned booke called 'Wright's Errors in Navigation' ... He made a table of Logarithmes befor Logarithmes were invented and printed, but he did not know he had donne it ...

In Sir Charles Scarborough's time (he was of Caius College) the head of that house would visit the boyes' chambers, and see what they were studying; and Sir Charles Scarborough's genius led him to the mathematics, and he was wont to be reading of Clavius upon Euclid. The old Dr. had found in the title '... e Societate Jesu', and was much scandalised at it. Sayd he, 'By all means leave-off this author, and read Protestant mathematicall bookes.'

(*Brief Lives*)

John Wallis, at Emmanuel in the early 1630s had a different experience:

I did therefore prosecute it not as a formal study, but as a pleasing diversion, at spare hours ... For I had none to direct me, what books to read, or what to seek, or in what Method to proceed . . . Amongst more than Two hundred students in our College at that time, I do not know of any two (perhaps not any) who had more of Mathematics than I, (if as much) which was then but little . . . For Mathematics, (at that time, with us) were scarce looked upon as Academical Studies, but rather Mechanical, as the business of Traders, Merchants, Seamen, Carpenters, Surveyors of Lands, or the like; and perhaps Almanach-makers in London.

(Costello, *The Scholastic Curriculum*)

Aubrey also has a note on William Harvey, whom Cambridge can partially claim.

William Harvey, M.D., natus at Folkestone in Kent: borne at the house which is now the post-house, a faire stone-built house, which he gave to Caius College in Cambridge, with some lands there . . .

He was always very contemplative, and the first that I heare of that was curious in anatomie in England. He made dissections of frogges, toades, and a number of other animals, and had curious observations on them, which papers, together with his goods, in his lodgings at Whitehall, were plundered at the beginning of the Rebellion, he being for the king.

(*Brief Lives*)

Anatomy always seems to have attracted the curious.

Joseph Mede, 16 April 1631:

Going on Wednesday from Jesus Colledge pensionary with Dr. Ward to his colledge through the closes and gardens and espying a garden dore open I entred and saw a hideous sight of the skull and all other bones of a man (with ligaments and tendons) hanging out drying in the sun by strings upon trees, etc. I asked what it meant. They told me it was the pedlar they anatomized this Lent and that when his bones were dry they were to be sett together againe as they were naturally and so reserved in a chest or coffin . . . It was the garden of one Seale a surgeon and a cheife in the dissection.

(Heywood & Wright, *Cambridge Transactions*)

Members of the University were not exclusively concerned with learning and by no means led entirely blameless lives, as various decrees and reports suggest.

One decree was entitled:

A DECREE FOR REFORMING NIGHT JETTERS, KEEPERS OF GREY-HOUNDS, &C.

In 1629 King Charles issued injunctions from Newmarket:

Whereas we have been informed, that of late years many students of that our University, not regarding their own birth, degree, and quality, have made diverse contracts of marriage with women of mean estate and of no good fame in that town, to their great disparagement, the discontentment of their friends and parents, and the dishonour of the government of that our University; we will and command you, that at all times hereafter, if any taverner, innholder, or victualler, or any other inhabitant of the town, or within the jurisdiction of the University, shall keep any daughter or other woman in his house, to whom there shall resort any scholers of that University, of what condition soever, to mispend their time, or otherwise misbehave themselves, or to engage themselves in marriage without the consent of those that have the gardiancie and tuition of them . . . that you command the said woman or women . . . to remove out of the University and four miles of the same . . . And if any refuse to . . . that you imprison them till they remove or put in such bonds with sureties.

(Heywood and Wright, *Cambridge Transactions*)

1636. Report in anticipation of visit of Archbishop Laud, entitled 'Common Disorders in the University' (Laud did not in fact come):

in all places among Graduates, & Priests also, as well as the younger Students, we have fair Roses upon the Shoe, long frizled haire upon the head, broad spred Bands upon the Shoulders, and long large Merchants Ruffs about the neck, with fayre feminine Cuffs at the wrist . . .

In KING'S COLL. some of the Quiremen cannot sing & are diverse of them very negligent. The Choristers are neare one half of them mutes, when they list they come to service with Surplices & when they list they come without them . . .

In CHRIST'S COLL. . . . Noblemen's Sonns have of late left of their Surplices there as they doe when they are in other Colledges. Hard by this House there is a Town Inn (they call it the Brazen George) wherein many of their schollers live, lodge, & study, & yet the Statutes of the Universitie require that none lodge out of the Colledge where no Governour or Tutor can looke after their Pupills as they ought.

(Cooper)

Letters and diaries of parents and their sons at university reflect many pre-occupations. Lady Katherine Paston wrote frequently to her son, 'sweet Will':

To my very wellbeloued sonne william Paston
these I pray at his lodginge in Corpus Christy Colledge:
Cambridge

My good will:

I doe much desire to heer how you doe . . . take heed to your selfe good child, that I may here a good report of your Ciuill and kinde behaiour. towards all. but cheeffly haue an espetiall care to fear and serue god: lett it be the first and last thinge you thinke of . . . and next beware of violent tennisinge or leapinge or any other thinge which shall hinder your healthe: take heed of frute of all sorts if you eate any. eate very moderately . . . I hop to heer you still hate the very smell of tobaca: I send you a pece of gowld for a token. and if thow doest well and be ruled by thy tutore in all things, for thy good: then thow shalt be sur to want nothinge that I can doe for the: and so the Lords blesinge be for euer more vpon thy sowle and body farwell good will:

thy most Louinge Mother
Katherine Paston

Comend me very kindly to the *master* and to good mr. Roberts. wright to me as oft as thow canst and so agayne farwell:
friday the 11th of June 1624.

25 June 1624

... good child, lett not a poor hungery siser want a reward from the. lett such not want bread or beer, in a moderat maner ... at the Commencement I will send a beaver hat to the but I feare it will be to bigge ore to littell or too broad verged or sumthinge amis.

July 1624

I doe send the a new sute of sattine to weare this commencement as also a payer of silke stokins poynts garters and shoe strings and a silver girdell ... have a great care to wear thy clothes neat and clean it is a great Comendation to se a yonge man spincs and neat, without spots and durtines upon his clothes.

March 1625

I haue sent the as thow desirest, some edeble Comodity for this Lent. to eate in your chamber your good tutor and you together: a Cake and Cheese a fewe pudinges and linkes: a turkey pie pasty: a pot of Quinces and sume marmelate wishinge all maye Come saffe hom to the ...

Remember my best respecte to the most worthy Doctor and thanke hime I pray the for his kinde wrightinge to me ... I send your *quarters*, rent 40s due at our Lady next your tamel gowne and damask sute, for that I know not what warme wether it maye be at easter. but be as sparinge of the wearinge of it as maye be.

March 1626

I sende the now thy New sute. a girdell, 2 shirts: 2 ruff bands: as for a beaver hate, if you cowld fitt your selfe *with* a spetiall good on I wold be very well content that thow sholdest haue on agaynst Easter ... moreover I sende the and thy tutor a turkey pasty and the other is a pateridge peie. a littell Cake and a Littell cheese for Robin the great Cake the Cheese and the pudinge for thy tutor and thy self and lett thy Cosine Robine Bell be partaker also of the rest sumtims *with* the.

(*Correspondence, 1603–1627*, ed. Ruth Hughey, 1941)

There was no lack of advice for those coming up to the University.

Henry Peacham in 'The Complete Gentleman' (1622) writes:

Chapter V 'Of a Gentleman's Carriage in the University'
Wherefore, your first care, even with pulling off your boots, let be the choice of your acquaintance and company ... For the companions of your recreation consort with gentlemen of your own rank and quality, for that friendship is best contenting and lasting. To be overfree and familiar with inferiors argues a baseness of spirit and begetteth contempt.

Travel to and from home was expensive, as was the cartage of food, trunks, books etc. Hobson the carrier was useful in this connection, as the following letter, written to the Chancellor on his behalf in 1628 or 1629, shows:

We are earnestly requested by our trusty and ancient carrier, Thomas Hobson, to be humble petitioners that your lordship will be pleased to procure him a toleration to travel between Cambridge and London with his waggons with four wheels, without incurring the danger of the penalty mentioned in his Majesty's late proclamation. Upon his information we have well considered of those inconveniences which will happen to his Majesty and the University carriages, without these waggons be suffered to go as they have done; for first, it is impossible for him to carry from us to London those great vessels of fish for provision for his Majesty's household; secondly, the passengers, whereof most are scholars, women and children, that travel to or from in them; thirdly, books, trunks, and other necessaries for our scholars, without danger of overthrowing, and great loss and spoil of such things as are committed to his charge in them: all of which have heretofore been safely conveyed at reasonable rates from the city of London hither ... which cannot be satisfactorily undertaken in carts without greater charge and inevitable danger; the way being deep in winter, and the carts more subject to overthrowing ...

*(The Fairfax Correspondence, ed.
George W. Johnson, 1848)*

Hobson was in demand not only as a carrier but for horses. Richard Steele, in 'The Spectator' (1712), explains the real meaning of the term, 'Hobson's choice':

... observing that the scholars rid hard, his manner was to keep a large stable of horses, with boots, bridles and whips to furnish the Gentlemen at once, without going from college to college to borrow, as they have done since the death of this worthy man ... but when a man came for a horse, he was led into the stable, where there was a great choice, but he obliged him to take the horse which stood next the stable-door; so that every customer was alike well served according to his chance ... from whence it became a proverb, when what ought to be your election was forced upon you to say, Hobson's choice ...

Milton made him famous:

On the University Carrier who sickn'd in the time of his vacancy, being forbid to go to London, by reason of the Plague

> Here lies old *Hobson*, Death hath broke his girt,
> And here, alas, hath laid him in the dirt,
> Or els the ways being foul, twenty to one,
> He's here stuck in a slough and overthrown.
> 'Twas such a shifter, that if truth were known,
> Death was half glad when he had got him down;
> For he had any time this ten years full,
> Dodg'd with him, betwixt *Cambridge* and the Bull.
> And surely, Death could never have prevail'd,
> Had not his weekly cours of carriage fail'd;
> But lately finding him so long at home,
> And thinking now his journeys end was come,
> And that he had tane up his latest Inne,

In the kind office of a Chamberlin
Shew'd him his room where he must lodge that night,
Pull'd off his Boots, and took away the light:
If any ask for him, it shall be sed,
Hobson has supt, and's newly gone to bed.

There was often worry about money:

Ralph Josselin, at Jesus College in 1632:

March. My father's love was such towards me that when I was neare 16 yeares
old I went to Cambridge to Jesus Colledge, entred pentioner under Mr. Tho.
Lant my loving and I hope godly and honest tutor; he dealt lovingly with me,
but I was forced to come from Cambridge many times for want of meanes &
loose my time in the country . . .

In 1640:

That spring I went up to Cambridge to visit for my degree of M^{str} arts as ^{r}
custome was: charges their and for my gowne and cassocke amounted to 19*l* 18*s*
& somewhat upwards: this was a hard pull.

> (*Ralph Josselin's Diary*, ed. E. Hockliffe,
> 1908)

and many begging letters:

*Robert Herrick the poet went to St. John's in 1613. His father was dead and
and he was dependent upon his uncle, to whom he wrote:*

Health from Heaven
Chambridg

Sr I have long since expected your return, in that your long absence hath made
me want that, which your presence could have remedied, (I trust you are not
ignorant what my meaning is) may it therefore please you to send me 10 guineas
for my ocasions require so much, and the long time that your worship hath been
absent from London hath compelled me to run somewhat deepe into my Tailours
debt; I entreat your worship to send me a part of my stipend, with all possible
sceleritie for want of which so necessarie helpe, cares greatly posses me, and
force me contrarie to my will, in some sort to neglect my study, whereas if you
would be pleased to furnish me with so much that I might keepe before hand
with my Tutor, I doubt not but with quicker dispatch to attaine to what I
ayme . . .

For ever readie to be comanded during mortalitie
Robert Hearick

To the right worship his carefull uncle Sr William Hearick these to be delired
at his house in London.

and later:

Trinitie Hall: Cam:

I have (as I presume you know) changd my colledg, for one, where the quantie
of expence wilbe shortned, by reason of the privacie of the house, where I

purpose to live recluce, till Time contract me to some other calling, striving now with myself (retayning upright thoughts) both sparingly to live, thereby to shun the current of expence.

(Works, ed. L. C. Martin, 1956)

George Herbert, at Trinity, was dependent on his step-father:

March 18, 1617

... you know I was sick last Vacation, neither am I yet recovered, so that I am fain ever and anon, to buy somewhat tending towards my health; for infirmities are both painful and costly. Now this Lent I am forbid utterly to eat any Fish, so that I am fain to diet in my Chamber at mine own cost; for in our public Halls, you know, is nothing but Fish and White-meats ... Sometimes also I ride to Newmarket, and there lie a day or two for fresh Air; all which tend to avoiding of costlier matters, if I should fall absolutely sick; I protest and vow, I even (*sic*) study Thrift, and yet I am scarce able to make one half year's allowance shake hands with the other. And yet if a Book of four or five Shillings come in my way, I buy it, though I fast for it; yea, sometimes of Ten Shillings.

(Works, ed. R. A. Willmott, 1854)

In 1626 Anthony Gawdy wrote from Caius College to his patron:

... As farre as I understand by my carrier you are disposed to bestowe a shute [suit] upon me. I confess it is the time now when nature doeth cloeth all hir cretures: the earth with grase, as the cloeth, and with diversitye of flowers as it were the triming or setting out of the garment: besides if you would be pleased to observe, in yor own yarde, you shall not see any creature but dame nature will afford him a new coete in summer; goe we a little higher and behowld the birdes of the aier, and yow shall see them in the springe drope down their feathers, as men cast off there oulde shuts, and then put on another. Not to trouble you I am not determined to com doune till after the commencement, because it is now our chuife time of arts and disputations, but if then you thinke it fitting to let mee come and waight upon you (with all my harte); in the mean time I shall make shuift, or if you be other wayes disposed, I think Robert Levall heath my measure, I am not growne since you did see me neyther in haith nor bigness, but only I hope to growe every daye more and more, by my pore indeavours, in to yor faviour.

Yor porre kinsman

(John Venn, Early Collegiate Life, 1913)

He was given his suit. Some patrons or parents might have reacted differently:

To my very loving son, Henry Fairfax, in Trinity College,
Harrie, I would to God you would forbear to write to me in this discomfortable style, or promise yourself my displeasure ...

(Fairfax Correspondence)

(Henry had been exceeding his allowance.)

Some men had other worries. John Williams (see p. 63 above) spent time on his Welsh accent:

At Cambridge his Countrymen receiv'd him with a hearty wellcome, and that must always be said for their Honour, that they are sincere and cordial in their Affections to one another, beyond most People. As they carress'd young Williams, so likewise did they never cease praising him, and speaking much in his Commendation up and down the University . . . There are few of our Welsh Youth but at their first coming abroad, would move almost any Man to Laughter with the Native Tone of their Voice, and by pronouncing all their English, as if they spoke it in a Passion. And thus it was with our Youngster, which would often put him to the Blush . . . this made him more the retired Student, because he was resolv'd to shut himself up from all Company as close as possible, till he had smooth'd his Tongue, and could manage it like others his Companions . . . And this he practiced the more earnestly . . . so that in a short time he overcame this National Defect of his so far, that when ever he had occasion to speak publickly, his Gesture and Pronunciation were as elegant as his Invention.

(Philips, Life)

and Joseph Mede of Christ's on his speech defects:

The letter R was Shibboleth to him, which he could not easily pronounce; so that a set speech cost him double the pains to another man, being to fit words as well to his mouth as his matter.

(Fuller, History)

Mede was a man of many interests:

He allowed himself little or no Exercise but *Walking*; and oftentimes, when he and others were walking in the Fields or in the College-Garden, he would take occasion to speak of the Beauty, Signatures, usefull Virtues and Properties of the Plants then in view. For he was a curious Florist, an accurate Herbalist . . . Here [in the Fellows' Garden] he hath been found very busy (at due hours) and sometime *knuckle-deep*, when he would say smiling, *Why? this was Adam's work in his Innocency.*

He had a quick tongue and turn of phrase:

Such Fellow-commoners who came to the University onely to see it and to be seen in it, he called The University-Tulips, that made a Gawdy show for a while &c.

When he saw others lavishly spending beyond their Income and not wisely proportioning their Expenses to their Receipts, he us'd to say (with a pleasant allusion to that Philosophical term) *they wanted the Estimative Faculty.*

(Worthington, 'Life of Mede')

Much of an undergraduate's (and indeed graduate's) time was taken up by attending chapel, listening to sermons and examining his conscience.

Ralph Josselin

1636   In Cambridge in my studyes I was close and diligent; my fault was to omitt too many mornings by reason of my tenderness, either in bed or by the fire: the superstitions of the Church were a perplexity then unto mee.

(Diary, ed. Hockliffe)

Nicholas Ferrar (of 'Little Gidding' fame):

During his being at Clare Hall (c. 1605–13) he had an only Sister then living – marry'd to one Mr. John Collett who lived at Borne some 5: Miles off Cambridge. This Sister he lov'd intirely she being a lover of learning – often resorted to her House and his Tutor and Fellows ... train'd up – in dayly reading Chapters in the Bible ... Being at Cambridge, that air was not very proper to his tender Constitution ... his aguish disposition grew yearly more and more upon him – physick not prevailing ... the Dr. advised Travell.

(The Ferrar Papers, ed. B. Blackstone, 1938)

Whilst he lived at the college, his life was the example not only of his equals but of his superiors. It must be no little indisposition that kept him at home when he heard the five o'clock bell ring to chapel. His chamber might be known by the last candle put out and by the first lighted in the morning.

(Dr. Jebb, 'Life of Nicholas Ferrar', in
Mayor, Cambridge in the Seventeenth
Century)

Conscience led people in different directions.

From notebooks in St. John's College Library:

Hee that would be a knowing, and well-grounded Divine (for 'tis a matter of sweat and industrie, notwithstanding the wild and willful contradictions of these unhappie times) should seriously apply himself to the study, and comprehension of that science wee call divinity, that twofold 1) Natural 2) Supernatural and revealed ... I call that knowledge of the duty and o' Deity towards him, which may be attained by the light of nature ... that naturall understanding, a law of reason writ into our hearts by the finger of God and Nature.

Qu. Whether rebus sic stantibus non conformists must of necessary duty still preach at all hazards or forbear.

If I must preach, then either as a separatist or a Communicant with the present Church. Not as a Separatist. If soe the Church of England from which I separate must then be Apostate & Ant-christian. If so now, then, ever so in K. Edward, Qu. Elizabeth, K. James raigns.

(Costello, Scholastic Curriculum)

An exemplary undergraduate, later a Colonel in the Parliamentary Army, is described:

[He was] a fellow Commoner in Peter-house under the tuition of one Mr. Norwich, an admirable scholler ... He kept not companie with any of the vaine young persons, but with graver men, and those by whose conversation he might gaine improvement. He never mist the Chappell, where he began to take notice of their stretching superstition to idolatrie; and was courted much into a more solemne practise of it than he could admitt, though yet he consider'd not the emptinesse and carnallitie, to say no more, of that publick service which was then in use. For his exercise he practis'd Tennis, and play'd admirable well att it; for his diversion he chose musick, and gott a very good hand, which afterwards he improv'd to a greate mastery, on the Violl; there were masters that taught to dance and valt, whom he practis'd with, being very agile and apt for all such beccomming exercises.

He was entic'd to bow to their greate Idoll Learning, and had a higher veneration for it a long time than can strictly be allow'd, yet he then look'd upon it as a handmaid to devotion, and as the greate emproover of naturall reason. His Tutor and the Masters that govern'd the Colledge while he was there were of Arminian principles, and that Colledge was noted above all the Towne for popish superstitious practises; yett through the mercy of God, notwithstanding the mutuall kindnesse the whole house had for him and he for them, he came away, after five yeares study there, untainted with those principles or practises.

(Lucy Hutchinson, The Life of Colonel
Hutchinson, 1973)

> *The Cambridge Platonists represented for some a middle way, being against the narrow dogmatism of the Puritans and for a more liberal and enlightened spirit. 'Truth is truth', Benjamin Whichcote said, 'whosoever hath spoken it.'*

If a new set of men had not appeared of another stamp, the Church had quite lost her esteem over the nation . . . These were generally of *Cambridge*, formed under some divines, the chief of whom were Drs. *Whitchcot, Cudworth, Wilkins, More*, and *Worthington. Whitchcot* was a man of a rare temper, very mild and obliging . . . He was much for liberty of conscience: and being disgusted with the dry systematical way of those times, he studied to raise those who conversed with him to a nobler set of thoughts . . . In order to this, he set young students much on reading the ancient philosophers, chiefly *Plato, Tully*, and *Plotin*, and on considering the christian religion as a doctrine sent from God, both to elevate and sweeten humane nature . . . *Cudworth* carried this on with a great strength of genius, and a vast compass of learning. He was a man of great conduct and prudence: upon which his enemies did very falsely accuse him of craft and dissimulation. *Wilkins* was of *Oxford*, but removed to Cambridge. His first rise was in the Elector Palatine's family, when he was in *England*. Afterwards he married *Cromwell*'s sister; but made no other use of that alliance, but to do good offices, and to cover the university from the sourness of *Owen* and *Goodwin*. At *Cambridge* he joined with those who studied to propagate better thoughts, to take men off from being in parties, or from narrow notions, from superstitious conceits, and a fierceness about opinions . . . *More* was an open hearted and sincere christian philosopher, who studied to establish men in the great principle of religion against atheism, that was then beginning to gain ground . . . *Worthington* was a man of eminent piety and great humility, and practised a most sublime way of self-denial and devotion. All these, and those who were formed under them, studied to examine farther into the nature of things, than had been done formerly. They declared against superstition on the one hand, and enthusiasm on the other. They loved the constitution of the church, and the liturgy, and could well live under them; but they did not think it unlawful to live under another form. They wished that things might have been carried with more moderation.

(Bishop Gilbert Burnet, A History of His
Own Times, 1753)

One of Nicholas Ferrar's 'travells' was to Virginia but unlike many of his generation he did not stay. There are precise figures of graduate immigrants in New England. One hundred and forty emigrated there before 1645, of whom no less than 104 came from Cambridge, 35 of them from Emmanuel, including John Harvard. S. E. Morison, in his 'Founding of Harvard' (1935) quotes Cotton Mather as saying:

If New England hath been in some respects Immanuel's land, it is well – but this I am sure of, Immanuel College contributed more than a little to make it so.

Morison also includes potted biographies, e.g.:

JOHN COTTON, son of Roland Cotton, an attorney of Derby, was born there 4 December 1584. Entered the University of Cambridge from Derby Grammar School; matriculated sizar from Trinity College 1598; admitted scholar 16 April 1602; B.A. 1602–03 or 1603–04. Migrated to Emmanuel; M.A. 1606; became fellow and head lecturer of the College; ordained 1610; vicar of St. Botolph's, Boston, 1612; B.D. 1613. His fame as preacher and theologian, already great at Cambridge, increased at Boston; Bishop Williams protected him from the consequences of non-conformity and Archbishop Ussher consulted him on theology; the Master of Emmanuel sent him divinity students to complete their studies. Preached farewell sermon to Winthrop's fleet at Southampton, 1630; resigned vicarage 8 July 1633, owing to unwillingness to conform, and emigrated in the *Griffin* with Hooker and Stone. Overseer of Harvard College from 1637 to his death on 23 December 1652, which took place in consequence of catching cold while preaching to Harvard students.

TIMOR MORTIS CONTURBAT ME

The plague was a constant source of terror, distress and inconvenience; colleges were closed for long periods; their remaining inhabitants lived in a state of siege.

Joseph Mede writes:

4 September 1625

All our market today could not supply us commons for night. I am steward; and am faine to appoint egges, apple-pyes, and custards, for want of other fare. They will suffer nothing to come from Ely. Eales are forbidden to be brought to our market, so are rootes. You see what tis to have a physitian among the heads. [This was John Gostlin, MD, Master of Caius.]

We cannot have leave scarce to take the aire. We have but one master of art in our colledg, and this week he was punisht 10d for giving the porters boy a box on the eare because he would not let him out at the gates. You may by this gather I have small solace with being here, and therefore will hast all I can to be in a place of more libertie and society, for I have never a pupil at home.

17 April 1630

I suppose you have heard of the like calamitie begun and threatened us here . . . It began at the further house, Forsters, a shoemaker; supposed by lodging a souldier who had a soare upon him, in whose bed and sheets the nastie woman layd 2 of hir sons, who are both dead, and a kinswoman. Some adde for a cause a dunghill on his backside, close by his house, in a little yard, in which the fool this lent-time suffered some butchers, who killed meat by stealth, to kill it there, and so bury the garbage in his dunghill, so to avoyd discovery, by which it became very noysome, even to Magdalene Colledge.

(Heywood and Wright, Cambridge Transactions)

April 1630

Our University is in a manner wholy dissolved; all meetings and Exercises ceasing. In many Colledges almost none left. In ours of 27 Mess we have not five. Our Gates strictly kept, none but Fellowes to go forth, or any to be lett in without the consent of the major part of our Society, of wch we have but 7 at home at this Instant, only a Sizer may go with his Tutors Ticket upon an errand. Our Butcher, Baker and Chandler bring the provisions to the Colledg. Gates, where the Steward & Cooke receive them. We have taken all our Officers we need into the Colledg & none must stirre out. If he doth he is to come in no more.

(Cooper)

Dr. Butts the Vice-Chancellor writes to Lord Coventry in 1630:

There are five thousand poor and not above one hundred who can assist in relieving them ... For the present state of the town the sickness is much scattered, but we follow your lordships counsell to keep the sound from the sick; to which purpose we have built nere 40 booths in a remote place upon our commons, whether we forthwith remove those that are infected, where we have placed a German physician who visitts them day and night and he ministers to them: besydes constables we have certain ambulatory officers who walk the streets night and day to keep our people from needless conversing, and to bring us notice of all disorders.

Dr. Butts, who was Master of Corpus Christi, seems to have acted with wisdom and foresight. He ends his letter to Lord Coventry:

Myself am alone a destitute and forsaken man, not a Scholler with me in College, not a Scholler seen by me without. God all sufficient (I trust) is with me, to whose most holy protection I humbly commend your Lordship with all belonging unto you.

(Cooper)

On Easter Day 1632 he was found hanged by his garters. His ghost is supposed to haunt the college.

Extracts from the audit books of St. Catharine's College

		£	s	d
1629–30	Given to severall poore people and towards the reliefe of the visited in tyme of the plague	4	6	9
	For allowance to the Butler for losses in beare in the time of infection	5	16	3½

1641-2	To the towne poore in the plague time after the Colledge rate	1	0	0
	Money and Commons to the Porter, the women, Wright & George in the plague time	2	0	5
	To Goodman Cloude for gate keeping in the plague time besides the quarters wages	2	0	0
1642-3	Payd for the visited of the plague	0	6	0

(W. H. S. Jones, The Story of St. Catharine's College, 1951)

Heads of houses (the generic name for masters, provosts, principals etc. of colleges) were not always popular.

Pembroke 1605-16

The fellows complained about Samuel Harsnett who had succeeded Lancelot Andrewes:

His absence was not like other Masters' absence, who keeping near Cambr. or att London had weekly intercourse of letters for directing and ordering of business, but he being 100 miles hence, much inconvenience has rose upon itt. poore schollers have binne fayne to send so farre of purpose for theire graces ... Being a bishop and by reason thereof, being to keep state at his meales in his lodgings, the College napery of very fayre diaper and damaske is extremely worn and spoyled. It having been observed, when his men have most negligently stayned it, and wyped ther shoes with itt, or worse ... he made both the Cookes at once his men, and at his pleasure used them, and carried them about wth him, so that sometimes the kitchen was without a cooke a whole day together ... leaving the College but one poore soull boy to dresse commons.

(A. Attwater, Pembroke College, 1936)

He was only got rid of when a petition was presented to King James at Thetford.

Choosing a master was often a difficult matter.

St. John's 1633

There is a great controversy in Saint Johns Colledg in Cambridg for the mastership of the colledg betwixt Mr. Oldsworth and Dr. Lane.

Dr. Lane spake to one of his pott companions, and did challenge his voyce by reason of their former familiarity. *Ile tell thee, Robin* (answered the fellow), *if I were to chewse a companion, I would chewse thee before any man; but thou shalt never be my master by my consent.*

(Heywood and Wright, Cambridge Transactions)

Cambridge has always nurtured poets. Those of the early decades of the seventeenth century seem to have sung louder under the storm of ideas which swept through the college courts, staircases and chapels of that time:

George Herbert, described by King James as 'the jewel of the University', was an illustrious Fellow of Trinity:

[76]

In the year 1619, he was chosen Orator for the University . . . and manag'd it with as becoming and grave a gaity, as any had ever before, or since his time. For, He had acquir'd great Learning, and was blest with a high fancy, a civil and sharp wit, and with a natural elegance, both in his behaviour, his tongue, and his pen.

(Isaac Walton, George Herbert, 1670)

He enjoyed his duties at first. He wrote to his step-father in 1617/18:

The Orator's place (that you may understand what it is) is the finest place in the University, though not the gainfullest: yet that will be about 30*l* per annum, but the commodiousness is beyond the Revenue; for the Orator writes all the University Letters, makes all the Orations, be it to King, Prince, or whatever comes to the University; to requite these pains, he takes place next the Doctors, is at all their Assemblies and Meetings, and sits above the Proctors, is Regent, or Non-Regent at his pleasure, and such like Gaynesses, which will please a young man well.

(Works, ed. R. A. Willmott)

but later longed to leave the University:

AFFLICTION

When I got health, thou took'st away my life,
    And more; for my friends die:
My mirth and edge was lost; a blunted knife
    Was of more use than I.
Thus thinne and lean without a fence or friend,
I was blown through with ev'ry storm and winde.

Whereas my birth and spirit rather took
    The way that takes the town;
Thou didst betray me to a ling'ring book,
    And wrap me in a gown.
I was entangled in the world of strife,
Before I had the power to change my life.

Yet, for I threaten'd oft the siege to raise,
    Not simp'ring all mine age,
Thou often didst with Academick praise
    Melt and dissolve my rage.
I took thy sweetened pill, till I came neare;
I could not go away, nor persevere.

Yet, less perchance I should too happie be
    In my unhappinesse,
Turning my purge to food, thou throwest me
    into more sicknesses.
Thus doth thy power cross-bias me, not making
Thine own gift good, yet me from my ways taking.

Now I am here, what thou wilt do with me
    None of my books will show:

I reade, and sigh, and wish I were a tree;
    For sure then I should grow
To fruit or shade: at least some bird would trust
Her household to me, and I should be just . . .

                                          (c. 1620)

*Not all poets were happy in their undergraduate days, including Milton,
though in later life he was eager to refute libels about his time in Cambridge:
the 'commodious lie' of his having been 'vomited out thence' gave him an
opportunity:*

to acknowledge publicly with all grateful mind, that more than ordinary favour
and respect, which I found above any of my equals at the hands of those courteous and learned men, the fellows of that college wherein I spent some years:
who at my parting, after I had taken two degrees, as the manner is, signified
many ways how much better it would content them that I would stay; as by
many letters full of kindness and loving respect, both before that time, and long
after, I was assured of their singular good affection towards me.

                                ('An Apology for Smectymnuus', 1642)

Earlier he had objected to being described as, 'the Lady of Christ's':

But why do I seem to those fellows insufficiently masculine? . . .

    Doubtless it was because I was never able to gulp down huge bumpers in
pancratic fashion; or because my hand has not become calloused by holding the
plough-handle; or because I never lay down on my back under the sun at
Mid-day, like a seven-year ox-driver; perhaps, in fine, because I never proved
myself a man in the same manner as those gluttons.

                                (from 'The Sixth Prolusion', 1628)

John Aubrey perpetuates the story:

Went to Christ's College in Cambridge at fifteen, where he stayed eight yeares
at least . . . was a very hard student in the University, and performed all his
exercises there with very good applause. His first tutor there was Mr. Chapell;
from whom receiving some unkindnesse (Whip't him) . . .

    His complexion exceeding faire – he was so faire that they called him *the lady
of Christ's college*. Ovall face. His eie a darke gray.

                                          (*Brief Lives*)

*Milton's memories of Cambridge are perhaps reflected in lines from 'Il
Penseroso':*

                But let my due feet never fail,
                To walk the studious Cloysters pale,
                And love the high embowed Roof,
                With antick Pillars massy proof,
                And storied Windows richly dight,
                Casting a dimm religious light.
                There let the pealing Organ blow,
                To the full voic'd Quire below,

In Service high, and Anthems cleer,
As may with sweetness, through mine ear,
Dissolve me into extasies,
And bring all Heav'n before mine eyes.

'Lycidas' commemorates a fellow poet and contemporary, Edward King:

For we were nurst upon the self-same hill,
Fed the same flock, by fountain, shade, and rill.
  Together both, ere the high Lawns appear'd
Under the opening eye-lids of the morn,
We drove a field . . .

Abraham Cowley at Trinity, like his friend Richard Crashaw at Peterhouse,
was driven into exile by the Civil War:

with . . . my heart wholly set upon Letters, I went to the University; But was
soon torn from thence by that violent Publick storm which would suffer nothing
to stand where it did, but rooted up every Plant, even from the Princely Cedars
to Me, the Hyssop. *(Abraham Cowley, The Essays and Other*
Prose Writings, ed. A. B. Gough, 1915)

His Cambridge friendships inspired some of his poems:

'On the Death of Mr. William Harvey'

Ye fields of *Cambridge*! our dear *Cambridge*! say,
Have you not seen us walking every day?
Was there a *Tree* about which did not know
The *Love* betwixt us Two?
Henceforth, ye gentle *Trees*! for ever fade,
On your sad Branches thicker join,
And into darksome Shades combine,
Dark as the *Grave* wherein my *Friend* is laid.
Henceforth no learned *Youths* beneath you sing . . .

and an early one by Crashaw:

UPON TWO GREENE APRICOCKES SENT TO
COWLEY BY SIR CRASHAW

Take these, times tardy truants, sent by me,
To be chastis'd (sweet friend) and chidd by thee.
Pale sons of our *Pomona!* whose wan cheekes
Have spent the patience of expecting weekes,
Yet are scarce ripe enough at best to show
The redd, but of the blush to thee they ow.
By thy comparrison they shall put on
More summer in their shames reflection,
Than ere the fruitfull *Phœbus* flaming kisses
Kindled on their cold lips. O had my wishes
And the deare merits of your Muse, their due,

The yeare had found some fruit early as you;
Ripe as those rich composures time computes
Blossoms, but our blest tast confesses fruits.

Crashaw wrote commemorative verses for Lancelot Andrewes, Master of Pembroke, who was Chairman of the Committee appointed by James I to produce the Authorised Version of the Bible:

UPON BISHOP ANDREWES HIS PICTURE BEFORE HIS SERMONS

See heer a *Shadow* from that setting *SUNNE*,
Whose glorious course through this Horizon runn
Left the dimm face of our dull Hemisphære,
All one great *Eye*, all drown'd in one great *Teare*.
    Whose rare industrious Soule, led his free thought
Through *Learning's* Universe, and (vainly) sought
Roome for her spacious Self; untill at length
She found the way home: with an holy strength
Snatch't herself hence to Heav'n; fill'd a bright place
'Midst those immortall Fires, and on the face
Of her Great MAKER, fixt a flaming eye,
Where still she reads true, pure *Divinitie*.
    And now that grave *Aspect* hath deign'd to shrink
Into this lesse appearance. If you think
'Tis but a *dead face* Art doth heer bequeath,
Look on the following leaves and see him *breath*.

Crashaw was fond of his college. He wrote from Leyden:

Feb. 20 1643/4

I have I assure you no desire to be absolutely and irrespectively rid of my beloved Patrimony in St. Peter. No man than myself holds more high the humble scepter of such a little contentfull kingdom . . .

(Basil Willey, *Richard Crashaw, A Memorial Lecture,* 1949)

Poets enjoyed friendship with other poets:

James, thou and I did spend some precious years
At Katherine Hall; since when, we sometimes feel
In our poetic brains (as plain appears)
A whirling trick, then caught from Katherine's wheel.

(*Thomas Bancroft's epigram on James Shirley,* 1639)

The monarch still believed that the Vice-Chancellor and heads of houses were at his beck and call.

In 1607 King James I ordered that the scholars of Trinity should be taken chiefly from Westminster School if duly qualified. This was deeply resented

and there is a memorandum, probably written by the Master, Thomas Nevile,
outlining the arguments, some of the most powerful of which are as follows:

Howbeit in that kind of fruitfulness we also are not destitute of God's gracious
blessing; for ... besides Doctors in all faculties to the number at the least of
sixty, Deans to the number of eleven, Publick Professors to the number of ten,
the two Archbishops, Canterbury and York, the most reverend Fathers Whitgift
and Hutton, and seven other principal Prelates of this kingdom, namely Fletcher
of London, Still of Bath and Wells, Babington of Worcester, Redman of
Norwich, Rud of St. Davids, Bennett of Hereford, and Gouldesborough of
Gloucester, all of them simul et semel Bishops of this kingdom ... are such a
demonstrative instance as we think no other College in either University can
afford the like – and not one of these chosen out of Westminster School.

It is to be doubted whether there can be the like success if our Elections out
of a private School shall be indubitate and certain; we rather think there can
be no readier means to make Droanes and Loyterers in Colleges, nor any worse
prejudice or more deadly bane unto learning and vertue, than when the rewards,
and means thereof are tyed to persons, times, and places, and made regular and
certain.

The proposal would do a grave injustice to other students who might be men
of great abilities.

(Rouse Ball, *Cambridge Papers*)

Choosing a Chancellor, 1626

Joseph Mede to Sir Martin Stuteville:

Christ Coll. Jun. 3
Our Chancellor my Lord of Suffolk died on Sunday about two a Clock in the
morning: which no sooner came to our ears on Monday, but about dinner time
arrives Dr. Wilson ... with a message ... that we should chuse the Duke (of
Buckingham); such being his Majesty's desire and pleasure. Our Heads meet
after Sermon, when by Dr. Wren, Beale, Maw, Pask, this motion was urged
with that vehemency and as it were confidence of authority, that the rest were
either awed or persuaded ...

Upon the news of this Consultation and Resolution of the Heads, we of the
Body murmur, we run to one another to complain, we say the Heads in this
Election have no more to do than any of us ... some durst be so bold as to visitt
for the contrary, in publick. Others more privily enquired how their friends and
others were affected ...

On Thursday morning ... he (the Bishop of London) makes a large speech
in the Colledge Chapel ... when the School Bell rang he caused the Colledge
Bell also to ring as an Act, and all the Fellows to come into the Hall and to
attend him to the Schools for the Duke ... and yet for all this stirre the Duke
carried it but by three votes from my Lord Andover whom we voluntarily set
up against him ...

Jun. 10
The Parliament was wonderfully exasperated by our Election, aggravating it as

[81]

an Act of Rebellion and had sent Letters to fetch up our Doctors to answer it; but the King stopped them and commanded them not to stir in this business of the University, which belonged not to them but to himself.

Buckingham came on a visit in March 1626/7:

March 10

The Duke is coming to our towne, which putts us all into a commotion. The bells ring. The posts wind their hornes in every streat. Every man putts on his cappe and whood ready for the congregation, whither they suppose his grace will come. He dines, they say, at Trinity Colledg; shall have a bankett at Clare Hall. I am afrayd some body will scarce worship any other god as long as he is in towne. For mine owne part, I am not like to stirre, but hope to heare all when they come home.

He was on the top of Kings Colledg chappell, but refused to have his foot imprinted there, as too high for him . . .

(Letters of Eminent Literary Men, ed. Ellis)

The Fellows of Pembroke College did not welcome the intervention of the King in choosing a fellow. In 1629 King Charles I recommended one Jasper Chomley, of Corpus Christi. The Master and Fellows replied:

The generall good report and well approved merit of Jasper Chomley was it that induced your Majestie to direct unto us your Gracious letters for his preferment. And we wish with all our hearts that his fame were as really sweete in Cambridge as it was charitably conceived at Whitehall. But in the University it is most certaine that he the said Jasper upon the importunity of a worthy Court friend was by the Mr. of Bennet College, wherein he was brought up propounded unto the fellows of that Societie, whom not one man no not his tutor Sterne vouchsafed a voice. Y^r Matie may therefore easilie conceive what credit another Societie can get by advancing him who was so much slighted in his owne College. Moreover it is notorious that once in a sodeine passion (which they say haunteth him often) upon verie slender provocation, with a pen knife he dangerously stabbed one Sr Palmer in the bellie: So that without much feare and jeopardie, there is little hope of safe converse with a man of his morosity . . . the College would be rent in pieces with brawles at home and law-suits abroad.

(Attwater, Pembroke College)

The Civil War: the garrison town

The Whig historians have made of Cambridge a Puritan university, coloring a place like Trinity with Emmanuel; the Tories, on the other hand, will urge the loyalty of Cambridge divinity, arguing that Emmanuel was a separatist little

Mill Lane (woodcut by Gwen Raverat)

seedbed, which can be ignored as far as the whole University is concerned. The truth lies somewhere between. Cambridge was as loyal, on the whole, as Oxford (we yield the confusion of orthodoxy with loyalty) and, if Cambridge be theologically suspect in the early decades of the 1600s, it is because two of her colleges, Emmanuel and Sidney Sussex, smelled of Puritanism.

(Costello, *Scholastic Curriculum*)

The academic world of Cambridge was no more insulated from the disturbances and tumults of the Civil War than other places. Indeed, whatever the colour of the allegiances in the University, the town was within the Parliamentary sphere of influence. Cromwell, who had been at Sidney Sussex for a year in

*1616/17, was MP for Huntingdon and Cambridge, and by December 1642
Cambridge was the natural choice for the headquarters of the 'Eastern Association' which comprised the East Anglian counties where puritanism was very
strong. The Association was the strategic heart of the Parliament position.*

Part of a letter from the King to the Vice-Chancellor 24 July 1642:

Whereas we have great reason to acknowledge the willing expressions of the
affections of both our Universities, In that late supply afforded to us, in this
time of necessity; and particularly being informed of the further readiness of all
or most of our Colleges in Cambridge, to make offer of depositing their Plate into
our Hands, for the better security and safety thereof . . . and lest the obligation
of their college statutes might hinder the effect of their good wills to this service
. . . we do hereby . . . dispense with any such statute.

(Cooper)

There was a mixed response. St. John's has the following record:

Agreed by the Master and Seniors *August* 8, 1642. that these pieces of Plate
underwritten should be sent to the King's Majesty, and deposited in his Hands
for the Security thereof, and Service of his Majesty, according to the Tenor of
his Majesty's late Letters, written to the Vice-Chancellor, and published to the
University.

Unc.

Pots with two Ears, *Clippesey, Crew, Theodore Beacon, John Lucat,
Thomas Wentworth,* &c. Number 22. Weight   559¾
Tankards, *Frances* Lord *Willoughby* of *Parham, Thomas Bourchier,
Thomas Fairfax,* &c. Number 17. Weight etc. etc.. . .   325
The Weight of the aforesaid Particulars, according to Grocers Weight
    is   2065½

(Peter Barwick, *The Life of the Rev. Dr.
John Barwick, 1724*)

*Other colleges provided some of their plate and it was planned to dispatch it
to the King:*

This could not be effected without first outwitting Cromwell, who had been
appriz'd of their Design by some of the Townsmen of Cambridge . . . and with
a disorderly Band of Peasants on Foot, lay in wait for the rich Booty at a Place
called *Lawler Hedges,* betwixt Cambridge and Huntingdon. But Mr. Barwick
and some other select Persons of the University, to whose Care and Prudence
the Management of this important Affair was committed, having got Intelligence
of Cromwell's Way-laying them, sent away the Royal Supply through By-Roads,
convoy'd by a small Party of Horse, that very Night in which Cromwell with his
Foot beset the common Road, or else the Spoil had the next morning certainly
fallen into the Enemy's Hands. He that was made choice of to conduct this
Expedition was the Reverend Mr. Barnaby Oley, a Man of Great Prudence, and
very well acquainted with all the By-Ways, through which they were to pass.
He was President of Clare-Hall; and none more proper to be the Messenger of
the University's Duty and Affection to their most gracious Sovereign . . . he

arrived safe at Nottingham, where he had the Honour to lay at his Majesty's feet this small Testimony and Earnest of the University's Loyalty.

Three heads of houses, Dr. Beale of St. John's, Dr. Martin of Queens', and Dr. Sterne of Jesus, were arrested and sent to London.

St. Steven's Day, Die Lunae 26 Decembris:
A Petition of Three Colleges in Cambridge was read: desiring, That their Lordships would be pleased to admit that their Governors, who are now in The Tower, may be permitted to come amongst them, for the Government of their Colleges . . . for the making up of our Audit Accompts now approaching, the Choice of Scholars and Officers, the renewing of Leases, and many other Businesses most nearly concerning the Welfare of our foresaid several Colleges.

(*Journals of the House of Lords*)

The petition was not successful and the three men spent several years in various prisons, part of the time on a ship called the 'Prosperous Sarah' on the Thames.

Some idea, probably exaggerated, of what it was like in the 'garrison town' of Cambridge, is given in 'Querela Cantabrigiensis', or 'a remonstrance by way of apologie for the banished members of the late flourishing university of Cambridge by some of the said sufferers':

How some of us (and many others with us) have been thrust out of bed in the night, that our Chambers might forthwith be converted into Prison Lodgings: How our young Scholars with terrour have been commanded to accuse and cut out the names of their owne Tutors . . . But (to passe higher) how often have our Colleges been beset, and broken open, and Guards thrust into them sometimes at midnight, while we were asleep in our beds? How often our Libraries and Treasuries ransackt and rifled . . . How often hath that small pitance of Commons which our Founders and Benefactors allotted for our sustenance, been taken off our Tables by the wanton Soldier? How often have our Rents been extorted from our Tenants, or if received, remanded of our Bursars and Stewards, and by force taken from them? and all this under the old odious title of Plundering, which word though they cannot endure to heare of, since that new terme of *Sequestration* was invented . . . prizing and selling away our Books at a tenth part of their value, which are our onely tooles and instruments whereby the trade and profession of Learning should be holden up . . . they have invented a pretty device to reserve out of their plunder all sorts of pictures, were they but paper prints of the 12 Apostles, and every market-day to burne them openly in the market-place, proclaiming them the *Popish Idols* of the University, untill we became so hated by the weaker sort of the deceived people, that a Scholar could have small security from being stoned or affronted as he walkt the streets . . .

For besides the cutting down of our Walks and Orchards . . . they have cut down the Woods and Groves belonging to our Colleges, and sold them before our eyes to a great value . . . they have pulled down, demolished and defaced five or six faire Bridges of Stone and Timber belonging to severall Colleges, and have spoyled a goodly Walk with a new Gate . . .

When the Kings Prisoners taken at *Hilsden-house* were brought famished and naked in triumph by *Cambridge* to *London*, some of our Scholars were knockt downe in the streets, onely for offering them a cup of small beere to sustaine nature, and the drinke throwne in the kennell, rather than the famished and parched throats of the wicked, as they esteem'd them, should usurp one drop of the creature. And it is much to be feared, they would have starved them in prison there, if a valiant Chamber-maid (Mistris *Cumbers* maid) had not relieved them by force, trampling under her feet in the kennell their great persecutor, a Lubberly Scotch Major.

(John Barwick)

Attempts were made however to restrain the troops:

Theis are to will require and command you and everie of you, to forbeare (under any pretence whatsoever) to prejudice, or offer any damage to the University of Cambridge, or to any the Schooles Colledges, Halls, Libraries Chappells or other places belonging to the said University; by plundering the same, or any part thereof in any kind whatsoever. Hereof faile not as you will answeare the contrarie at your perills. Given under my hand and Seale this Seaventh daie of March 1642.

ESSEX.

To all Colonells, Leiuetenant Colonells, Captaines and all other Officers and souldiers of the Armie under my command.

(J. R. Wardale, Clare College Letters and Documents, 1903)

Trinity College Steward's Accounts – first quarter of 1644:

To diverse souldiers at severall times that behaved themselves very devoutly in the chappell 00. 05. 00. To some of Major Scot's souldiers who defended the chappell from the rudenesse of the rest 00. 05. 00. (W. & C.)

The University petitioned both Houses of Parliament on 5 June 1643 saying how:

Our Schools daily grow desolate, mourning the absence of their Professors and their wonted Auditories; how, in our Colleges, the numbers grow thin, and our Revenues short . . . how, frighted by the Neighbour Noise of War, our Students either quit their Gowns, or abandon their Studies; how our Degrees lie dis-esteemed, and all Hopes of our Public Commencements are blasted in the Bud.

(Journals of the House of Lords)

Eleven heads of houses were ejected by the Earl of Manchester 'by vertue of an Ordinance of Parliament', including of course Beale, Martin and Sterne.

In 1643 Mr. William Dowsing was appointed to demolish altars, images, etc. He kept a journal:

At Queen's colledge, Decemb: 26

We beat downe about a 110 Superstitious Pictures besides Cherubims & Ingravings, where none of the Fellowes would put on their Hatts, in all the time they were in the Chapell, & we digged up the Steps, for 3: howers & brake downe 10, or 12 Apostles & Sts: within the Hall.

Kings Coledg Decemb: 26

Steps to be taken, & 1: thousand Superstitious Pictures the layder of Christ & theves to goe upon many Crosses, & Jesus write on them.

Madlin Coledge Dec: 30 1643

We brake downe about 40: Superstitious Pictures, Joseph & Mary stood to be espoused in the wyndowes.

(William Dowsing, *Cambridge Journal*, 1643)

ANARCHUS: Wee'l down with all the 'Varsities
　　　　　　 Where Learning is profest;
　　　　　　 Because they practice and maintain
　　　　　　 The Language of the Beast:
　　　　　　 Wee'l drive the Doctors out of doores,
　　　　　　 And Arts whatere they be;
　　　　　　 Wee'l cry both Arts, and Learning down
　　　　　　 And, hey! then up goe we . . .
PHILARCHUS: Heaven keep such *vermin* hence.

(Francis Quarles from 'The Shepheards Oracles', 1646)

Extract from the Journals of the House of Lords:

Die veneris, 26 Februarii (1646/7)

This Day William Wotton, One of the Fellows of Trinity Colledge of Cambridge, was brought to the Bar as a Delinquent; and John Lawrance and Henry Graves were produced as Witnesses, who proved that the said Wm. Wotton did say at Cambridge, 'That the Rebellion of the Parliament of England was worse than the Rebellion of Ireland'.

On the other hand, on 12 March 1646/7, when Sir Thomas Fairfax, the Parliamentary General, came to Cambridge:

he was highly caressed and a Latin Oration made to him by a Fellow of Trinity Colledge who had been a Souldier in his Regiment. In the Chapel they presented him with a rich Bible; in the Hall with a sumptuous banquet. Then the Town entertained him with a stately Banquet and at the Schools he was made a Master of Arts.

(Bulstrode Whitelocke, *Memorials of the English Affairs*, 1682)

Some Royalists captured by Parliamentary forces in East Anglia were sent first to Cambridge. Thomas Knyvett writes to his wife (his 'mouse') about what was happening:

March 23　1642

We are billited in the rose, the cheefest Inn in the towne, 16 of us together, where we have very good lodging & a very good ordinary at 18*d* a meale. I knowe not how long we shall continue here. We hope well, because we heard last night the Commisioners have some design to remove us to Jesus Colledg . . . If we goe to the Colledg, there some of us will studdy like pigg-hoggs. We are nowe in the midst of the schoole of mars, nothing but drums and Trumpets all the day long . . .

March 24   1642

Little alteration since my last letter, only the mallice of the townsmen by complaints to the Committee hear have bereft us of the society of any scholler comming to us . . . Olde Do[tr] Ward [Master of Sidney Sussex College] is in prisson & the proctor of Pembrook Hall . . .

I do not desier to have Jack come hether yet, till I knowe when we shalbe settled, but I would have Mun: Hovell come to me and bringe my cloake. I will have no more cloaths 'till I knowe where I shalbe. If in a colledg, then I must send for bed linnen & other commodityes. I praye send me some conserve of roses for I have got a greate cold . . .

April 6   1643 [?42]

. . . I heer Just nowe that we are designded for Peter house, Dr. Cousens coll. We desier no better fortune in this condition. Indeed Mus [Mouse]: I was never so wearye of a Tavern in my life.

All the D[rs] heer in the university stands out stifly. And are like to be in our condition. They wear lockt up, all but towe, on fryday night, in ther regent house, till past 12 of the clock, but the olde blades would not yeeld to lend a penny . . . 6000l was demanded of them but not A penny is gotten.

(*The Knyvett Letters 1620–44*, ed. Bertram Schofield, 1949)

The 'olde blades' were certainly under orders:

The Earl of Manchester's notice, Feb. 26   1643/4

Theis are to will and require you upon sight hereof to give speedie advertisement to the Master Fellowes Schollers and Officers of your Colledge to be resident at your said Colledge the Tenth day of March next ensuing to give an Accompt wherein they shalbe required true to answer such things as may be demanded by mee or such Commissioners as I shall appoint.

Given under my hand & seale this 26th of Febr. 1643

Manchester

To the President or Locum tenens of Clare Hall

(Wardale, *Clare College Letters and Documents*)

By the Committee for the Association

Cambridge

You are hereby Ordered that according to the order of Parliament, you celebrate friday next in your Society as a day of thanksgiving with exceedings at dinner and a supper, provided that neyther consist of theire ordinary fish commons in part And to have a bonefire in the evening.

June 26   1645

To the fellows and manciple of Clare hall

Nath[n] Bacon
Samuell Plumme
Robt Clocke
Robt Vinter

[To celebrate victory at Naseby ?]

For six quarts of clarett wine in the Hall at dinner upon the day of thanksgiving for the rowting of Lord Goring's forces at Langport.

Undergraduate life of a sort continued.

Born in the North Riding, Matthew Robinson, a Parliamentarian, went to Edinburgh because of the war and left there for Cambridge because of the plague. He writes in the third person:

Therefore ere the end of May he took his venture again for Hull, designing to slip to Cambridge through the washes of Lincolnshire . . . and getting to Spalding . . . thought it not safe to lodge there that night (the enemie's army having just then taken Leicester) but hastened for Crowland, a garrison whither no enemies could come but by water. There he was kindly received . . . and appointed to a mean quarter but could take no rest for swarms of night enemies, the gnats and hummers, thousands of which he left slain on his bed . . . by break of day made to Peterborough, where he took his rest a little and kept his sabbath that day devoutly; but that night the city was alarumed . . . so that our student was forced to fly again, leaving the troops to make good his rear; and to Huntingdon he got by noon and to Cambridge safely ere night.

He was at that time about seventeen years of age; yet was mightily ravished with the beauty of the colleges of Cambridge and with the exercises of the schools and colleges, much despising all that he had seen or learned in Scotland . . . he entered himself freshman of the first year in St. John's College, under the tuition of that darling of men Mr. Zachary Cawdrey . . . the tutor doted on his new pupil and he on his tutor; and to his study thus he fell . . . But he had not settled himself many nights in quiet, till the king's army broke into the associated counties, took Huntingdon and in parties came near to Cambridge on which alarum the bells rung backwards and the beacons were fired as if Hannibal had been at the gates; all the Cantabridgian students in four hours' time were all fled, two and three on an horse, and the rest footed it to friends in safe places.

Therefore to the castle in Cambridge he goeth, addressing himself to the then governor, who was a master of arts and a captain, offering his service in that juncture to live and die in the defence of that citadel. The governor armed him with sword firelock and bandoliers, taking him into his own post. In this castle he was upon his military duty every night, and in the mornings stole into the college with his gown, none knowing this his new adventure, until the king's forces were driven away.

('Autobiography of Matthew Robinson', in Mayor, *Cambridge in the Seventeenth Century*)

Some fled to Oxford and, according to Anthony Wood, as refugees were making their impact in 1647/8:

Undergraduates and Bacchelaurs of Arts wore the sleeves of wide sleev gowns as wide as those of surplices, a fashion brought into the Universitie by the Cantabrigians . . . The newcommers also (who mostly were very meane and poore at their first comming) having gotten into good fellowships, became

7. The Castle Hill and Gatehouse, 1730 (engraving by Samuel and Nathaniel Buck)

wondrous malopert and saucy, especially to the old stock remayning. They went in half shirts, appearing at their brest and out at sleeves, great bands with tassell strings, and Spenish leather boots with lawne or holland tops . . .

(Life and Times of Anthony Wood,
ed. Andrew Clark, 1891)

On 12 October 1649 it was decreed that no person could take a degree or hold office in the University who had not subscribed to the following engagement:

I do declare and promise, That I will be true and faithful to the Commonwealth of England, as the same is now established, without a King or House of Lords.

Three more heads of houses were ejected for not signing. William Sandcroft of Emmanuel College (later Archbishop of Canterbury) writes to his brother on 13 September 1650, as he ties up his luggage.

This day, it seems, the committee here sat; and I, amongst the rest of the non-subscribers, was summoned to appear at the Bear. I went not . . . It is said they will give us yet a fortnight's time to come in, before they pin the door with their last and inexorable doom. For my part . . . I fear nothing more than their indulgence; for if we should be continued here till the man in the north hath done his business, and comes back triumphant, we must look for impositions of a higher nature, and under far stricter penalties. This makes me almost long to be displaced, that I may hide my head in some hole so obscure, whither our jolly conquerors may scorn to descend to seek me. In order to this design, I truss up my baggage as fast as I can, and send it towards you. To the books I sent lately I add now, by Rogers, my viol, wrapt up in a dozen flaxen napkins, and two table cloths of the same, with two old half shirts, and over all a carpet. Also, in a little box, my hanging watch and alarum, with lines and weights . . .

Many signed. Samuel Dillingham of Emmanuel writes to William Sandcroft:

Some have subscribed that were never dreamed on; others quite contrary: whence I have learned not to think of men by this touchstone . . . some of them . . . thought themselves only bound negatively, and but so long till a party should appear against the present power. Happy men that can so construe it.

(Cooper)

Even those who supported Cromwell were anxious about the effect on the University:

Oct 2 1649   The engagement is prest in Cambridge to out many honest men, and to admit divers young and rude blades because engagers.
Oct 23   The engagement outs many deserving men from the fellowships; its thought there will fall a sad blowe upon the ministry, the universities and their meanes.

(Josselin's *Diary*, ed. Hockliffe)

Interference from above continued as from a monarch:

Gentlemen,
   I am given to understand that by the late decease of Dr. Duck, his chamber is become vacant in the Drs. Comons, to which Dr. Dorislaus now desireth to be

your Tenant: who hath done service unto the Parliament from the beginning of these warrs, and hath bene constantly imployed by the Parliament in many weighty affaires, and especially of late beyond the seas, with the States Generall of the United Provinces. *If you please to preferr him before any other, paying rent & fine to your Colledge,* I shall take itt as a curtesie at your hands, whereby you will oblige

Your assured freinde and servant
O. CROMWELL

XVIII Decem: 1648.

Directed thus,

To the right worshipfull the Master and Fellowes of Trinity Hall in Cambridge.

Seal'd with a Head having two faces, one of a Philosopher, the other of a Soldier.

(Warren's Book, ed. Dale)

Restoration, refulgence and rebellion

On Saturday the 12th May 1660 the King was proclaymed at King's College; all the souldiers were placed round on the topp of their chappell from whence they gave a volley of shott.

(Alderman Newton's Diary, ed. J. E. Foster,
1890)

May 12. 1660
To Mr. South for his club at the boonfires and exceedings at the voting of the King and at his proclamation . . .10s 0d.

(W. J. Harrison, Life in Clare Hall,
1658–1713, 1958)

Eleven heads of houses were restored to their colleges, including Dr. Sterne at Jesus. John Worthington, who had been made Master in 1650 rather against his will, did his best to welcome Sterne back and to expedite the handover of house and orchard.

Worthington to his wife:

Aug. 6, 1660.

I have not heard of thee, how thou doest in body; but I am glad that thy minde is cheerfull. I received this day from Dr. Sterne a civil letter . . . desiring to know, what time I would please to make way for his return to the college. I told him, I did obey the order . . . I told him, it should be by the end of August. If Ditton business be not determined till then, some house or chambers must be hired in the town, till we see the issue of things. Bid him welcome, when he comes, & as for the fruits of the orchard then ripe, or near ripe, tell him, it shall not be meddled with but as he appoints.

Worthington to Sterne:

October 1660

I was not in the least unmindfull of the fair benignity & candour which appear'd (besides several other instances) in your kind complyance with my conveniences, for the removing of myself & family . . . I had about 3 or 4 years since layd out a great deal of money upon the house . . . yet upon further view, there appeared more to be done by masons & carpenters . . . to make it more warm & safe: it standing bleek & alone, & therefore more obnoxious to the cold weather now approaching & to that violence from men, of which there have been some late proofs in parts adjacent, & I wish the disbandment of the soldiers this winter may not increase the instances. I could not procure the carpenters, till Sturbridge Fair (which is their harvest) was over. They are now . . . near finishing what is necessary . . .

I was thinking here to conclude, but I must not omit the giving you an account of your orchard fruit. A little after your going hence, I caused the summer fruit to be gathered, which were layd up, & lookt to every day, that none might hurt the other. Glad should I have been, that you had enjoyed them in their perfection, which you might, if you had returned, as we expected: but now summer apples have lost both the fair look & tast. As for the winter fruits . . . I employed some to gather these, as the uncertain weather would permit. I think the last will be gathered today. They are more than they have been of late years, though the mud wall has been climed more than once, & the last week a thief escaped taking very hardly. The apple loft over the founder's chamber will be filled with them. I mean with those that are gathered from the trees. As for those that fell in the gathering, or fell by the winds, they are layd up in another place. It is one of the dayly employments of my wife, to look that none of them hurt their fellows.

Sterne replies:

London, Oct. 17, 1660

I return you many thanks for your kind letter & the care you have taken for me. My coming to Cambridge will be now something uncertain, in regard of mine attendance upon my business here . . . The apples I have desired Dr. P. to take order may be beaten for cyder.

Worthington to Sterne:

October 19, 1660

For mine owne part, as I never had any ambitious desires to such a place at first (being far from the least seeking it, or desire to retain it; for when I was brought in, I could with as much chearfulness have left it for you, nay with more willingness, than I entered upon it . . .) my disposition chiefly inclining me to a life of devotional retirement, about which I did love to talk with worthy Mr. Thristcross, who knew Mr. Ferrar & Little Gedding.

(*Diary and Correspondence*, ed. James Crossley, 1847)

He had his wish and retired to the parish of Fen Ditton. Presumably Sterne drank the cider.

[93]

Despite political change, the University flourished and numbers rose. Under-graduates came in all varieties with differing inclinations and problems, and colleges tried to cope with them. James Duport, a Fellow of Trinity, had compiled a list of rules, probably just before the Restoration. Here are some of them:

Be diligent & constant at Chappell every morning. Use to be at Chappell at the beginning & come not drooping in ... when almost all is done.

Beware of sleeping at prayers and sermons for that is the sleep of death.

Use to walke often in the fields, and to walke alone, because that will put good thoughts in you, and make you retire into your self, and commune with your owne hearts.

Carry yourself civily in your Tutors Chamber, not laughing or lolling, or leaning or whispering, or using any other childish gesture or posture.

When you reade or speake in your Tutors Chamber, or else where, take heed of picking your Nose, or putting your Hatt or Hand to your face, or any such odd, uncouth, or unseemely gesture.

Use often to dispute & argue in Logick, and Phylosophy with your Chamber-fellow, and acquaintance when you are together.

If at any time in your Disputation you use the authority of Aristotle, be sure you bring his owne words & in his owne language.

Touch not, handle not Cards, nor dyes, both being expressly against the statutes. Play not at Chesse or very seldome, for though it be an ingenious play, yet too tedious and time-devouring.

Refraine foot-ball, it being as it is commonly used a rude, boisterous exercise, & fitter for Clownes then for Schollers.

Goe not a gadding and gossiping from Chamber to Chamber, for that is no recreation, but meere idlenesse and losse of time.

Goe not into the water at all or very wareily once or twice in a Summer at most, but better it were I thinke if you could quite forbeare.

I am no great friend to going downe the water, because I observe oftentimes it hath occasioned the going downe of the wind too much, and some under colour of going a fishing, drop into a blind house and there drink like fishes.

(G. M. Trevelyan, 'Undergraduate Life',
Cambridge Review, 22 May 1943)

Not all heeded such admonitions:

Dec. 19 A Senior Soph. of Peter House being complain'd of, by the Proctors for his disturbances, uncivil actions in the schools &c. (as the blowing of a horn in the Sophister's schools, when they were hudling) he confesseth, & is suspended a gradu suscipiendo.

(Worthington, *Diary and Correspondence*, ed. Crossley)

Note: 'huddling' was hurrying through certain formal exercises in lieu of those regularly required for a degree.

A useful little list ?

1675/6

That hereafter no scholar whatever (excepting officers of the University performing their duty in searching houses) upon whatsoever pretence shall enter into the house of Abraham Achersely at the green dragon in Trinity parish, or of William Shepheard at the three feathers in saint Edward's parish, or of the Widow Gilson at the saracen's head upon the causeway to Queen's College, or of Henry Skilback at the boot in Trumpington street, or of Richard Fuller at the salutations near the Castle, or of widow Grigson in little St. Maries lane, or of Richard Lindley at the Challis gardens by Pembroke hall, or of William Copeland at the carpenters arms over against Peterhouse, or into any other house of bad repute in Cambridge; and that if any scholar shall presume to disobey this order, he shall for his misdemeanour and for his contumacy immediately be expelled from the university.

(Cooper)

J. Peachell, Master of Magdalene, felt constrained to issue the following orders in 1679:

That no senior dare to hale or compell any his juniors, at the time of the yeare, eyther in the Colledge or out of it, to give them cherries, berries, or any other expence of fruit whatsoever, nor set others on to do it.

(E. K. Purnell, *Magdalene College*, 1904)

At Clare, John Walcott behaved badly in 1663:

	s	d
To Sr. Lowe for mending his viall which he brake	3	0
For books which he borrowed of Sr. Lowe and sold	6	0
To Sr. Lowe for a looking glass which he brake	3	6
Selbys Riders dictionary borrowed and sold by him	7	2
Selbys hatt lent and never returned	4	0
Becketts Scrivelius lexicon borrowed and sold by him	7	0
[Robert Lowe was an Exeter Fellow of the College]		

(Harrison, *Life in Clare*)

A parent worried about his son at St. Catharine's, writes to the Master, John Eachard:

23 April 1680

Let the milliners etc be forbidden to trust him: he hath clothes enough for a quarter of a year, or two months. Take him off from tobacco, he hath forced it on himself, he neglecteth his study, would run after wenches: I hope you will laugh him out of these things. Task him well for his book; if a strict hand be not kept over him he will do but little. Let him not know of this my writing. I will endeavour to get money, as soon as I can, when I know my charge: I desire care to be used in casting up the accounts, and that the profit of his scholarship may be allowed.

Postscript. I have given my son much good counsel, but he very much slighteth it. Watch him for speaking untruths to which he is so prone: as also to chop and change his clothes so as to cut and alter them to my great detriment: if he be not more moderate, I cannot hold.

<div align="right">(Jones, <em>The Story of St. Catharine's</em>)</div>

<p align="center"><em>Some undergraduates spent industrious lives:</em></p>

<div align="right">1667</div>

I did most extremely envy the common scholars for the joy they had at football, and lament my own condition, that was tied up by quality from mixing with them . . .

As to study there, I followed my own appetite, which was to natural philosophy, which they call physics, and particularly Descartes, whose works I dare say I read over three times before I understood him . . . And at that time new philosophy was a sort of heresy, and my brother cared not to encourage me much in it. I had the old physics, as Majirus and Senectatus, but could not thresh so at them . . . I joined with this study some mathematics, to which also I had an inclination . . . I had books of ethics and metaphysics also to peruse, but my delight was in philosophy and mathematics . . . Logic I did not touch upon there, having had enough at home.

<div align="right">(Roger North, <em>Lives of the Norths</em>,
ed. A. Jessopp, 1890)</div>

<p><em>Some, like John Strype at St. Catharine's, wrote detailed accounts of their lives to their mothers:</em></p>

We have roast meat, dinner and supper, throughout the weeke; and such meate as you know I not use to care for; and that is Veal: but now I have learnt to eat it. Sometimes, neverthelesse, we have boiled meat, with pottage; and beef and mutton, which I am glad of; except Fridays and Saturdays, and sometimes Wednesdays; which days we have Fish at dinner, and tansy or pudding for supper. Our parts then are slender enough. But there is this remedy; we may retire unto the Butteries, and there take a half-penny loafe and butter or cheese; or else to the Kitchen, and take there what the Cook hath. But, for my part, I am sure, I never visited the Kitchen yet, since I have been here, and the Butteries but seldom after meals; unlesse for a Ciza, that is for a Farthing-worth of Small-Beer: so that lesse than a Peny in Beer doth serve me a whole Day. Neverthelesse sometimes we have Exceedings: then we have two or three Dishes (but that is very rare): otherwise never but one:

We go twice a day to Chapel; in the morning about 7, and in the Evening about 5. After we come from Chapel in the morning, which is towards 8, we go to the Butteries for our breakfast, which usually is five Farthings; an halfepenny loaf and butter, and a cize of beer. But sometimes I go to an honest House near the College, and have a pint of milk boiled for my breakfast.

<div align="right">(<em>Letters of Eminent Literary Men</em>,
ed. Ellis)</div>

or, like him, worried about their rooms and the 'chamberers' (or 'chums') they shared them with. One found the décor trying to his eyes:

while I was an undergraduate, an accident happened to me . . . I one summer observed, that my eyes did not see as usual, but dazzled after an awkward manner. Upon which, I imagined this might arise only from my too much application to my studies and I thought proper to abate of that application for a fort-night, in hopes of recovering my usual sight by walking, during that time, much abroad in the green grass and green fields but found myself disappointed . . . At this time I met with an account . . . that Mr. Boyle had known of a person who had new whited the wall of his study or chamber, upon which the sun shone, and used to read in the glaring light, and thereby lost his sight for a time, till upon hanging the place where he studied with green, he recovered it again, which was exactly my own case . . . For I and my chamber-fellow had newly whitened our room, into which all afternoon the sun shone, and where I used to read. I therefore retired to my study, and hung it with green, by which means I recovered my usual sight.

(William Whiston, *Memoirs*, 1753)

John Strype to his mother:

as yet, I am in a Chamber that doth not at all please me. I have thoughts of one, which is a very handsome one, and one pair of stairs high, and that looketh into the Master's garden.

At my first Coming I laid alone: but since, my Tutor desired me to let a very clean lad lay with me, and an Alderman's son of Colchester, which I could not deny, being newly come: he hath laid with me now for almost a fortnight, and will do till he can provide himself with a Chamber.

Rooms had to be fitted out. In 1688, John Gibson of St. John's had the following expenses:

	£	s	d
ffor a bedstead	0	2	6
ffor 2 paper books	0	0	10
ffor a study table	0	2	0
ffor paper	0	0	6
ffor Whole Duty of Man sent to my sister Prudence	0	4	0
ffor Letters	0	1	6
spent	0	1	6
ffor a paper booke	0	0	4
sum	0	13	2

(*The Eagle*, XVII, no. 98, June 1892)

Some feared ghosts. Dr John North was a youth at Jesus in 1661:

when he was in bed alone he durst not trust his countenance above the clothes. For some time he lay with his tutor, who once, coming home, found the scholar in bed with only his crown visible. The tutor . . . pulled him by the hair; whereupon the scholar slunk down, and the tutor followed, and at last with a great outcry the scholar sprang up, expecting to see an enormous spectre.

Another time, which was after he was fellow of the college, in a moon-shine night, he saw one standing in a white sheet. He surveyed it with all his optics and was confirmed it was a spirit . . . and resolved with himself if he could find out what it came for. He got out of his bed . . . went nearer and nearer till he might touch it; and then reaching out his hand he perceived it was only his towel hung against the wall with the moon shining full upon it; and then he went to bed and slept well.

(North, Lives, ed. Jessopp)

Colleges looked after their invalids.

Clare College accounts (kept by Dr. Samuel Blithe, Fellow 1658–78, Master 1678–1713):

John South:
August 13, 1660
caudells, grewell, chickens, connys, broths, sugar, pruins and other
   diett in the time of his sicknesse   £2 9s 4d
Richard Haworth:
May 17, 1678, he broke his legg at Chesterton by a fall

	£	s	d
June 3, for boat hire to bringe him to the Colledge		1	6
4th to him to give Mr. Desborow for gloves for setting his bone	2	0	0
June 12th, paid to his landlady at Chesterton for drink 6s and for diett, washing and tendance 12 dayes £1	1	6	0

(Harrison, Life in Clare)

Some undergraduates came from unusual backgrounds:

For it is a common fashion of a great many, to complement, and invite inferiour Peoples Children to the University, and there pretend to make such an all-beautiful provision for them, as they shall not fail of coming to a very eminent degree of Learning: But when they come there, they shall save a Servants Wages. There took therefore heretofore a very good method to prevent Sizars over-heating their Brains: Bed-making, Chamber-sweeping, and Water-fetching, were doubtless great preservations against too much vain Philosophy. Now certainly such pretended favours and kindnesses as these, are the most right down discourtesies in the World. For it is ten times more happy, both for a Lad and the Church, to be a Corn-cutter, or Tooth-drawer, to make or mend Shoes, or to be of any inferiour Profession, than to be invited to, and promised the Conveniences of a learned Education, and to have his Name only stand airing upon the College Tables, and his chief business shall be to Buy Eggs and Butter.

(John Eachard, The Grounds and Occasions
of the Contempt of the Clergy, 1670)

1657 Dec. 16 was the congregation for ending of the term. At that time Mr. G. Haynes his brother, who was bachelor of arts in New England of a year standing, and now admitted in Pembroke Hall, was incorporated here. His testimoniall of degree and carriage was under the hand and seal of Mr. Chaney, B.D. (sometime fellow of Trinity College here), now master of the college in New England, and others.

(Worthington, *Diary and Correspondence*, ed. Crossley)

1673 (Blithe's account book):

Henry Perrott borne at Rapahanocke in Virginia admitted by Mr. Alston in my absence under my care.

April 23 1675

Thomas Sargeant borne at Dublin in Ireland (he was four yeares in the Universitye of Dublin; and one yeare at the Coll: called Collegium Harvard-inum at Cambridge in New England, where he commenced Bachelor of Arts, 1674, as his testimonialls shew) admitted Pentioner under my care.

(Harrison, *Life in Clare*)

Some were not fondly remembered:

In the year 1664, I was admitted into Caius Colledge . . . where I continued until 1668; I remember Titus Oates was enterd into our Colledge; by the same token that the *Plague* and *he* both visited the University in the same year. He was very remarkable for a Canting Fanatical way conveyed to him with his *Anabaptistical* Education, and in our Academical exercises, when others declaim'd, *Oates* always preach'd . . . I moreover remember, that he staied not above a year in our Colledge, but removed to *Saint Johns*; what the occasion was, I cannot call to mind.

(Adam Elliott, *A Modest Vindication of Titus Oates*, 1682)

Others had too brief a life to be remembered (except by John Aubrey):

Richard Stokes. His father was fellow of Eaton College. He was bred there and at King's College. Scholar to Mr. Oughtred for Mathematiques (Algebra). He made himselfe mad with it, but became sober again, but I feare like a crackt glasse . . . Became a Roman Catholique; married unhappily at Liege, dog and catt, etc. Became a sott. Dyed in Newgate, prisoner for debt, 1681.

(*Brief Lives*)

Others left abruptly:

Mr. Alderman Crabb . . . alledged that december 1677 he mett Leigh of Trinity College, andrew Feltwell, and Charles Slayd, Barbers, about tenn of the Clock at night at the end of Shoemakers Roe and they did unhorse him twice, and did strike him with a stick till it did breake; And when he said that he was a Justice of the Peace they made answer, You shall have one blow the more for that . . . Then the Vicechancellour and Heads aforesaid did goe to the Schole Gates, and at the command of Mr. vice-chancellour Titus Tillett Yeoman Bedle of the University did pull off Leighs Gowne and take away his Capp.

(*The Esquire Bedells*, 1981)

Christ's College

there are some things wanting which I must trouble you to furnish me with. I sent for the trunkes which were my uncle Ro. in which I thought to have found a paire of sheets, but there were none. I want also half a douzen of napkins which are to be used in the hall which in the meantime I am constrained to borrow, and some small table clothes and towells and a piece of plate ...
Sir, I desire you to send me twelve shillings for to cleare the cookes bill. I hope you will excuse me for being so short. So I rest ...

Your most obedient son,
Bassingbourne Gawdy

I pray bid my brother John send me some of his pictures to dress up my study.

(Venn, *Early Collegiate Life*)

If you are not too straight of money, send me some such thing by the woman, and a pound or two of Almonds and Raisins ...

(Strype in *Letters of Eminent Literary Men*, ed. Ellis)

but sometimes there were thank-you letters too. John Dryden, at Trinity, sends a well-turned one to a cousin, Honor Dryden:

Yet though I highly vallue your Magnificent presents, pardon me if I must tell the world they are but imperfect Emblemes of your beauty; For the white and red of waxe and paper are but shaddowes of that vermillion and snowe in your lips and forehead. And the silver of the Inkhorne if it presume to vye whitenesse with your purer Skinne, must confess it selfe blacker than the liquor it containes. What then do I more then retrieve your own gifts? and present you that paper adulterated with blotts which you gave spotlesse?

For since 'twas mine the white hath lost its hiew
To show t'was n'ere it selfe but whilst in you;
The Virgin Waxe hath blusht it selfe to red
Since it with mee hath lost its Maydenhead.

You (fairest Nymph) are waxe; oh may you bee
As well in softnesse so as purity;
Till Fate and your own happy choise reveale
Whom you so farre shall blesse to make you seale.

Fairest Valentine the unfeigned wish of yo[r] humble votary,

Jo: Dryden

Cambridge May 1653

(*Letters*, ed. C. E. Ward, 1942)

Good conversation was highly regarded:

The old Court (in Christ's) till after the return of K. Charles the Second was rail'd in and there was no common Combination Room below Staires, for the Fellows every day to meet in; But at dinner and supper in Summer they met upon the Regent Walk ... and there they waited until they knew what Seniors would come down, and then they went into the Hall. In Winter they always met in the Hall and stood about the Fire . . . After Dinners and Suppers they had no common Combination Room, but went into the Orchard in Summer, or at other times to one anothers Chambers.

(Dr. Covel's Account in W. & C.)

Some conversations were in Latin:

Queens'

Octob. 26 1676   It was decreed by the unanimous consent of the President and Fellows that nothing but Latin be spoken in the Hall at dinner and supper (not only in Term but out of Term) by all Gownmen constantly (excepting All Scarlet-days, the twelve days at Christmas and Commemoration of benefactors). Sept. 13 1680   It was desired and consented to that English may be spoken on Sundays and Holidays, and the Decree in force as to all other times.

(J. H. Gray, The Queens' College, 1899)

The coffee-house fashion was just beginning.

In 1664 the Vice-Chancellor and heads decreed:

that all in pupillari statu that shall go to coffee-houses without their tutors leave shall be punished according to the statute for haunters of taverns and ale-houses.

(Cooper)

though Roger North, writing much later, says:

Whilst he [John North] was at Jesus College [1661] coffee was not of such common use as afterwards, and coffee-houses but young. At that time, and long after, there was but one, kept by one Kirk. The trade of news also was scarce set up: for they had only the public Gazette, till Kirk got a written news-letter circulated by one Mudiman. But now the case is much altered; for it is become a custom after chapel to repair to one or other of the coffee-houses (for there are divers) where hours are spent in talking; and less profitable reading of news-papers, of which swarms are continually supplied from London.

(North, Lives, ed. Jessopp)

Other distractions included tennis:

Sir William Temple

the disorders of the time haveing hindred his goeing to the university till seventine where he was placed at Emanuel Colledge in Cambridge, under the care of Dr. Cudworth, who would have engaged him in the harsh studies of logick and phylosophy which his humor was too lively to pursue. Entertainments (which agreed better with that & his age, especially Tennis) past most of his time there, soe that he use to say, if it had bin possible in the two years time he past there to forget all he had learn't before, he must certainly have done it.

(Life and Character, by Martha, Lady
Gifford, 1690, ed. G. C. Moore Smith, 1930) *and Emmanuel College, 29 October 1651:*

For the better regulating of the Tennis Court it is ordered by the Master and Fellows *unanimi concensu* that the key of it shalbe in the keeping of the Deane, who is to take care that the door be kept lockt, and never suffered to play dureing the howers hereafter mentioned, vizt from one of the clock till three in the afternoone and from eight of the clock at night till tenn the next morning; unless any of the fellows shall desire to play there in any of these howers, who may take any fellow commoner with them; yet soe as they cleare the Court, shutt the doore and returne the key to the Deane at their comeing away.

(Shuckburgh, Emmanuel College)

And there was ever-pervasive music:

Dr. Covel of Christ's recollects:

Many of the Fellows when I was a Freshman (1654) were Musical, and old Robt Wilson taught them, and often bore them Company in some of their Chambers where they diverted themselves with singing.

(W. & C.)

Blithe's account book:

	£	s	d
(George Cooke)			
Feb. 18, 1680 For a violin and case	2	0	0
For entrance with Crispe the musician		10	0
April 27. For the Musicke Master	1	10	0
Oct. 1681. For his flute master		10	0
(Griffith Boynton)			
Nov. 18, 1681. To him to pay Mr. Crispe for violin	2	0	0
and for entrance		10	0
Feb. 22, 1682. To himselfe to pay Mr. Crispes quarterage	1	10	0
June 15. To him to pay Mr. Wilkins for entrance to learn the			
base violl		15	0

(Harrison, Life in Clare)

There was a dark side to life always; calamity, sudden death and the plague.

Anthony Wood writes in Oxford:

Feb/March 1666   Many that could not go to Cambridge came hither [because of the plague]
June/July   The plague raging againe in Cambridge: many came here.

(Life and Times, ed. Clark)

Robert Lowe writes to S. Blithe, Fellow of Clare, who was staying in Norfolk:

1665
Alderman Mywell the Brewer and one of his children dyed of the plague this last Munday, he hath had 4 children in all dead of it. Clayton the Barber in petty

Cury and one of his children dyed last Satturday of the sickness. It is newly broken out sadly by Christs (though they are all fled from that Colledge upon Mr. Bunchly their Manciple's dying of the plague).

Poore Mr. Brown the old man that is one of the university Musitians and Mr. Saunders that sings the deep base are shut up in Mr. Saunders's house in Green Street, whose child dyed last week suspected.

(Wardale, Clare College Letters and Documents)

John Strype wrote to his mother in 1662:

Here in the college hath died a lad whom I loved better than any since I came to Cambridge; some say of the spotted fever, which I think proved false; every one in the College, as also his acquaintance in Town, had gloves and ribbons: he was buried very nobly. The small pox and these fevers are very much about Town; so that it is dangerous being here.

(Letters of Eminent Literary Men, ed. Ellis)

Alderman Newton in his diary:

1664 Dec. 17   Saturday: in the morning betimes dyed Roger Nightingale Manciple or Caterer and singing man of Kings College . . . The same day in the morning from about 2 of the clock to 5 was seene in the ayre a Comett wch several days lately before had bin alsoe seene, the star it selfe was very little or not at all bigger than an ordinary starr, but it had a ray which came from it that appeared to the judgemt of some to be 20 yards in length, to the others the length of a pike, to others the length of Kings Col Chappell . . .

1664/Jan. 5   Thursday. This morning being a great frost, Mr. Griswold mar. of Arts and Fellow of Trinity Coll in Cambr' Fell downe the stayres wch are next the chappell north by the Kings gate, and with the fall was killed, being found dead there lyeing, (about 5 in the morning by the bedmakers) and was cold and stiff, he had the key of the garden dore in his hand and lay with his head downwards at the feet of the stayres and his heels upwards upon the stayres, with his neck (as was supposed) choked with his high coller, and bloud had come out of his nose, being seene on his head. Humfry Prychard the Coll porter lett him into the Coll about 2 of the clock that morning and was supposed to have bin drinking somewhere, and haveing bin as was supposed through the garden at the house of easement at his retourn goeing up the said stayres to his chamber fell downe and was killed as aforesaid.

1712 May 21   Wednesday morning Dr. Syke, a German, of Trinity College . . . and Hebrew Professor of the University, was found dead in his Chamber uppon the floor, having hanged himselfe with his Girdle or shash which he girded himself in his morning Gowne . . . he was the night before in the College Hall at supper and eate Sperragrasse . . . he was observed for some time lately to be melancholy.

(Alderman Newton's Diary, ed. Foster)

The University still had problems with the Court.

Cambridge complaint:

1674 14 July   Tewsday in the morning at a Congregation in the Regent House in the University, was chose his Grace James Duke of Monmouth (the Kings naturall sonne) Chancelour of the University of Cambridge.

(Alderman Newton's Diary, ed. Foster)

On 3 July 1685 the Vice-Chancellor and Heads proposed a grace, unanimously approved by the Senate, that the portrait of the Chancellor, the rebellious Duke of Monmouth, should be publicly burned on Commencement Day – 6 July.

(The Esquire Bedells)

Cambridge rebellious:

The King [James II] sent his letter, or *mandamus*, to order *F. Francis*, an ignorant Benedictine Monk, to be received a Master of Arts, once to open the way for letting them into the degrees of the University. The truth is, the King's letters were scarce ever refused, in conferring degrees: and, when Ambassadors, or foreign Princes, came to those places, they usually gave such degrees, to those who belonged to them, as were desired. The *Morocco* Ambassador's secretary, that was a Mahometan, had that degree given him; but a great distinction was made between honorary degrees given to strangers, who intended not to live among them, and those given to such as intended to settle among them . . .

They refused the *mandamus* with great unanimity, and with a firmness, that the Court had not expected from them.

(Bishop Gilbert Burnet, History of the
Reign of King James II, 1852)

*Nevertheless John Peachell, the Vice-Chancellor, had to play for time when
in April 1687 he was summoned to Lord Chancellor Jeffreys:*

L.C. Now Mr. Vice Chancellor, what have you to say, why you did not obey His Majesty's Command, in behalf of the Gentleman mentioned there?

V.C. My Lord, you enquire of me why I did not admit Mr. Francis, according to the King's Letters?

L.C. Yes, that's the Question I ask you.

V.C. Is this the only Question your Lordship is pleased to ask me?

L.C. Nay, Mr. Vice Chancellour, we will not capitulate in the very beginning; pray answer the first, and then you shall know what we have to say more.

V.C. It is but a little while since we met in Town, and this is a question of great Concern; I am not prepared to answer it on a sudden.

L.C. Why, Mr. Vice Chancellour, my Lords specified it in their summons what would be prepared, on purpose you should not come unprepared, but it may be Mr. Vice Chancellour did not attend sufficiently to that part of the Summons, therefore let it be read to him once more – (which was done).

Now Sir, you hear it is for refusing to comply with the King's Commands.

V.C. My lords, I beg time to answer you; my lords, I am a plain Man, not used to appear before such an Honourable Assembly and if I should answer hastily, it may be I might speak something indecent or unsafe, which I should afterwards be sorry for, therefore I beg Leave, my lords, to have time allowed us, for giving in such an answer, as may be both for our own safety and your Lordship's Honour.

L.C. (smiling)   Why, Mr. Vice Chancellour, as for your own Safety, my Lords are willing you should take all the care you can, but for what concerns our Honour, do not trouble yourself, we are able to consult that without any Interposition of yours.

(Cooper)

(Peachell's punishment for his non-cooperation was to be deprived of his office as Vice-Chancellor: an unpaid office, as Cooper observes.)

Papists were unpopular:

In the reign of K. James II when by reason of the Master's being in the decline of life, it was feared lest both the College and their Mss might fall into the hands of Papists, Mr. Corey, one of the Fellows . . . was employed . . . carefully to copy some of those relating to the Establishment of the Protestant Religion . . .

Clement Scot one of the Fellows, had already declared his Inclinations towards Popery; for which the Mob at the Revolution, were so much irritated against him that they brake into his Chamber, and would probably have destroyed him, had he not at that time secreted himself in the Cupola from their Rage. It discharged itself however . . . upon his Books and Papers, when 'tis imagined many belonging to the College (he being then Bursar) perished with them. 'tis reported also, that upon finding Boyle's Experiments on Blood, some of them cried out, see what a bloody-minded Dog he is, his books are full of nothing else. He was obliged to retire into the Country for further safety, and resigned his Fellowship soon after.

(R. Masters, *History of Corpus Christi*,
ed. Lamb, 1831)

There were expensive state visits and other junketings:

Trinity 1669   for Oranges spent upon the Prince & strangers at the two times of publick acting 14s 4d

1670   for wine at the Comedy before the Duke of Ormond 12 qts of Canary 12 qts of Claret £1 18 0
6 qts of Canary & 6 qts of Claret for the Actors 19s.

(G. C. Moore Smith, *College Plays*, 1923)

1671 Oct. 4   Wednesday being a very cleere sunshiney day, his Majestie King Charles the 2nd came to Cambridge the 1st time . . . The Conduit ran claret wine when his Majestie passed by who was well pleased with it.

(*Alderman Newton's Diary*, ed. Foster)

October 1678   The King returned from Newmarket to London. Some days before which Nell Gwyn with Fleetwood Shepard were entertained by certaine scholars at Cambridge (either by the vice-chancellor or proctors) and had verses presented to her.

(*Life and Times, of Anthony Wood*,
ed. Clark)

Clare College Accounts (1688)

Pd in money to Edw. Hucke for Xmas greens 1s od.

(Harrison, Life in Clare)

1688/9 19 Feb. The Vice-chancellor and heads of Colleges and Doctors in scarlett on Foot being Tewsday morning about 10 of the Clock with the rest of that body there in their Habitts, at the Market Crosse and on the Hill against the Rose Taverne proclaimed King William and Queen Mary Prince and Princess of Orange to bee King and Queene of England France and Ireland etc. The Officers and some part of their Troops then in Towne attended the service, the officers were invited by the Vice-chancellor to dinner, the souldiers etc. had I heare 10 guineas given them to drinke, likewise the Towne waytes played before them.

(Alderman Newton's Diary, ed. Foster)

There were many ceremonies connected with examinations and degree giving.

Abraham de la Pryme's Diary:

1694 January. This month it was that we sat for our degree of batchelors of arts. We sat three days in the colledge and were examin'd by two fellows thereof in retorick, logicks, ethics, physicks, and astronomy; then we were sent to the publick schools, there to be examined again three more days by any one that would. Then when the day came of our being cap'd by the Vice-Chancellor, wee were all call'd up in our soph's gowns and our new square caps and lamb-skin hoods on. There we were presented, four by four, by our father to the Vice-Chancellor, saying out a sort of formal presentation speech to him. Then we had the oaths of the dutys we are to observe in the university read to us, as also that relating to the Articles of the Church of England, and another of allegiance, which we all swore to. Then we every one register'd our own names in the university book, and after that, one by one, we kneel'd down before the Vice-Chancellour's knees, and he took hold of both of our hands with his, saying to this effect, 'Admitto te', &c. 'I admitt you to be batchellour of arts, upon condition that you answer to your questions; rise and give God thanks.' Upon that as he has done with them one by one they rise up, and, going to a long table hard by, kneel down there and says some short prayer or other as they please.

About six days after this (which is the end of that day's work, we being now almost batchellors) we go all of us to the schools, there to answer to our questions, which our father always tells us what we shall answer before we come there, for fear of his puting us to a stand, so that he must be either necessitated to stop us of our degrees, or else punish us a good round summ of monny. But we all of us answer'd without any hesitation; we were just thirty-three of us, and then having made us an excellent speech, he (I mean our father) walk'd home before us in triumph, so that now wee are become compleat battchellors, praised be God!

(Diary of Abraham de la Pryme, the
Yorkshire Antiquary, 1870)

8. The Pepysian Library, Magdalene College in 1841 (drawing by F. Mackenzie)

A licensed humourist or jester, at some time known as 'Mr. Tripos', provided light relief:

One Cook being prevaricator or umbra in Cambridge commencement...
seemed to be verie wittie in his speech, but in the middle thereof seeing Jack
Glendall an Oxford wit peeping out of a private hole, the prevaricator saw him
and called out saying 'Salve, Mr. Glendall' to which Glendall replyed 'Salve
tu quoque'.

(Life and Times of Anthony Wood,
ed. Clark)

Many visitors enjoyed themselves. Pepys certainly did when he came back to his old university:

24 Feb. 1660 . . . we two came to Cambrige by 8 a-clock in the morning, to the
Faulcon in the Petty Cury. Where we found my father and brother very well.
After dressing myself, about 10 a-clock, my father, brother and I to Mr. Widdrington at Christ's College, who received us very civilly and caused my brother
to be admitted (as a sizar) while my father, he and I sat talking. After that done,
we took leave. My father and brother went to visit friends, Pepys's, scholars in
Cambridge, while I went to Magdalen College . . .

26. *Sunday*. My brother went to the college to Chappell.

   My father and I went out in the morning and walk out in the fields behind
King's College and in King's College chapel yard; and there we met with Mr.
Fayrbrother. Who took us to Butolphes Church, where we heard Mr. Nicholas
of Queen's College (who I knew in my time to be Tripos with great applause) . . .

I took leave of all my friends and so to my Inn. Where, after I had wrote a note and enclosed the certificate to Mr. Widdrington, I bade good-night to my father; and John went to bed but I stayed up a little while, playing the fool with the lass of the house at the door of the chamber; and so to bed.

15th July 1661   Up by 3 a-clock this morning and rode to Cambrige, and was there by 7 a-clock. Where after I was trimmed, I went to Christ College and find my brother John at 8 a-clock in bed, which vexed me. Then to King's College chappell, where I find the schollers in their surplices at the service with the organs – which is a strange sight to what it used in my time to be here . . .

10th October 1662 (Ware)   Up, and between 8 and 9 mounted again. But my feet so swelled with yesterday's pain, that I could not get on my boots, which vexed me to the blood; but was forced to pay 4s for a pair of old shoes of my landlord's, and so rid in shoes to Cambrige; but the way so good that but for a little rain I have got very well thither – and set up at the beare. And there, being spied in the streets passing through the town, my Cosen Angier came to me, and I must needs to his house; which I did and there find Dr. Fairebrother, with a good dinner – a barrel of good oysters – a couple of lobsters, and wine. But above all, telling me that this day there is a Congregacion for the choice of some officers in the University, he after dinner gets me a gowne, Capp, and hoode and carries me to the Schooles, where Mr. Pepper, my brother's Tutor, and this day chosen Proctor, did appoint a Master of art to lead me into the Regent-house, where I sat with them and did (vote) by subscribing papers thus: '*Ego Samual Pepys eligo Magistrum Bernadum Skelton*' (and which was more strange, my old schoolfellow and acquaintance, and who afterwards did take notice of me and we spoke together) '*alterum e taxatoribus hujus Academiae in annum sequentem*'. The like I did for one Biggs for the other Taxor and for other officers as the Vice-proctor, Mr. Covell, for Mr. Pepper, and which was the gentleman that did carry me into the Regent-house.
   This being done and the congregacion dissolved by the Vice-Chancellor, I did with much content return to my Cosen Angiers, being much pleased of doing this jobb of work, which I have long wished for and could never have had such a time as now to do it with such ease.

8th October 1667   . . . away to Cambridge, it being foul, rainy weather; and there did take up at the Rose, for the sake of Mrs. Dorothy Drawwater, the vintener's daughter, which is mentioned in the play of *Sir Martin Marr-all*. Here we had a good chamber and bespoke a good supper; and then I took my wife and W. Hewer and Willett (it holding up a little) and showed them Trinity College and St. Johns Library, and went to King's College chapel to see the outside of it only, and so to our Inne; and with much pleasure did this, they walking in their pretty morning gowns, very handsome, and I proud to find myself in a condition to do this; and so home to our lodging, and there by and by to supper with much good sport, talking with the drawers concerning matters of the town and persons whom I remember; and so after supper to cards and then to bed, lying, I in one bed and my wife and girl in another in the same room; and very merry talking together and mightily pleased both of us with the girl. Saunders, the only Viallin in my time, is I hear dead of the plague in the late plague there.

9th. Up, and got ready and eat our breakfast and then took coach; and the poor, as they did yesterday, did stand at the coach to have something given them, as they do to all great persons, and I did give them something; and the town musique did also come and play; but Lord, what sad music they made – however, I was pleased with them, being all of us in very good humour; and so set forth and through the town, and observed at our College of Magdalen the posts new-painted, and understand that the Vice-Chancellor is there this year.

23 May 1668   after supper to bed and lay very ill by reason of drunken scholars making a noise all night . . .

25 May 1668   . . . and so we away and got well to Cambridge about 7 to the Rose, the waters not being now so high as before. And here lighting, I took my boy and two brothers and walked to Magdalen College; and there into the Butterys as a stranger and there drank my bellyfull of their beer, which pleased me as the best I ever drank; and hear by the butler's man, who was son to Goody Mulliner over against the College that we used to buy stewed prunes of, concerning the College and persons in it; and find very few, only Mr. Hollins and Peachell I think, that were of my time.

(Diary, ed. R. C. Latham and W. Matthews,
1970–83)

Humfry Wanley was sent to Cambridge to look at various MSS on behalf of the Master of University College, Oxford. He wrote back to Dr. Charlett, describing his reception:

Cambridge, Septemb. 2, 1699

Reverend & Honoured Sir,

. . . On Thursday morning I waited on Mr. Laughton, at Trinity College, who was very busie, but however, at last, took me with all freedom into the College Library . . . Some of the books I enquired after could not be found on the sudden; but I made a shift to probe out a few of them myself, being left alone . . . After I had satisfied my curiositie there for the present, I went to the Schools, and found Mr. Laughton in the Publick Library. He was pleased to show me presently most of the books that I shall have occasion to use, which satisfied me very much . . . I met at Trinity College with Mr. Buckeridge, Mr. Norgrove, (etc.) who engaged me to dine with them, which I did. After dinner, we all went together to visit some of the College Libraries and Chapels . . . At night we were regaled with a very good concert of Music; where I was much taken with some Italian songs, which Mr. Pate brought from Rome, and a Gentleman here sang very well.

There I met with Mr. Annesley, who did me the honour to desire my acquaintance, &c. We came away together, and betimes in the morning I waited on him at his Chamber (preventing his calling at mine, as he purposed). We went to Bennet College . . . and with some difficulty all the books were found that I shall use. Take 'em all together, and they'l appear to be a most noble parcel of books.

(Letters of Eminent Literary Men, ed. Ellis)

Some visitors were more critical.

John Evelyn in his diary, 31 August 1654:

The Schools are very despicable, and Public Library but mean, though some-what improved by the Bishop Bancroft's library and MSS. They showed us little of antiquity . . .

The market-place is very ample, and remarkable for old Hobson, the pleasant carrier's benefaction of a fountain. But the whole town is a low dirty unpleasant place, the streets ill-paved, the air thick and infected by the fens, nor are its churches (of which St. Mary's is the best) anything considerable in compare to Oxford.

James Bonnell writes to John Strype about a not very satisfactory visit to their old college, St. Catharine's:

17 November 1679

By ill fortune it proved Gosling day and Mr. Blackall preached; I came when he had done; and was taken up in company all of the time, at a long dinner of ill-dressed meat (under the rose) and a formality of being served by gowned waiting-men, little dirty-pawed sizars, with greasy old fashioned glasses, and trenchers that would hold no sauce; but this only for merriment between you and I: the end of the College next Queens' is finished, and the gate is plain next the street; but very handsome of the inside; they talk of going on, but whether next Spring or no, I can't tell.

(Jones, *St. Catharine's College*)

Celia Fiennes appreciated the buildings (1697):

Trinity Colledg is the finest yet not so large as Christ-church College in Oxford; in the first Court there is a very fine fountaine in the middle of the Quadrangle with a carved top and Dyals round; there are large Cloysters [in] the Second and the Library runns all the rang of building at the end and stands on 3 rows of stone pillars; it opens into the Gardens and Walk with 3 large Gates or doores of iron carv'd very fine with flowers and leaves; the river runs at the back side of most of the Colleges; they have fine stone bridges over it and gates that lead to fine walks, the rivers name is Cam; the Library farre exceeds that of Oxford, the Staires are wanscoated and very large and easye ascent all of Cedar wood, the room spacious and lofty paved with black and white marble, the sides are wanscoated and decked with all curious books off Learning their Catalogue and their Benefactors; there is two large Globes at each end with teliscopes and microscopes and the finest Carving in wood in flowers birds leaves figures of all sorts as I ever saw; there is a large Balcony opens at the end that answers to the Staires . . .

St. Johns College Garden is very pleasant for the fine walks, both close shady walks and open rows of trees and quickeset hedges, there is a pretty bowling green with cut arbours in the hedges . . . Claire Hall is very little but most exactly neate; in all parts they have walks with rows of trees and bridges over the river and fine painted gates into the fields . . .

(*The Journal of Celia Fiennes*, ed. Christopher Morris, 1947) as we passed through Trumpington, when the Scholars at their leisure hours are some or other of 'em usually refreshing themselves; we saw several Black Gowns pop in and out of the little Country-hovels, like so many Black Rabbits in a Warren, bolting out of their Coney-Burroughs . . .

There is one very famous Inn, distinguished by the sign of the Devils Lap-dog in Petty-Cury – where I found an Old grizly Curmudgeon corniferously wedded to a Plump, Young, Brisk, Black, Beautiful, good Landlady, who I afterwards heard had so great a kindness for the University, that she had rather see two or three Gown-men come into her House, then a Cuckoldy Crew of Aldermen in all their Pontificalibusses; and indeed I had reason to believe there was no love lost, for the Scholars crept in as fast and as slily, for either a Kiss, a kind Look, or a Cup of Comfort, as Hogs into an Orchard after a High-wind, or Flys into Pig-sauce, for the sake of the Sugar . . .

Cooks-row . . . great number of booksellers . . . are now crept into possession of their greasinesses division; this learned part of the fair is the scholars chief rendezvouz, where some that have money come to buy books, whilst others, who want it, take 'em slily up, upon condition to pay if they're catch'd, and think it a pious piece of generosity, to give St. *Austin* or St. *Gregory* protection in a gown sleeve till they can better provide for 'em . . .

As for the town itself, it was so abominably dirty, that *Old-street* in the middle of a winter's thaw, or *Bartholomew-fair* after a shower of rain, could not have more occasion for a scavenger, than the miry streets of this famous corporation, and most of them so very narrow, that should two wheel-barrows meet in the largest of their thoroughfares, they are enough to make a stop for half an hour before they can well clear themselves of one another, to make room for passengers . . . The buildings in many parts of the town were so little and so low, that they look'd more like huts for pigmies, than houses for men.

> (Edward Ward, *A Step to Stir-Bitch-Fair;*
> *with Remarks upon the University of*
> *Cambridge,* 1700)

The seventeenth century was, despite upheavals, a great period of building and benefaction:

Now began the University to be much beautified in building, every college either casting its skin with the snake, or renewing its bill with the eagle, having their courts, or at least their fronts and gatehouses repaired and adorned.

> (Fuller, *History*)

Some building projects had been started before the Civil War:

Christ's

Memoir of Dr. Covel:

A very considerable part of the Schollars of Christ College lodged in the Brazen George [south side of St. Andrew's churchyard in Preacher Street] and the Gates there were shut and open'd Morning and Evening constantly as the

College gates were. In the year 1640 the Foundations of the new Building [The Fellows' Building] were laid and the College at that time added a room or two to the Master's private Lodge, which before was only a washhouse or Laundery with a Close or two for Drying-yards. All was encompassed at first with only Hedges or Mud-wall, but afterwards they were made of brick as they now stand.

(W. & C.)

Orders for the New Building, 8 November 1642 include:

Every Chamber shall be made handsomelye habitable by the Colledge, or by those who desyre to inhabit it: and, the charge shall be an Income, to be enterd into a Booke.

Some were interrupted:

Clare – the Butt Close controversy

Clare wanted to move the old quadrangle further to the west and to build a bridge over the river as had King's, Trinity and John's and a passage to the fields through Butts Close. There was a reasonable request to King's accompanied by an appeal to the King c. 1637–8. This caused bitter controversy.

King's: This little peice of ground, (commonly called Butt-close) is all we have both for the walkes and exercise of at least an hundred persons, and allso for the feeding of Tenne horses which we are enjoyned to keepe by Statute . . .

Clare (to the King): your petitioners doe humblie begg of your most sacred Majesty, that they may be suffered at their own chardge to land a bridge over the river, and enjoy a passage through the said But-close into the feilds, which would be litle or noe prejudice to them, and of great benefitt to your petitioners, especially in tymes of infecion, having noe passadge into the feilds, but through the Chappell yard of your said Kings Colledge, the gates whereof are shutt up in these tymes of danger.

The parties were eventually reconciled by the King in 1638 and Clare then embarked on building:

The bridge

Jan 18 1638–9	To Tho: Grumball for a Draught of a Bridge	00 03 00
March 4	To Richard Chamberlayne in pt of a Bargaine for the Gates and Bridges into and out of K Coll. Butclose	60 00 00
Feb 1 1639–40	To Grumbald for working the Rayle and Ballisters xl shill Febr 8th 40 shill Febr 22. 45s	06 05 00

Received of Mr Oley, November 12 1642. Fifty shillings and I promise with all Speed to make an end of all the plummers worke that is to be done about the new Built South Range in Clare hall for other three poundes and to do it very well and sufficiently before the feast of the nativity of Xt next comeng. I say so.

John Kendall   02 10 00

9a. and 9b. Before and after: St. John's Bridge

COLLEGIUM DE GONEVILL et CAIUS Cant

10. Gonville and Caius College, 1688 (engraving by D. Loggan)

Unfortunately building materials were seized for the fortification of the Castle and work was not really resumed until the Restoration. The new Hall was inaugurated by a banquet, 20 April 1693:

Accounts

May the 5 1693. to Ch: Bumstead for the use of pewter at the treat	01 18 06
May the 11. 93. pd. Henry Green his Cookes bill for all his pro- visions at the dinner	29 01 00
– 13. 93. paid Edw: Huckes bill for 3 choristers, tobacco, sugar, knives, linnen, glasses, pipes, etc.	02 03 00
June the 30. 1693. paid Edw: Huckes bill for Beer, bread and cheese upon account of this treat	07 18 08
Octob: 12. allow for Canary and white Port wine to Mr. Rob: Herne wch he paid to Mrs. Hinton	02 02 00
– 24 paid to Mr. Herne for so much of a hogshead of red Port as was then spent	10 11 03
Total	53 14 05

A concern for college amenities had continued through troubled times:

St. Catharine's

Accounts 1637–8

For 2 keyes to the bowling-green	00 02 00
For painting the seats in the Bowl:	01 03 00
Making the bowlinge greene	05 00 00
Mending the backe gate of the Bowl: and a key to the same for the Master	00 01 02
1640–1	
For boards to the seats in the bowlinge ally	00 01 00
1642–3	
Payd for making up the bowlinge greene	02 07 09
1638–9	—
For 3 hookes for the sweete briar in the court	00 00 09
1640–1	
To the Gardiner for rosemary sweetbriers and worke	00 06 00

Pembroke (under the mastership of Mr. Serjeant Moses, Master from 1658 to 1660)

After the displacing of Mr. Vines and death of Mr. Simson who succeeded, the Fellows unanimously chose him for their Master, wch yet came under a great contrast at Whitehall. For the then called Protector would needs have imposed upon them another. But the fellowes by representation of his worth and service-ableness to the College gayned their poynt, and got a revocation of his Order.

In the five years of his mastership he bestird himself for the advancement of his College, as if it had been his onely business and proper estate . . . That old and withered face of that ancient and pious foundation, he refreshed and made it look young agayn. The building over the Library, which was ready to tumble

11. Emmanuel College Chapel, 1688 (engraving by D. Loggan)

down, and the walles of the College which were so decayed, ruefull and ill-favoured that they would rather affright students from them than invite them thither, hee brought to this pleasant aspect that they have ever since had . . . And all this at a time when Universityes and Colleges were devoted to ruin in the desires of some, and apprehensions of most men.

The chapel. On 17 March 1659 Bishop Matthew Wren was released from the Tower after eighteen years:

The first Money he receiv'd after his Restitution, he bestow'd on Pembroke-Hall and to the Honour of Almighty God . . . for the Ornament of the University, which he always affected with a fervent and passionate Love; and in grateful remembrance of his first Education . . . he built that most elegant Chapel there, at the expence of above five Thousand Pounds. [The architect was his nephew, Christopher Wren, whose first building this was.]

Christopher Wren was also engaged by Emmanuel. The Master wrote to Dr. Sandcroft, then Dean of St. Paul's:

19 Feb 1667/8

Dr. Wren hath sent me a very civill ansure of the letter which you was pleased to send him from me, he sayth it is possible he may be in London by Midlent (which is now near) and that he may then make a start to come here, but desires I would not delay one day in expectation of him. Truely, sir, though I am in some readiness to begin, I will stay many days rather than want his advice upon the place. His presence will be a great reputation (besides other advantages) to the whole work. Give me leave to ask earnestly of you to use your power with him, which I know is great, to procure it. [The Chapel was opened in 1677.]

Wren gave his services free as architect of Trinity's Wren Library (1676–90). The concept was that of Isaac Barrow, then Master:

The tradition of this undertaking runs thus. They say that Dr. Barrow pressed the heads of the university to build a theatre; it being a profanation and scandal that the speeches should be had in the university church, and that also be deformed with scaffolds, and defiled with rude crowds and outcries. This matter was formally considered at a council of the heads; and arguments of difficulty and want of supplies went strong against it. Dr. Barrow assured them that if they made a sorry building, they might fail of contributions; but if they made it very magnificent and stately, and at least exceeding that at Oxford, all gentlemen of their interest would generously contribute; it being what they desired and little less than required of them; and money would not be wanted as the building went up and occasion called for it. But sage caution prevailed, and the matter, at that time, was wholly laid aside. Dr. Barrow was piqued at this pusillanimity, and declared that he would go straight to his college and lay out the foundations of a building to enlarge his back court and close it with a stately library, which should be more magnificent and costly than what he had proposed to them, and doubted not but upon the interest of his college in a short time to bring it to perfection. And he was as good as his word; for that very afternoon he, with his gardeners and servants, staked out the very foundation upon which the building now stands; and Dr North saw the finishing of it . . . and divers benefactions came in upon that account; wherewith, and the liberal supply from the college, the whole is rendered complete; and the admirable disposition and proportion on the inside is such as touches the very soul of any one who first sees it.

(North, Lives, ed. Jessopp)

Christopher Wren explains his design:

I have given the appearance of arches as the Order required fair and lofty: but I have layd the floor of the Library upon the impostes, which answar (*sic*) to the pillars in the cloister and the levells of the old floores, and have filled the Arches with relieves of stone, of which I have seen the effect abroad in good building, and I assure you where porches are lowe with flat ceilings is infinitely more gracefull then lowe arches would be and is much more open and pleasant, nor need the mason freare (*sic*) the performance because the Arch discharges the weight, and I shall direct him in a firme manner of executing the designe. By this contrivance the windowes of the Library rise high and give place for the deskes against the walls, and being high may be afforded to be large, and being wide may have stone mullions and the glasse pointed, which after all inventions is the only durable way in our Climate for a publique building, where care must be had that snowe drive not in.

(W. & C.)

Property and possessions still came to colleges from benefactors, some rather oddly:

Extract from Dr. Gostlin's will, 9 October 1626

Fiat voluntas Domini. In the name of God, Amen. I, John Gostlin, Doctor of Physick and Master or Keeper of Gonville and Caius College in Cambridge, being sick of body, but of sound perfect memory (praise be to God) desirous to settle my poor estate, and prepare myself for a better world, do make this my last will and testament . . . Item, I do give the rents and profits of the common Inn in Cambridge, called and known by the name of the Black Bull, for the first seven years after my death unto my executor . . . after those seven years expired for ever, I do give [it] unto the Master and Fellows of Catharine Hall and to their successors for the uses following.

(Philpott, St. Catharine's College)

It is said that the Society of Caius used annually to drink confusion to the memory of:

Dr. Gosling, who was such a goose as to leave the Bull to Catharine.

Two colleges did not have the Masters they originally chose:

Clare (1680)

A letter was sent to Barnabas Oley offering him the mastership, though he was 77 at the time. He later wrote to Dr. Blithe, the new Master:

[118]

I have been told by persons of Good note, that the College was so kinde as to offer me the mastership. I must desire their pardon for not returning thanks for it, and they can-not well deny it, Because I never knew it till very few days since; that they did so: I never Received, either letter, or message, to that effect. I must confess, when I came home from Woster, I heard there was a letter came, The Day, (or next day after) I sett out, from the College, which some said was to that intent: but from the Coll: joyntly, or any one single member of it, I heard nothing at all. But it is better in the Hand that Holds it.

(Wardale, Clare College Letters and Documents)

Pembroke (1693)

Extract from the diary of William Sampson:

1693.   Dec. 24   Geo Norton's wife Buryed being Sunday & the Sunday after George himself.

Dec. 28   Entertained Parishioners.

1694   Jan. 18   Mr. Anthony & Mr. Tyrwhit two of the Fells of Pemb Hall in Cambr. (upon the death of Dr. Coga) brought me Letters of my being Elected to the Mastership of the College. But I excused myself to them.

Feb.   We headed 2 Rows of Willows in Parson Hern, being the 1st fruites o' my Plantg.

Mar. 1   We plow'd a peece o' my Orchyard & sow'd Beans wch did very well.

(Attwater, Pembroke College)

Learning flourished in an unfolding world of ideas, stimulated by men of independent and original thought:

JEREMY: Sir, I have the seeds of rhetoric and oratory in my head. I have been at Cambridge.

TATTLE: Ay, 'tis well enough for a servant to be bred at a University; but the education is a little too pedantic for a gentleman.

(Congreve, Love for Love, 1695)

'Cedars or seraphims?' The Arabic professorship was founded by Thomas Adams, Alderman of London. He wrote to Abraham Wheelocke of Clare, the first professor:

1631

I have received your Letter, with the enclosed from the Vice-Chancellour and Heads of your famous University, myself an unfit object in such manner to be saluted by such reverend persons. I am right glad of their good acceptance of the Worke intended . . . I am right glad also of their good acceptance of your self . . . being the only person our friends here purposed and designed for the honor and burthen of that Oriental Chair. And now, with the leave and favour of those worthy Cedars, or Seraphims rather, of your learned Academy, I wish you much joy in the execution of that hopefull employment.

(Letters of Eminent Literary Men, ed. Ellis)

The Lucasian professorship of mathematics was founded in 1663:

The Professor must be of good fame, and honest conversation, well learned, and especially skilled in Mathematical science . . .
  He must be a Master of Arts at least . . .

(Henry Gunning, *Ceremonies Observed in the Senate House*, 1828)

Isaac Barrow, the first Lucasian professor, was a man of enthusiasm. In his Preface to Euclid (1655) he wrote:

God always acts Geometrically!

How great a geometrician art thou, O Lord! For while this Science has no Bound; while there is forever room for Discovery of New Theorems, even by Human Faculties, Thou art acquainted with them all at one View . . . without any wearisome Application of Demonstration . . .

and in his Oration (1654):

At what time, I ask you, since the foundation of the University, has a murderous curiosity wrought savageries of death and dismemberment against so many dogs, fishes, birds, in order to notify you of the stature and functions of the parts of animals? A most innocent cruelty! An easily excusable ferocity! What am I to say about the history of plants, a subject eagerly explored by your freshmen?

John Ray, the botanist and zoologist, was a scholar of St. Catharine's in 1644, transferred to Trinity in 1646 where he shared rooms and tutor with Isaac Barrow and subsequently became a fellow. John Worthington writes to Samuel Hartlib:

He [Ray] is a person of great worth; and yet humble, and far from conceitedness and self-admiring . . . I think there are not many who have attained to so great a knowledge in this part of natural philosophy; which he is still adding to. He hath a little garden by his chamber which is full of choice things as it can hold: that it were twenty times as big I could wish for his sake.

(*Diary and Correspondence*, ed. Crossley)

In Ray's 'Catalogus Plantarum circa Cantabrigiam nascentium' (1660) there is a Preface to the reader:

I became inspired with a passion for Botany, (following a convalescence spent in 'riding and walking contemplating the varied beauty of plants and the cunning craftsmanship of nature') and I conceived a burning desire to become proficient in that study . . . I searched throughout the University looking everywhere for someone to act as my teacher and guide . . . But, to my astonishment, among so many masters of learning and luminaries of letters I found not a single person who was deeply versed in Botany, and only one or *two* who had even a slight acquaintance with the subject.

Some of the English and local references from the book:

Allium sylvestre   Crow garlic
On Jesus Colledge wall, nigh the gate which opens out of the road into Garlick fair; also about a gravell pit near the foot way leading from Christ's Colledge to Cherry Hinton, and in many other places.
Atripox olida   Stinking Orrache or Notchweed
Under the wall that joynes Peter-house Tennis Court, and at the Tennis-court end and backside, and in several other places.
Blitum rubrum minus   the small wild red Blite – *variis in locis,* as in some other holts by the river: also in a ditch on the backside of S. Johns Colledge in a close on the north of the back-gate.
Cirsium Anglicum primum   the English soft or gentle Thistle, Melancholy Thistle, for the most part single headed. In the first close you pass through, as you go in the footway from Cambridge to Cherry-hinton, near a little ditch or gripe that crosseth the close from corner to corner.
Eupatorium aquaticum folio integro   Water-hempe, or Agrimony with an un-divided leafe. In the ditches cut out of the river behind Peter-house.
Sambucus aquatilus sive palustris   March or Water Elder
By the ditch of one of the closes on the back-side of Clare-hall. In many places in moist woods or by water courses.
Trifolium majus flore purpureo sive   Great purple Trefoil. Common Clover-grasse. Lately in an enclosed ground near the river Cam, not farre from Newn-ham by the footway to Grantcester.

Ray became Greek lecturer in 1651 and mathematics lecturer in 1653, but resigned his fellowship in 1662 rather than accept the precise wording of the new Anglican oaths, though he remained to his death in communion with the Established Church.

Newton was the unchallenged luminary of his time: voyaging through strange seas of thought alone:

> Nature, and Nature's Laws lay hid in night:
> God said, *Let Newton be!* and all was light.

> (Pope, *Epitaphs*)

A few years before he died Newton said:

I do not know what I may appear to the world; but to myself I seem to have been only like a boy playing on the sea-shore, and diverting myself in now and then finding a smoother pebble or a prettier shell than ordinary, whilst the great ocean of truth lay all undiscovered before me.

He was admitted sub-sizar in Trinity College in 1661. He was made scholar in 1664, took his Bachelor of Arts degree in 1665 but in 1666, because of the plague, retired to Woolsthorpe. In the next year he was made junior fellow and in 1668 Master of Arts and senior fellow. In 1669 Isaac Barrow resigned the Lucasian professorship in favour of Newton, who was then 27.

On 20 June 1686 Newton wrote to Dr. Halley about 'Principia':

The proof you sent me I like very well. I designed the whole to consist of three books; the second was finished last summer, being short, and only wants transcribing, and drawing the cuts fairly. Some new propositions I have since thought on, which I can as well let alone. The third wants the theory of comets. In autumn last I spent two months in calculation to no purpose for want of a good method, which made me afterwards return to the first book, and enlarge it with diverse propositions, some relating to comets, others to other things found out last winter. The third I now design to suppress. Philosophy is such an impertinently litigious Lady that a man had as good be engaged in law suits, as have to do with her. I found it so formerly, and now I can no sooner come near her again, but she gives me warning. The first two books, without the third, will not so well bear the title of Philosophiae Naturalis Principia Mathematica; and therefore I had altered it to this, De Motu Corporum Libri duo. But after second thoughts, I retain the former title. 'Twill help the sale of the book, which I ought not to diminish now 'tis yours. [He did however relent and send the third book.]

(Sir David Brewster, *Life of Newton*, 1855)

I have bethought myself about Sir Isaac's life as much as possibly I can. About 6 weeks at spring, and 6 at the fall, the fire in the elaboratory scarcely went out, which was well furnished with chymical materials as bodyes, receivers, heads, crucibles, &c., which was made very little use of, the crucibles excepted, in which he fused his metals; he would sometimes, tho' very seldom, look into an old mouldy book which lay in his elaboratory. I think it was titled *Agricola de Metallis*, the transmuting of metals being his chief design, for which purpose antimony was a great ingredient. Near his elaboratory was his garden, which was kept in order by a gardiner. I scarcely ever saw him doing anything as pruning, &c. at it himself. When he has sometimes taken a turn or two has made a sudden stand, turn'd himself about, run up the stairs like another Archimedes, with an 'Eureka', fall to write on his desk standing without giving himself the leisure to draw a chair to sit down on. At some seldom times when he designed to dine in the hall, would turn to the left hand and go out into the street, when making a stop when he found a mistake, would hasily turn back, and then sometimes instead of going into the hall, would return to his chamber again. When he read in the schools he usually staid about half an hour; when he had no auditors he commonly returned in a 4th part of that time or less ... He would with great acuteness answer a question, but would very seldom start one.

(Humphrey Newton, account in Brewster's *Life of Newton*)

Notes on Newton's college expenses at Trinity:

	£	s	d
Stilton		2	0
Cambridge White Lion		2	6
A chamber pot		2	2
A table to set down the number of my clothes in the wash		1	0
A paper book			8
For a quart bottle and ink to fill it		1	7

and after he graduated:

	£	s	d
Drills, grovers, a hone, a hammer and a mandril		5	0
A magnet		16	0
Compasses		3	6
Glass bubbles		4	0
At the tavern several times	1	0	0

Items in 1667 include:

	£	s	d
The Hist. of the Royal Society (presumably Sprat's which came out that year)		7	0
Spent on my cousin Ayscough		12	6
Lost at cards twice		15	0
Four ounces of putty		1	4
Philosophical Intelligence		9	6
Bacon's Miscellanies		1	6
For oranges for my sister		4	2
To three prisms	3	0	0
For aquafortis, sublimate, oyle pink, fine silver, antimony, vinegar, spirit of wine, white lead, salt of tartar	2	0	0
A furnace		8	0
Lent Warwell 3s & his wife 2s		5	0

(from J. G. Crowther, *Founders of British Science*, 1960)

The eighteenth century:
was reason sleeping?

Let lazy hermits dream in college cells,
Severely great, and indolently good.

(John Taylor)

A contemplation of the eighteenth century encourages generalisations, some not altogether accurate. The image of the dozing don or the befuddled fellow-commoner sleeping off boredom, hunting and college port, is only part of the picture. The liberating renaissance of learning of the previous century spilled over into its successor: people and ideas do not enclose themselves tidily in centuries. Beneath the surface of accepted opinions and practices, ferment both the decaying past and the bubbling future. All kinds of ways of life and modes of thinking co-existed in the University, causing occasional conflict and uproar but never resulting in more than the martyrdom of exile. Fellowships were at risk, not liberty or life. The University engaged itself in politics, both domestic and national; power was sought after, greed was assuaged and exacerbated. Many professors gave no lectures or were absentees; yet the pursuit of learning and the nurture of the young continued; college tutors and 'pupil-mongers' saw to them faithfully.

The Jacobites provided the last stirrings of old controversies; the biographer of Bentley claims that:

A vulgar error has represented this University as the headquarters of Whig politics. At the General Election in 1715, the Town representatives were re-elected ... It is however equally certain that only a small proportion of the High Church party at Cambridge were Jacobites ... the Non-jurors were not numerous ... But on the night of the Pretender's birthday, and again on that of King George, disturbances did take place through some young men, who had either imbibed Jacobite principles, or thoughtlessly availed themselves of these occasions for juvenile license; some windows were broken, and some cries were heard of 'No Hanover'. But the excesses, being few and trivial, were censured by the Vice Chancellor as ordinary breaches of discipline, without reference to their political tendency.

(J. H. Monk, Life of Richard Bentley, 1830)

A non-juror was one who refused to take an oath of allegiance to the (non-Stuart) monarch. There were forty-two in Cambridge, twenty-eight of whom were in St. John's. There were only fourteen in Oxford.

John Byrom writes to John Stansfield:

Trin. Coll.   May 3rd 1715

Our Vice-chancellor has forbid the coffee-houses taking in any other papers but the Daily Courant, Evening Post, Gazette, and Votes, so that our written letters, Postboy, Flying Post, Examiner, Spectator, &c. are all banished, and we must have news without politics. The abjuration oath hath not been put to us yet, nor do I know when it will be; nobody of our year scruples it, and indeed in the sense they say they shall take it, I could; one says he can do it and like the Pretender never the worse . . . You know my opinion, that I am not clearly convinced that it is lawful, nor that it is unlawful; sometimes I think one thing, and sometimes another.

(*The Private Journal and Literary Remains of John Byrom*, ed. Richard Parkinson, 1854–7)

Nonchalance.

Gray writes on 3 February 1746:

I heard these people, sensible and middle-aged men (when the Scotch were said to be in Stamford and actually were at Derby) talking of hiring a chaise to go to Caxton to see the Pretender and the highlanders as they passed.

(Christopher Wordsworth's *Social Life at the English Universities*, 1874)

Reigning monarchs were welcomed.

Queen Anne:

Feb: 1705. The Queen was at Cambridg, came from Newmarket, returned at night, the prince being there. The scholars were placed on one side of the way from Emmanuel Coll. to the Regent Walk. A speech made in the Regent house. She dined at Trinity . . . Provost of Kings made a speech to her in the Chappell, I was by, he presented her with a Bible. She knighted Sr Isaac Newton after Dinner at Trinity, & the Vice Chancellor Dr. Ellis of Caius.

(William Stukeley, *Family Memoirs*, ed. W. C. Lukis, 1882–7)

Orders to be observed by all students in the University at the approach and during the Continuance of Her Majesty here –
 – That as Her Majesty passeth by, they all kneel down, and say with loud and audible voices, Vivat Regina
 – That at the Congregation the Regents and Non-Regents be present in their Caps, Hoods and Habits as the Statute requires . . .
 – That both Regents and Non-Regents keep their places, that they stand not upon the Benches or Seats, or look over the Partition of the Houses, or gather together in Companies, but deport themselves with such Gravity as becomes so Great and Venerable a Senate . . .

(John Ellys, Vice-Chancellor, in Cooper)

King George I did not visit until 1717. He had previously however given the University Dr. John Moore's Library. This gift occasioned this exchange of verses:

> The King, observing with judicious eyes,
> The state of both his universities,
> To Oxford sent a troop of horse; and why?
> That learned body wanted loyalty;
> To Cambridge books he sent, as well discerning
> How much that loyal body wanted learning.
>
> (Dr. Joseph Trapp of Oxford)

> The King to Oxford sent a troop of horse,
> For Tories own no argument but force;
> With equal skill to Cambridge books he sent,
> For Whigs admit no force but argument.
>
> (Sir William Browne of Cambridge)

There was a muddle at his visit. All went well at first:

The procession then left the chapel for Trinity College, where his Majesty was to lodge, and where a banquet was prepared for the whole company. A distressing mistake now occurred. The Vice-Chancellor wishing that his own beautiful college should have its share of the royal admiration, chose to conduct the procession the back way to Trinity, in order that it might pass by Clare Hall. Thus his Majesty, after a passing glance at that House, was led to the Queen's-gate of Trinity: but no intimation having been given of Grigg's design, and his arrival being of course expected at the King's-gate, the Master and the whole college were drawn up there for his reception, while all the inhabitants of the town were assembled on the outside: meantime the other entrance had been closed to prevent the irruption of the populace into the quadrangle. Thus did the King find the entrance of his Royal college barred against him, and was compelled to stand five minutes in the lane, which is described to have been at that time 'a most dirty, filthy place', before the tidings of his arrival could reach the Great Gate, and the postern be thrown open for his reception. At length his Majesty obtained admission, and Dr. Bentley at the head of his society, meeting him about the middle of the court, bade him 'welcome to a college which he might call his own' . . .

(Monk, *Life of Bentley*)

The status quo in University government and discipline was not without its critics. William Whiston in his Memoirs recommended:

All old statutes to be repealed: yet so that their useful parts be taken into the new statutes; and the designs of the founders preserved as much as may be. The new statutes to be

> Few in number:
> Plain in words:
> Practicable in quality:
> Known by all.

The University would be very thin, if the next Statute was to be strictly put in Execution:... It enjoins, That Dice are never to be us'd, or Cards, unless in Christmas Time, and that only in the College-halls, on pain of Expulsion, after the second Admonition. There is to be no Fencing, or Dancing-School; or Cockfighting, Bear or Bull-baiting, in Cambridge... None under the Degree of Master of Arts, unless poor Scholars, who are sent of Errands by their Tutors, may go out of his College unto the Town, unless with a Companion (as a Witness of his Behaviour) of the same College, Order and Degree...

Anyone who has ever been at Cambridge, but for one Night, may be a Witness how this Statute is observ'd.

He was enlightened enough to want to expunge those Statutes imposing Holy Orders on fellows:

As nobody can say, That this Nation is over-stocked at present, or ever was, but rather deficient in Men who understand Fortification, Gunnery, Navigation, Draining, Architecture, Experimental Philosophy, or any other Parts of Learning, except Divinity.

(An Account of the University of Cambridge, 1717)

There was a continuing leaven of new ideas, sometimes nervously contemplated, as in a Matthew Prior poem, written when he was at St. John's:

> Man does with dangerous Curiosity
>   These unfathom'd Wonders try:
> With fancy'd Rules and Arbitrary Laws
>   Matter and Motion he restrains,
> And study'd Lines and fictious Circles draws;
> Then with imagin'd Soveraignty
> Lord of his new *Hypothesis* he reigns.
> He reigns: How long? 'till some Usurper rise,
> And he too, mighty Thoughtful, mighty Wise,
> Studies new Lines, and other Circles feigns.
> From this last Toil again what Knowledge flows?
>   Just as much, perhaps, as shows,
>   That all his Predecessors Rules
> Were empty Cant, all *Jargon* of the Schools;
> That he on t'other's Ruin rears his Throne;
> And shows his Friend's Mistake, and thence confirms his own.

(Poems on Several Occasions, 1709)

sometimes with enthusiasm: William Whiston in his Memoirs:

After I had taken holy orders (1693), I returned to the college, and went on with my own studies there, particularly the mathematicks, and the Cartesian philosophy; which was alone in vogue with us at that time. But it was not long before I, with immense pains, but no assistance, set myself, with the utmost zeal, to the study of Sir Isaac Newton's wonderful discoveries in his Philosophae Naturalis Principia Mathematica, one or two of which lectures I had heard him read in the publick schools, though I understood them not at all at that time.

But Whiston went too far for the establishment:

I have a piece of very ill news to send you, i.e. viz. that one *Whiston* our Mathematicall Professor, a very learned (and as we thought pious) man has written a Book concerning the Trinity and designs to print it, wherein he sides with the Arrians; he has showed it to severall of his friends, who tell him it is a damnable, heretical Book and that, if he prints it, he'll lose his Professorship, be suspended *ab officio et beneficio*, but all won't doe, he saies, he can't satisfy his Conscience, unless he informs the world better as he thinks that it is at present, concerning the Trinity.

(William Reneu to John Strype quoted in Christopher Wordsworth, Scholae Academicae, 1877)

I Charles Roderick, Vice-Chancellor of this University, do decree, declare and pronounce, that Mr. William Whiston, Mathematick Professor of this University, having asserted and spread abroad divers Tenets contrary to Religion, receiv'd and establish'd by Publick Authority in this Realm, hath incurred the Penalty of the Statute, and that he is Banished from this University, 1710.

(Cooper)

He was succeeded by Saunderson:

1711 Nov. 19   A mandate from the Queen to make Mr. Nicholas Saunderson (a blind man from his infancy, but who had taught Mathematicks in Christ's College about four years) Master of Arts . . .
        20.   He was chosen Mathematicks Professor in the room of Mr. Whiston.

(Edward Rud's Diary, ed. G. H. Luard, 1860)

The Cambridge scene was illuminated by outstanding and unusual men, not without their quirks and controversies, but marked by industry and genius.

Richard Watson of Trinity, first sizar, then scholar, then second wrangler and tutor, became Professor of Chemistry in 1764, Professor of Divinity in 1771, Bishop of Llandaff in 1782 and in 1787 Bishop of Carlisle. Something of a polymath, he saved the government money by a new method of manufacturing gunpowder. The King's comment on this was:

'Let not that affect your conscience, for the quicker the conflict, the less the slaughter.'

Watson himself wrote:

1757   . . . returned to College at the beginning of September, with a determined purpose to make my Alma Mater the mother of my fortunes. *That*, I well remember, was the expression I used to myself, as soon as I saw the turrets of King's College chapel, as I was jogging on a jaded nag between Huntingdon and Cambridge.

1764   ... I was unanimously elected by the Senate, assembled in full congregation, Professor of Chemistry ... At the time this honour was conferred on me,
I knew nothing of Chemistry, had never read a syllable on the subject; nor seen
a single experiment in it; but I was tired with mathematics and natural philosophy ... I buried myself as it were in my laboratory ... and in fourteen months
from my election, I read a course of chemical lectures to a very full audience.
... I now look back with a kind of terror at the application I used in the younger
part of my life. For months and years together I frequently read three public
lectures in Trinity College, beginning at eight o'clock in the morning; spent four
or five hours with private pupils, and five or six more in my laboratory, every
day, besides the incidental business of presiding in the Sophs schools ...

In October 1771, when I was preparing for another course of chemistry, and
printing a new chemical syllabus, Dr. Rutherforth, Regius Professor of Divinity,
died. This Professorship ... had long been the secret object of my ambition ...
On being raised to this distinguished office, I immediately applied myself with
great eagerness to the study of divinity.

When made Bishop of Llandaff, he wrote:

the puff of lawn was never any object of my ambition

but as Bishop of Carlisle he was as active as ever:

as an improver of land and a planter of trees.

(*Anecdotes from the Life of Richard Watson,
written by himself,* 1817)

*Richard Bentley, scholar and controversial figure was at St. John's before he
was appointed in 1699 to be Master of Trinity.*

Tradition says that, being congratulated upon a promotion so little to have been
expected by a member of St. John's, he replied, in the words of the Psalmist,
'By the help of my God, I have leaped over the wall'.

(Monk, *Life*)

He incurred Pope's malice:

—As many quit the streams that murm'ring fall
  To lull the sons of Marg'ret and Clare-hall,
  Where Bentley late tempestuous wont to sport
  In troubled waters, but now sleeps in Port.
  Before them march'd that awful Aristarch;
  Plow'd was his front with many a deep Remark:
  His Hat, which never vail'd to human pride,
  Walker with rev'rence took, and lay'd aside ...
  Thy mighty scholiast, whose unwearied pains
  Made Horace dull, and humbled Milton's strains.

(*Dunciad,* IV)

As for the hat, I must acknowledge, it was of formidable dimensions, yet I was accustomed to treat it with great familiarity, and if it had ever been further from the hand of its owner than the peg upon the back of his great arm-chair, I might have been despatched to fetch it ... but the hat never strayed from its place, and Pope found an office for Walker, that I can well believe he was never commissioned to in his life.

(Richard Cumberland, *Memoirs*, 1806)

As Master of Trinity he was unpopular and fell out with the fellows:

When Bentley first came to Trinity, the Seniors, who did not yet know with what manner of man they had to deal, gratified the new Master by signing him a blank cheque in the following terms:

'Ordered then by the Master and Seniors, that the Master's Lodge be repaird and finished with new Seeling, Wainscot, Flooring and other convenient improvements; towards which Expense the Master will contribute *de proprio* the Summ of one hundred pounds sterling.

The Seniors afterwards alleged that Bentley had obtained this order from them by promising that the whole work on the Lodge would not cost more than £300 – which he denied...he had soon spent £1600...But worse was yet to come. Bentley suddenly determined that there must be a new staircase of the spacious eighteenth-century type, to match the modern style of windows and panelling which he had introduced into the rooms. The little old Tudor staircase presumably stood in the entrance hall. Bentley pulled it down and built out a new brick shell on the west side of the entrance hall, to contain the present grand staircase which he proceeded to build. The Fellows refused to pay for it, and the Bursar came to bid the workmen desist. The Master appeared on the scene, angrily bade the workmen proceed and shouted at the Bursar, 'I will send you into the country to feed my turkeys' ...

Bentley's own defence of his improvements, not only in the Lodge ('Master's Apartment') but elsewhere in the College, was put forward to the Visitor in 1710 in the following flamboyant and provocative terms:

'It has been often told me by Persons of Sense and Candour, that when I left them I might say of the College, what *Augustus* said of *Rome, Lateritium inveni, marmoreum reliqui*. The *College-Chappel*, from a decay'd antiquated Model, made one of the noblest in *England*; the College-Hall, from a dirty, sooty, Place, restor'd to its original Beauty, and excel'd by none in Cleanliness and Magnificence. The Master's Apartment (if that may be nam'd without Envy) from a spacious Jail, from want of room in an excess of it, made worthy of that Royal Foundation, and of the Guests it's sometimes honour'd with: An elegant Chymical Laboratory, where Courses are annually taught by a Professor, made out of a ruinous Lumber-Hole, the thieving House of the Bursars of the old Set, who in spite of frequent Orders to prevent it, would still embezzle there the College-Timber: the College-Gatehouse rais'd up and improved to a stately Astronomical Observatory, well stor'd with the best Instruments in Europe. In a word, every Garret of the House well repair'd and inhabited, many of which were wast and empty before my coming.'

(G. M. Trevelyan, *Trinity College*, 1943)

Workmen were sent for from London; the whole house was wainscotted; a chimney was constructed according to a peculiar notion of his own, having a window behind it, that he might have light for reading while he sat by the fire.

(Monk, *Life*)

Van Uffenbach reflects the masculine view of women in Cambridge:

1710 3. *Aug. Sunday* we dined with Dr. Bentley, who sent the invitations the day before, and were very sumptuously entertained. As his wife dined with us, we did not converse upon serious matters.

(J. E. B. Mayor, *Cambridge Under Queen Anne*, 1911)

But Mrs. Bentley was a robust personality, the first of many such ladies to inhabit Trinity Lodge: she writes to her daughter:

1732 March 27th

I know not whether we shall go to London or not. I think 'tis better staying because neither Dr. B's health nor inclination incline him to visit and 'tis better staying at home here ... He and Dr. Walker went on Monday morning to Fullbourn to try how the Air would agree with him; we think he has eatt better since, and my head is much better, tho' not quite well.

May 11th

I hope we shall soon come to you. Dr. B has gott a book as well as fishing tackling to bring to you. I thank God he is wel as usueall and so am I; but I want to see my little Jug as well as my great one, and I am glad the boy is well.

(*Cambridge Antiquarian Society*, 1860)

Dr. John Taylor was appointed Librarian in 1732. He had been sent to St. John's by a Mr. Owen:

That gentleman was accustomed to converse with his barber concerning his family, and his future prospects for his children: to all which the old man used to answer cheerily, except as to his son, *Jack*, whom, he said, he could not get to take to the business or to handle either the razor or comb. Hence, Mr. Owen was determined to give young Taylor a learned education.

(John Nichols, *Literary History*, 1817–58)

He was a scholar; but a hospitable one. A friend remembers him:

If you called on him in college after dinner, you were sure to find him sitting at an old oval walnut-tree table, entirely covered with books, in which, as the common expression runs, he seems to be buried. You began to make apologies for disturbing a person so well employed; but he immediately told you to advance (taking care to disturb, as little as you could, the books on the floor) and called out, 'John, John, bring pipes and glasses', and then fell to procuring a small space for the bottle just to stand on ... he instantly appeared as cheerful, good-humoured, and dégagé, as if he had not been at all engaged or interrupted. Suppose now you had staid as long as you would ... you took your leave, and got half way down the stairs; but recollecting somewhat that you had more to say to him, you go in again; the bottles and glasses were gone, the books had expanded themselves so as to re-occupy the whole table, and he was just as much buried in them as when you first broke in on him.

(Ackermann, *History*)

Richard Porson was the son of a parish clerk and was sent to Eton by a local wealthy man. He then went to Trinity, became a fellow and in 1792 Regius Professor of Greek. When asked why he had written so little, he replied:

I doubt if I could produce any original work which would command the attention of posterity. I can be known only by my notes: and I am quite satisfied if, three hundred years hence, it shall be said that 'one Porson lived towards the close of the eighteenth century, who did a great deal for the text of Euripides'.

(Samuel Rogers, *Table Talk*, 1887)

Lord Byron remembers him:

Venice
20 February 1818

I remember to have seen Porson at Cambridge, in the hall of our college, and in private parties, but not frequently; and I never can recollect him except as drunk or brutal ... He was tolerated in this state amongst the young men for his talents, as the Turks think a Madman inspired, and bear with him. He used to recite, or rather vomit pages of all languages, and could hiccup Greek like a helot.

(To John Murray in *Letters and Journals*, ed. L. A. Marchand, 1973–82)

There are endless stories about him:

Porson was walking with a Trinitarian friend; they had been speaking of the Trinity. A buggy came by with three men in it: 'There,' says he, 'is an illustration of the Trinity.' 'No,' said his friend Porson, 'you must show me one man in *three* buggies, if you can.'

Porson called on a friend, who was reading Thucydides and wished to consult him on the meaning of a word. Porson, hearing the word, repeated the passage. His friend asked how he knew it was that passage. 'Because,' said Porson, 'the word occurs only twice in Thucydides, once on the right hand, and once on the left. I observed on which side you looked, and therefore knew the passage to which you referred.'

(E. H. Barker, *Literary Anecdotes and Contemporary Reminiscences*, 1852)

But few doubted his greatness:

But Mr. Porson, the republisher of Heyne's Virgil, is a giant in literature, a prodigy in intellect, a critic whose mighty atchievements leave imitation panting at a distance behind them, and whose stupendous Powers, strike down all the restless and aspiring suggestions of rivalry into silent admiration and passive awe.

(S. T. Coleridge, *The Notebooks*, ed. K. Coburn, 1957)

Nov. 1734 ... there is not a soul in our Colledge (a body I should say) who does not smoke or chew: there's nothing but Whiffing from Fellow to Sizar.

Jan 1735 ... tho' in Cambridge there is nothing so troublesome, as that one has nothing to trouble one. every thing is so tediously regular, so samish, that I expire for want of a little variety.

March 20 1738 ... I don't know how it is, I have a sort of reluctance to leave this place, unamiable as it may seem; 'tis true Cambridge is very ugly, she is very dirty, & very dull; but I'm like a cabbage, where I'm stuck, I love to grow.

Jan: 9. Cambridge. 1756

you who give yourself the trouble to think of my health, will not think me very troublesome if I beg you to bespeak me a Rope-Ladder (for my Neighbours every day make a great progress in drunkenness, wch gives me reason to look about me) it must be full 36 Foot long, or a little more, but as light & manageable as may be, easy to unroll, & not likely to entangle. I never saw one, but I suppose it must have strong hooks, or something equivalent, a-top, to throw over an iron bar to be fix'd withinside of my window. however you will chuse the properest form, & instruct me in the use of it.

(Letter to Wharton)

His fear of fire made him the victim of many practical jokes and he moved to Pembroke in 1756, continuing to enjoy the unfolding of the human comedy:

Pembroke Hall, August 12, 1760

I would wish to continue here (in a very different scene it must be confessed) till Michaelmas; but I fear I must come to town much sooner. Cambridge is a delight of a place, now there is nobody in it. I do believe you would like it, if you knew what it was without inhabitants. It is they, I assure you, that get it an ill name and spoil all. Our friend Dr. Chapman (one of its nuisances) is not expected here again in a hurry. He is gone to his grave with five fine mackerel (large and full of roe) in his belly. He eat them all at one dinner; but his fate was a turbot on Trinity Sunday, of which he left little for the company besides bones. He had not been hearty all the week; but after this sixth fish he never held up his head more, and a violent looseness carried him off. – They say he made a very good end.

There was an actual fire in Pembroke in 1768:

28 Jan: 1768: P: Coll:

I and mine are safe, & well, but the chambers opposite to me (Mr. Lyon's) wch were getting ready for Mason, are destroy'd. Mr. Brown was in more immediate danger than I; but he too is well, & has lost nothing. We owe it to Methodism, that any part (at least of that wing) was preserved: for two Saints, who had been till very late at their nocturnal devotions, & were just in bed, gave the first alarm to the college & the town. We had very speedy and excellent assistance of engines & men, and are quit for the fright, except for the damage above-mention'd. I assure you it is not amusing to be waked between 2 & 3 in the morning & to hear, Don't be frighten'd, Sr: but the college is all of a fire.

Jermyn-Street
(at Mr. Roberts's)

1 Aug. 1768

It is only to tell you that I profess modern history and languages in a little shop of mine at Cambridge, if you will recommend me any customers. on Sunday Brocket died of a fall from his horse, drunk, I believe, & (as some say) returning from Hinchinbroke. On Wednesday the D: of Grafton wrote me a very hand-some letter to say, that the King offer'd the vacant place to me.

(Letter to Mason)
(*Correspondence*, ed. P. Toynbee and
L. Whibley, 1935)

Christopher Smart was a sizar at Pembroke in 1739, became a fellow, and stayed until 1749. Among his poems is one on the Long Vacation:

At length arrives the dull Vacation,
And all around is Desolation;
At noon one meets unapron'd Cooks,
And leisure Gyps with downcast Looks.
The Barber's Coat from white is turning,
And blacken's by degrees to Mourning;
The Cobler's Hands so clean are grown,
He does not know them for his own;
The Sciences neglected snore,
And all our Bogs are cobweb'd o'er;
The Whores crawl home with Limbs infirm
To salivate against the Term;
Each Coffee-house, left in the Lurch,
Is *full* as *empty* – as a Church.

In 1747 Gray wrote to Wharton:

as to Sm:, he must necessarily be abîmé, in a very short Time. his Debts daily increase . . . he takes Hartshorn from Morning to Night lately; in the mean time he is amuseing himself with a Comedy of his own Writeing, wch he makes all the Boys of his Acquaintance act . . . he can't hear the Prologue without being ready to die with Laughter. he acts five Parts himself, & is only sorry, he can't do all the rest . . . all this, you see, must come to a Jayl, or Bedlam, & that without any help, almost without Pity.

(*Correspondence*, ed. Toynbee and Whibley)

The play was 'A Trip to Cambridge', only the Prologue of which remains. Gray was right about 'Jayl' and 'Bedlam': 'poor Kit' spent four years in Potter's madhouse and died in prison in 1771.

Despite the reputed torpor and languor of the period, poised between the 'despised learning of the schoolmen' and a 'vigorous and manly system of instruction', enthusiasm existed for the development of scientific knowledge and for mathematics. Of the ten professorships founded in the century, no less than seven of them were in this field.

William Stukeley, pensioner of Corpus Christi in November 1703, wrote in what he called his 'Commentaryes' in 1720:

All this while I turnd my mind particularly to the study of Physick, & in order thereto began to make a diligent & near inquisition into Anatomy & Botany, in consort with Hobart, a senior Lad of our College who was enterd into that study, & since dead. With him I went frequently a simpling, & began to steal dogs & dissect them & all sorts of animals that came in our way. We saw too, many Philosophical Experiments in Pneumatic Hydrostatic Engines & instruments performed at that time by Mr. Waller, after parson of Grantchester, where he dy'd last year beeing professor of chymistry, & the doctrine of Optics & Telescopes & Microscopes, & some Chymical Experiments, with Mr. Stephen Hales then Fellow of the College, now of the Royal Society. I contracted acquaintance with all the Lads (& them only) in the University that studyd Physic, & Swallow of Pembroke who took his Batchelor of Physics degree while I was there . . . and Dr. Addenbrook, now dead [In 1719 he left £4,000 to found a physical hospital] . . . With these I used to range about once or twice a week the circumjacent country, & search the Gravel & Chalk pits for fossils. Gogmagog Hills, the moors about Cherry Hinton, Grantchester, Trumpington, Madingley Woods, Hill of health, Chesterton, Barnwell, were the frequent scenes of our simpling toyl, armed with Candleboxes & Rays catalogus. We hunted after Butterflys, dissected frogs, usd to have sett meetings at our chambers, to confer about our studys, try Chymical experiments, cut up Dogs, Cats, & the like . . .

1705   I used to frequent, among the other Lads, the River in sheeps Green, & learnt to swim in Freshmens and Sophs pools as they are called, & sometimes in Paradice, reckoning it a Beneficial Exercise . . .

At that time [1706] my Tutor [Fawcett] gave me a Room in the College to dissect in, and practice Chymical Experiments, which had a very strange appearance with my furniture in it, the wall . . . hung round with Guts . . . I had Sand furnaces, Calots, Glasses, & all sorts of Chymical Implements . . . I sometimes surprizd the whole College with a sudden explosion. I cur'd a lad once of an ague with it by fright . . .

In my own Elaboratory I made large quantitys of sal volatile oleosum, Tinctura Metallorum, Elixir Proprietatis, & such matters as would serve to put into our drink. I used to distribute it with a plentiful hand to my Tutors Fawcet & Danny . . . & any of the Lads I kept Company withal. At this time Dr. Bentley made a New Chymical Laboratory at Trinity College, & Seign.r Vigani directed it, & was chosen Professor of Chymistry by the University & was the first. I usd to visit Dr. Ashenhurst of Trinity, who kept in the chambers that had been S.r Isaac Newtons. I took particular pleasure in being there where he composed his Immortal Principia.

(Stukeley, *Family Memoirs*)

The first Professor of Botany in the University was Richard Bradley. He hoped to establish a Botanic Garden, as is clear from the Preface of his 'Survey of the Ancient Husbandry and Gardening', published in 1725:

I think Britain might yet be brought to a much greater perfection in agriculture than it is at present, if our farmers had opportunities and judgment to try experiments, or had some fixed place, where they might see examples of all kinds of husbandry, as a School for their information . . . This I hope to compass, as soon as a Physic Garden is completed at Cambridge, where, besides collecting such plants as are used in physic, and choice vegetables from foreign countries, a little room may be spared for experiments tending to the improvement of land, which may be the means of increasing the estate of every man in England; for in such an undertaking every kind of soil must be used, and every situation imitated.

The Botanic Garden was eventually founded by Richard Walker, Bentley's Vice-Master, in 1762. In stating what the garden was for he referred to the fact that:

about fifteen years ago, the learned physician, Dr. Heberden, was so kind as to oblige the University with a course of experiments, upon such plants as he then found among us, in order to show their uses in medicine . . . But this Doctor's great abilities in his profession soon after called him from us, much lamenting the want of a Public Garden.

Dr. Heberden's course of thirty-one lectures:

began on 7 April and finished on 22 May 1747 . . . with a week off between the tenth and eleventh lecture for the Newmarket races.

(S. M. Walters, *The Shaping of Cambridge Botany*, 1981)

Dr. Walker, a great 'florist', when told of a brother florist's death by shooting himself in the Spring, exclaimed:

Good God! is it possible? Now, at the beginning of tulip time!

(Ackermann, *History*)

Anatomy: Alas, poor Sterne!

During Collignon's professorship a strange and gruesome incident occurred in the history of our school. Near the end of the Lent Term of lectures in 1768, the professor invited two friends to see an interesting dissection...The friends accompanied him to the room and during the dissection one of them uncovered the face of the dead man, and recognised it as that of Laurence Sterne, whom he had known in his lifetime. Poor Tristram Shandy had died of phthisis in an obscure lodging, and had been followed to his grave by two friends. His place of interment was St. George's Burial-Place at Tyburn, a favourite spot for the operation of the resurrectionists and it had probably been disinterred that night, brought to Cambridge, and sold to Collignon.

(A. Macalister, *History of the Study of Anatomy in Cambridge*, 1891)

The most far-reaching development at this time was the emergence of mathematics as a predominant subject to be studied. This was Newton's legacy to Cambridge and it was largely brought about by the activities of one man:

In 1709–10, when Mr. *Laughton of Clare hall,* a zealous Newtonian, was proctor, instead of appointing a moderator, he discharged the office himself; and by the most active exertions, stimulated still farther the progress of mathematical science. He had previously published a paper of questions on the *Newtonian* philosophy, apparently as theses for the disputations. He had been tutor in *Clare hall* from 1694 . . . the credit and popularity of his college had risen very high in consequence of his reputation.

> (William Whewell, quoted in Mayor,
> *Cambridge Under Queen Anne*)

Mathematics had just begun to gain ground in the university of Cambridge in the year 1707, when I was admitted a student there at the age of 15 . . . Sir *Isaac Newton's Mathematical Principles of Natural Philosophy* or *Knowledge,* a book originally but of ten or twelve shillings price, had risen so high above par, that I gave no less than two guineas for one, which was then esteemed a very cheap purchase . . .

and

For in my Soph's year, 1711, being a student at *Peterhouse* . . . and having performed all my exercises in the schools . . . on mathematical questions, at the particular request of Mr. proctor *Laughton* . . . I was then first informed, that subscribing these articles was a necessary step to taking my degree of B.A.

> (Sir William Browne, FRS, quoted in Mayor,
> *Cambridge Under Queen Anne*)

But mathematics was not found easy, then or later.

Ambrose Bonwicke writes to his father from St. John's in 1712:

I'm returned very luckily for lectures, for on *Saturday* our sub-tutor, Mr. *Newcome,* begun *Taquet's* Euclid to us . . . I'm very glad I brought the *De Chales,* 'twill help me, I hope, in mathematicks, which I find somewhat difficult.

> (Mayor, *Cambridge Under Queen Anne*)

Horace Walpole to Sir Horace Mann, 13 December 1759:

When I first went to Cambridge, I was to learn mathematics of the famous blind professor Sanderson. I had not frequented him a fortnight, before he said to me, Young man, it is cheating you to take your money: believe me, you can never learn these things; you have no capacity for them. – I can smile now, but I cried then, with mortification. The next step, in order to comfort myself, was not to believe him: I could not conceive that I had not talents for anything in the world. I took, at my own expense, a private instructor, who came to me once a day for a year. Nay, I took infinite pains, but had so little capacity, and so little attention . . . that after mastering any proposition, when the man came the next day, it was as new to me as if I had never heard of it.

(*Correspondence*, ed. W. S. Lewis, 1937–67)

Examinations for the ambitious were both an exacting and highly competitive end to years of study, and a quasi-theatrical performance.

John Jebb describes the system as it was in 1772:

Upon the first of the appointed days, at eight o'clock in the morning, the students enter the senate-house, preceded by a master of arts from each college, who . . . is called the 'father' of the college . . .

The examination is varied according to the abilities of the students. The moderator generally begins with proposing some questions from the six books of Euclid, plain (*sic*) trigonometry, and the first rules of algebra. If any person fails in an answer, the question goes to the next. From the elements of mathematics, a transition is made to the four branches of philosophy, viz. mechanics, hydrostatics, apparent astronomy, and optics.

If the moderator finds the set of questionists, under examination, capable of answering him, he proceeds to the eleventh and twelfth books of Euclid, conic sections, spherical trigonometry, the higher parts of Algebra, and sir Isaac Newton's Principia . . .

When the clock strikes nine, the questionists are dismissed to breakfast: they return at half-past nine, and stay till eleven; they go in again at half-past one, and stay till three; and, lastly, they return at half-past three, and stay till five . . .

The father of a college takes a student of a different college aside, and, sometimes for an hour and an half together, strictly examines him in every part of mathematics and philosophy, which he professes to have read.

After he hath, from this examination, formed an accurate idea of the student's abilities and acquired knowledge, he makes a report of his absolute or comparative merit to the moderators . . .

The moderators and fathers meet at breakfast, and at dinner. From the variety of reports, taken in connection with their own examination, the former are enabled, about the close of the second day, so far to settle the comparative merits of the candidates, as to agree upon the names of four-and-twenty, who to them appear most deserving of being distinguished by marks of academical approbation.

These four-and-twenty [wranglers and senior optimes] are recommended to the proctors for their private examination; and, if approved by them, and no reason appears against such placing of them from any subsequent inquiry, their names are set down in two divisions, according to that order, in which they deserve to stand; are afterwards printed; and read over upon a solemn day, in the presence of the vice-chancellor, and of the assembled university.

(Rouse Ball, *Cambridge Papers*)

William Gooch in 1791 scribbled in his journal:

Monday $\frac{1}{4}$ aft. 12.

We have been examin'd this Morning in pure Mathematics & I've hitherto kept just about even with Peacock which is much more than I expected. We are going at 1 o'clock to be examin'd till 3 in Philosophy.

From 1 till 7 I did more than Peacock; But who did most at Moderator's Rooms this Evening from 7 till 9, I don't know yet; – but I did above three times as much as the Senr Wrangler last year, yet I'm afraid not so much as Peacock.

Between One & three o'Clock I wrote up 9 sheets of Scribbling Paper so you may suppose I was pretty fully employ'd.

Tuesday night.

I've been shamefully us'd by Lax today ... he gave Peacock a long private Examination & then came to me (I hop'd) on the same subject, but 'twas only to *Bully* me as much as he could, – whatever I said (tho' right) he tried to convert into Nonsense by seeming to misunderstand me. However I don't entirely dispair of being first, tho' you see Lax seems determin'd that I shall not.

Wednesday evening.

Peacock & I are still in perfect Equilibrio & the Examiners themselves can give no guess yet who is likely to be first; – a New Examiner (Wood of St. John's, who is reckon'd the first Mathematician in the University, for Waring doesn't reside) was call'd solely to examine Peacock & me only. – but by this new Plan nothing is yet determin'd. – So Wood is to examine us again to-morrow morning.

Thursday evening.

Peacock is declar'd first & I second.

I'm perfectly *satisfied* that the Senior Wranglership is Peacock's due, but *certainly* not so very indisputably as Lax pleases to represent it – I understand that *he* asserts 'twas 5 to 4 in Peacock's favor.

(Wordsworth, *Scholae Academicae*)

Gooch was one of the first scientific travellers sent out from Cambridge. He went on a voyage of investigation to assign bounds to the English territories in South America, but was murdered by natives in May 1792 in the Sandwich Islands.

In 1786 Trinity instituted a written examination for fellowships, which was something of a milestone in educational progress, though these 1797 questions might appear eccentric:

Questions Historical

4. Why was the southern part of Italy called Magna Graecia? and whence in the middle, or more northern parts, did the Etruscans proceed?

7. How many were the families of the Caesars, and with whom did they begin and end?

8. By what Nation was the Roman Empire finally destroyed? and what were the principal causes which brought it to it's fall?

[139]

1. What is meant by the River and the Sea in the Sacred writings?

7. What places in the earth appear to have been contiguous to Continents, and are now divided by some great convulsions of nature?

8. What are the principal volcanoes on the surface of the globe?

Questions Grammatical

1. Is language most probably a gift of the Creator, or an effect of human institution?

2. Whence arises the diversity of languages, and in what manner was it most likely effected?

Other colleges introduced their own annual examinations. Some of the mathematical questions set by St. John's survive:

4. A shepherd had two flocks of sheep, the smaller of which consisted entirely of ewes, each of which brought him 2 lambs. Upon counting them he found that the number of lambs was equal to the difference between the two flocks, and that if all his sheep had been ewes and had brought him 3 lambs apiece, his stock would have been 432. Required the number in each flock.

5. A countryman, being employed by a poulterer to drive a flock of geese and turkeys to London, in order to distinguish his own from any he might meet on the road, pulled 3 feathers out of the tails of the turkeys and 1 out of those of the geese, and upon counting them found that the number of turkey feathers exceeded twice those of the geese by 15. Having bought 10 geese and sold 15 turkeys by the way, he was surprised to find as he drove them into the poulterer's yard, that the number of geese exceeded the number of turkeys in the proportion of 7:3. Required the number of each.

6. Two persons, *A* and *B*, comparing their daily wages, found that the square of *A*'s wages exceeded the square of *B*'s by 5; and that if to the square of the sum of the fourth powers of their wages, there was added 4 times the rectangle contained by the square of the product of their wages and the square of the difference of the squares of their wages, augmented by 12 times the 4th power of the product of their wages, the aggregate amount would be 1428£ 1*s*. Required the wages of each.

(Wordsworth, *Scholae Academicae*)

Some students were not obliged to take examinations or indeed to work, as is shown by the following passage from Cantabrigia Depicta in 1763:

In the beginning of January one of the Proctor's servants goes round to every college (King's College excepted) and requires of the Tutors a list of the Students, denominated Sophs, who intend to offer themselves candidates for the degree of Bachelor of Arts. The names thus collected are delivered to one of the Moderators, who transcribes them into a book, with appropriate marks given them by the several Tutors, such as Reading, Non-Reading and Hard-Reading Men etc. etc.

Others also escaped:

Degrees of Noblemen, and of those who proceed
to their Degrees 'tanquam Nobiles'

May 31, 1786. It was determined, by an Interpretation of the Vice-Chancellor and Heads of Colleges, that the following Persons are entitled to Honorary degrees: viz.

1. Privy Counsellors.
2. Bishops.
3. Noblemen { Dukes, Marquises, Earls, Viscounts, Barons.
4. Sons of Noblemen.
5. Persons related to the King's Majesty by Consanguinity or Affinity; provided they be also Honorable.
6. The eldest Sons of such Persons.
7. Baronets } are to be entitled to the degree of M.A. only.
8. Knights }

The Sons of Privy Counsellors or Bishops, as such, are not entitled to any Honorable degree by the Statute.

(Gunning, Ceremonies)

Undergraduate reaction to first 'coming up' varied:

I like the Colledge very well and I find my Commons with the addition of an half penny worth of Cheese or butter full enough for the most part. The Lads are very civil and kind to me, and now and then they ask me to come to their Chambers and I do the same to them again . . .

> (William Reneu to his former tutor, Strype, in 1705 quoted in Wordsworth, *Scholae Academicae*)

I find the college, where I am, infinitely the best in the university; for it is the smallest, and it is filled with lawyers, who have lived in the world, and know how to behave. Whatever may be said to the contrary, there is certainly very little debauchery in this university, especially among people of fashion, for a man must have the inclinations of a porter to endure it here.

> (Philip Stanhope, later Lord Chesterfield, from Trinity Hall in 1712 in *Letters*, ed. Bonamy Dobrée, 1932)

Cambridge,   Oct 31, 1734

now what to say about this Terra Incognita, I don't know; First, then it is a great old Town, shaped like a Spider, with a nasty lump in the middle of it, & half a dozen scrambling long legs: it has 14 Parishes, 12 Colledges, & 4 Halls . . . there are 5 ranks in the University, subordinate to the Vice-chancellour, who is chose annually: these are Masters, Fellows, Fellow-Commoners, Pensioners, &

Sizers; The Masters of Colledges are twelve grey-hair'd Gentlefolks, who are all mad with Pride; the Fellows are sleepy, drunken, dull, illiterate Things; the Fellow-Com: are imitatours of the Fellows, or else Beaux, or else nothing: the Pension: grave, formal Sots, who would be thought old; or else drink Ale, & sing Songs against the Excise. The Sizers are Graziers Eldest Sons, who come to get good Learning, that they may all be Archbishops of Canterbury: these 2 last Orders are qualified to take Scholarships; one of which, your humble servt has had given him

(Thomas Gray to Walpole, in *Correspondence*, ed. Toynbee and Whibley)

Some arrived painfully, as William Paley did (later Paley's 'Evidences' were to be a 'set book' for decades):

Soon after he had completed his fifteenth year, (in 1758) went to Cambridge, accompanied by his father, to be admitted a sizar of Christ College; to which society his father had belonged before him. He performed this journey on horse-back, and used often thus humourously to describe the disasters which befel him on the road: – 'I was never a good horseman, and, when I followed my father on a pony of my own, on my first journey to Cambridge, I fell off seven times. I was lighter than I am now, and my falls were not likely to be serious: – my father, on hearing a *thump*, would turn his head half aside, and say "Take care of thy money, lad".'

(*Facetiae Cantabrigiensis*, by 'Socius' (R. Gooch), 1836)

Some bolted:

Mr. Churchill was admitted of St. John's College in this university under a Tutor of great Eminence; a Day or two after his Admission he requested his Leave to go & meet some Friend at Ely; but this being refused, took the Liberty of making his Exit without Leave, & never returned again to College.

(*Cambridge Chronicle*, 15 Dec. 1764)

24 Oct: 1770 Pemb: Hall
our friend Foljambe has resided in college & persevered in the ways of godliness till about ten days ago, when he disappear'd, & no one knows, whether he is gone a hunting or a fornicating. the little Fitz-herbert is come a Pensioner to St. John's, & seems to have all his wits about him. your Elève Ld Richard Cav:sh having digested all the learning and all the beef this place could afford him in a two month's residence is about to leave us, & his little Brother George succeeds him.

(Thomas Gray to William Mason, in *Correspondence*, ed. Toynbee and Whibley)

Parents were anxious about their sons' welfare. John Stukeley to his son William at Corpus Christi College:

14 December 1705
Pray take Mr. Dodson's advice as to your wigg. As to the want of a watch, I am sure that cannot be considerable, for in regard you know the houres you are to go to prayers, the butteryes, & meale times, tis impossible for to be ignorant of the time of day, in such a town especially . . .

(*Family Memoirs*)

12. The hopes of the family: an admission at the University, 1774
(engraving by J. W. Bunbury)

The hazards of sharing rooms. Ambrose Bonwicke to his son at St. John's:

4 February 1711

I thank you and your tutor for the promise of a chamber for *Phil.* and think there may be some conveniences in admitting a third, but there may also be some inconveniences which I shall lay before you. By the grace of God this lad may continue very good, but should it be otherwise, you will not know how to get clear of him again. Besides, if he be not exactly of your principles, tho' he be otherwise very good, 'twill be very inconvenient; and you cannot at all times converse so freely with your brother, as 'twill be necessary you should. I had hopes that your brother might share with you in Mr. *Roper*'s favour, and fear this third chum may be an obstacle to that. Another thing is, if *Phil.* should have the small-pox, there will be no room for you to set up a bed for you for that time; and you know I do not care you should lye with any other but your brother. If this lad has never had that distemper, he may unhappily bring the infection into your chamber. Besides, I should not like him for a chum for you, if his dialect be ungenteel, for fear that infection should reach you, as well as your brother.

His son tries to allay these fears:

If my brother should have the small-pox, we must both remove, lest by staying with him, and then coming at meals, &c. into the company of others, we spread the infection: so that we shall not need to lie together at all, but go into different chambers, or some one together that happens to be empty. He has had the small-pox, and I think is genteel enough in his dialect, being neither a northern nor western lad, out of which two quarters bad dialects usually come.

(Mayor, *Cambridge Under Queen Anne*)

[143]

I make it my request that you will forbear drawing, totally, while you are at Cambridge: and not meddle with Greek...nor to meddle with Italian...

As to the carriage of your person, be particularly careful, as you are tall and thin, not to get a habit of stooping; nothing has so poor a look: above all things avoid contracting any peculiar gesticulations of the body, or movements of the muscles of the face. It is rare to see in any one a graceful laughter; it is generally better to smile than laugh out, especially to contract a habit of laughing at small or no jokes.

(*Letters to his Nephew*, 1804)

Some parents were difficult to approach. Lord Blandford, the Duke of Marlborough's son, was at King's. He wrote to Lord Sidney Godolphin on 3 August 1702:

My lord, I received your letter last night which was so obliging that I can't tell how to thank you enough for it. You desired to know how I liked the way of living here and the method of my learning which I think is both very agreeable. My Lord, if you would put my Mama in mind of sending the tea things and my ring I should be very much obliged to your Lordship. I live in hopes of seeing you here in October which is a great comfort to your Lorship's humble servant, J. Churchill.

(Iris Butler, *Rule of Three: Sarah, Duchess of Marlborough*, 1967)

and to his father on 2 January 1703:

I would have writ to my Mama now but that by what she said to me in her letter I am afraid she never will throughly forgive me, which has greived me so much that I cannot tell how to write till I have some hopes of being freinds with my dear Mama; and I hope my Dear Papa will be so kind as to intercede for me with Mama and to be perswaded that no body can be more heartily sorry for having done amiss than, Dear Papa, your most dutyfull son.

On 9 February he wrote to his mother:

I received a letter from Mr. Godolphin last post and the joy I had when I found I had some hopes of being freinds with my Dear Mama is not to be express'd; but I can't think my self so happy till my Dear Mama can find some time to lett me have a letter from her and I am sure there can be no greater pleasure than [that] would be to, my Dear Mama, your most dutyfull son.

(David Green, *Sarah, Duchess of Marlborough*, 1967)

He died at King's on 20 February, to his parents' lasting sorrow.

Another undergraduate had various anxieties:

I have been blooded in the Temple & in the Arm, been purged almost a dozen times & been blistered, and used all the remedies imaginable for this last qr of the year & have hardly diverted the Humour, so much, but that upon the least Cold it threatens me with a return. I have left off all the exercises as shooting, hunting, coursing, football etc. which can possibly endanger my catching cold; so that I hope I may have an opportunity of fixing to hard Study now; which I have left off so long . . . To draw the Rheum and humours from my eyes I am advised to smoak very much, which I dare not let my Father know, he's so averse to it I beleive he had as live see me dead or at least blind (and to be so is death to a Student) as with a pipe in my mouth. I have smoaked, so that I can receive no prejudice any other way but by his anger, but I'll take care to conceal it from him, if possible, whenever I take a pipe.

(Reneu to Strype, February 1709/10, in
Wordsworth, *Scholae Academicae*)

For many of the young life was agreeable enough:

Caius College   Aug: 17, 1767

I generally rise at five, and then read for an hour; at six I take a pretty long walk, but so as to be back at chapel at seven. After chapel is done, three times a week I go to the cold bath, and after that I come home to breakfast, which I take care to have over before nine. Then I sit down to read for three hours and a half, and at half an hour after twelve my hair-dresser comes to me, and I begin to dress for commons. You will be obliged to comply with the custom of putting on a clean shirt every day and of having your hair dressed. After commons, if ever, 'tis allowable to lounge away an hour at a friend's room and drink a glass of wine, but this is what I seldom do. At five I sometimes go to a Coffee-house, where you meet with all the new pamphlets, magazines, newspapers, &c., and drink a dish of tea, coffee or chocolate. At six I return to chapel, and after that I take a walk on the walks if it be fine weather, if not, in some college cloisters. At eight, your bedmaker comes to ask you what you please to have for supper, and gives you a bill of fare, which they call here a size bill. They have always very good things, but they are exorbitantly dear, as you may guess by 3*d* for a common tart. Persuade your father to let you have a good allowance.

Aug. 29, 1767

I have been somewhat more gay and idle than I should have been this last fortnight, in making parties to go on the water, and in riding out to Newmarket and the country round about Cambridge in little one-horse chaises they call Bougeès [?Buggy]. This is a very pleasant way of making a journey; and going upon the water with a set of no more than four friends for about three miles to drink tea is what I like exceedingly; but have been once caught in a violent shower of rain and ducked pretty frequently. If you are fond of going on the water you will have a fine opportunity of indulging your inclination, as Magdalen is close by the river side, and the men of Magdalen from being so much on the water are called Magdalen rats.

(Venn, *Early Collegiate Life*)

Henry Gunning loved shooting. He had come up to Christ's in 1784 and became Esquire Bedell in 1789. He wrote his Reminiscences in his old age.

1786.   The great source of idleness, which consumed more time than all my other employments put together, was my *passion* for shooting, for which diversion

Cambridge afforded the most extraordinary facilities. In going over the land now occupied by Downing-terrace, you generally got five or six shots at snipes. Crossing the Leys, you entered on Cow-fen; this abounded with snipes. Walking through the osier-bed on the Trumpington side of the brook, you frequently met with a partridge, and now and then a pheasant. From thence to the lower end of Pemberton's garden was one continued marsh, which afforded plenty of snipes, and in the month of March a hare or two. If you chose to keep on by the side of the river, you came to Harston-Ham, well known to sportsmen; and at no great distance from this you arrived at Foulmire Mere, which produced a great variety of wildfowl. The heavy coach changed horses at the Swan, and would set you down, between seven and eight o'clock, at the Blue Boar. If you started from the other corner of Parker's Piece, you came to Cherryhinton Fen; from thence to Teversham, Quy, Bottisham, and Swaffham Fens. In taking this beat, you met with great varieties of wildfowl, bitterns, plovers of every description, ruffs and reeves, and not unfrequently pheasants. If you did not go very near the mansions of the few country gentlemen who resided in the neighbourhood, you met with no interruption. You scarcely ever saw the gamekeeper, but met with a great number of young lads, who were on the look-out for sportsmen from the University, whose game they carried, and to whom they furnished long poles, to enable them to leap those very wide ditches which intersected the Fens in every direction.

(Gunning, *Reminiscences of Cambridge*, 1854)

Advertisement in the 'Cambridge Chronicle', 1 September 1787

We poor farmers who hire lands in the parish of Grantchester and fields of Coton, having some of our corn still standing, and some lying on the ground, do most humbly beg the favour of the Cambridge Gunners, Coursers and Poachers (whether Gentlemen, Barbers or Gips of Colleges) to let us get home our crops, even after the First of September, without riding or hunting their dogs over *our* property.

(Cooper)

There were coffee-houses:

From thence we went to the *Greek's Coffee house*, so called because the host is a born *Greek* . . . In this coffeehouse, particularly in the morning and after 3 o'clock in the afternoon, you meet the chief professors and doctors, who read the papers over a cup of coffee and a pipe of tobacco, and converse on all subjects; and thus you can make their acquaintance.

(Visit to Cambridge by Zacharias Conrad von Uffenbach, July and August 1710, quoted in Mayor, *Cambridge Under Queen Anne*)

High jinks, low life and wilder escapades were enjoyed:

But now to come to Cambridge: I must first tell you that I have not yet seen Miss Neville, but it will not be long first, for the sagacious ballock, her father, is at London, so if the daughter and the greyhound be not locked up, I will take this opportunity of a tête-à-tête, where I will endeavour, if possible, by talking very

[146]

much of you to her, to work her up to such a pitch as I could wish. The Tippins appeared last night at the fair, where Pat and I, after a damned quarrel we have had these two months, were reconciled. She's a fine girl, faith, and seems to have good dispositions. Oh! how I could! *sed me reprimo*, I consider the sin of fornication, and won't so much as indulge myself in the thought of it. Jack Cowper is more and more in love every day, passes three parts in four of his life with the nymph, and is gay or sad just as it pleases her Ladyship to frown or smile. Our old buggering Heads would not let us have a public commencement, to the great disappointment of all our young folks, whether male or female.

> (Lord Chesterfield from Trinity Hall to George Berkeley, 25 June 1713, o.s. in *Letters*, ed. Dobrée)

one evening, getting into Battie's room before Canonical hours [from close of morning chapel to 8 a.m. and from 8 p.m. to 9 p.m.], we locked him out and stuck up all the candles we could find in his box, lighted, round the room; and while I thrummed on the spinnet, the rest danced round me in their shirts. Upon Battie's coming and finding what we were at, he fell to storming and swearing, till the old Vice Provost – Dr. Willymott – called out from above, 'Who is that swearing like a common soldier?' 'It is I', quoth Battie. 'Visit me', quoth the Vice Provost, which indeed we were all obliged to do next morning, with a distich, according to custom ... he punished me with a few lines of Homer and Battie with the whole third book of Milton to get by heart.

> (Thomas Morell, from A. A. Leigh, *King's College*, 1899)

Emmanuel (1754)

strolling round the boundary, I perceived a key left in the gate at the lower end of the adjoining close, through which the gardener was wheeling dung. I took the opportunity, whilst he was at dinner, to take this key to a neighbouring smith, got an impression struck off in thin iron, brought it back, and replaced it unnoticed. From this impression I had a key made, and as our gates were locked at six in winter and nine in summer, and the name of everyone who entered after these hours was carried up by the porter to the Master of the College, with the time of his coming in, and he was reprimanded and punished according to his irregularity, everyone wished to become my friend, with a view of benefiting occasionally by this my ticket of admission.

> (Rev. Dr. J. Trusler, *Memoirs*, 1806)

Trinity (1780s)

There was a barber's shop just within the gate of Trinity, near Bishop's Hostel, where the Fellows were powdered and the wigs dressed. It existed even in my day. Sykes and some others bribed the barber one Saturday night, when he had the Sunday wigs to dress, to give them up; and getting out upon the library parapet, placed them on the heads of the four statues which face the hall. The next day the Seniors missing their best wigs were in a state of great excitement and obliged to go to dinner in their old ones. Coming out of hall into Nevile's

13. Academic dress, 1748 (*Universal Magazine*)

Court, and looking up, they saw them on the statues. The perpetrators were never found out.

(George Pryme, Recollections, 1870)

It was doubtless with some undergraduate practices in mind that in 1750 the Chancellor, the Duke of Newcastle, issued a Code of Orders for undergraduates which contained the following provisions:

3.4. No one to keep a servant or a horse, without the consent of parents or guardians and the head of his college.

5. No person to go to a coffee-house, tennis-court, cricket-ground &c. between 9 and 12 a.m.

7.8. Tavern-keepers and coffee-house keepers not to allow bills above 20*s.* Nor to serve wine, punch, or any other strong liquor after 11 p.m.

9.10. No one to ride or drive out of Cambridge without leave of his tutor or master of the College. Nor to be out of his College after 11 p.m.

11. Name and College to be given to superiors when asked.

12. Guns and sporting dogs forbidden.

The regulations provoked an immediate reply in the form of a squib entitled:

THE HAPPINESS OF GOOD ASSURANCE

A dog he unconcern'd maintains, (12)
And seeks with gun the sportive plains
Which ancient Cam divides;
Or to the hills on horseback strays (4 and 9)
(Unask'd his Tutor) or his chaise
To fam'd Newmarket guides.

For in his sight (whose brow severe
Each morn the coffee-houses fear, (5)
Each night the taverns dread; (7)
To whom the tatter'd Sophs bend low,
To whom the gilded tossils bow
And Graduates nod the head;) (11)

Ev'n in the Proctor's awful sight
On Regent-walk at twelve last night (10)
Unheedingly I came ... etc.

(Wordsworth, Social Life)

Life upstairs could be very enjoyable; it was satirised in 'The Idler' of December 1758:

SIR, – You have often solicited correspondence. I have sent you the *Journal* of a *Senior Fellow,* or *Genuine Idler,* just transmitted from *Cambridge* by a facetious correspondent, and warranted to have been transcribed from the common-place book of the journalist.

Monday, Nine o'Clock. – Turned off my bed-maker for waking me at night. Weather rainy. Consulted my weather-glass. No hope of a ride before dinner.

Ditto, Ten. – After breakfast transcribed half a sermon from Dr. *Hickman.*

[149]

N.B. – Never to transcribe any more from *Calamy*; Mrs. *Pilcocks*, at my curacy, having one volume of that author lying in her parlour-window.

Ditto, Eleven. – Went down into my cellar. *Mem.* – My *Mountain* will be fit to drink in a month's time. N.B. – To remove the five-year old port into the new bin on the left hand.

Ditto, Twelve. – Mended a pen. Looked at my weather-glass again. Quicksilver very low. Shaved. Barber's hand shakes.

Ditto, One. – Dined alone in my room on a soal. N.B. – The shrimp-sauce not so good as Mr. *H.* of *Peterhouse* and I used to eat in *London* last winter, at the *Mitre* in *Fleet Street*. Sat down to a pint of *Madeira*. Mr. H. surprised me over it. We finished two bottles of port together, and were very cheerful. *Mem.* – To dine with Mr. *H* at *Peterhouse* next Wednesday. One of the dishes a leg of pork and peas, by my desire.

It also had its rituals:

Trinity Hall (1 January 1739)
Order'd by the Master & Fellows that the Account of the Xtmas Exceedings at the Pensioners Table be kept separate fm that of the Fellows.

That every Pensioner upon the usual Exceeding Days be allow'd Twelve pence, & no more than a Bottle of red wine to each Mess. That whenever any Brawn is sent fm the Fellows Table, a Pint of sack be allow'd to each Mess upon that Day & no other.

(*Warren's Book*, ed. Dale)

its scandals:

9 March 1739 in the Vice-Chancellor's Court:

A 'sect of atheists' had been discovered: Tinkler Duckett, a Fellow of Caius, was accused of proselytising in his college; the evidence was obtained through a dropped letter found and read by the Esquire Bedell, a Mr. Burrough; other immorality was alleged.

He had been endeavouring to seduce a female, who was the object of his affections; and strove to remove her conscientious and religious scruples, by persuading her that matrimony was but an institution of human authority, that it was an affront to God to imagine that he would first implant passions in his creatures and then forbid the gratification of them; adding . . . that her compliance, instead of a sin, would be the highest act of benevolence; at the same time, he endeavoured to remove her fears of discovery by assuring her that he possessed drops which were a sovereign preventive against pregnancy . . .

Dr. Bentley's liability to catch cold did not suffer him to leave his house; accordingly . . . the court was adjourned to Trinity Lodge . . . Tradition in the University still records a jest then uttered by Bentley: he enquired of those about him, 'which was the atheist?' and on Duckett being pointed out, who was a small and spare personage, he exclaimed, 'What, is that the atheist? I expected to have seen a man as big as Burrough the beadle.'

The Senate voted to expel him. 'He was a vicious as well as a vain man.'

(Monk, *Life of Bentley*)

its firmness of purpose:

The will of Sir Nathaniel Lloyd, Master of Trinity Hall, 1740

To be carried from the place where I shall Dye by break of day, within 4 days to the Undertakers at London – after 2 or 3 days, to be carried thence by break of day to Cambridge – an Hearse wth 6 – Coach with 4 – with C. Jones and one more to be brought into Cambridge by night – No Escutcheons or other Fooleries on the Hearse and Horses.

To be directly carried to Trin-Hall and layd in the Outward Chapel that night.

In a morning before Colledge Prayers to be layd in the Vault I made.

The Minister Scholar of the Week and the Butler only attending 3–4 more to help.

(Warren's Book, ed. Dale)

and its eccentrics to be gossiped about:

1780s. When the Term ended, the University was far from being deserted. No college was entirely without resident members during the long vacation. At King's and Trinity, a certain number of the Scholars were obliged to reside during the summer; and many Fellows of colleges never slept out of the University for a great number of years altogether. The last of this class was Mr. Burrell, the Bursar of Catharine Hall, who used to take his daily walk in what is called 'The Grove', and who never travelled further than the Senate House, except once, during the long vacation, when the Master of the College prevailed upon him to walk half-way to Grantchester.

(Gunning, Reminiscences)

but was emphatically celibate:

11 February 1766

At Cambridge they seem to be going mad. Last week a grace was actually prepared in the Senate House in order to petition the Parliament for leave that the Fellows of colleges might marry: you may easily conceive that it was promoted by the junior part of the University. How it will proceed I know not, but they are in earnest. I hope the several overseers of the poor of the different parishes in Cambridge will prepare a petition also at the same time, requesting that a way may be found out that the wives, children and servants (if they can keep any) may not become burdensome to their respective parishes to which they may belong. For surely this scheme must not only end in misery and beggary to the Fellows themselves, but greatly to the discredit of the University, where, upon this plan, each college will become a sort of hospital.

(Rev. William Cole to Walpole, in
Walpole's Correspondence, ed. Lewis)

Colleges sometimes had problems choosing their heads:

King's (1742/3)

The Election of a *Provost of King's* is over. – *Dr. George* is the man.

The Fellows went into Chapel on Monday before noon in the morning as the

Statute directs. After prayers, and sacrament they begin to vote – 22 for *George*; 16 for *Thackeray*; 10 for *Chapman*.

Thus they continued, scrutinizing, and walking about, eating, and sleeping; some of them smoaking. Still the same numbers for each candidate; till yesterday about noon (for they held that in the 48 hours allowed for the Election no adjournment could be made); when the Tories, *Chapman*'s friends, refusing absolutely to concur with either of the two other parties; *Thackeray*'s votes wen1 over to *George* by agreement, and he was declared.

A friend of mine, a curious man, tells me, he took a survey of his brothers at the hour of two in the morning; and that never was a more curious, or a more diverting spectacle.

Some wrapped in blankets, erect in their stalls like mummies; others, asleep on cushions, like so many Gothic tombs. Here a red cap over a wig; there a face lost in the cape of a rug. One blowing a chafing-dish with a surplice sleeve; another warming a little negus, or sipping *Coke upon Littleton*, i.e. tent and brandy. – Thus did they combat the cold of that frosty night; which has not killed any one of them, to my infinite surprize.

(Nichols, *Literary History*)

To be a head of house was to be envied.

Peterhouse (1749)

Sir Benjamin Keene, KB (Envoy Extraordinary and Minister Plenipotentiary to Philip V of Spain) writes:

2 June 1749   Antigola

I will not forget your compliments to my brother, who is the happiest man in Europe. The Mastership of Jesus College was promised him upon the death of the present possessor who is very old, but in the mean while the Master of Peterhouse dyes. He was Fellow of this College (Peterhouse) and was immediately proposed to the Bishop of Ely by the Society, for their Head. That old gentleman was glad of this opportunity to change, according to his own terms to me, an uncertain small reversion into a sure and valuable possession. He is now in London getting a small living to be joyned to the Mastership by Act of Parliament. And he tells me he was just come from the Speaker, who has put his oldest son under his care at Cambridge.

To his brother:

Jany. 20 1750   Madrid

My house is as big as your Colleges. I believe my cook is a better one than yours.

(*Private Correspondence*, ed. R. Lodge, 1933)

Ceremony and ritual lent colour to life:

The Duke of Newcastle's installation (1749)

When the persons who went first, arrived at the foot of the steps leading into the Hall of Trinity College, they stopt, and opening to the right and left, made

[152]

a lane for his Grace the Chancellor, the Vice-Chancellor, the Nobility, Bishops, Doctors of the several Faculties, and the rest to enter according to their respective ranks ... In the Hall a splendid and elegant entertainment was provided for a most numerous and polite Company. Not less than 800 gentlemen dined in the Hall and the Master's Lodge. Great plenty of Champaign, Burgundy and Claret flow'd, in which loyal healths were drunk, and prosperity to literature in all its branches.

(Gentleman's Magazine)

The Duke to his wife:

I have this moment received my dearest's most kind letter. I am just come from King's Col. Chappell. Nothing ever went so well, & so magnificently, as our ceremony yesterday. Near two thousand people, & all the Joy and Satisfaction, that could be seen in all faces. The University appeared in the highest splendour. The Nobility, & persons of Quality were very numerous.

(R. A. Kelch, Newcastle, 1974)

The Duke of Grafton's installation (1769)

Pemb: Coll: 24 June. 1769

Odicle [The Installation Ode] has been rehearsed again & again, & the boys have got scraps by heart: I expect to see it torn piece-meal in the North-Briton, before it is born. the musick is as good as the words: the former might be taken for mine, & the latter for Dr. Randal's ... Dr. Marriott is to have Ld Sandwich & the Attorney-General at his Lodge, not to mention foreign Ministers, who are to lie with Dr. Hallifax, or in the stables. Ld North is at King's, Ld Weymouth at Mrs. Arbuthnot's, they talk of the D: of Bedford, who (I suppose), has a bed in King's-Chappel. the Archbishop is to be at Christ's, Bps of London at Clare-Hall, of Lincoln at Dr. Gordon's, of Chester at Peter-House, of Norwich at Jesus, of St. David's at Caius, of Bangor, at the Dog & Porridge-pot, Marq: of Granby at Woodyer's. The Yorkes & Townshends will not come. Soulsby the Taylor lets his room for 11 guineas the 3 days, Woodyer aforesaid for 15, Brotherton asks 20. I have a bed over the way offer'd me at 3 half-crowns a night, but it may be gone, before you come. I believe, all that are unlett will be cheap, as the time approaches. I wish it were once over.

(Thomas Gray to Norton Nicholls, in
Correspondence, ed. Toynbee and Whibley)

I should not at all like to be catched in the glories of an installation, and find myself a doctor, before I knew where I was. It will be much more agreeable to find the whole caput asleep, digesting turtle, dreaming of bishoprics, and humming old catches of Anacreon and scraps of Corelli.

(Walpole to Cole, 26 June 1769, in Letters,
ed. C. B. Lucas, 1904)

Von Uffenbach admires the organ-playing, interrupted though that was:

1710. 9. *Aug.* On Sunday afternoon we went again to *Trinity college* for the sermon, and also heard fine music, especially on the organ. The *English* excel specially herein, whereas on all other instruments they are mean performers; though they also make much ado of their chimes, and aim at an artistic and agreeable style of ringing; but we could not fancy the clatter, rather were much annoyed, to hear it so often: for the *scholars* or young students mount the towers and ring when they please, often for hours together. Accidents often happen in bell-ringing, some students being struck, or falling down and breaking leg and arm.

(Mayor, Cambridge Under Queen Anne)

There was much music to be heard:

Many of your schoolfellows are here; among the rest Hamilton, who is of Benet College; he is now gone to Hinchinbrook, where Lord Sandwich is entertaining the county and University with Musick for a whole week . . . I have been pressed to go to these Oratorios, but have my hands, as usual, so full of work, that Orpheus himself could hardly tempt me to leave college.

(Letter to Viscount Althorp, in Letters of
Sir William Jones, ed. Garland Cannon,
1970)

and a country clergyman visiting in 1793 writes:

I enjoyed my friend's tête-á-tête and music of the best kind almost every evening, public concerts and private quartett parties.

(Thomas Twining, Recreations and Studies
of a Country Clergyman, 1882)

Early in the century travel could be hazardous:

July 5 1712 . . . to Cambridge, after a prosperous journey. Escaped a great danger in the town itself, one of the wheels of the coach being just off, and the man driving at full career, as is too usual with them.

(Ralph Thoresby's Diary, 1830)

By 1763 there was a choice of transport:

Post to London,
Sets out on Mondays, Wednesdays and Fridays, at Five o'clock in the Evening through Royston
Sets out on Tuesdays, Thursdays, and Sundays, at Six o'clock in the Evening thro' Walden
The Fly for Four Passengers at 12s. each
Which goes to London every Day by Chesterford, Hockerill, and Epping, sets out at seven o'clock from the Rose in the Market-Place
Stage-Coach for Six Persons at 10s. each
Sets out from the Red-Lion in the Petty Cury at Seven in the Morning on Mondays, Wednesdays and Fridays
Lynn Passage-Boats
Go down from hence every Tuesday Morning and return on Sunday *and*:
A Man from Linton comes every Saturday to the Brazen-George in St. Andrew's Parish with a cart.

(Cooper)

Feb 4, 1735

I am forming the image to myself of your journey hither; I suppose you will come down Essex way, & if you do, first you must cross Epping forest, & there you must be rob'd: then you go a long way, & at last you come to Gog-magog hills, and then you must be overturn'd: I hope, you have not hurt yourself; but you must come at last to Foulmoor fields, & then you must fall Squash into a bog, pray, don't be frighted, for in about an hour and a half you may chance to get out; now perhaps if it is not dark, you may see the top of King's Chappel; tho' if it should be night, it is very likely, you won't be able to see at all: however at last you get into Cambridge, all bemudded & tired, with three wheels and a half to the coach, four horses lame, and two blind: the first thing, that appears, is a row of Alms-houses, & presently on the right-hand you'll see a thing like two Presbyterian Meeting-houses with the backside of a little Church between them, & here you must find out by Sympathy, that this is Peter-house, & that I am but a little way off, I shall soon feel how near you are; then you should say – no, no, I should say – but I believe I shall be too overjoy'd to say anything, well; be that, as it will, I hope, you will be almost as much so; dear Sr, you are welcome to Cambridge;

(*Correspondence*, ed. Toynbee and Whibley)

Von Uffenbach was highly critical of the state of many college libraries:

7. *Aug.* We were in *Peterhouse*, which, though the oldest college, is yet new and well built. The library is a poor room of moderate size. The manuscripts stand partly over the door, and at the very top of the cases, and were so buried in dust, that the librarian was forced to send for a towel, for me to wear as a pinafore, that I might not dirty myself too much.

(Mayor, *Cambridge Under Queen Anne*)

Many visited King's Chapel.

Ralph Thoresby in 1712:

I forgot to note that I was at the most stately fabric in the University, viz. King's College Chapel, where I got little benefit by the prayers, because of the music and noble architecture, which too much diverted my thoughts.

(*Diary*)

Parson Woodforde in 1776:

May 22 . . . Bill & myself went after breakfast and saw King's Chapel, the finest I ever saw, all fine carved Stone, the Roof of the same – most capital piece of Architecture indeed, gave a man that showed it to us 0.1.0. The gentlemen Commoners were [wear] black Gowns and gold trimmings made slight upon the sleeves of the same and very small gold Tossills to their square Caps of cloth. The members of Trinity Coll: undergraduates all wear Purple Gowns – gentlemen Commoners were purple Gowns trimmed with silver instead of gold and silver tossills. The Buildings are grand at Cambridge but few of them.

(*Diary of a Country Parson*, ed.
J. Beresford, 1924–31)

14. King's College Chapel and Clare Hall from Erasmus's Walk, 1762
(engraving by P. J. Lambourn)

Haydn in 1791:

Saw the universities there, which are very conveniently situated, one after another, in a row, but each one separate from the other; each university has back of it a very roomy and beautiful garden, besides beautiful stone bridges, in order to be able to cross the circumjacent stream – the King's Chapel is famous because of its stuccoed ceiling. It is all made of stone, but so delicate that nothing more beautiful could have been made of wood. It is already 400 years old, and everyone thinks that it is not more than 10 years old, because of the firmness and peculiar whiteness of the stone. The students there bear themselves like those at Oxford, but it is said that they have better teachers. There are in all 800 students.

(H. C. Robbins, *Notebooks of Haydn*, 1959)

Two visitors in 1719 were critical.

Hon. John Byng, later Viscount Torrington:

July 6th. It was with difficulty a bed cou'd be procured: had I known of this commencement I had gone 20 miles another way. The rain continued thro' the night with unabating violence, to the mischief of the corn, and to the destruction of the young partridges. The town is newly paved (*after a fashion*) which unluckily gives the walker an opportunity of viewing the houses.

My walk was much lengthen'd, by my meandring thro' several of the shady walks at the back of the greater colleges; which, with Kings College Chapel (into which, from the clerks absence I could not enter) constitute the only beauties of Cambridge.

I saw all the gownsmen handing ladies; and much crop-ear'd country company, hustling to The Senate-House . . . I know *nothingsh of commencements*!

(*Torrington Diaries*, ed. C. B. Andrews and Fanny Andrews, 1954)

Robert Hall:

In one of my early interviews with him, before I had been a month at that place, he said to me 'What do you think of Cambridge, Sir?' 'It is a very interesting place.' 'Yes, the place where Bacon and Barrow, and Newton studied and where Jeremy Taylor was born, cannot but be *interesting*. But that is not what I mean; what do you say to the scenery, Sir?' 'Some of the public buildings are very striking and the college walks very pleasing; but –' and I hesitated; he immediately added – 'but there is nothing else to be said. What do you think of the surrounding country, Sir? Does it not strike you as very insipid?' 'No, not precisely so.' 'Aye, aye: I had forgotten; you come from a flat country; yet you must love hills, there are no hills . . .

"'Tis a dismally flat country, Sir; dismally flat. Ely is twelve miles distant, but the road from Cambridge thither scarcely deviates twelve inches from the same level; and *that's* not very interesting. Before I came to Cambridge, I had read in the prize poems, and in some other works of fancy, of "the banks of the Cam", of "the sweetly flowing stream", and so on; but when I arrived here, I was sadly disappointed. When I first saw the river as I passed over King's College

[157]

Bridge, I could not help exclaiming, Why, the stream is standing still to see people drown themselves! and that I am sorry to say is a permanent feeling with me.' I questioned the correctness of this impression, but he immediately rejoined, 'Shocking place for the spirits, Sir; I wish you may not find it so; it must be the very focus of suicides. Were you ever at Bristol, Sir? there is scenery.'

(Olinthus Gregory, *Works and Memoir of Robert Hall*, 1832)

The happiest visitors were perhaps those who came back to their Alma Mater.

Horace Walpole, 1763:

I made myself amends with the university, which I have not seen these four-and-twenty years, and which revived many youthful scenes, which, merely from there being youthful, are forty times pleasanter than my other ideas. You know I always long to live at Oxford: I felt that I could like to live even at Cambridge again. The colleges are much cleaned and improved since my days, and the trees and groves more vulnerable; but the town is tumbling about their ears.

1777
I doat on Cambridge, and would like to be often there. The beauty of King's College Chapel, now it is restored, penetrated me with a visionary longing to be a monk in it.

(*Letters*, ed. Lucas)

The Rev. T. Twining, 1793:

In the morning I walked about viewing improvements, lounging in bookshops and music-shops, and with singular delight brushed up reminiscences of old walks and places and things.

(*Recreations*)

There were pleasures for residents too.

St. John's
Out of this third court you pass by an elegant stone bridge of three arches into the public, and through these into the private, walks of the society; which have long been . . . the favourite parade of the town, and the admiration of strangers. In those which are open to every visitor till the evening, the eye of taste is gratified, as it traces one of the finest windings of the Cam, with an assemblage of every image that can administer rural delight, from wood, water and a group of venerable turrets . . . The stately elms which flank the squares of two small meadows, are allowed to be the largest and tallest in the kingdom . . . In the private walks . . . is a neat summerhouse, looking into the fields; and a spacious bowling-green. From a proper spirit of liberality, many families of the university and town have keys and access to these as well as other walks.

(Richard Harraden, *Cantabrigia Depicta*, 1778)

Some of the improvements in Cambridge in the century were due to various benefactions:

I believe you have not heard of a noble Charity left us by Mr. Wm Worts deceased, formerly Master of Arts of Caius College ... This gentleman left £3,000 in the Bank thus to be disposed of ... £1,500 is to be laid out to build Galleries for the Bachelours of Arts and undergraduates in St. Maries Church ... £1,500 is to be spent in making a Causeway from Emmanuell College to Hog Magog ... Now I think no Charity of the value could have been better disposed of. For as to the Building of Galleries in St. Maries, it you know was as much wanted as any thing could be; for besides the undecency of seeing so many Gentlemens sons *standing* in the Isles; the want of seats brought in the ill custom of talking & walking about ... Then ye know the causeway to the Hills is very necessary, for by means of Coaches & Carts and the Chalkiness of the Road in winter time 'tis hardly possible to get into them; and they are the Pleasantest places as well as wholesomest that we have about us.

> (Reneu to Strype, quoted in Wordsworth,
> *Scholae Academicae*)

Gifts came in all sizes.

Lord Stanhope's bowl and cover – given in 1714 when he left Trinity Hall.
(It was the custom for fellow-commoners to bestow a piece of plate on leaving.)

Quarterly Ermin & Ruby. The Crest, on a Wreath Pearl & Ruby, a Castle Pearl, in the top of it a Demi-Lyon rampant Topaz, Crown'd Ruby, holding between his Paws a Fireball inflam'd proper. Supporters, on the Dexter side a Wolf Topaz crown'd with a Ducal coronet Ruby; on the Sinister a Talbot Ermin. Motto 'Exitus Acta Probat'. This Lord Stanhope is now Earl of Chesterfield, (A.D. 1729). He was lately Ambassador in Holland.

Clause in Mr. Samuel Bagnall's will dated 5 May 1733:

I do also give & bequeath unto the College or Hall called Trinity Hall in the University of Cambridge ... the sume of ten pounds of like lawfull money, which £10 my will is, shall be laid out in the purchasing of silver spoons for the use of the scholars of Trinity Hall aforesaid.

> (*Warren's Book*, ed. Dale)

Some bequests were quite specific:

Mr. Seaton's prize poem:

Mr. SEATON gives his Kingslingbury estate to the University of Cambridge for ever; the rents of which shall be disposed of yearly by the Vice-Chancellor for the time being; as he the Vice-Chancellor, the Master of Clare Hall, and the Greek Professor for the time being, or two of them, shall agree: which three Persons aforesaid shall give out a subject; which subject shall, for the first year be one or other of the perfections or attributes of the Supreme Being; and so the succeeding years, till that subject is exhausted. And afterwards the subject shall be either Death, Judgment, Heaven, Hell, Purity of Heart, &c. or whatsoever else may be judged by the Vice-Chancellor, Master of Clare Hall, and Greek

15. The river: colleges and commerce, 1790

Professor, to be most conducive to the honour of the Supreme Being, and recommendation of virtue.

(Gunning, *Ceremonies*)

The University and colleges continued to build.

The design for a Senate House and attached buildings to be built in the form of a quadrangle was drawn up by James Gibbs, and the foundation stone of the Senate House was laid in 1722. The scheme caused great controversy. Its greatest critic was the Master of Caius, who wrote to the Vice-Chancellor in May 1727:

Reverend Sir,

I am inform'd that at a late Meeting of the Syndics a Resolution was taken for digging Trenches etc to carry on (what is call'd) the attaching Scheme. 'Twill be good News to Me, should I find at my return, that You have Mony enough, or a Prospect of Mony enough, to finish the new Senate-house, to fit up the old one for a Royal Library, and to buy in the Benet-College Lease on the South-side of the Regent Walk ... Were these Things first done, Gentlemen might upon longer Deliberation change their Minds, (as some have already done) about the intended Scheme ... For my own Part, I am on many Accounts against your last Resolution of proceeding ... I am afraid you will involve yourself and Successors in inextricable Difficulties: and what I am particularly concern'd for, all this will be done to execute a Scheme for which I do in my Conscience believe the whole World will condemn Us; a Scheme that will so effectually shut out all View of that noble fabrick Kings-Chapell, that I wonder how the University or that College can bear it; and a Scheme so injurious to Caius College, that I am fully resolv'd not to bear it.

(W. & C.)

The plan to build the quadrangle and other university buildings was eventually abandoned.

Gardens were laid out and stocked.

Trinity Hall
The Fellows Terras Garden

This Garden is in Length from the Wall (joyning the Master's Gallery to the Library) to the outside of the opposite Wall that is wash'd by the River 236 Feet. In Breadth about 106 Feet in the middle.

The Horse Chestnut Trees by the Wall next Clare Hall were set about 1710, except two or three of them which were set some years later.

£   s   d

The Yew Hedges were planted A.D. 1705. Cost 16. 03. 01½.

The four Leaden Figures representing the Four Seasons were set up on the Terras Wall . . .

(*Warren's Book*, ed. Dale)

King's

A vote, 14 April 1772

Agreed to proceed in the further improvement of the Chappel yard on the West side of the New Building, by laying down the same with Grass seeds and afterwards feeding it from time to time with sheep as occasion may require in order to get it into good and ornamental condition; to complete the Gravelling the Walks round the same as now laid out, and not for the future to put any horses there.

(Leigh, *King's College*)

Gray noted the progress of spring in college gardens:

August 1763

I kept an exact account of Heat & Cold in the Spring here: the sum and substance of wch is, that (at 9 in the morning) on the 18th of January, the Therm: was at 31, & the small birds were so tame you might take them up with your hand. this was the greatest cold. on the 15th of April it was at 58, & the same afternoon, at 65, wch was the greatest heat from Jan: 1 to May 1st.

Feb.   3. Snowdrops flower'd.
         12. Crocus & Hepatica fl:, the snow then lieing, & Therm: at 45.
         18. Chaffinch sings. Bees appear.
         21. White butterfly abroad.
         25. Gnats flie, & large Flies. Mezereon fl:
         27. Honeysuckle & Gooseberry unfold their leaves.
March   1. Violet flowers (in the garden). Rose opens its leaf.
         3. Daffodil & single Hyacinth fl: Spider spins.
         5. Thrush singing.
         6. Elder in leaf, Currant & Weeping Willow in l:
         8. Apricot blows. Sky-Lark singing.
         11. Wind very high at S:E:, wch continued with hard frost.
         16. Frost gone.
         18. Abricot in full bloom.
         19. Almond flowers. Lilac, Barberry, & Gelder-rose in leaf.

16. Academic groves: the Wren Library and St. Johns', 1855 (engraving by B. Rudge)

April 2. Standard-Abricot, & Wall-Pears flower. Quince, Apple, and Sweet-briar, in leaf. Currant flowers. Dutch-Elm opens its leaf.
4. Plumb in leaf.
5. Crown Imperial fl:
6. Plumb flowers. Hawthorn, Horse-Chestnut, Mountain-Ash, in leaf.
9. Lime-tree in leaf. Jonquil & single Anemone flower. Lady-birds seen.
11. Cowslip flowers, & Auricula. Swallow appears. young rooks caw in the nest.
14. Red-Start appears. Cherries in full bloom.
15. Frontignac Vine in leaf. Double Wall-flower blows.
16. Nightingale sings. Apple blossoms.
19. Chaffinch & Red-Start sit on their eggs.
20. Elm, Willow, & Ash, in flower (with the Black-thorn) Hawthorn in full leaf.
21. Sycomore quite green. Oak puts out.

(Letter to Thomas Wharton, in *Correspondence*, ed. Toynbee and Whibley)

The turning century: giants in the groves

The last decade of the eighteenth century and the first few decades of the nineteenth saw no dramatic changes; many dons slumbered on but there were stirrings and twitches. Long-held ordinances on the exclusion of Dissenters began to be challenged and there had even been a proposal to allow fellows to marry. Reforms in the way degrees were awarded and in the nature of examinations were initiated. People did hold unorthodox political opinions and were indeed prosecuted for them. Nevertheless, though the establishment views prevailed, there was a whispering undercurrent of liberal change. Cambridge, like the rest of the country, reflected both the fears fanned by the French Revolution and the ideas that fuelled those fears.

1792 In the evening of the last day of the year, Thomas Paine was burnt in effigy by the populace on the Market Hill.

Peterhouse, £100	Corpus Christi, £100	St. John's, £525
Clare, £200	King's, £525	Magdalene, £100
Pembroke, £200	St. Catharine's, £100	Trinity, £525
Caius, £210	Jesus, £105	Emmanuel, £210
Trinity Hall, £105	Christ's, £200	Sidney, £100

and:

At a meeting of housekeepers and inhabitants of the town held at Emmanuel College on the 7th of May, it was agreed to form an armed association to be called 'The Patriotic Association of Cambridge Volunteers'. Busick Harwood M.D. Professor of Anatomy was appointed captain . . . On the 3rd of October, the Town and University were generally illuminated on account of the Battle of the Nile, the Volunteer Associations paraded the town preceded by their band, and there was a public supper in the Town Hall.

(Cooper)

> *In 1793 William Frend, Fellow and Tutor of Jesus College, published a pamphlet entitled 'Peace and Union recommended to the Associated bodies of Republicans and Anti-Republicans'. He was accused by his Master of, amongst other things, degrading the doctrines and rites of the Church of England and 'that there is a tendency in the said Pamphlet to disturb the harmony of society'. His expulsion from college was voted for by seven to four. Later there was a long trial in the Vice-Chancellor's court, which led to his exile from the University.*

The other day he was barred out of Jesus with an iron chain . . . And now he is publicly baited in the Senate-house! Why, at moments there today I could have believed I was in the Holy Inquisition – or at Oxford – as I watched the doltish malignancy of that old mumpsimus Dr. Kipling, as prosecutor, and all the petty spite of those red-robed, red-faced Daniels sitting there in judgment. Only the undergraduates in the gallery cheered poor Frend to the echo. They at least are young enough to have some sense . . .

Imagine, my dear, that noble hall, fit for better things than this. Round the table on the dais at its upper end, ten owls; with the arch-owl, Milner, in their midst. (How fitly was Queens' College first founded on Goose Green!) At a separate table the weasel's snout of Dr. Kipling, endeavouring to look wise, magnanimous, and compassionate – all three at once; and all with like success. At another table, poor Frend. The gallery black with excited youth, bless them! I could see our venerable Court was uncomfortably aware of the rage of the young barbarians above their heads.

You should have heard the Homeric mirth from the gallery, when Frend referred to Dr. Kipling's famous bad Latin – 'those beautiful changes of cases, those noble deviations in the mood of verbs' . . . Then, as they had accused him under some cobwebby statute of Queen Elizabeth's day, he turned and accused them of infringing canons of more recent date themselves, by the dress they were wearing at that very moment. He read out some hoary ordinance that prescribed for Masters of Arts and the like 'no new-fangleness', but 'priests' cloaks' and 'plain night-caps'! 'Surely, Mr. Frend,' interrupted the Vice-Chancellor, 'you cannot imagine this buffoonery will help you?' 'Certainly not,' said Frend gaily, and proceeded to point out that Dr. Kipling was incorrigibly given to riding out with no 'priest's cloak' to cover his disreputable nakedness; and that Lort Mansell of Trinity was sitting in front of them at that instant most indecorously attired in light-coloured fustians and white stockings.

(F. L. Lucas, *Doctor Dido*, 1938)

The Undergraduates were unanimous in favour of Mr. Frend, and every satirical remark reflecting upon the conduct and motives of his prosecutors was vociferously applauded. At length the Court desired the Proctors to interfere. Mr. Farish, the Senior Proctor, having marked one man who had particularly distinguished himself by applauding, and noted his position in the gallery, selected him as a fit subject for punishment. He went into the gallery, and having previously ascertained the exact situation of the culprit, he touched a person, whom he supposed to be the same, on the shoulder, and asked him his name and college. The person thus addressed assured him that he had been perfectly quiet. Farish replied, 'I have been watching you for a long time, and have seen you repeatedly clapping your hands. 'I wish this was possible', said the man, and turning round, exhibited an arm so deformed that his hands could not by any possibility be brought together; this exculpation was received with repeated rounds of applause, which continued for some minutes. The name of the young man was Charnock, and his college Clare Hall; the real culprit was S. T. Coleridge, of Jesus College, who having observed that the Proctor had noticed him, and was coming into the gallery, turned round to the person who was standing behind him, and made an offer of changing places, which was gladly accepted by the unsuspecting man.

(Gunning, *Reminiscences*)

Gunning has an interesting postscript to his account of the trial:

That the Vice-Chancellor was desirous that the prosecution of Frend should be considered as instituted against the prevalence of Jacobinism in the University, and that he took great pains to impress this on Mr. Pitt, is evident from a letter of his to Mr. Wilberforce, in which are the following words: –

'I don't believe Pitt was ever aware of how much consequence the expulsion of Frend was: it was the ruin of the Jacobinical party as a *University thing*, so that that party is almost entirely confined to Trinity College.'

Gunning himself had 'radical' sympathies:

As my political opinions so materially affected my prospects, I consider it right to state them without reserve. Whence I derived them I know not, but I cannot remember the time when I was not a Reformer. In 1780, when only twelve years old, I mixed with the multitude who were assembled opposite the steps of the Senate-house to listen to the speeches that were delivered on that occasion by the following persons: – John Wilkes, Esq., Thomas Day Esq., Crisp Molineux, M.P. for Lyme Regis, the Duke of Manchester, and many others.

[165]

And there were other threads of unorthodoxy under the smooth surface:

In March (1811) the Duke of Grafton, Chancellor of the University, died. The Duke of Gloucester, nephew to the King ... was a candidate for the vacant office. His hostility to West Indian Slavery gave him many supporters among those who, for political reasons, would have preferred his opponent, the Duke of Rutland, and he was elected by a majority of 117.

(Pryme, *Recollections*)

1792   On the 9th of March, the Senate voted a petition to the House of Commons, for the Abolition of the Slave Trade.

(Cooper)

In 1796 the first University Calendar was published. Various university offices were defined:

A VICE-CHANCELLOR, who must, by an Act passed in 1587, be *head* of some College. He is chosen yearly on the *fourth* of November; his office embraces the execution of the Chancellor's powers, and government of the University, according to her Statutes. – TWO PROCTORS, chosen annually on the *tenth* of October, who must be *Masters of Arts*: their business is to attend to the discipline and behaviour of all *in statu pupillari*, search houses of *ill* fame, commit women of *loose* and *abandoned* character, or even those, *de malo suspectæ*; read the graces, attend at taking of degrees, and take the votes in the *White-hood house*★ – TWO TAXORS† appointed to regulate the Markets, and take cognizance of weights and measures. – TWO MODERATORS,† who are appointed and paid by the Proctors; acting as their substitutes and assistants, superintending the exercises and disputations in philosophy, and the examinations previous to the degree of A.B. –

A PUBLIC ORATOR, who is, on all public occasions, the voice of the University, writes their letters, and presents Noblemen to their degrees with an appropriate speech. – THE CAPUT, chosen yearly on the *twelfth* of October, consists of the Vice-Chancellor, a Doctor of each faculty, viz. *Divinity, Law, and Physic, a regent and non-regent* Master of Arts. They are to consider and determine what graces are proper to be laid before the Senate, as none can be offered without first receiving their *unanimous* approbation; each Member having a *negative* voice. –

THREE ESQUIRE BEDELLS, chosen by the Senate, whose office is to wait upon the Vice-Chancellor on all public occasions and solemnities, whom they precede with their silver Maces. – There are *five* orders by which Students are distinguished in this University, viz. *Noblemen, Hat Fellow Commoners, Fellow Commoners, Pensioners, and Sizars.*

★ The *regents* or *white hoods*, are Masters of Arts during five years immediately following that degree, the *non-regents* or *black hoods*, are all above that standing.

† Annual Officers.

There was much building in the early part of the century, though a new college, founded by Sir George Downing, took some time to be built:

27 October 1784

Mr. Ainsly [Annesley] the new Master of Downing has been here to fix on a site for his new College, for, though many has been proposed to him, yet objections are made to all – Mr. Wyat the architect wishes much that it should be opposite to some of the colleges on the River, for then he thinks he shall not be crampt for Room, and may make four fine façades: but how will they here get an access to, and communication with, the Town? The most promising Spot seems to be that between Bp Watsons house and the Tennis Court, but here is said they cannot dig cellars, a material object, I presume, to such a college. The King has recommended two particulars – that it may not be a Gothic building, and that the Professors be obliged to publish their lectures.

> (William Lort, Fellow of Trinity, to
> Rev. Ashby, in W. & C.)

The foundation stone was eventually laid on 18 May 1807.

Work began on the Observatory in 1822 but in 1824 the Observatory Syndicate reported to the Senate:

that the expenses (£2,766 16s 1d) of the Dome and the Shutters (for which, on account of their peculiar construction, no accurate estimate could previously be given) have very far exceeded what the Syndicate were led to expect . . .

. . . that in the Grounds, Out-buildings, Gates &c . . . an heavy expense has been incurred.

> *(Cambridge Pamphlets)*

(The bill for the gates was indeed £652 14s out of a total bill of over £19,000.)

The foundation stone of the Fitzwilliam Museum was laid in 1837:

The Vice-Chancellor, Dr. Ainslie of Pembroke, then took a silver trowel and proceeded to lay the stone. The multitude then set up nine hearty cheers . . . The Public Orator then made a Latin speech, elegant enough, but very long-winded, but it was heard with patience. Another *faint* cheer followed.

> (*Memorials of George Elwes Corrie*, ed.
> Michael Holroyd, 1890)

Sir George Downing had also founded professorships of law and medicine: among other things it was decreed that:

Professors must be chosen . . . from colleges of Oxford or Cambridge . . . but a gentleman of a Scottish University may also be chosen to be professor of medicine.

> (George Dyer, *History of the University*,
> 1814)

We the undersigned Tutors of Colleges beg leave respectfully to express to the
Vice-Chancellor that we decidedly disapprove of our Pupils attending the Public
Lectures of any person who is neither a Member of the University nor a Member
of the Church of England.

> (J. E. Smith, *Considerations respecting
> Cambridge more particularly relating to its
> Botanical Professorship*, 1818)

Lectures and lecturers came in all kinds:

By the way at the meeting of the Philosophers last Monday Hopkins was
delivering a long prosy lecture on Geology, & before it was over the Master of
Downing (who had been snoring some time) fell flat on his face in the middle
of the room to the delight of the company.

> (Joseph Romilly, *Cambridge Diary 1832–42*,
> ed. J. P. T. Bury, 1967)

I attended a course of Lectures on Anatomy ... Dr. Clark, who was then
professor, had a high reputation as a lecturer. He was the only survivor of the
three Professors Clark, whom Cambridge had once seen in the chairs of Geology,
Music and Anatomy, and who therefore were distinguished as Stone-Clark,
Tone-Clark, and Bone-Clark.

> (Harvey Goodwin, *A Memoir*, 1880)

Come with me to hear Professor Farish; the hour will be well employed. The
experimental philosopher has laid out all his apparatus of cog-wheels, cylinders,
bars, pulleys, cranks, screws, blocks etc, and, with a complacent smile, is contemplating the ingenious combination of all the parts. In the simplest, almost
approaching to infantine, manner, he explains all the intricate modes by which
these wheels work upon one another, their multipliers, their momentums, and
their checks. His sawing-machine, his hat manufacturing, his oil press, and
cannon-foundry, are abundant stores of entertainment ... His explanations of
the art of mining and ship-building are perfect in clearness and precision ...
Under all this appearance of simplicity, it is discoverable that he is a great man.

> (*Facetiae Cantabrigiensis*, by Socius)

Dons' lives continued to be agreeable and undemanding:

Trinity (1809)

I was often a visitor to the Lodge. The Master, Bp Mansel, was a widower, and
had three daughters nearly grown up, and three much younger. Mrs. Pearson,
wife of the Master of Sidney, acted as lady of the house when he gave parties.
We had frequently music, Blomfield played on the violin, and if a dance was
improvised, the Master would himself turn an organ.

> (George Pryme, *Recollections*)

There were bets in the Combination Room at Christ's, usually laid in bottles:

1812 that the Gentleman in Bridge Street is the son of the man with the large
     nose in Clapham Common (lost)
     that Lord Liverpool was not at school at Eton (won)
     that Mr. Doncaster will not be the next incumbent of Canfield Parva
     (won)
1813 that Milton's name was in the College Admission Book (won)
     that the race between Hambletonian and Diamond was run before the
     year 1800 (won)
     that the Armistice now supposed to have been proposed by Bonaparte
     will be or has been accepted by the Russians and Prussians (won – at
     five bottles to one)
1814 that the Poem beginning with the words 'All in the land of Essex' is the
     production of Denham and not of Cleveland (won)
     that a Gooseberry Pye appeared in the Hall eight days ago (lost)
     that there is no such Parish as Wimpole in Cambridgeshire (lost to
     Gunning)
1818 that one of the 2 ships intended to get to the Pole succeeds in its object
     (lost)
     that the Tiger Cat is spotted and not striped (lost)
     that in Bewick's British Birds there is a print of a man leaping over the
     Water with a Pole (lost)
     that a person having 9 or more unmarried Daughters can claim an
     exemption from part of the Hair-powder Duty (won)
     that Mr. Pearson kills more moor-game on the 12th of August than
     Mr. Coe kills partridges on the 1st of September (won)
     that Mr. C is sick on his passage to France (won)

(Anthony Steel, *The Custom of the Room,*
1949)

Suppers for the clergy:

most of the churches within ten miles of Cambridge were served by Fellows of
colleges. In some cases the curate hastened back to dine in hall; there were
others who undertook two or three services . . . During this period suppers were
served in the halls of several of the colleges. At Trinity they were not abolished
until after the death of Renouard, the Vice-Master, who was a regular attendant,
as also Carr the Bursar, and Pugh the incumbent of Bottisham. In those colleges
where there were no suppers, the officiating clergy formed Sunday-evening
Clubs. At St. John's it was called 'The Curate's Club'. At King's, 'The Neck
or Nothing', so named from the supper consisting of necks of mutton cut into
chops. At Christ's, the meeting was called 'The Apostolic'; the supper was
always tripe, dressed in various ways.

(Gunning, *Reminiscences*)

Ritual and feasting at Stourbridge Fair:

On the 18th of September, the ceremony of proclaiming Stourbridge Fair took
place. At 11 a.m., the Vice-Chancellor, with the Bedells and Registrary, the

17. Site of the present Botanic Gardens, 1809, viewed from Trumpington Road. (From S. M. Walters, *The Shaping of Cambridge Botany*, 1981)

Commissary, the Proctors, and the Taxors, attended in the Senate-House, where a plentiful supply of mulled wine and sherry, in black bottles, with a great variety of cakes, awaited their arrival. This important business ended, the parties proceeded to the Fair, in carriages provided for the occasion. The proclamation was read by the Registrary in the carriage with the Vice-Chancellor, and repeated by the Yeoman Bedell on horseback, in three different places. At the conclusion of this ceremony, the carriages drew up to the *Tiled Booth* (which is still standing), where the company alighted for the dispatch of business – and of oysters . . .

At this repast we were joined by numbers of Masters of Arts, who had formed no part of the procession, but who had come for the express purpose of eating oysters. This was a *very serious part* of the day's proceedings, and occupied a long time. We then left the *dining-room*, that the waiters might remove the shells and cover the boards with a cloth, in preparation for dinner . . . The scene which presented itself on entering the room I can describe most accurately, for the dishes and their arrangement never varied. Before the Vice-Chancellor was placed a large dish of herrings; then followed in order a neck of pork roasted, an enormous plum-pudding, a leg of pork boiled, a pease-pudding, a goose, a large apple-pie, and a round of beef in the centre. On the other half of the table, the same dishes were placed in similar order (the herrings before the Senior Proctor who sat at the bottom). From thirty to forty persons dined there; and although the wine was execrable, a number of toasts were given, and mirth and good humour prevailed, to such an extent as is seldom to be met with at more modern and more refined entertainments. At about half-past six the dinner party broke up, and, with scarcely an exception, adjourned to the theatre.

(Gunning, *Reminiscences*)

Some undergraduates arrived nervous, some blasé.

1821   Edward Bulwer (later Lord Lytton) at Trinity:

There was a crowd collected on the steps leading into the Hall; and, as I walked up the immense quadrangle, I felt as if every eye was fixed upon me. You know how nervous my private education has made me. But when I found myself actually last in the throng of purple gowns which haunted the approach, and stunned by the clatter of dishes and babel of voices, I felt very much as a shoe-black might feel if transplanted to Almack's . . . When the dishes were all placed on the table, there was a hungry and eager look, a murmur, and a sudden rush. I found myself borne down the current, till, following the example of my immediate precursor, I dropped into a place by an enormous sirloin of beef. This was abruptly seized, and a fork stuck into it. A pile then suddenly rose on the plate of my opposite neighbour. Scarcely had he relinquished the sirloin before it was pounced upon by another. The same operation took place. A third succeeded, and I began to cast a disconsolate glance at a hacked and maimed shoulder of mutton . . . when I found the beef before me, and, so far as I could in my inexperience perceive, no rival fork at hand, I therefore brandished mine, and was just going to make up for lost time – when, like the Fata Morgana, it vanished in a trice.

(Edward Bulwer Lytton, *Life, Letters and Literary Remains, by his Son*, 1883)

1827 Richard Monckton Milnes (Lord Houghton). His mother writes:

Arranged Richard's books in his rooms and the old butler showed me a gallery where I could see him dine in Hall for the first time. He sat by Wentworth, who was also just arrived, and seemed as much at home among all the dons as if he had been there for years.

(T. Wemyss Reid, *Richard Monckton Milnes: Life, Letters and Friendships*, 1890)

In 1804 J. B. Scott of Bungay had an agreeable preview and a kind reception:

June 28 1806 ... My parents being anxious to fix my inclinations either for or against college life, took me up to Cambridge with the idea that I might thus judge for myself. On the 28th I started from Bungay in the gig, with the servant George Cole ...

July 1 ... We fixed our quarters at the Hoope Inn. Mr. Gilbert of Emmanuel called and gave us very kind assistance in seeing the University. It was Commencement week. Everything appeared in gala dress. I was sure to like Cambridge under such circumstances ...

I was enchanted with this visit and with all I saw and heard; but among the enchantments was the pretty little bar-girl of the Hoope (Miss Curtis) who made the leaving Cambridge quite painful to me.

He was soon in the social swim:

1810

Cambridge October 18   The aspect of the college pleased me. The tone of Emmanuel society at that time was gay, gentlemanly and classical.

The bustle and importance of furnishing my rooms excited and amused me ...

Fresh acquaintances full of youthful joy and energy poured daily into my rooms. Sir Busick Harwood, Professor of Anatomy, invited me to a supper party of 20 and there I found myself unexpectedly popular. All tempted me away from study. Blackhall, after examining me, pronounced me first in mathematics, not only of the new men of my own year but of those of the year above me. Slade also reported favourably of my classical acquirements. I was told I did not want to read for lectures, and that I could answer all Lecture Room questions without study. I soon became gay and idle. Invitation followed invitation. I gave a supper to 22 before the end of the term, and sat playing cards till 5 in the morning.

I resumed my old love for dancing both at the Cambridge and Huntingdon County Balls, from the latter of which I returned only in time to attend morning chapel. I joined too in gallops on hired hacks over the Gogmagogs with large parties, and played Billiards at Chestertons with my companions.

(*An Englishman at Home*, ed. Ethel Mann, 1930)

As a freshman there was a lot to do:

Tuesday September 19 (1826)   Here I am lying on my sofa, with my drab reading coat on, in the upper rooms of the Lodge-Turret Staircase, a freshman of Trinity College, Cambridge ...

From Friday to this time I have been from the Upholsterer to the Ironmonger, and from the Ironmonger to the Upholsterer - ordering Pembroke tables, Round do. Small do. Sofa, Chairs, Easy do. book shelves, Curtains (scarlet) Fire Irons, Snuffers, Teapots, Coffee Machine, Candlesticks, Coal-scuttle to fill the Coal scoop and a Coal scoop to fill the Coal shovel, and a great many more useless things.

(*Christopher Wordsworth, Bishop of Lincoln, 1809–86: Diaries*, ed. J. H. Overton and E. Wordsworth, 1888)

(*This is Christopher Wordsworth, the third son of Christopher Wordsworth the Master of Trinity.*)

For noblemen life was easy, if expensive:

the reins of authority were relaxed in favour of noblemen and fellow-commoners, especially the former, who were exempt from attendance at chapel, except on Sundays, and altogether from Hall. One of them passed a great part of his time in the green-room of Covent Garden, and another in driving stage-coaches by night . . . The cost of a nobleman's outfit amounted to £100; that of a single gown which he wore on gaude (festival days) to be between £50 and £60 . . . the attendance at Trinity Chapel was too much required as a roll call. The gownsmen dropped in till the Creed.

(Charles John Shore Teignmouth, Baron, *Reminiscences of Many Years*, 1878)

and sometimes rowdy:

Lord Mount Charles, son of the Marquis of Conyngham, of my year at Trinity (1813), was a tall, stout, good-humoured fellow, with the rattle of whose boisterous laugh the drowsy echoes of our principal quadrangle sufficiently familiarised us . . . He had taken his place at Cambridge for London in the Telegraph coach, driven by Hellfire Dick. There were at this time some agrarian disturbances at Ely. Mount Charles, probably under the influence of an early potation, finding a stout, farmer-like man seated opposite to him, charged him at once with being a rioter. A retort was followed by words, and at length, blows. Mount Charles, after the ancient fashion of his countrymen, astonished his bucolic antagonist by producing a pair of pistols, and insisting on their exchanging shots across the high-road. Dick . . . a master of tact, continued at length to pacify the combatants . . . and to drive his 'happy family' to their destination in Fetter Lane.

Sport was a major occupation for many. A father writes to his son's tutor:

Dear Sir,

I do not understand the tenour of your communication. When I was an undergraduate at Queens' (about 1808–11) it would have been counted a disgrace to the college if any man had been present in hall on a Newmarket day.

Yours faithfully

(A. G. Bradley, *Our Centenarian Grandfather 1790–1890*, 1922)

Rowing

In the summer of 1826, just before I came into residence, there were only two 8-oars on our water, a Trinity boat and a Johnian, and the only idea of encounter they had that was each should go, as it were casually, downstream and lie in wait, one of them, I believe, sounding a bugle to intimate its whereabouts, when the other coming up would give chase with as much animation as might be expected when there were no patrons of the sport or spectators of the race. In the year 1827 this flotilla was increased by the accession of a Trinity ten-oar . . . and of two or three 6-oars from other colleges, and then regular rowing began . . . In 1829 we aspired to compete with Oxford.

(Dean Merivale, in *The University Boat Race: Official Centenary History, 1829–1929,* by G. C. Drinkwater and T. R. B. Sanders, 1929)

Cricket

Herbert Jenner-Fust, who played in the first University match in 1827, recalls:

it was not to be expected that we could play many matches. Our only competitors were Cambridge Town Club and Bury St. Edmunds . . .

We had no colours and dressed *ad libitum*. I often played in a white beaver hat, but people used to call those of us who did so 'post boys', and that caused us to drop the practice . . . we wore pretty much what we liked, but fancy jackets were not favoured. I kept wicket without pads or gloves; in fact, pads were not heard of . . . and the player would have been laughed at who tried to protect his shins. Knee-breeches, and thin gauze silk stockings, doubled up at the ankles, formed a popular costume. When the ball was wet, I occasionally used a kid glove, but that was all.

(W. J. Ford, *The Cambridge University Cricket Club 1820–1901,* 1902)

A sporting man's rooms in 1820:

Well, we will suppose that you have arrived at the door of the apartment. It is no sooner opened by your host, than a strong smell, as of a menagerie, strikes upon your olfactory nerves. At the same time, three or four enormous dogs, such as Scotch greyhounds, for example, glide playfully through your legs, and sniff around you in a way which tends on the whole to render a man unaccustomed to the canine race, uncomfortable. You sink down upon a chair, but rise with a shriek, having sat upon a ferret. Your host lays down his *Bell's Life* and runs up to the ferret, hoping he has not been hurt.

(John Smith, 'Sketches of Cantabs', 1849, quoted in Oskar Teichman, *The Cambridge Undergraduate 100 Years Ago*, 1926)

Most of us had dogs. Dogs and King's were in a manner identical. None of us ever went a single step out of College in cap or gown. Dog, top-hat, and walking-stick. Why not? we had nothing to do beyond a Greek or English lecture at 11, – not always that . . . To be sure we had Chapel at 8, – our great grievance.

(Rev. W. H. Tucker, quoted in Leigh, *King's College*)

Dons too went riding and shooting.

Edward Pote, a resident Fellow of King's is described by Tucker:

He was to be seen throughout the year in strong, stout, white Russia ducks –
mostly a little frayed at the heel; but – coat, always black, which had a degree of
merit at a time when every one else had swallow-tailed coats of blue, green, olive,
or various shades of brown with gilt buttons. He was a constant attendant in
Hall except on shooting days, when he dined in his rooms . . . The writer not
unfrequently went out shooting with him. One day as we were out two or three
miles from Cambridge an unpreserved ground, he said to me, 'We must go a
little to the right to such-and-such a church, as I have promised to take a funeral
there at 3 o'clock.' We reached it in time, and stopped at the outer gate. 'Keep
the dog and my gun', quoth he. He leaned the gun by the gate; tucked up his
trousers into shorts; went in; performed the funeral; came forth; took up his
gun; patted doggie on the head, and we went on as before, shooting our way
home.

A fellow of St. John's College walking with a friend, who was a stranger in
Cambridge, by chance met the master of his college, Dr. Wood,* on horseback;
and, on his friend asking who the gentleman on horseback was, he facetiously
replied, 'It's St. John's head on a charger.'

(*Facetiae Cantabrigiensis*, by Socius)

Ballooning

*Richard Monckton Milnes went up in a balloon with Mr. Green, a well-known
aeronaut, and another undergraduate. Whewell, giving permission, recorded:*

Ascendat Mr Milnes, May 19 1829

Milnes wrote to Arthur Hallam:

19 May 1829

Your friend in the skies speeds this note to you at an elevation of about a mile
and a half from the base earth, where you are grovelling. Oh if the spirit of
Adonais would sail with me in my little boat, my very crescent moon. The sun
has given me a little headache, but a light breeze comes playing along. Now we
cross St. Neot's. The whole country looks a beautiful model; the wind near the
earth is tremendously high . . . now the shout rises from the earth, in a sort of
distant wail.

(Reid, *Milnes: Life*)

There were always problems over money:

Macaulay writes home, referring to his tutor's bill:

31 December 1818

It is most grossly erroneous, surcharging in some points and not mentioning
others . . . There is a charge of five pounds for a shoe-maker's bill though I have
employed no shoe-maker, and of 7 pounds for a tailor though I have not had
one stitch put in for me.

* Son of a weaver, sizar in 1778, Master of St. John's 1815–39.

Nov. 24 1819

My tea-canister and purse are exhausted together, and for a fortnight I have been living without money, and drinking a decoction of chopped hay.

23 ? February 1820

I had almost forgot to mention that I am destitute of money.

13 January 1821

P.S. I forgot to mention that the Chandler's bill is not for candles alone but for the glasses and decanters with which I was compelled to fit myself over at the beginning of the October term and that the 5£ for Cash were paid to the Vintner, who sells no wine without ready money, and who was employed at a time when all my stock was lent to Malden.

(Letters, ed. Thomas Pinney, vol. I, 1974)

My father, with a view of acquiring some information which might be of use to me in Cambridge, had consulted a tutor of one of the colleges ... The advice of the Rev. Doctor was quite sound, but very limited. It might be summed up in one short sentence: 'Advise your son not to purchase his wine in Cambridge'.

(Charles Babbage, Passages from the Life of a Philosopher, 1864)

Not all undergraduates came from wealthy homes.

A 'Trinity man', in his 'Advice to parents':

If you are wealthy send him as a Pensioner (I repeat it) to Trinity. Here, if he be clever, he will meet with abundant incitement to display his abilities and will be best instructed; if a dunce, something good will necessarily be driven into him. In either case he will here be introduced to the best society, and will have widest scope for knowledge of life as well as for a selection of friends.

If you are ever so needy, provided your son is possessed of *uncommon* talents (of which you yourself solely ought not to judge), still let him go to Trinity. Let his name be on the college boards as a *Sizar* (if you cannot spare him two hundred a year) three years or thereabouts before he is old enough to reside. By thus 'taking time by the forelock', he becomes a foundation Sizar, and as such entitled to much assistance from the college. Sixteen of this order, although like the Sizars generally, wearing the same cap and gown as the Pensioners, and in no way otherwise degraded by outward distinctions, are allowed rooms and commons gratis. They dine and sup, indeed, after the Fellows, but from the rich overplus of the feastings from the Fellows' table, there is '*satis superque*', to satisfy the palate of the greatest epicure of them.

(J. M. F. Wright, Alma Mater, or Seven Years at Cambridge. By a Trinity Man, 1827)

and 'Gradus ad Cantabrigiam':

whoever has resided any little time at Cambridge must know that, in point of rank, the distinction between *Pensioners* and *Sizars* is by no means considerable. Between *Commoners* and *Servitors* there is a great gulph. Nothing is more common than to see *Pensioners* and *Sizars* taking sweet counsel together and walking arm in arm to St. Mary's . . . In respect to their academical habit: At Trinity College, the *Sizars* wear precisely the same dress with the Pensioners. At other colleges, the only difference is that their gowns are not bordered with velvet.

In every College, the *Sizars* invite, and are invited by, the *Pensioners* to wine parties; and some of them (the former) to vie with the latter in fashionable frivolity.

(by 'A Pembrochian', 1803)

The authorities thundered about riotous conduct and took steps to deal with malefactors:

Tu. 11. Feb.   An awful long Seniority: we expelled Hon. G. A. Murray & Hunter for gambling (Murray won near £800 of Hunter, who confessed to Whewell): we confined to Gates & Walls Lord Cl. Hamilton, Ld J. Beresford, 2 Ponsonbys & 8 more for a riot in the Court at 2 o'clock on Sunday Morning after a supper at Ld Claud Hamiltons: 2 lamps and part of the balustrade in Nevile's Court were pulled down, but by whom of the party unknown: 3 of the party, Conyngham, Herbert & Ponsonby (3 Fellow Crs) were very drunk & confined for a longer time than the rest.

(Romilly, *Diary*, ed. Bury)

One young man paid with his life for a drunken party:

On Thursday, 5th February, 1818, Lawrence Dundas, Esq. an Under-graduate of Trinity College, dined with K. A. Jackson, Esq. Fellow-commoner of St. John's College, and the following gentlemen – Messrs. Musgrave, Bach and Messrs. Wigram, Pym, and the Hon. Wm. Thelluson, Under-graduates of Trinity College, at Mr. Jackson's lodgings, at the house of Dyball, in Bridge Street, Cambridge.

They sat down to dine about half past seven, and remained drinking till near eleven, when two of the party (Mr. Wigram and the deceased) set off, BY AGREEMENT, TO GO TO BARNWELL.* Mr. Wigram, as soon as he was out of doors, ran off to Barnwell; the deceased was so drunk that he could not get his gown on alone, and Mrs. Dyball helped him on with it, when he proceeded to follow his companion – never, however, to reach him – for when he arrived at Parker's Piece he seems to have missed his way, and tumbled into a muddy ditch, not much above knee-deep, out of which he struggled once or twice; but at length, after stripping every thing off, saving his pantaloons and his stockings, which nevertheless were drawn over his feet and completely fettered him, he fell to rise no more; for he was found dead on Friday morning in a sitting posture in the ditch, in a part of it where there was about eighteen inches of water, with his head and side reclining on the bank, and with the water nearly up to his mouth, so that he does not appear to have been drowned, but to have perished from the inclemency of the weather.

* I believe Barnwell, some years back, was little more than the resort of women of the town; now it is greatly improved, and these characters are chiefly in its outskirts.

*The author of a pamphlet about the death of Dundas, the Rev. F. H. Maberley
of Chesterton, described other disgraces and a controversy with Mr. Lawson
ensued:*

Maberley

On the Monday night immediately following his death, was an Under-graduate
led home from a house, hard by Dyball's, in a drunken state . . . With regard to
women of the town; I have not been in Cambridge for some time since after six
o'clock in the evening; but I have seen them parading the streets in the most
impudent manner, accosting many that they met and talking with men of the
University in a drunken state . . .*

* Since writing the above, one evening at about eight o'clock, in less than five minutes,
  two prostitutes met me, ran against me and separated; two more came behind me and
  pushed against me, and two more ran hollooing by me.

Answered by M. Lawson Esq., Fellow of Magdalene College and a JP:

Now is it not pretty evident these six were the same two, three times over? We
can easily conceive how perplexed Mr. M must have been by the gloom of the
evening, to which he owns he is unaccustomed, and how unable to identify the
persons of these professional ladies, from the rapidity of their movements, and
their proverbial levity.

Maberley's concern for morals extended itself to the Fitzwilliam:

pictures of naked women, beautifully painted . . . let the licentious pictures,
exhibited in the Fitzwilliam Museum be removed . . . The effect of such
exhibitions upon the passions of the most phlegmatic . . . cannot but be highly
injurious. But upon the passions of those in youth, and in the vigour of life,
and when those passions are heated, how highly inflammatory will be the effect.

Lawson counters:

is he not aware of the licentious tendency of the classics? . . . Are not Ovid and
Anacreon at least as dangerous as the pictures in the Fitzwilliam Museum?

> (F. H. Maberley, *The Melancholy and
> Awful Death of Lawrence Dundas Esq.*, 1818)

Three poets all up about this time had quite disparate views on the University:

Coleridge came up to Jesus in 1791:

early November 1791

We go to Chapel twice a day – every time we miss, we pay twopence, and
fourpence on Surplice days – *id est*, Sundays, Saints' days and the eves of Saints'
days. I am remarkably religious upon an economical plan.

23 November 1791

Cambridge is a very damp place – the very palace of winds

14 February 1792

The quiet ugliness of Cambridge supplies me with very few communicables in
the news way . . .

The River Cam is a handsome stream of a muddy complexion, somewhat like Miss Yates . . . In Cambridge there are 16 colleges, that look like Workhouses, and 14 Churches, that look like little houses. The Town is very fertile in alleys, and mud, and cats, and dogs, besides men, women, ravens, cattle.

P.S. A party of officers had been drinking wine together . . . As we were returning homewards, two of them fell into the gutter (or kennel). We ran to assist one of them – who very generously stuttered out – 'Nnn, no, nn no! ssave my ffrfrfriend there – nnever mind me – I can swim.'

> (*This is a common story about the two flowing gutters along Trumpington Street, known as the Pot and Pem.*)

13 January 1793

I owe about 50£ to my Tutor – and about 8£ elsewhere. The debt to my Tutor is entirely the arrears of my two first Quarters – and I have owed it to him ever since! – My income from the school is 40£ – from the Rustat Scholarship this year it will be about 23£ – or perhaps a little more – from the Chapel clerkship 33£ – And as I eat no Supper, or Tea, and keep little company my expences this year *excluding* Travelling into Devonshire will be about 50£ – so that I shall be 26£ plus. My commons I have for nothing . . . they being included in the Chapel clerkship – so that it is little expence to be resident.

> (*Collected Letters*, ed. Earl Leslie Griggs, 1956)

> *Christopher Wordsworth notes in his diary:*

Time before supper was spent in hearing Coleridge repeat some original poetry (he having neglected to write his essay, which therefore is to be produced next week).

> *On 2 December 1793, harassed by Cambridge debts, Coleridge enlisted in the King's Light Dragoons as Silas Tomkyn Comberbache:*

My *number* I do not know – it is of no import.

> *Extricated by his brothers, he returned to Cambridge in May 1794.*

A month's confinement to the precincts of the College, and to translate the works of Demetrius Phalareus (*sic*) into English – it is a thin quarto of about 90 Greek pages . . . The confinement is nothing – I have the fields and Grove of the college to walk in – and what could I wish more.

> *There were other schemes, which came to nothing:*

27 August 1794

Sir, . . . A small but liberalized party have formed a scheme of emigration on the principles of an abolition of personal property . . . The minutiae of topographical information we are daily endeavouring to acquire; at present our plan is, to settle at a distance . . . from Cooper's Town on the banks of the Susquehannah . . . For the time of emigration we have fixed on next March. In the course of the winter those of us whose bodies, from habits of sedentary study or academic indolence, have not acquired their full tone and strength, intend to learn the theory and practice of agriculture and carpentry . . .

Your fellow Citizen,

S. T. Coleridge

He left Cambridge in December 1794. He had had liberal treatment from Jesus: his name was not removed from their boards until June 1795. He had the most affectionate regard for Cambridge in later life.

William Wordsworth, at St. John's from 1789 to 1791, has left in 'The Prelude' his record of life in Cambridge:

> I was the Dreamer, they the Dream; I roamed
> Delighted through the motley spectacle;
> Gowns grave, or gaudy, doctors, students, streets,
> Courts, cloisters, flocks of churches, gateways, towers:
> Migration strange for a stripling of the hills,
> A northern villager.

> The Evangelist St. John my patron was:
> Three Gothic courts are his, and in the first
> Was my abiding-place, a nook obscure;
> Right underneath, the College kitchens made
> A humming sound, less tuneable than bees,
> But hardly less industrious; with shrill notes
> Of sharp command and scolding intermixed.
> Near me hung Trinity's loquacious clock,
> Who never let the quarters, night or day,
> Slip by him unproclaimed, and told the hours
> Twice over with a male and female voice.
> Her pealing organ was my neighbour too;
> And from my pillow, looking forth by light
> Of moon or favouring stars, I could behold
> The antechapel where the statue stood
> Of Newton with his prism and silent face,
> The marble index of a mind for ever
> Voyaging through strange seas of Thought, alone.

> . . . Yet from the first crude days
> Of settling time in this untried abode,
> I was disturbed at times by prudent thoughts,
> Wishing to hope without a hope, some fears
> About my future worldly maintenance,
> And, more than all, a strangeness in the mind,
> A feeling that I was not for that hour,
> Nor for that place . . .

> *Caverns* there were within my mind which sun
> Could never penetrate, yet did there not
> Want store of leafy *arbours* where the light

Might enter in at will. Companionships,
Friendships, acquaintances, were welcome all.
We sauntered, played, or rioted; we talked
Unprofitable talk at morning hours;
Drifted about along the streets and walks,
Read lazily in trivial books, went forth
To gallop through the country in blind zeal
Of senseless horsemanship, or on the breast
Of Cam sailed boisterously, and let the stars
Come forth, perhaps without one quiet thought.

    Such was the tenor of the second act
In this new life. Imagination slept,
And yet not utterly. I could not print
Ground where the grass had yielded to the steps
Of generations of illustrious men,
Unmoved. I could not always lightly pass
Through the same gateways, sleep where they had slept,
Wake where they waked, range that inclosure old,
That garden of great intellects, undisturbed.
Place also by the side of this dark sense
Of noble feeling, that those spiritual men,
Even the great Newton's own ethereal self,
Seemed humbled in these precincts thence to be
The more endeared . . .

Among the band of my compeers was one
Whom chance had stationed in the very room
Honoured by Milton's name. O temperate Bard!
Be it confest that, for the first time, seated
Within thy innocent lodge and oratory,
One of a festive circle, I poured out
Libations, to thy memory drank, till pride
And gratitude grew dizzy in a brain
Never excited by the fumes of wine
Before that hour, or since. Then, forth I ran
From the assembly; through a length of streets,
Ran, ostrich-like, to reach our chapel door
In not a desperate or opprobrious time,
Albeit long after the importunate bell
Had stopped, with wearisome Cassandra voice
No longer haunting the dark winter night.

    All winter long, whenever free to choose,
Did I by night frequent the College groves
And tributary walks; the last, and oft
The only one, who had been lingering there
Through hours of silence, till the porter's bell,

[181]

A punctual follower on the stroke of nine,
Rang with its blunt unceremonious voice,
Inexorable summons! Lofty elms,
Inviting shades of opportune recess,
Bestowed composure on a neighbourhood
Unpeaceful in itself. A single tree
With sinuous trunk, boughs exquisitely wreathed,
Grew there; an ash which Winter for himself
Decked as in pride, and with outlandish grace:
Up from the ground, and almost to the top,
The trunk and every master branch were green
With clustering ivy, and the lightsome twigs
And outer spray profusely tipped with seeds
That hung in yellow tassels, while the air
Stirred them, not voiceless. Often have I stood
Foot-bound uplooking at this lovely tree
Beneath a frosty moon.

Byron began as he meant to go on and went on till he left:

26 October 1805

Dear Sir - I will be obliged to you to order me down 4 Dozen of Wine, Port – Sherry – Claret, & Madeira, one Dozen of Each; I have got part of my furniture in, & begin to *admire* a College Life. Yesterday my appearance in the Hall in my State Robes was *Superb*, but uncomfortable to my Diffidence.

(To John Hanson)

27 December 1805

like all other young men just let loose ... I have been extravagant, and consequently am in want of Money.

(To Augusta Byron)

Chapel time:
'A num'rous crowd arrayed in white
Across the green in numbers fly.'
(Byron)

(*Cambridge Scrapbook*, 1859)

18. Academic habiliments, 1800

16 Piccadilly   26 February 1806

I have also discharged my College Bills, amounting to £231 – £75 of which I shall trouble Hanson to repay, being for Furniture . . . I find it inconvenient to remain at College, not for the Expence, as I could live on my Allowance, (only I am naturally extravagant) however the mode of going on does not suit my constitution, improvement at an English University to a Man of Rank is you know impossible, and the very Idea *ridiculous*.

(To Mrs. Catherine Gordon Byron)

8 July 1806

I am detained in Cambridge by the painting of my Carriage, nor take my departure till Saturday.

(To Mrs. Elizabeth Massingberd)

Southwell   14 February 1807

I certainly do not feel that prediliction for Mathematics, which may pervade the Inclinations of men destined for a clerical, or collegiate Life . . . The subjects for your present Lectures, are undoubtedly interesting, but the '*Demonstration of the Being of a God*', is (to me, at least) unnecessary – To expatiate on his 'attributes' is superfluous, we do not know them? he who *doubts* them, does not deserve to be instructed. – To *bewilder* myself in the mazes of Metaphysics, is not my object . . . I have other Reasons for not residing at Cambridge, I dislike it; I was originally intended for Oxford.

(To his tutor, Rev. Thomas Jones)

30 June 1807

I am almost superannuated here, my old friends . . . all departed, & I am preparing to follow them, but remain till Monday to be present at 3 *Oratorios*, 2 Concerts, a *fair*, a boxing match, & a Ball . . . I got awkward in my academic habilaments, for want of practice, got up in a Window to hear the Oratorio at St. Mary's, popped down in the middle of the *Messiah*, tore a *woeful rent* in the Back of my best black silk gown, & damaged an *egregious pair* of Breeches, mem. never tumble from a church window during Service.

I have determined to reside *another year* at *Granta* as my Rooms etc. etc. are finished in *great Style* . . . I shall return to College in October if still *alive* . . . The *Music* is all over at present, met with another '*accidency*', upset a *Butter Boat* in the *lap* of a *lady* . . . This place is a *Monotony* of *endless variety*.

26 October 1807

This place is wretched enough, a villainous Chaos of Dice and Drunkenness, nothing but Hazard and Burgundy, Hunting, Mathematics and Newmarket, Riot and Racing . . . I have got a new friend, the finest in the world, a *tame Bear*, when I brought him here, they asked me what I meant to do with him, and my reply was 'he should *sit* for *Fellowship*'.

(To Elizabeth Bridget Pigot)
(*Letters*, ed. Marchand)

He delighted in castigating his University:

The sons of science these, who, thus repaid,
Linger in ease in Granta's sluggish shade;
Where on Cam's sedgy banks supine they lie,
Unknown, unhonour'd live, unwept-for die:
Dull as the pictures which adorn their halls,
They think all learning fix'd within their walls:
In manners rude, in foolish forms precise,
All modern arts affecting to despise;
Yet prizing Bentley's, Brunck's, or Porson's note,
More than the verse on which the critic wrote:
Vain as their honours, heavy as their ale,
Sad as their wit, and tedious as their tale.

('Thoughts Suggested by a College
Examination', 1806)

Mathematics gave problems to many reading men.

Cambridge. Their hearts hardened by mathematics.

(R. S. Hawker, *Thought Books*)

'*A Trinity Man*':

I knew a man of this sort, of Trinity, who fagged, poor devil, night and day to get on, but failed with all his efforts. He used to read, upon an average, about 14 hours a day, his fond and foolish father having persuaded him that if he did so he must inevitably become *Senior Wrangler*. But, alas! at the expiration of three years he was *plucked*, and plucked, and plucked, three several times, and at last was given his B.A. out of sheer compassion. Nevertheless, this dunce, in a drawing-room, would out-talk nine tenths of the truly great ones of the day upon *ordinary* topics, and has become a most popular preacher, in a populous town in Sussex. His father, poor man, still ascribes his failure at Cambridge, to the excessive nervousness of his son's constitution and to the partiality of the examiners.

(Wright, *Alma Mater*)

3 March 1823

Our change of purpose respecting John, has been entirely caused by his own inclinations – the mathematical education of Cambridge – especially at St. John's (the Coll. in which he was entered) is so contrary to the course of studies which is most agreeable to himself that he sickened at the thought of how much time he must give to Mathematics, which he has no taste or talent for. His father, therefore, has taken some pains (which are fortunately successful in Exeter Coll) to meet with an accidental vacancy in Oxford.

(*Letters of Mary Wordsworth*, ed. M. E. Burton, 1958)

and, above all, Macaulay:

Trinity College
Wednesday (postmark 1818)

I can scarcely bear to write on Mathematics or Mathematicians. Oh for words to express my abomination of that science, if a name sacred to the useful and embellishing arts may be applied to the perception and recollection of certain properties in numbers and figures! Oh that I had to learn astrology, or demonology, or school divinity! Oh that I were to pore over Thomas Aquinas, and to adjust the relation of Entity with the two Predicaments, so that I were exempted from this miserable study! 'Discipline' of the mind! Say rather starvation, confinement, torture, annihilation! But it must be. I feel myself becoming a personification of Algebra, a living trigonometrical canon, a walking table of Logarithms . . . My classics must be Woodhouse, and my amusements summing an infinite series. Farewell, and tell Selina and Jane to be thankful that it is not a necessary part of female education to get a headache daily without acquiring one practical truth or beautiful image in return. Again, and with affectionate love to my Father, farewell wishes your most miserable and mathematical son.

(*Letters*, ed. Pinney)

Charles Darwin, who went up to Christ's in 1827, also disliked mathematics and found his interests elsewhere.

I attempted mathematicks, and even went during the summer of 1828 with a private tutor (a very dull man) to Barmouth, but I got on very slowly. The work was repugnant to me, chiefly from my not being able to see any meaning in the early steps in algebra. This impatience was very foolish, and in after years I have deeply regretted that I did not proceed far enough at least to understand something of the great leading principles of mathematicks; for men thus endowed seem to have an extra sense. But I do not believe that I should ever have succeeded beyond a very low grade. With respect to classics I did nothing except attend a few compulsory college lectures, and the attendance was almost nominal.

I was so sickened with lectures at Edinburgh that I did not even attend Sedgwick's eloquent and interesting lectures. Had I done so I should probably have become a geologist earlier than I did. I attended, however, Henslow's lectures on Botany, and liked them much for their extreme clearness, and the admirable illustrations; but I did not study botany. Henslow used to take his pupils, including several of the older members of the University, field excursions, on foot, or in coaches to distant places, or in a barge down the river, and lectured on the rarer plants or animals which were observed. These excursions were delightful.

But no pursuit at Cambridge was followed with nearly so much eagerness or gave me so much pleasure as collecting beetles. It was the mere passion for collecting, for I did not dissect them and rarely compared their external characters with published descriptions, but got them named anyhow. I will give a proof of my zeal: one day on tearing off some old bark, I saw two rare beetles and seized one in each hand; then I saw a third and new kind, which I could not bear to lose, so that I popped the one which I held in my right hand into my mouth. Alas it ejected some intensely acrid fluid, which burnt my tongue so that I was forced to spit the beetle out, which was lost, as well as the third one. I was very successful in collecting and invented two new methods; I employed a labourer to scrape during the winter moss off old trees and place [it] in a large bag, and likewise to collect the rubbish at the bottom of the barges in which reeds are brought from the fens, and thus I got some very rare species. No poet ever felt more delight at seeing his first poem published than I did at seeing in Stephen's 'Illustrations of British Insects' the magic words 'captured by C. Darwin, Esq.'

(*Autobiographical Recollections,* ed. F. Darwin, 1887)

But mathematics was regarded as essential; and even when, in 1824, a classical tripos was instituted, it could only be taken after passing the mathematical honours examination (except for noblemen and Kingsmen).

Whewell wrote to Archdeacon Hare:

I do not want *much* mathematics from them, but a man who either cannot or will not understand Euclid, is a man whom we lose nothing by not keeping among us.

It was indeed enjoyed by some. Sir Frederick Pollock, Senior Wrangler in 1806:

I fell in love with the cone and its sections, and everything about it. I have never forsaken my favourite pursuit; I delighted in such problems as two spheres touching each other and also the inside of a hollow cone.

(Rouse Ball, *Cambridge Papers*)

But all examinations were taxing. Macaulay after his Fellowship examinations:

3 Oct. 1821

The last three weeks have been, till within a few days, a continued series of petty indispositions, mortifying accidents, tormenting anxieties, sleepless nights, and days of nervous depression. With a feverish body and a harassed mind, I have been compelled to go through an examination which required great mental and great corporeal exertion. Success, distinction, and the kindness of my friends here have restored my cheerfulness. Calomel, flannel and fine weather have dispelled my maladies. But I am still weak; and pant, like a slave in a mine, for liberty, rest, and fresh air.

and Richard Monckton Milnes after a Tripos paper in 1829:

Thank heaven the examination is over, and the result is just what I expected, though from causes I hardly anticipated. I had been reading very hard before it, but found when I got a paper before me, that I could indeed write down what I had got by heart; but as for thinking, and deducing, and collecting my scattered knowledge, it was perfectly useless. I was so nervous and agitated, that it was a great exertion even to write down anything *memoriter* accurately, and as it happened, hardly anything that I could do so was set. It was much the same on the second day, but I still hoped I should do tolerably in my differential, and I sat up nearly all the preceding night getting it up. It came on in the afternoon, when, what with fatigue (I had written for four hours incessantly in the morning) and the heat of the hall, I soon became excessively faint and giddy, and could hardly see before me. My agitation increased every moment, and I went out for some minutes, hoping to collect myself. When I returned it was all in vain, and when, after trying some very simple things, I found even my memory quite gone, I lost all self-possession, and rushed out of the hall in a most miserable state, and cried myself to sleep on my sofa.

(from Reid, *Milnes: Life*)

There were worse casualties:

Mon. 7 January 1839.   Last night a hurricane . . . A stack of Chimnies was blown down at Magdal. into the sitting room of Mr. Spinks just as he had gone to bed: – he became so nervous in conseqce that he could not go into the Exn for degrees wch began today: – I refunded his fees to him . . .
Tu. 20 Oct. 1840 . . .   Last night an unfortunate young man (Holman Cath) was plucked at the Little Go & destroyed himself with Laudanum.

(Romilly, *Diary*, ed. Bury)

Despite Macaulay's horror of mathematics, Cambridge was a delight to him, especially Trinity:

24 Jan 1841

Of all the titles which I have a right to add to my name that of late Fellow of Trinity is the one of which I am proudest.

(To Joseph Edleston, Fellow and Bursar of Trinity)

1 Dec 1856

I wish from the bottom of my soul that Milton had been a Trinity man. But, as his parents were so stupid and perverse as to send him to Christ's, I must admit that your arguments against putting up a statue of him in our Chapel are of great weight.

(To William Whewell)

When on a visit to Lord Lansdowne at Bowood, years after they had left Cambridge, Austin and Macaulay happened to get upon college topics one morning at breakfast. When the meal was finished they drew their chairs to either end of the chimney-piece, and talked at each other across the hearthrug as if they were in a first-floor room in the Old Court of Trinity. The whole company, ladies, artists, politicians, and diners-out, formed a silent circle round the two Cantabs, and, with a short break for lunch, never stirred till the bell warned them that it was time to dress for dinner.

(G. O. Trevelyan, *Life and Letters of Lord Macaulay*, 1876)

This enthusiasm was shared by those who wrote about the colleges and those who came to enjoy them.

Trinity

The walk along the north side is completely covered from the sun by a row of exceedingly noble chestnut-trees, which have, of late years, suffered much from age and rough weather. The western gateway of the New Court leads, over an elegant stone bridge with cycloidal arches, the work of the well-known James Essex, along an avenue of lime-trees, whose branches, at a great elevation, intersect and form, as it were, a gateway of light open iron-work, and in the distance is seen the steeple of the village of Coton. It was the prospect along this walk, that the witty critic, Porson, compared to a college fellowship, which, he said, was a long dreary road, with a church in the distance.

(John Le Keux, *Memorials of Cambridge*, 1841)

George Dyer, historian of the University, describes Cambridge as he knew it:

Queens': in the fellows' garden were formerly espaliers, now removed, and its present appearance, it being open, and consisting principally of a kitchen garden, looks, perhaps, more like a country, than a college garden. An *improver*, perhaps, might say, give those strait walks a more curving direction, and plant them round with a shrubbery; beat down that brick wall, and exchange it for palisades, or an iron fence railing, that there may be some sort of connection between garden and grove: perhaps a poet or a painter, without too much fondness for the petit embellishments, the architecture of gardening, or taking a receipt, how to awaken by the scenery on a small spot, a *sublime melancholy*, might wish a little done here: but be it recollected, that Queen's has been rather famous for mathematicians and divines, than poets; and it has been observed, that mathematicians and divines are apt to walk in straight lines, and poets in curves, as the former are apt to be more uniform and regular in their literary pursuits than the latter.

Emmanuel: as a building, it is elegant, without being frivolous, and varied, without being crowded.

Jesus gardens though they contain but little of shrubbery, they are, at least, the best fruit gardens in the university . . . in the fellows' garden is a good proportion of flowers and plants, which, to assist the botanical student, are marked with their scientific names, according to the system of Linnaeus.

Sidney Sussex: here is a good garden, an admirable bowling-green, a beautiful summer-house, at the back of which is a walk, agreeably winding, with a variety of trees and shrubs intertwining, and forming, the whole length, a fine canopy overhead; with nothing but singing, and fragrance, and seclusion: a delightful summer retreat; the sweetest lover's or poet's walk, perhaps, in the University.

King's: this college attracts the notice of strangers beyond most.

(George Dyer, A History of the University,
1814)

Charles Lamb, a great friend of Dyer's, loved coming to Cambridge with his sister Mary, who writes in 1815:

In my life I never spent so many pleasant hours together as I did at Cambridge. We were walking the whole time, – out of one College into the other. If you ask me which I like best I must make such an answer as your little two year old girl would, being the traditional unoffending reply to all curious enquirers – 'Both'. I liked them all best. The little gloomy ones because they were little gloomy ones. I felt as if I could live and die in them – and never speak again . . . I certainly liked, St. John's College best . . . I got up at six o'clock and wandered into it by myself – by myself indeed for there was nothing alive but one cat who followed me all about.

(Letters of Charles and Mary Lamb, ed.
Edwin W. Marrs, 1978)

Lamb enjoyed a present from a college kitchen once:

You knew Dick Hopkins the swearing Scullion of Caius'? This fellow by industry and agility has thrust himself into the important situations (no sinecures believe me) of Cook to Trinity Hall & Caius College: and the generous creature has contrived with the greatest delicacy imaginable to send me a present of Cambridge Brawn. Richard knew my blind side when he pitched upon Brawn. Tis of all my hobbies the supreme in the eating way. He might have sent, sops from the pan, skimmings, crumplets, chips, hog's lard, the tender brown judiciously scalped from a fillet of veal (dextrously replaced by a salamander) the tops of asparagus, fugitive livers, runaway gizzards of fowls, the eyes of martyr'd Pigs, tender effusions of laxative woodcocks, the red spawn of lobsters, leveret's ears, and such pretty filchings common to cooks: but these had been ordinary presents, the every-day courtesies of Dish-washers to their sweethearts. Brawn was a noble thought. It is not every common Gullet-fancier than can properly esteem of it. It is like a picture of one of the choice old Italian masters. It's gusto is of that hidden sort.

(Letter to Manning, 1805)

Maria Edgeworth came too:

1 May 1813

In Sidney College we found your friend in neat, cheerful rooms, with orange-fringed curtains, pretty drawings and prints: breakfast-table as plentifully prepared as you could have it – tea, coffee, tongue, cold beef, exquisite bread, and many inches of butter ... All the butter in Cambridge must be stretched into rolls a yard in length and an inch in diameter, and these are sold by inches, and measured out by compasses, in a truly mathematical manner, worthy of a university ...

Went into Trinity College Library: beautiful! I liked the glass doors opening to the gardens at the end, and trees in full leaf ...

Shockingly windy walk: thought my brains would have been blown out.

Professor Farish, newly that day elected Professor of Natural Philosophy had dinner with them.

The bells were ringing in honour of Professor Farish's election, or, as Mr. Smedley said, at the Professor's expense. Farish insisted upon it very coolly that they were not ringing for him, but for a shoulder of mutton.

'A shoulder of mutton? What do you mean?'

'Why, a man left to the University a shoulder of mutton for every Thursday, on condition that the bells should always ring for him on that day.'

(*Life and Letters*, ed. by Augustus J. C. Hare, 1894)

Farish, of Magdalene, Senior Wrangler at the age of 19, was a distinguished and inventive man, but very absent-minded:

One of his ingenious contrivances is still in existence. It consisted of a movable partition which could be screwed up and down, so as to convert a large bedroom into two separate rooms when two guests were on a visit. Tradition has it that with his usual absence of mind he one night proceeded to remove the partition when both rooms were occupied, one by a lady and the other by a gentleman.

On one occasion when his servant brought his horse to the door (of Merton House) he mounted it, and to the surprise of his servant, dismounted it again on the other side and walked quietly away, till the shouts of his servant brought him back again.

(John Venn, *Annals of a Clerical Family*, 1904)

Another, but quite different, eccentric of the time was William Pugh of Trinity:

Soon after he became a Fellow [c. 1796], he was applied to by Dr. Farmer to make a catalogue of the books in the University Library, for which his acquaintance with various languages, and his habits of intense application, particularly qualified him. He almost lived in the Library, and so absorbed did he appear in his occupation that he occasionally forgot his dinner.

The Librarian, from time to time, advanced him money on account without hesitation, not doubting but that he had earned more than he applied for. At length Dr. Farmer expressed a wish to see what progress he had made in the catalogue, when he discovered to his great astonishment that very little had been done; and no wonder, for it appeared, whenever he came to a work with which he was unacquainted, he was not content with looking at the title-page, but applied himself to reading the contents.

(Gunning, *Reminiscences*)

Possibly because of his dismissal, oddities began to appear:

he dreaded the society of everybody; he never left his room for any purpose whatever; he would not let his bedmaker enter it: but used, at a stated hour every day, to open the door a little, take in his breakfast, and slam it to again. One morning, very early, he was seen by the porter walking across the court in a mistrustful manner, looking behind him and to the right and left with the utmost circumspection . . . On his shoulders he carried a large, white bundle. This he was seen to carry to the terrace overlooking the river, and then pitch it over. Some one made search for it and fished it up. On opening it, it was found to contain all his dirty linen and everything which had become too foul to be endured longer; so he put them all in a table cloth and pitched them into the Cam.

(Cambridge Papers – Squibs and Crackers,
collected by J. W. Clark, 1939)

For a time he was expelled but returned to the college and lived a studious and useful life.

'Maps' Nicholson flourished at this time:

Mr. John Nicholson, formerly a well-known bookseller in Cambridge (a full-length portrait of whom, painted by Reinagle, hangs in the entrance to the public library), originally hawked *prints* and *maps* round the colleges for sale, and it was his custom to bawl at the entrance to the staircases which led to the

19. Rowlandson's cartoon of the Old University Library, 1800

20. 'Maps' Nicholson, 1790 (by A. Reinagle)

rooms where the students kept, 'Maps!' From this circumstance he was, by the gownsmen, so named.

(Facetiae Cantabrigiensis, by Socius)

> *Two giants dominated the university both in the manner of their lives and the nature of their ideas, heralding and influencing the Victorian age and adding to its mythology. One was Charles Simeon, who was born in 1759, went to Eton and became a scholar of King's in 1778. He describes in a Memoir what happened to him on arrival:*

It was but the third day after my arrival that I understood I should be expected in the space of about three weeks to attend the Lord's Supper. What! said I, *must* I attend? On being informed that I *must*, the thought rushed into my mind that Satan himself was as fit to attend as I; and that if I must attend, I must *prepare* for my attendance there. Without a moment's loss of time, I bought the old *Whole Duty of Man* (the only religious book that I ever heard of) and began to read it.

(Memoirs, ed. W. Carus and R. Carter, 1847)

> *From then on he became a convinced Evangelical. Even so, his influence on Cambridge would have been non-existent had the vicar of Trinity Church not died just as Simeon was leaving Cambridge in 1782 and had he not, largely by influence, been appointed to succeed. After initial opposition from the congregation, he filled the church at his sermons, mostly with undergraduates, soon to be called 'Simeonites' or 'Sims'.*

An undergraduate view:

P. Riding to the Gogmagogs to-day I fell foul of old Simeon. The gay old cushion-thumper was amusing himself with leaping over the ditches. He's as good a horseman as a preacher, and that's saying much for his jockeyship; for much as he's sneered at for his works of supererogation – for his evangelization, he's the most powerful expositor and advocate I have ever heard. But, as I was saying, he was leaping, and making his servant follow him. One, however, which he took, the servant dared not attempt, at which the fine old fellow roared out, 'You cowardly dog, why don't you follow?' . . .

But much as I like old Simeon, the Simeonites I hate indiscriminately, as I do all serpents . . .

M. Well, what have they done?

P. Bitching with me one evening, they won't pollute their holy lips with stronger waters than tea, mind ye – when I *kept* over the Queen's Gate, they discovered the important fact, that the snobs and snobbesses are in the habit of making love in that sequestered spot, Trinity-lane, and immediately under my window. Now, to put down this crying sin (for such they deem 'all love unknown to Pa and Ma'), they collected all the slops about my rooms, and poured it ruthlessly forth upon a happy pair, who that moment, were doubtless naming the wedding day.

(Wright, Alma Mater)

21. Charles Simeon, the preacher, 1828 (silhouette by Edouart)

Magdalene contained several Simeonites. One undergraduate there, Romaine Hervey, kept a diary:

11 Dec 1797. A famous row in the hall which called the attention of the President: it was about guarding the freshmen against Bird, Jerram, Jones etc. [three Evangelical ordinands]; the President had the impudence to ask who attended Simeon's church: and the Master [Dr. Gretton] was heard to growl that he thought there must be something in the air of Magdalene that made men 'Methodists', 'for', said he, 'we have elected Fellows from Clare Hall, from Trinity, and other Colleges, whom we considered to be Anti-methodistical, but in a short time they all became Methodists'.

(*Magdalene College Magazine*, December 1937, article by Charles Smythe)

Simeon's influence remained for some time:

The first boat that Magdalene put on the river in 1828 was called The Tea Kettle owing to the preference that the Simeonites, who abounded in that college, had for tea over ale; so much so that it was alleged that the Cam which

bathed the very walls of the college is said to have been rendered unnavigable
by tea-leaves.

(Wright, *Alma Mater*)

Even the Second Trinity Boat crew was at one time known as Hallelujahs.

Many people disliked Simeon:

My uncle remembered . . . a student coming in one Sunday evening during
service, and at a momentary pause opening the door and shouting out, 'Charley!'
in a way which completely disturbed the preacher. They would also come in
after their wine, stroll up the aisle and deliberately stare at him.

(Venn, *Annals*)

Simeon's chief legacy was a way of life:

6 Park Street
22 October 1832

I went last night, with several more, to Mr. Carus's rooms, where about 25 or
30 were assembled. We sit round, and tea is brought, Mr. Carus being the chief
speaker. And before we left he read a chapter, and prayed. Our Sunday routine
of duty is to attend chapel at 8 o'clock, the University church at two, where a
sermon only is preached; dinner at 4; and chapel at a quarter past six. This
throws a great deal of vacant time into our hands and it enables those who like
to attend Mr. Simeon's church at a quarter before eleven; which many do.

(Rev. S. Thornton to his mother, in
W. R. Fremantle, *Memoir of Rev. S.
Thornton*, 1850)

There were still a good many Simeonites, or as they were more briefly called
'Sims', in Ernest's time. Every college contained some of them but their
headquarters were at Caius . . . and among the sizars of St. John's.

Behind the then chapel of this last-named college, there was a 'labyrinth'
(this was the name it bore) of dingy, tumble-down rooms, tenanted exclusively
by the poorest undergraduates, who were dependent upon sizarships and
scholarships for the means of taking their degrees. They were rarely seen except
in hall or chapel or at lecture, where their manners of feeding, praying and
studying were considered alike objectionable; no one knew whence they came,
whither they went, nor what they did, for they never showed at cricket or the
boats; they were a gloomy, seedy-looking *confrérie* . . .

Unprepossessing then, in feature, gait and manners, unkempt and ill-dressed
beyond what can be easily described, these poor fellows formed a class apart,
whose thoughts and ways were not as the thoughts and ways of Ernest and his
friends, and it was among them that Simeonism chiefly flourished . . . they
would have meetings in one another's rooms for tea and prayer and other
spiritual exercises. Placing themselves under the guidance of a few well-known
tutors, they would teach in Sunday Schools, and be instant, in season and out
of season, in imparting spiritual instruction to all whom they could persuade to
listen to them.

(Samuel Butler, *The Way of All Flesh*,
1903)

The other giant was William Whewell. Son of a master carpenter of Lancaster, he spoke with a northern burr and was once said to have described Tennyson's northern farmer as a 'wurthless pussonage'. He became Fellow of Trinity in 1824 until he married in 1841. Marriage could have meant the end of his career but in that same year he was made Master of Trinity. A fanatical mathematician, he held his ideas with great firmness:

Universities, so far as they are schools of *general* cultivation, represent the permanent, not the fluctuating elements of human knowledge . . . They ought not, therefore, rapidly or easily to introduce changes into the subjects of their study. They ought to wait till novelties have been well discussed and firmly established, before they adopt them into their elementary course. I am here, of course, not speaking of *professional* education . . . But in that fundamental education, of which I have principally treated, the old ways are not lightly to be abandoned.

(Quoted in M. M. Garland, *Cambridge Before Darwin*, 1980)

Sir Robert Peel disagreed with Whewell in a letter to the Prince Consort:

I think Dr. Whewell is quite wrong in his position – that mathematical knowledge is entitled to *paramount* consideration because it is conversant with indisputable truths – that such departments of science as chemistry are not proper subjects of academic instruction, because there is controversy respecting important facts and principles and constant accession of information from new discoveries – and danger that students may lose their reverence for Professors when they discover that the Professors cannot maintain doctrines as indisputable as mathematical or arithmetical truths. The Doctor's assumption that a *century should pass* before new discoveries in science are admitted into the course of academic instruction, exceeds in absurdity anything which the bitterest enemy of University education would have imputed to its advocates.

(D. A. Winstanley, *Early Victorian Cambridge*, 1940)

There are countless stories about him:

Whewell, when Master, objected in his arbitrary manner to people standing on Trinity Bridge. Seeing an undergraduate one day leaning over its northern parapet he accosted him thus: 'Sir, do you know what this bridge was made for?' The answer he expected was 'To go over it', to which Whewell would retort, 'Then, sir, do so.' But the undergraduate happened to be a Johnian, who promptly replied, 'I understand this bridge was erected to give the public the best possible view of the new buildings of St. John's' . . .

It is a well-authenticated Trinity tradition that Whewell, when Master, jumped up the Hall steps at one leap, a feat that is very seldom accomplished even by youthful athletes. Sir George Young told his son Geoffrey Young that he had actually witnessed this performance; Sir George said that the Master, in cap and gown, found some undergraduates trying in vain to accomplish the feat. He clapped his cap firmly on his head, took the run, and reached the top of the steps in one bound.

There is a story that a well-known pugilist looking at Whewell said, 'What a bruiser was lost when that man became a parson.'

(Trevelyan, Trinity College)

Whewell coined a new word:

We need very much to describe a cultivator of science in general. I should incline to call him a scientist.

(The Philosophy of the Inductive Sciences,
1840)

and inspired comment:

Someone having said of Whewell that his forte was science, 'Yes,' assented Sydney Smith, 'and his foible is omniscience.'

(Isaac Todhunter, William Whewell, 1876)

> Though you through the regions of space should have travelled,
> And of nebular films the remotest unravelled,
> You'll find, though you traverse the bounds of infinity,
> That God's greatest work is – the Master of Trinity.

(Sir Francis Doyle, 1866)

In many of his attitudes he was reactionary. Of the junior fellows who supported radical reforms in 1856:

It is a very sad evening of my College life, to have the College pulled in pieces and ruined by a set of schoolboys. It is very nearly that kind of work. The Act of Parliament gives all our Fellows equal weight for certain purposes, and the younger part of them all vote the same way, and against the Seniors. Several of these juveniles are really boys, several others only Bachelors of Arts, so we have crazy work, as I think it.

And decidedly 'Victorian'. Late in 1855, as Vice-Chancellor, he removed some pictures from the Fitzwilliam Museum and wrote:

The exhibition of nude figures in a public gallery is always a matter of some embarrassment. Even when the gallery is visited by those only who are habituated to regard merely the pictorial interest of such objects, they ought not, it would seem, to be obtruded on the eye of the visitor. But since in recent times we have opened the Fitzwilliam Gallery to the public indiscriminately, and to very young persons of both sexes, it appears to be quite necessary for the credit of the University that it should be possible to pass through the gallery without looking at such pictures, and therefore they should not be in prominent places in the large room by which the spectator enters.

There was a row. Thomas Worsley, Master of Downing, who was mostly responsible for hanging the pictures, wrote in January 1856:

I am informed that you have given orders for the entire subversion of the existing arrangement of the pictures, and for their entire rearrangement on your own single authority, and without the consent, or even the privity, of the Management Syndicate.

[197]

that the Fitzwilliam Syndicate should consist of the Vice-Chancellor and 8 elected members and should 'provide for the care of the collection, and . . . make arrangements for the placing of the various articles at any time composing it'.

(Winstanley, *Early Victorian Cambridge*)

March 1866. Apropos of accidents, poor Dr. Whewell was thrown from his horse, fell upon his head, and, after living for ten days, died . . . Poor old Whistle! You will recollect that his equitation was a standing joke; he was notoriously the worst horseman in the University or out of it. He was certainly the embodiment of a Trinity man. Lightfoot, who was in the year below us, and who is now Regius Professor of Divinity, preached Whewell's funeral sermon last Sunday in the College Chapel, and told some interesting traits of our old master . . . how he loved his college, how he spent large sums of money in adding a hostel to it, how he thought the blue sky had a brighter blue in his eyes when seen bounded by the walls of the Great Court . . . He never won the affections of us undergraduates, but we were all proud of him.

(Sir William Hardman, *The Hardman Papers, a Further Selection* ed. S. M. Ellis, 1930)

G. M. Trevelyan sums up:

Those who were classics first and foremost came from the south; the northerners, Adam Sedgwick and Whewell, were the mathematicians, and were destined to give to the physical sciences their importance in modern Cambridge. But all were men of the twofold learning, classical and mathematical. Their minds were therefore very different from those of their contemporaries on the Isis, who were indeed classical scholars, but were soaking the other half of their minds not in mathematics but in patristic theology. And so, ere long, Oxford gave England the Oxford Movement, and Cambridge helped to give her science.

(*Trinity College*)

Tennyson's sojourn in Trinity (he left in 1831 without taking a degree) coincided with the emergence and flowering of two important societies: the Union and the Cambridge Conversazione Society, known as the Apostles and, later, as the Society. Both encapsulated a new and fashionable seriousness and were characterised by liveliness and camaraderie.

Tennyson did not take happily to Cambridge. In his second term he wrote to his aunt:

I am sitting owl-like and solitary in my rooms (nothing between me and the stars but a stratum of tiles). The hoof of the steed, the roll of the wheel, the shouts of drunken Gown and drunken Town come up from below with a sea-like murmur. I wish to heaven I had Prince Hussain's fairy carpet to transport me along the deeps of air to your coterie. Nay, I would even take up with his brother Aboul-something's glass for the mere pleasure of a peep. What a pity it is that the golden days of Faerie are over! What a misery not to be able to consolidate our gossamer dreams into reality! . . . When, dearest Aunt, may I hope to see you again? I know not how it is, but I feel isolated here in the midst of society. The country is so disgustingly level, the revelry of the place so monotonous, the studies of the University so uninteresting, so much matter of fact. None but dry-headed, calculating, angular little gentlemen can take such delight in $a + \sqrt{b}$, etc . . .

Mathematics was not Tennyson's strong suit:

Whewell, who was his tutor, he called 'the lion-like man', and had for him a great respect. It is reported that Whewell, recognizing his genius, tolerated in him certain informalities which he would not have overlooked in other men. Thus, 'Mr. Tennyson, what's the compound interest of a penny put out at the Christian era up to the present time?' was Whewell's good-natured call to attention in the Lecture Room while my father was reading Virgil under the desk.

The interests of the Apostles were more to his liking; though he was only a 'fringe' member, they all cherished their poet:

These friends not only debated on politics but read their Hobbes, Locke, Berkeley, Butler, Hume, Bentham, Descartes and Kant, and discussed such questions as the Origin of Evil, the Derivation of Moral Sentiments, Prayer and Personality of God . . . Three questions discussed by the Society were: (1) Have Shelley's poems an immoral tendency? Tennyson votes 'No'. (2) Is an intelligible First Cause deducible from the phenomena of the Universe? Tennyson votes 'No'. (3) Is there any rule of moral action beyond general expediency? Tennyson votes 'Aye'.

I have a note to my father from Tennant saying: 'Last Saturday we had an Apostolic dinner when we had the honour, among other things, of drinking your health. Edmund Lushington and I went away tolerably early; but most of them stayed till past two. John Heath volunteered a song; Kemble got into a passion about nothing but quickly jumped out again; Blakesley was afraid the Proctor might come in; and Thompson poured large quantities of salt upon Douglas Heath's head because he talked nonsense.'

(Hallam Lord Tennyson, *Tennyson: A Memoir*, 1899)

The real founder of the Apostles was F. D. Maurice, who was first at Trinity and then Trinity Hall from 1823 to 1827 and returned to Cambridge later as Professor of Moral Philosophy:

The effect which he has produced on the minds of many in Cambridge by the single creation of that society of 'Apostles' (for the spirit if not the form was created by him) is far greater than I dare to calculate, and will be felt, both directly and indirectly, in the age that is upon us.

(Arthur Hallam to Gladstone)

John Sterling, also of Trinity Hall, wrote:

Commend me to the brethren, who, I trust, are waxing daily in religion and radicalism.

(both letters quoted in Hallam Lord Tennyson, *Tennyson: A Memoir*)

To my *education* given in that society I feel that I owe every power I possess, and the rescuing myself from a ridiculous state of prejudice and prepossessions with which I came armed to Cambridge. From 'the Apostles' I, at least, learned to think as a free man.

> (Quoted in R. B. Martin, *Tennyson: The Unquiet Heart*, 1980)

In the summer of 1830, Tennyson with his great friend Arthur Hallam made a leisurely journey to the Pyrenees to hand over money and coded messages to Spanish revolutionaries. (This Cambridge and English involvement in an abortive insurrection was ended disastrously in Malaga a year later.)

Arthur Hallam wrote to Tennyson in October 1830:

I cannot find that my adventures have produced quite the favourable impression on my father's mind that his letter gave me to expect. I don't mean that he blames me at all; but his odd notions about the University begin to revive, and he does not quite seem to comprehend, that after helping to revolutionize kingdoms, one is still less inclined than before to trouble one's head about scholarships, degree and such gear. Sometimes I sigh to be again in the ferment of minds, and stir of events, which is now the portion of other countries. I wish I could be useful; but to be a fly on that great wheel would be something.

> (Hallam Lord Tennyson, *Tennyson: A Memoir*)

Later in 1830, the year of the Reform Bill, there were riots in the Michaelmas term, special constables were sworn in, and the Apostles prepared for action. James Spedding describes the preparation:

Blakesley is Captain of Poets and Metaphysicians, – & visions of broken heads and arms, scythes and pitchforks disturbed the purity of our unselfish contemplations and the idealism of our poetical imaginings. But the threatened army did not make the threatened attack; and our heads are still sound to talk nonsense and metaphysics; very much to my satisfaction and the disappointment of the more adventurous spirits among us.

> (Martin, *The Unquiet Heart*)

Tennyson commemorated the Apostles in 'In Memoriam', written in memory of Arthur Hallam:

> Up that long walk of limes I past
> To see the rooms in which he dwelt . . .
>
> Where once we held debate, a band
> Of youthful friends, on mind and art,
> And labour, and the changing mart,
> And all the framework of the land;
>
> When one would aim an arrow fair,
> But send it slackly from the string;
> And one would pierce an outer ring,
> And one an inner, here and there;

And last the master-bowman, he
Would cleave the mark. A willing ear
We lent him. Who, but hung to hear
The rapt oration flowing free

From point to point, with power and grace
And music in the bounds of law,
To those conclusions when we saw
The God within him light his face,

And seem to lift the form, and glow
In azure orbits heavenly-wise;
And over those ethereal eyes
The bar of Michael Angelo.

The first debate of the Union Society was held on 20 February 1815:

in a low, ill-ventilated, ill-lit apartment at the back of the Red Lion Inn –
cavernous, tavernous – something between a commercial room and a district
branch meeting house.

(Reid, *Milnes: Life*)

*Political matters being in the early days forbidden, some of the subjects of
debate were:*

1824. Do theatrical entertainments tend to improve the morals of the people?
(carried 88 to 31)
1829. Has the spirit of Shelley's poetry been beneficial to mankind? (defeated
30 to 19)

(*Union Minute Book*)

*In 1829 a debate against Oxford was held at Oxford on Cambridge's motion
that, 'Mr. Shelley was a greater poet than Lord Byron.' Monckton Milnes
(later Lord Houghton) was deputed to obtain an 'Exeat' from Dr. Wordsworth, the Master of Trinity.*

I have always had a dim suspicion – though probably I did not do so – that I
substituted the name of Wordsworth for Shelley. Nevertheless, I so wrapped up
in my language the definition of our object – which was mainly, as I put it, the
destruction of the wicked influence of Lord Byron – as to make Dr. Wordsworth
believe that what we intended to substitute for Byron was not Shelley, but
Wordsworth . . .

(Lord Houghton, *Some Writings and
Speeches*, 1888)

So, with the full permission of the authorities, we went to Oxford – in those days
a long, dreary post-chaise* journey of ten hours – and we were hospitably entertained by Milnes Gaskell . . . and by a young student of the name of Gladstone
. . . we were much shocked, and our vanity was not a little wounded, to find that
nobody at Oxford knew anything about Mr. Shelley.

(Reid, *Milnes: Life*)

* By what was then called the Pluck Coach, so called because the 'plucked' men of
Cambridge used to go by coach to seek better luck at Oxford.

*Edward Bulwer, later Lord Lytton, first at Trinity, then at Trinity Hall in
1821, describes Macaulay:*

the greatest display of eloquence I ever witnessed at the Club was made by a
man some years our senior . . . The first of these speeches was on the French
Revolution; and it still lingers in my recollection as the most heart-stirring effort
of that true oratory which seizes hold of the passions, transports you from
yourself . . . During these visits to Cambridge, I became acquainted with
Macaulay. I remember well walking with him, Praed, Ord, and some others of
the set, along the College Gardens; listening with wonder to that full and
opulent converse, startled by knowledge so various, memory so prodigious. That
walk left me in a fever of emulation. I shut myself up for many days in intense
study, striving to grasp at an equal knowledge.

(Edward Lytton, *Life, Letters*)

Praed on Macaulay:

Then the favourite comes, with his trumpet and drums,
And his arms and his metaphors crossed;

(W. M. Praed, *The Union in 1823*)

Thackeray on himself:

Trin: Coll: Cam:
Sunday night. 22 March 1829

Monday. I have made a fool of myself! – I have rendered myself a public
character, I have exposed myself – how? I spouted at the Union. I do not know
what evil star reigns to day or what malignant daemon could prompt me to such
an act of folly – but however up I got, & blustered & blundered, & retracted, &
stuttered upon the character of Napoleon. Carne had just been speaking before
me and went on in a fluent & easy manner but it was all flam – as for me I got
up & stuck in the mud at the first footstep then in endeavoring to extract myself
from my dilemma, I went deeper and deeper still, till at last with one desperate
sentence to wit that 'Napoleon as a Captain, a Lawgiver, and a King merited &
received the esteem & gratitude & affection of the French Nation.' I rushed out
of the quagmire into wh. I had so foolishly plunged myself & sat down like
Lucifer never to rise again with open mouth in that august assembly – So much
for the Union –

(Percy Cradock, *Recollections of the
Cambridge Union*, 1953)

Lytton on Praed, the darling of the Union:

The quickest and easiest debater in the Union; carrying everywhere into our
private circles a petulant yet graceful vivacity . . . passionately fond of dancing;
never missing a ball, though it were the night before an examination . . .

What the last news? – the medal Praed has won;
What the last joke? – Praed's epigram or pun;
And every week that club-room, famous then,
Where striplings settled questions spoilt by men,

When grand Macaulay sat triumphant down,
Heard Praed reply, and long'd to halve the crown.

(poem from St. Stephen's, quoted in
Edward Lytton, *Life, Letters*)

(Praed died at the age of 36.)

Recurrent challenge to the obligation of subscription to the thirty-nine Articles before being allowed to take a degree (a non-subscriber – Dissenter, Roman Catholic, Jew etc. – was not prevented from being a member of a college which accepted him, unlike at Oxford where subscription was required at matriculation) was accompanied by a revolt against compulsory chapel. Connop Thirlwall, then Fellow of Trinity, proposed that chapel attendance should be voluntary:

The epithet compulsory applied to religion appears to me contradictory, the difference between a compulsory religion and no religion at all is too subtle for my grasp.

He was deprived of his fellowship and went to the important living of Kirkby-under-Dale in 1834 and later became Bishop of St. David's. The rules were stiffened in 1838:

Agreed that . . . all Undergraduate Scholars, and Foundation Sizars do attend Chapel eight times at the least in every week, that is twice on Sundays and once every other day; the Scholars on pain of losing *ipso facto* their statutable allowance for Commons, and such additions as have since been made by the College in the way of augmentation to the Commons, for every week when there has been a failure of such attendance.

There was a scale of punishments, culminating in being sent down. A deputation of undergraduates remonstrated and were unwisely told that their attendance was a privilege, appreciated most by those who were oldest. This led to the formation of a Society for the Protection of Cruelty to Undergraduates, who kept a register of attendance of the dons. These marking-sheets were regularly printed and circulated. Bulletins were issued:

The Society regret much that during the last week great laxity has prevailed among the Fellows in general with regard to their attendance in Chapel. This is the more to be lamented, as they had been for the previous two weeks so much more regular than usual. This irregularity cannot proceed from ill health, for they have been constantly to Hall, although they are not compelled to go there more than five times in each week. The Society, however, still hopes that in the ensuing week they will be able to make a more favourable report . . . As was before stated, any Fellow who shall, owing to any wine-party, or other sufficient reason, be prevented from attending, will be excused on sending a note previously to the Secretary of the Society.

The examination of the Fellows is now finished: and in arranging the different classes the Secretary has attached to each person's name his number of marks, in order to do away with any appearance of favour shown more to one than another, as is too often the case in other Examinations . . .

The Prize Medal for regular attendance at chapel and good conduct when there, has been awarded to Mr. Perry, who has passed an examination highly creditable to himself and family. He was only 18 marks below the highest number which he could possibly have gained . . . In consequence of the New Agreement the Chapel Lists will be discontinued in future.

(Rouse Ball, *Cambridge Papers*)

But the university establishment was still busy with ancient rite and ceremonial, such as in the appointment and installation of a new Chancellor, and in the next decade receiving their new Queen:

December 1834

Sat. 13. At 11 we went to the Thatched House drest in our cassocks & full academic costume . . . The form of Installation was exceedingly well conducted, as the Vice-Ch. spoke remarkably well & the Chancellor elect read his letter of thanks with much feeling. I did not much like the Orator's speech in Latin as it represented the Univy in a state of perfection: to be sure there were some slight defects; for example: Gunning when he had to swear the Marquis could not get his glove off & was obliged to put the oath-board in his mouth and tug away with the other hand: it was in vain, & Crouch came up to the rescue: Gunning's hood also was awfully dirty & the string tied in knots: it was scarcely decorous on such an occasion: And in spite of all the rehearsals that I gave Potter he made most pottering work of reading the Patent . . . We departed about 2. – At 3 we got into the carriage to return to Camb . . . It was very cold as it froze sharply – We reached Camb. at 10 & ate a pheasant at Philpott's: Hopkins like a good husband went home at once –

and the installation in July 1835:

Sun. 5 . . . Much plagued with applicants for tickets. Cuthb. and I went to St. Mary's where there was a very bad sermon from that great fool Dr. Foord Bowes: it was a Commem. of Benefrs & the whole affair was insuffy long, particy as we were standing & the weather was hot. (We slipped out during the Communion & returned again for the Anthem . . .) We then went to Kings Chapel: the admission tickets were very limited today & that beast Hinde would not give me one . . .

Tu. 7 . . . the whole S. House was crammed to suffocation . . . The impatience of the people was extreme & the conduct of the young men . . . disgraceful in the extreme. They proposed a howl for the present ministry, 3 groans for Ld. J. Russell & others of the ministry, & at the end of the day called for 'God save the King' & interrupted it at 'Confound their knavish tricks' to give a round of applause . . . many persons fainted away, the men in far greater numbers than the women.

Th. 9 . . . The grand Public Breakfast in Trinity Cloisters today . . . There was a grand tent in the middle of the grass of Nevile's Court for a Band . . . Tables were set up round the 3 inclosed sides of N's Ct., the left (or South) was for solid viands, the right (or North) was for jellies, ice, fruits etc.

(Romilly, Diary, ed. Bury)

Romilly cast a cold eye too on peacocks and fellow-commoners:

April 1836
Tu. 26 . . . Long Seniority today at wch we past sentence of expulsion on the Peacocks for the intolerable screeching they make, & rejected the Protest of the Noblemen & F.C. on the new order of not walking over the Grass.

Victoriana

In 1843 the Queen and Prince Albert made the first of several visits.
A lady in waiting, The Hon. Eleanor Stanley, writes:

The students inside were sometimes difficult enough to keep back, and when it came to the common people in the streets, even the Scots Greys escort, making their horses prance in every direction, with their swords drawn, had great difficulty in keeping any sort of passage for her, though the crowd was very quiet and orderly, and cheered immensely. The gownsmen took it into their heads to show loyalty by throwing down their gowns on every occasion for the Queen to walk upon, but, as they did not like us to tread upon them, it was really a service of danger following her, tripping up every moment upon these. At the Senate House, where the Prince was to have the degree of D. of Laws conferred upon him, there were, as usual, when royalty are concerned, loads of mistakes; the Queen and he came ten minutes sooner than was expected, they having taken a punctual fit, so that there were no oaths ready, and the Vice-Chancellor administered the oaths from memory, and of course forgot half and boggled the rest; there was no Bible, to swear upon, and I do not know where they would have got one if Lord Arthur Hervey had not had a little Church service in his pocket.

(Mrs. Stewart Erskine, Twenty Years at Court)

'Punch' reports, November 1843:

Directly it was known that Her Majesty intended going to Cambridge, and that Prince Albert was to be made a Doctor of Civil Law, Punch felt that his presence would be expected at the University . . . we were certain that his Royal Highness would establish his claim to the beefeater's hat and crimson dressing-gown, which form the academical costume of a legal doctor . . .

When His Royal Highness was led out to be made a Doctor of, Crick, the public orator, immediately commenced a long tirade in Latin . . . The oration

22. The Queen leaving the Senate House, 1843 (*The Pictorial Times*)

was annotated by the noise of the mob outside, the braying of a jackass in the west, an occasional burst of juvenile laughter through an open window in the east, and the sudden smash of a pane of glass in the gallery. We did not catch the oration . . . but we heard enough of it to ascertain that Crick was pitching it – what is vulgarly but expressively termed – strong; that he called Albert *praestantem inter praestantissimos*, and that he talked of the University as a place where lucre was abhorred, as a pestilence. For a reverend gentleman on the look-out for a bishoprick, these sentiments were 'pretty well'. The 'heads of houses', who are most of them sensible to Prince's Mixture, or more familiarly speaking, 'up to snuff', winked at each other when the public orator touched on the topic of disinterestedness . . .

The grand ceremony being concluded, the remainder of the day was occupied in running about after the royal couple, who kept popping into their lodgings at Trinity for refreshment, and then popping out again to see some church, museum or library. The Fitzwilliam was made a bonne bouche between luncheon and dinner – a species of intellectual sandwich . . . His Royal Highness observed to the Queen that there were some interesting manuscripts in the library, when her Majesty made a reply at once worthy of the woman, the wife and the sovereign. Her answer . . . was simply this – 'Yes, my dear, but don't stay.'

Four years later Prince Albert was installed as Chancellor:

William Barnes, the Dorset poet, a 'Ten Year Man' up for a term at St. John's, writes to his wife:

By hardship I got into the Senate House today and saw the queen and heard the Installation ode. I have been also to the grounds of Downing College where she walked on within three or four steps of me. This small chat is for the children. I am told there were twenty thousand persons all, of course, well dressed, in the ground together . . .

It is a mercy you have a husband with sound limbs as we have had such a squeeze in Trinity College as you can hardly conceive. Members of the University, up to many hundreds, possibly nearly two thousand, assembled in the outer square to receive the Queen, who arrived soon after one o'clock, and on its being announced that we were to go into the Hall to present our addresses to her, a great rush was made to get in. I went with an impetuous wave that carried everything before it; and in which Doctors with their red robes were pushed into scarecrows, and Masters had their hoods torn off and your worthy admirer got his silver chain broken . . . I got up to the head of the hall near the queen before she withdrew. Our noble old college has appeared in its glory today. We have had two Halls (dinners), one for the pensioners and sizars at four o'clock, and a Fellows' Hall at six, when I sat down to a superb dinner with about 200 sons of our Alma Mater; most of these men come up from the provinces to the Installation . . .

(Giles Dugdale, *William Barnes of Dorset*, 1953)

Queen Victoria writes in her journal:

The evening being so beautiful we proposed to walk out, and accordingly at ten set out in curious costumes: Albert in his dress coat, with a macintosh over it; I in my evening dress and diadem, and with a veil over my head, and the two Princes in their uniform, and the ladies in their dresses, and shawls, and veils. We walked through the small garden, and could not at first find our way, after which we discovered the right road, and walked along the beautiful avenues of lime-trees in the grounds of St. John's College, which is like the Bridge of Sighs at Venice. We stopped to listen to the distant hum of the town; and nothing seemed wanting, but some singing, which everywhere but here in this country we should have heard. A lattice opened, and we could fancy a lady appearing, and listening to a serenade . . .

(David Duff, *Victoria Travels*, 1978)

The Prince Consort did not regard his chancellorship as a sinecure. Conscious of developments in European universities, he was anxious to help bring Cambridge into the modern world and for the University to reform itself without outside interference:

Windsor Castle
14 October 1847

My dear Vice-Chancellor [Dr. Philpott] – Naturally anxious to trace the course of studies and scientific enquiries pursued at Cambridge at this time, I feel desirous of being furnished with a comprehensive table, showing the scheme of tuition in the Colleges separately and the University for the ensuing year. I mean the subjects to be taught in the different Colleges, the authors to be read there, the subjects for examination, those selected for competition and prizes, and the lectures to be given by the different professors in their different branches.

Russell confided his intention of appointing a Royal Commission in November. The Prince, agitated, replied:

Feeling that it was time to move a little in the matter, and at the same time aware of the susceptibility of the academic body and their dread of any innovation, I confined myself to writing a letter to the Vice-Chancellor desiring him to have prepared for me a complete scheme of tuition at Cambridge for the ensuing year ... [Dr. Philpott says] that any innovation tending (as they imagine) to lessen the attention to this science [mathematics] is viewed with the greatest suspicion. Moreover the College tutors and private tutors would not be able to teach or to examine in anything else.

(Theodore Martin, *Life of H.R.H. The Prince Consort*, 1875)

In 1848 some Graces were passed by the Senate leading to moderate reforms. Nevertheless progress seemed slow and in 1850 the appointment of a Royal Commission to enquire into improvements both at Oxford and Cambridge was announced by Lord John Russell, to the Prince's vexation.

The mirror into which the University had long been looking, and which presented such a pleasing picture of a venerable institution, proceeding at its own pace, and unmolested by the State along the path of reform, had cracked from side to side; and those who had so long gazed upon this bewitching vision may be forgiven for thinking in the first shock of disillusionment that the curse had come upon them.

(Winstanley, *Early Victorian Cambridge*)

The decay of Cambridge as a place of learning threatened to overwhelm the university. I believe that for the first half of the century the scholarship and science of Cambridge were a laughing stock on the Continent. Naturally, the dulness of the fellows was in some sort reflected among the undergraduates. There were certain colleges which seemed never to show any intellectual life at all.

In the fifties, the now universal habit of travel was unknown; the lads who came up to Cambridge had seen no other place than the small country town or country village from which they came. They were the sons of country gentlemen, but infinitely more rustic than their grandsons of the present day; they were the sons of the country clergy, well and gently bred, many of them, but profoundly ignorant of the world; they were the sons of manufacturers; they were the sons of professional men; they came from the country grammar school, which had not yet been converted into a public school after the one pattern now enforced; they had gone through the classical mill; they had learned a little mathematics; they played cricket with zeal; they were wholly ignorant of the world, of society, of literature, of everything.

(Sir Walter Besant, *Autobiography*, 1902)

Some reforms were still needed even after the new Statutes. Many fellowships and college offices were still restricted to those in holy orders and it was not until the Test Act of 1871 that such restrictions were abolished.

According to these new statutes there will in future be about 360 Fellowships at Cambridge, and a sum of about 30,000L a year will be annually voted to Scholarships . . . A Dissenter is now permitted to hold a scholarship, but he cannot be elected to a fellowship . . . Many most distinguished students have by this religious disability been excluded from fellowships. Their place has been occupied by men of inferior talents.

(Henry Fawcett in MacMillan's Magazine,
March 1861)

I wandered up and down the King's Parade, watching the tall gables of King's College Chapel, and the classic front of the Senate House, and the stately tower of St. Mary's, as they stood, stern and silent, bathed in the still glory of the moonlight, and contrasting bitterly the lot of those who were educated under their shadow to the lot which had befallen me.

'Noble buildings!' I said to myself, 'and noble institutions; given freely to the people, and the Saviour who died for them. They gave us what they had, those mediaeval founders: whatsoever narrowness of mind or superstition defiled their gift was not their fault, but the fault of their whole age. The best they knew they imparted freely, and God will reward them for it. To monopolise those institutions for the rich, as is done now, is to violate both the spirit and the letter of the foundations . . .

'It is not merely because we are bad churchmen that you exclude us, else you would be crowding your colleges, now, with the talented poor of the agricultural districts, who, as you say, remain faithful to the church of their fathers. But are there six labourers' sons educating in the universities at this moment? No! the real reason for our exclusion, churchmen or not, is, because we are poor.'

(Charles Kingsley, Alton Locke, 1850)

A contrary view had prevailed.

It is a very common practice, however, to send young men to the university, who have no claims but those of poverty to urge, and who are thus forced by the mistaken benevolence of their patrons out of their proper sphere of life, into professions for which they are neither qualified by their habits nor attainments, though the provisions of the ancient statutes would appear in many cases to point out such persons as the proper objects of the bounty of our foundations . . . The very general diffusion of wealth, and the complete graduation of the social rank and condition of the various classes of society . . . which is characteristic of modern times, affords a more than sufficient supply for the learned professions, without the necessity of meeting the demand by a nearly gratuitous education in the university, except in those cases when extraordinary merit and industry constitute a just and honourable claim to encouragement and support.

(Peacock, Observations on Statutes)

There was, however, some measure of general tolerance:

On a certain Degree day in 1850 or thereabouts, a West African undergraduate named Crummell, of Queens', a man of colour, appeared in the Senate House to take his degree. A boisterous individual in the gallery called out, 'Three groans for the Queens' nigger' . . . A pale slim undergraduate . . . shouted in a voice which re-echoed through the building, 'Shame, shame! Three groans for you, Sir!' and immediately afterwards, 'Three cheers for Crummell!' This was taken up in all directions . . . and the original offender had to stoop down to hide himself from the storm of groans and hisses that broke out all around him. [Crummell's champion was E. W. Benson.]

(A. C. Benson, *Life of E. W. Benson, Archbishop of Canterbury*, 1901)

Prince Albert had only fourteen years as Chancellor and it is ironic that a visit to Cambridge to see his son was at least partly the cause of his death in 1861:

Although sleepless, aching all over, and without appetite, on 22 November Albert travelled to Cambridge, and father and son had a serious talk in the country lanes round Madingley. It was to be their last. There had been many sad passages of arms between them, not all Albert's fault by any means, but this time Albert forgave his son and returned home with an easy mind. But he also returned near collapse. Typically, the Prince of Wales had never before been tempted to explore the Cambridge countryside, and was soon completely lost, with the result that he made his sick father walk an unnecessarily long way, again in the rain, thereby draining Albert of his last drop of energy.

(Daphne Bennett, *King Without a Crown*, 1977)

Henry Sidgwick was elected into a fellowship at Trinity at the age of 21 in 1859. A year later he wrote:

Do you know that I am considered at Cambridge to have become irretrievably donnish – probably I am the last person to hear of the fact, and am not the least amused by it – I dare say it is true, and it gives me another inducement to stay up at Cambridge and discover what are the internal arrangements of that being whose external phenomena I have so long gazed at with interest and admiration.

Tolerance and doubt seeped into the system:

1864. I went to Oxford last Saturday and saw William. I enjoyed it excessively! the Sunday was delicious and the intellectual excitement of the conversation there almost fatiguing. Oxford presents a striking contrast to Cambridge in respect of the much greater stir and activity of the intellectual life that is kept up there. It is partly due to the hot controversies that are always raging there, which keep people's minds always thinking; so we have perhaps a compensative advantage in the scholarlike quiet and toleration of Cambridge, where a man may on the whole 'speak the thing he will'.

(Arthur Sidgwick, *A Memoir by A. S. and E. M.*, 1906)

My Cambridge life was cut short by my inability, unfortunate or otherwise, to come to terms with the Thirty-nine Articles. I was not, indeed, cast out by the orthodox indignation of my colleagues. At Cambridge, I have said, there was no bigotry; I was treated with all possible kindness, and for a time continued to reside and to take some part in college work. But I had to resign my tutorship.

(Leslie Stephen, *Some Early Impressions*, 1924)

We are in a considerable state of agitation here, as all sorts of projects of reform are coming to the surface, partly in consequence of having a new master – people begin to stretch themselves and feel a certain freedom and independence ... There is much that needs alteration, as I suspect there is in every old and wealthy Corporation; and it is the merit of Cambridge that though there is in it very little reforming spirit, there is also very little of what Carlyle calls hidebound Toryism; people judge every new proposal really on its own merits – without enthusiasm and without prejudice.

The Apostles reflected this, as Sidgwick recalls:

I can only describe it as the spirit of the pursuit of truth with absolute devotion and unreserve by a group of intimate friends, who were perfectly frank with each other, and indulged in any amount of humorous sarcasm and playful banter, and yet each respects the other, and when he discourses tries to learn from him and see what he sees. Absolute candour was the only duty that the tradition of the society enforced ... The gravest subjects were continually debated, but gravity of treatment, as I have said, was not imposed, though sincerity was. In fact it was rather a point of the apostolic mind to understand how much suggestion and instruction may be derived from what is in form a jest – even in dealing with the gravest matters ...

I had at first been reluctant to enter this society when I was asked to join it. I thought that a standing weekly engagement for a whole evening would interfere with my work for my two Triposes. But after I had gradually apprehended the spirit as I have described it, it came to seem to me that no part of my life at Cambridge was so real to me as the Saturday evenings on which the apostolic debates were held; and the tie of attachment to the society is much the strongest corporate bond which I have known in life. I think, then, that my admission into this society and the enthusiastic way in which I came to idealise it really determined or revealed that the deepest bent of my nature was towards the life of thought – thought exercised on the central problems of human life.

Henry Sidgwick resigned his fellowship in 1869.

To E. W. Benson, 13 June 1869.

The thing is settled. I informed the Seniority that it was my intention to resign my Fellowship at the end of the year, in order to free myself from dogmatic obligations. With great kindness and some (I hope not excessive) boldness they have offered me, on this understanding, the post of lecturer on Moral Sciences (*not* Assistant Tutor), which I have accepted. I do not, as at present advised, intend to secede from the Church of England: I have taken Lightfoot's advice on this point (as a sufficiently unconcerned reasonable orthodox clergyman). I explained to him that, as far as sympathy and goodwill go, I had no wish to secede, but I could not accept the dogmatic obligation of the Apostles' Creed, which *primâ facie* I have bound myself (in confirmation) to accept ...

He remained in Cambridge as a lecturer, devoting much of his time to the project of higher education for women, not just to the theory but to the practical details:

1871 ... I have been detained here by trifling matters connected with the ladies' lectures. We are just now in rather a peculiar position – we have given exhibitions, and induced one or two young persons to come to Cambridge, but the Committee as such does not provide them any accommodation. This is done advisedly, because some of us, though they do not object to girls coming up to Cambridge to attend lectures, yet do not wish formally to encourage them: still less to be responsible for them. The result is that I have semi-officially to make arrangements for the comfort of these persons, or at least to see that no difficulty is thrown in their way by absence of provision.

(A Memoir)

The loss of orthodox faith for Sidgwick and others like F. W. H. Myers was amongst other things responsible for the founding of the Society for Psychical Research, which had great importance for its members:

It must be remembered that this was the very flood-tide of materialism, agnosticism, – the mechanical theory of the Universe, the reduction of all spiritual facts to physiological phenomena ... We were all in the first flush of triumphant Darwinism ...

I believe then that Science is now succeeding in penetrating certain cosmical facts which she has not reached till now. The first is the fact of man's survival of death. The second is the registration in the Universe of every past scene and thought.

(F. W. H. Myers, Fragments of Inner Life, 1961)

1892 On Saturday Nora [his wife] was made Principal of Newnham ... I am doubtful whether she did right in accepting ... I fear that she may not find time for the work of the S.P.R. .... If it turns out that she must sacrifice some of this work, I shall have to take her place; but my intellect will be an inferior substitute for this work, and I shall give up with reluctance the plans of literary work for which I am better fitted. Still, if it must be so, I shall give them up without hesitation, just as I should give them up to fight for my country if it was invaded (by the way, though, I believe I am too old for that).

(Henry Sidgwick, A Memoir)

'The Turban of Proof', 1880:

Like many young men who are discovering themselves and the world, Dickinson wondered whether there may not be a super-normal path to knowledge. He was by no means credulous or unable to sift evidence, and he had taste and humour, so that Esoteric Buddhism could not detain him long, but for about a year he was intrigued with it. 'My idea I believe was that one must first discover absolute standards of good and evil, and then descend to govern mankind.' So he attended the meetings of the Society of Psychical Research to hear Colonel Olcott describe how he had once been visited by a mahatma who had dematerialised through a closed door, but had left his turban behind him as proof. 'And here', said the Colonel passing it round, 'is the turban.' This sort of thing does not go down in Cambridge.

(E. M. Forster, *Goldsworthy Lowes Dickinson*, 1934)

Lady Jebb took a robust view:

the most arrant nonsense and imposture in my mind, but it amuses these great geniuses who think they can see some distance into a mill stone. Henry Sidgwick and Fred Myers . . . are the head of the investigation as they call it, but they both seem as easy to delude and as anxious to believe as any infant.

(Mary R. Bobbitt, *With Dearest Love to All, The Life and Letters of Lady Jebb*, 1960)

Dons and college coaches could work very hard. Leslie Stephen describes Isaac Todhunter, the college coach:

He was a striking case of a man designing a scheme of life and carrying it out systematically. When I was his pupil he was beginning to execute it by living the life of an ascetic recluse. His chief room in St. John's College was devoted to his pupils and furnished only with benches and tables at which we were always scribbling our lucubrations. Two little closets opened out of it, one his bedroom, the other the den where he examined our work. A table and a couple of chairs were the only furniture of the den, and the walls were covered with books, each in a brown paper cover inscribed in exquisite handwriting with the title. The little man with his large head and delicate little hands always reminded me of a mouse, dressed in superlatively neat though certainly not fashionable costume. He laboured from morning till night, taking indeed an hour's constitutional round the so-called 'parallelogram' of footpaths – an essential part of our Cambridge habits – and spending another hour or so upon his dinner in the college hall at four. The rest of the day was devoted to the unremitting labours of teaching and of writing very successful text-books. Some fifteen years of such work enabled him to carry out the plan of life upon which he had resolved. He had saved money enough to give up the drudgery of teaching, married, and wrote books for the learned upon the history of mathematics . . . I can still hear his regular adjuration, 'Push on'.

(*Some Early Impressions*)

The story goes that Todhunter was asked how much time it was morally permissible for a 'hard reading man' to take off in the course of a year. He replied, 'The forenoon of Christmas Day would be in order, gentlemen.'

Giving lectures could be taxing too.

To many people's surprise, Charles Kingsley was appointed Regius Professor of Modern History. Of his inaugural lecture in 1860 he wrote:

I was so dreadfully nervous, I actually cried with fear up in my own room beforehand . . . Had a *very* successful lecture . . . Never spoke better in my life . . . Received 90 cards . . .

Justin McCarthy did not agree:

Rather tall, very angular, surprisingly awkward, with his thin staggering legs, a hatchet face adorned with scraggy whiskers, a faculty for falling into the most ungainly attitudes and making the most hideous contortions of visage and frame; with a rough provincial accent and an uncouth way of speaking which would be set down for caricature on the boards of a theatre . . .

J. R. Seeley of Christ's, who succeeded him in 1875,

did not receive much kinder treatment when he delivered his inaugural lecture. As he left the lecture hall Dr. Thompson [Master of Trinity] declared, 'Dear, dear, who would have thought that we would so soon have been regretting poor Kingsley.'

(Susan Chitty, *The Beast and the Monk*, 1974)

But J. C. Powys, reading history at Corpus Christi, said:

I must confess I was only once really thrilled by any of the university teachers. This was by Professor Seeley, a far-sighted and indeed a rather Goethean person . . . Seeley was already failing in health, and I think he died soon after; but I shall never forget – as he gave one particular lecture on the Athenian way of life – the reverberating unction with which from his seat on the dais, for he was too weak to stand, he uttered the word 'Ecclesia'.

(J. C. Powys, *Autobiography*, 1934)

Professor Newton (1829–1907):

The Professor sat before a reading desk and read every word of his discourse from a MS, written in his minute hand with a broad quill, so that all the letters looked the same, like the Burmese script. At long intervals there was drawn the outline of a tumbler . . . whenever the Professor came to these outlines he religiously took a sip of water.

(A. Shipley, *Cambridge Cameos*, 1924)

Work for examinations was equally taxing and waiting for the results perhaps even more so.

Mixed ability classes:

The 'Little-Go' then occurred just in the middle of our career, and we had in consequence regular and frequent lectures both in classics and mathematics. During the first few terms we had to attend these every day from 9 to 11. So far, good; but what will now seem odd is that we all alike had to attend the same lecture. There was no selection or discrimination . . . the destined high wrangler, who had read his conic sections as a schoolboy, and the youth to whom Euclid and his mysterious pictures were a daily puzzle, sat side by side on the benches of our lecture room, and tried to make the most of the lecture . . . This arrangement . . . was probably one of the worst features in the system.

(Venn, *Early Collegiate Life*)

A victim recalls the cold:

The examination in January, 1840, took place in the Lecture Rooms of Trinity College . . . Complaints of the coldness of the Schools and the Senate-house had long been current, and at that time no attempt had been made to remedy the evil. And the evil was a real one: the cold was in some seasons so intense, that one wonders that the brains of the candidates were not frozen . . . I remember seeing O'Brien, to whom I have already referred as being delicate, so wrapped up in coats and comforters that when he came out of the Schools he looked like an Arctic traveller.

(Harvey Goodwin, A Memoir)

There was much excitement.

Albert Pell in 1839:

In the year I took my degree the usual rivalry between Trinity and St. John's for the Senior Wrangler's place was as keen as ever. Our man was Cayley . . . While the examination was going on in the Senate House a small crowd was frequently in attendance outside by the door, discussing the merits of the examined and waiting to get the latest intelligence of their work. I, among them, went for this purpose, and on a Johnian in our group saying, 'I wonder how our man is getting on', Barstow in a loud, contemptuous voice said he did not know, not did he care, but he could tell him that 'Cayley had finished his papers a quarter of an hour ago, and was now licking his lips for more.'

(Reminiscences, ed. T. Mackay, 1908)

An American at Trinity waits for the result of a scholarship examination in the 1840s:

The examiners . . . meet after chapel to compare results and elect the Scholars. About nine a.m. the new scholars are announced from the chapel gates. On this occasion it is not etiquette for the candidates themselves to be waiting – it looks too 'bumptious'; but their personal friends are sure to be on hand, together with an humbler set concerned – the gyps, coal-men, boot-blacks, and other College servants – who take great interest in the success of their masters, and bet on them to the extent of five shillings and less . . . Just before nine, my coach went off to chapel to wait for the announcement of the result; and I returned to my rooms to superintend breakfast arrangements . . . A long, very long fifteen or twenty minutes elapsed, and then my gyp, first to bring the tidings, rushed in at full trot to assure me that it was all right . . . Soon after, our Plato lecturer, my College tutor, stalked in direct from the scene of action (he had been one of the examiners) in his full academicals, like Tragedy in a gorgeous pall, to tender me his congratulations in a majestic and Don-like manner; and after him Professor Sedgwick.

(C. A. Bristed, Five Years in an English
University, 1873)

For the undergraduate the Victorian scene embraced both the expected and the unexpected; some patterns of life continued as for centuries, but there were new preoccupations.

Sermons continued to attract many. Richard Wilton, in 1847, his first year at St. Catharine's College, writes home:

I shall not soon forget my first Sunday in Cambridge. At 9.30 a.m. we had the full morning service in our chapel. At two we went to Great St. Mary's, the University Church, where the undergraduates are expected to attend, and heard Dr. Christopher Wordsworth preach a sermon 75 minutes in length to prove that the Epistle to the Hebrews was written by St. Paul. He proved his point most conclusively, but most of us would have been content with an argument 50 minutes shorter! The spacious galleries of this noble church were crowded with gownsmen. Opposite the preacher sat the Vice-Chancellor, Dr. Philpott, who is Master of our College, and the other heads of houses in a recess by themselves which men call Golgotha or the place of skulls or heads (of houses!). We then had a short walk in the beautiful grounds behind the colleges along the banks of the Cam and under the rows of magnificent elms. We dined and attended evening chapel and then repaired to St. Mary's again where Mr. Carus preaches on Sunday evenings, and at the conclusion of a delightful service we walked directly to Mr. Carus's rooms in Trinity College.

(Mary Blamire Young, *Richard Wilton*, 1967)

Much was expected. William Cory, master at Eton, writes to F. Warre Cornish, undergraduate at King's in 1858:

I hope [Browning] will not forget to urge upon you the expediency of giving up the piano in your room as a total destroyer of reading.

If you worked five hours a day in term time, besides Lectures, allowing one weekday as a holiday, and gave up two months of the vacations to extra reading in College, or in some rural retreat in England or abroad (only not at home) working seven hours a day all but one weekday, there would remain plenty of time for kinsfolk and acquaintances, for alternative pursuits, such as music, French or drawing, and for (what I am very glad to see you value) active bodily exercise. But I can assure you that habitual dwelling at or near a piano, and standing irresolutely at 11 a.m. and sitting at wine later than 7 p.m., and spending all the immense and absurd vacations at home – all this is incompatible with *high* success.

(*Letters and Journals*, ed. F. W. Cornish, 1897)

The magistrate chastises Ernest Pontifex:

Ernest Pontifex, yours is one of the most painful cases that I have ever had to deal with. You have been singularly favoured in your parentage and education ... At Cambridge you were shielded from impurity by every obstacle which virtuous and vigilant authorities could devise, and even had the obstacles been fewer, your parents probably took care that your means should not admit of your throwing money away upon abandoned characters. At night proctors patrolled the streets and dogged your steps if you tried to go into any haunt where the presence of vice was suspected. By day the females who were admitted within the college walls were selected mainly on the score of age and ugliness.

but cheerfulness kept breaking in, or out, according to disposition:

As I was talking to Ernest one day not so long since he said that . . . Cambridge was the first place where he had ever been consciously and continuously happy.

How can any boy fail to feel an ecstasy of pleasure on first finding himself in rooms which he knows for the next few years are to be his castle? Here he will not be compelled to turn out of the most comfortable place as soon as he has ensconced himself in it because papa or mamma happens to come into the room, and he should give it up to them. The most cosy chair here is for himself, there is no one even to share the room with him, or to interfere with his doing as he likes in it – smoking included. Why, if such a room looked out both back and front on to a blank dead wall it would still be a paradise, how much more than when the view is of some quiet grassy court or cloister or garden.

(Butler, The Way of All Flesh)

Samuel Butler (as opposed to Ernest Pontifex) wrote to his father from St. John's in 1857:

I don't care about beginning small print candle-reading too soon as it seems to try them – Daylight reading does not in the least affect them, so I have been out of bed by a quarter past five every morning lately and into bed by ten at night, get a cup of tea by six in the morning . . . music from one to two and exercise from two to four and music from four to five and dinner at five – I am exceedingly well in every respect but my eyes, and they are mending. This is all about myself but I can think of no more agreeable topic! It is pouring wet, the river is flooded, and Snow says I am to steer at two o'clock, which hour is just on the point of approaching.

(Philip Henderson, Butler, The Incarnate Bachelor, 1953)

Thackeray wrote in 1847:

I wonder what has become of Emily Blades, daughter of Blades, the Professor of the Mandingo language? I remember her shoulders to this day, as she sat in the midst of a crowd of about seventy young gentlemen, from Corpus and Catherine Hall, entertaining them with ogles and French songs on the guitar. Are you married, fair Emily of the shoulders? What beautiful ringlets those were that used to dribble over them! – what a waist! – what a killing sea-green shot-silk gown! – what a cameo, the size of a muffin! There were thirty-six young men of the University in love with Emily Blades: and no words are sufficient to describe the pity, the sorrow, the deep deep commiseration – the rage, fury and uncharitableness, in other words – with which the Miss Trumps (daughters of Trumps, the Professor of Phlebotomy) regarded her, because she *didn't* squint, and because she *wasn't* marked with the small-pox.

(Book of Snobs, 1869)

Joseph Chater, a Cambridge draper's assistant, writes in his diary:

Early March 1846: About half past nine Mr. Blumson came and rapped at the counting house window and told us there was a row between Town and Gown. So we cut out directly, and a rare row there was, just in the Crescent. Four

[217]

23. View from a roof in St. John's College, 1840 (drawing by G. Dodgson)

gownsmen were taken to the Station House. It lasted till eleven. Lord Stamford was one of the leading men, but Tooker of Jesus was taken first. I went to the Station House with him. The last they took had a poker in his hand.

9 March

The four University men were tried this morning at the Town Hall. One was fined £1. o. o., one ten shillings and one 2/6d, and pay their costs. The other was let off. There were a great many people on the Market Hill and the University men vow vengeance to the police tonight. About half past eight the gownsmen assembled in the Rose Crescent to the amount of, as near as I could guess, 300, and from there they paraded the streets till a little after nine; they began to kick up a row; they had tremendous cudgels . . . The Proctors and Masters were all out, but to no purpose . . . the gownsmen threw glass bottles on to the townsmen's heads, and water and stones, which so enraged the townsmen that they went to all the Colleges and smashed the windows to pieces. Christ's have got it worst. There are about 80 panes broken.

3 November 1854

A man intended to give a lecture at the Town Hall against tobacco smoking this evening, but a lot of gownsmen went up and interrupted him and made an uproar, upon which the Mayor went in and dissolved the meeting, which was not effected without blows and three of the gentry being taken into custody.

(Enid Porter, Victorian Cambridge, 1975)

W. E. Heitland of St. John's remembers:

In the election of November 1868 there was a serious row at the meeting of streets near Christ's College. The town roughs had the upper hand and drove back a number of undergraduates. Two Johnians were penned against the gate of Christ's, which had been closed for good reason. The College Porter generously opened the wicket and rescued them from the angry mob. As he was shutting it again, a heavy stone struck him on the head and killed him.

(After Many Years, 1926)

Food and drink were topics of perennial interest.

(*'The Family'*, *possibly of Jacobite origins, deriving from the toast drunk to 'the family over the water', was an élite dining club to which most heads of houses belonged.*)

18 Dec 1834   Dined for the first time at the Family where I have succeeded Thirlwall. We dined at Caius Lodge . . . the dinner and wines were very good, and the Pineapple – I thought the introduction of pipes and spitting boxes most filthy, but as it is the invariable custom, one must bear it . . .

30 Oct 1835   I violated the club rules and gave Champagne which was drunk con amore by my guests. We had a rubber of whist and the company staid much longer than usual. Lodge said it had been by far the best Family he had been at. The vile smoking did not agree with Dr. Graham and he went away early. The Provost and Haviland were vastly good company. T. Mortlock never uttered and the Master of Caius was as tiresome as ever.

(S. C. Roberts, The Family, 1963 – quoting Romilly)

Albert Pell in 1839 (he was supposed to be in training for one of the Trinity boats):

Now the food put before the Pensioners in Trinity for dinner and the way it was served was abominable . . . We had three-pronged steel forks to eat with; before using them we passed the prongs through the table-cloth and at once three black spots indicated the wounds on the cloth. For any soup we had to 'size', or pay extra, the same for pudding. The inelegant bedmakers who waited at table generally announced the sizings to be 'Julia' soup and custard pudding . . . I broke away . . . and appeased my hunger at an eating-house out of observation of the training spies. They reported, however, on my insubordination and on my inveterate habit of eating pastry, and this caused my removal from the boat.

(Pell, *Reminiscences*, ed. Mackay)

T. G. Bonney of St. John's in 1852:

'Wines' then were occasional after-dinner entertainments, the number of guests depending on the size of the host's table. The decanters contained port and sherry, claret and burgundy being unknown in my undergraduate days; the dessert came from a fruiterer. College tutors invited their pupils to wine: the marker coming round in Hall and saying *sotto voce* 'Mr. X would be glad to see you to wine.' This was regarded as a 'command', superseding other engagements. When the chapel bell rang (the evening service was at six) some of the guests left to attend it, occasionally returning afterwards.

Supper parties were commoner, but for reading men they were rather rare indulgencies; luncheons were unknown; breakfasts were the usual entertainments other than wines. A dealer outside provided coffee, tea, and muffins; the college kitchen sent up hot dishes to order. I remember the usual menu – *soles à l'indienne*, 'pulled fowl', spread-eagle (a fowl, split and stewed with small mushrooms), cutlets *à la soubise*, and perhaps a steak or chops, for any guest in partial training. A dish of ruffs and reeves, when they were in season, was a favourite

College fare:
Dinner in hall. Trinity College

(*Cambridge Scrapbook*, 1859)

delicacy. They came then in numbers to the fens, but I have not seen them for years in the poulterers' shops. After breakfast, pipes were lighted, and a tankard of ale, or, for a large party, a 'cup' with cider or copus was circulated. The regular hour was nine, and a ten o'clock lecture had a dispersive effect. I could then do justice to such a breakfast, the tankard excepted, and work at mathematics afterwards. Needless to say that power has long been lost.

(T. G. Bonney, *Memories of a Long Life*, 1921)

Letter to 'The Times':

Trinity College

15 May 1863

Sir, it seems a question whether matters of College discipline ought ever to be made the subject of comment in the public press. But after much long-suffering, and no redress, what can a man do but 'write to the Times'?

My complaint is the Trinity College Hall, and my case is as follows: – Last Sunday I wanted some dinner; I went to Hall. I was in good time, but could only get one joint (a cold one): having cut myself some meat, I waited nearly a quarter of an hour before I got the smallest bit of any vegetable, or before a waiter came near me . . . Well, then came the sweets; I took a little jelly, or rather I did not take it, for I could not get a plate; at last a hot one was brought me . . . I ate my rapidly dissolving jelly, and left Hall not a little disgusted. It was a dinner(?) I should have been ashamed to have given my servant.

But it is not the dinner, it is the price I complain of. In the Times of Monday, there was a letter showing what an excellent dinner could be got for 6d incomparably better than what I paid 2s for.

Why should gross injustice be done to 500 undergraduates, for the sake of one cook.

I enclose my card.

Your obedient servant

Justly Indignant

(*Cambridge Papers – Squibs and Crackers*, collected by J. W. Clark)

'Pall Mall Gazette'   9 November 1868:

We hear from Cambridge that the old quarrel between the undergraduates and the college authorities about the college dinners has been revived . . . Matters have gone so far at Sidney Sussex College that the undergraduates have 'struck'. On Monday after the grace was read they left the hall in a body and dined together at an hotel. This step was repeated on Tuesday . . . At St. John's, too, there are symptoms of a rising, and the disaffection, it is said, is spreading to other colleges . . . At Trinity the undergraduates appear to be scarcely less dissatisfied than at Sidney Sussex. Several correspondents assure us that the meat is of very indifferent quality, and the beer undrinkable.

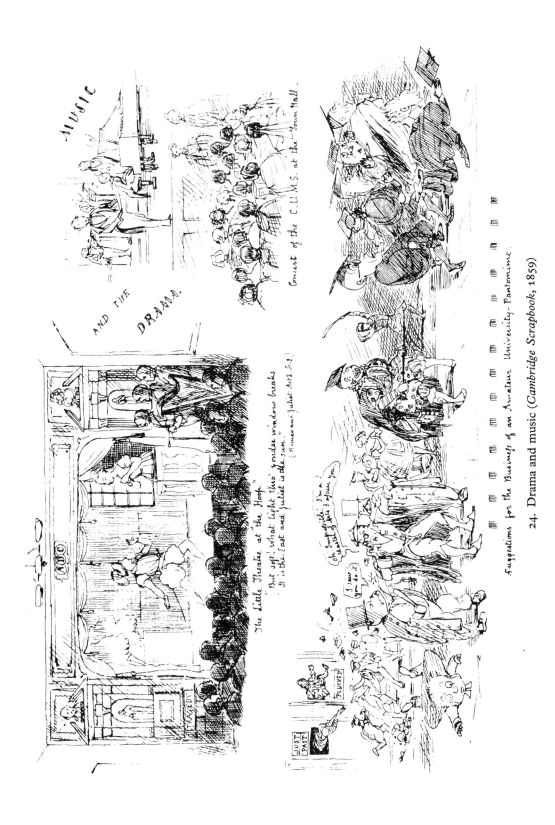

24. Drama and music (*Cambridge Scrapbook*, 1859)

Walter Besant of Christ's remembers:

The undergraduate's life in the fifties differed in many respects from that of his successor in the nineties. To begin with, there was a far more generous consumption of beer. Many reading men began the day with beer after breakfast; every Sunday morning breakfast was concluded with beer; there was more beer for lunch; nothing but beer was taken with dinner; and there was beer with the evening pipe. Every college had its own brewer. Four kinds of beer were brewed: the 'Audit' ale, old and strong, the 'Strong' ale, the 'Bitter', and the 'Small' beer, or 'Swipes'; the common dinner drink was 'Bitter and Swipes'.

(Autobiography)

and a Christ's 'scullion' remembers:

Down at the tables are seated
Scores of Men with appetites sharp
The waiters all running about
And many with tongues there do carp

Wisken's name in Hall oft sounded
A message from some one is pop't
Meat tough, or something else wanting
Or knife in the gravy is drop't

Wisken, Potatoes I do want
Wisken, do bring the greens this way
Wisken, ask if there's any soup
Wisken, do hear me what I say

(John Wisken, scullion at Christ's – born 1798, died 1873. One of his sons went to the Perse School, then to Caius and was eighth Wrangler in 1848. *Christ's College Magazine,* May 1967)

Etiquette in clothes and manners mattered to undergraduates.

Advice to freshmen:

First, he must not alight on the Cambridge platform with high hat on head, or hat-box in hand; chimney-pots and their cases must on all accounts be left at home. In the matter of hats, there is safety in the ordinary hard round felt; even a straw hat should not be brought up, as the colour of the straw and of the ribbon will depend on the College Club which is eventually joined. Scotch bonnets, wide-awakes, and other soft things may be donned later according to taste, but the diffident ones had better begin with billycocks . . .

Only one other accoutrement must be mentioned as absolutely to be left behind, along with boyhood, viz., sugar-tongs; for lump sugar, in Cambridge, is generally passed round and taken with the clean finger and thumb. The hands have little other social use, for there is total abstinence from handshaking, except on the first and last occasion of seeing an acquaintance in any term. When two men meet in the street or road who have nothing to say, they do not stop and

say it, nor even mutter in passing, 'Do?' but the tiniest nod or the least per-
ceptible motion of the near eyelid suffices.

(Charles Dickens the younger, *A Dictionary
of the University of Cambridge*, 1884)

A light touch in verse was appreciated:

HIC VIR, HIC EST

Once, an unassuming Freshman,
Through these wilds I wandered on,
Seeing in each house a College,
Under every cap a Don.
Each perambulating infant
Had a magic in its squall,
For my eager eye detected
Senior Wranglers in them all . . .

(C. S. Calverley (Christ's) 1862)

Plays had been acted throughout the century:

*Richard Monckton Milnes played Beatrice in a remarkable performance of
'Much Ado About Nothing' in 1830 at the Hoop Inn, with Hallam as Verges
and J. M. Kemble as Dogberry. Milnes himself wrote the epilogue, which
ended:*

But ere *our* pageant disappear,
We ask one boon – if, in some after-year,
In evening hours, your eye should chance to light
On any name you recognise tonight –
On some brief record of their mortal lot –
Married, or murdered, ruined, or what not?
While natural thought returns upon its track,
Just pause, and murmur, ere you call it back,
With pleasant memory, sipping your liqueur –
'Yes, yes, he was a Cambridge Amateur.'

*It was at The Hoop that the ADC was founded in 1855, largely by the
inspiration of Frank Burnand of Trinity:*

we naturally took such precautions at first that to ensure our safety by flight in
case of a raid of Proctors, we had a speaking tube run through from the Hoop
bar to our greenroom, by which 'the office could be given' in an emergency, and
outside the windows of our stage we had a ladder placed . . . This never
happened . . .

The first night's bill

Why all the actors were 'Misters', when the acting manager, stage manager, and even 'prompter' were 'Esquires', I don't know.

This invidious distinction disappeared from our bills after this first term.

(F. C. Cowley Burnand, *Personal Reminiscences of the A.D.C. Cambridge*, 1878)

As in past centuries, music echoed through the chapels, courts and staircases:

I must here just hint that music, sweet music, finds favour in our ears a little oftener than once a year. Each term we have concerts, for two or three successive evenings, and at the close of the Academical Year in July, oratorios in the Senate-house.

(Wright, *Alma Mater*)

[225]

Charles Darwin:

I also got into a musical set, I believe by means of my warm-hearted friend, Herbert, who took a high wrangler's degree. From associating with these men and hearing them play, I acquired a strong taste for music, and used very often to time my walks so as to hear on week-days the anthem in King's College Chapel. This gave me intense pleasure, so that my back-bone would sometimes shiver. I am sure that there was no affectation or mere imitation in this taste, for I used generally to go by myself to Kings College, and I sometimes hired the chorister boys to sing in my rooms. Nevertheless I am so utterly destitute of an ear, that I cannot perceive a discord or keep time and hum a tune correctly; and it is a mystery how I could possibly have derived pleasure from music.

(*Autobiographical Recollections*, ed. F. Darwin)

Becoming a King's Chorister:

What a time of nursing it was by my Coach, who was one of the senior boys (six were seniors), a near neighbour, his and my parents being servants at the same College ('Keys'), we were closely acquainted. I can remember his taking me several times to the 'backs' for a shouting stroll, viz., causing me to shout to him at lengthening distances, and if there were any crowds into which he could take me to shout, he embraced the opportunity of strengthening my voice, and, meanwhile, was practising me on the piano . . .

The eventful day arrived for the trial of the four. Oh! what a time! That morning was for mother, father, aunts, uncles, sisters, brothers, *all so most* very anxious that one of the family should wear a hat and gown (top hats only allowed to be worn). Oh! the excitement as my dear mother mixed the yolk of an egg in a glass of sherry, which it was intended should make my voice mellow and strong, and probably as an anti-nervous draught! . . .

Any way, I was taken to St. Mary's organ, and there the bewildering Do, Re, Mi, Fa, with the additional test Do, Mi, – Re, Fa, and so on, at the end of which one other boy and myself were adjudged equal . . .

Thus, on the 7th of July, 1836, I became a King's boy, was introduced to a 'Bishop' (Tailor) at the corner of St. Edward's Passage, on King's Parade, and was measured for my first gown. Father had to take me to a Hatter for a top hat (my! what an expense those hats were, the *wear* being of short duration).

(Thomas H. Case, *Memoirs of a King's College Chorister*, 1899)

The Cambridge University Musical Society (CUMS) was founded in 1843 from the Peterhouse Musical Society.

Their very first concert came close to being their last; the junketings at supper later that evening somehow contrived, after certain hilarious proceedings, to finish on the college roof, and their next concert had to be given in the Red Lion Hotel in Petty Cury because the Master of Peterhouse would no longer allow them use of a suitable room within the college.

(Gerald Norris, *Stanford, The Cambridge Jubilee and Tchaikowsky*, 1980)

New music was played and composers honoured. 8 March 1877: first per-
formance of Brahms' First Symphony conducted by Joachim. Stanford wrote:

The Cambridge performance of the C Minor Symphony attracted almost every
musician of importance in England and much interest was excited among
Cambridge men by the curious coincidence that the horn theme in the introduction to the last movement was nearly note for note a quotation of the famous
hour-chimes of St. Mary's bells.

In June 1893 at the time of the CUMS Jubilee, Tchaikowsky conducted
'Francesca de Rimini' in the Guildhall.

I remember his serious set expression as he faced round to his band, his wildly
energetic baton, and the awful fury and madness of his music. I fancy, to most
of us present, it was our first introduction to the music of this master.
　The concert finished a little after 4.30. Normally the college boat races would
have begun at 5.00, but they were put back until 5.30, so as not to draw people
away from the concert at the interval.

(Ernest Markham Lee quoted in
Gerald Norris, *Stanford*)

Grieg, Saint-Saens, Bruch, Boito and Tchaikowsky were given honorary
degrees (Grieg was the only one not there in person) and a CUMS Jubilee
dinner followed in King's.

There was domestic music too:

This devoted four (an undergraduate string quartet) used to practise assiduously,
often into the small hours of the morning, in rooms in the Great Court tower of
Trinity facing the chapel. They played steadily through all the quartets of
Haydn and many of those of other great masters. I well recollect hearing about
midnight a blood-curdling sound issuing from the upper windows, which
resolved itself into the 'Terremoto' from Haydn's 'Seven last Words'.

(C. V. Stanford, *Pages from an Unwritten*
Diary, 1914)

Sport of every kind was a predominant, not to say obsessive, interest.

Rowing

Bumping races 1851:

We walked along the Fields by the Church ... crossed the Ferry, and mingled
with the Crowd upon the opposite Shore. Townsmen and Gownsmen, with the
tassel'd Fellow-commoner sprinkled here and there – Reading men and Sporting
men – Fellows, and even Masters of Colleges – all these, conversing on all sorts
of topics, from the Slang in Bell's Life to the last new German Revelation, and
moving in ever-changing groups down the Shore of the River, at whose farthest
visible bend was a little Knot of Ladies gathered up on a green Knoll faced and
illuminated by the beams of the setting Sun. Beyond which point was at length
heard some indistinct shouting, which gradually increased until 'They are off –

they are coming', suspended other Conversation among ourselves: and suddenly the head of the first Boat turned the corner; and then another close upon it; and then a third; the Crews pulling with all their Might compacted in perfect Rhythm; and the Crowd upon the shore turning round to follow along with them, waving hats and caps, and cheering, 'Bravo, St. John's', 'Go it, Trinity'.

(Edward Fitzgerald, *Euphranor*, 1851)

The Boat Races

After a long series of Oxford victories, Cambridge at last won in 1870; the crew contained the famous J. H. D. Goldie of St. John's:

Oft had we seen by the ait of old Chiswick
Dark Blue on Light Blue relentlessly gain;
Oft had we swallowed (detestable physic!)
Tears of disgust, disappointment, and pain;
But now the age of gold,
Oft by our bards foretold,
Brightly has beamed through the cloud of dark blue;
Cam, Eton, Putney, then,
Echo his praise again,
Three cheers for Goldie, and three for his Crew!

(*The Eagle*, VII, 1871)

25. The Cambridge University Eight training on the Cam, 1866
(*The Illustrated London News*)

Many of the dons coached their college crews:

I really believed that I was acting from a high sense of duty when I encouraged my pupils in rowing, and I enjoyed the supreme triumph of seeing our boat at the head of the river as much as the great victory in the mathematical tripos, when, for once, we turned out a senior wrangler . . .

The college boat club was a bond of union which enabled me to be on friendly terms with young gentlemen whose muscles were more developed than their brains, and so far favourable to the development of the wider human sympathies. Interest in such pursuits is, at any rate, antagonistic to the intellectual vice of priggishness.

(Leslie Stephen, *Some Early Impressions*)

There was more informal boating and sailing, often based at the inn 'Five Miles from Anywhere' where there was an 'Upware Republic Society':

1 Apr 1853   An 'out' jolly sail very squally, stopped all day, did a chop dinner, quoits and paddy's songs to follow . . .

31 Mar 1855   Sculled in a 'funny' to Ely . . . Left Ely in the 'Tiddledy Widdledy' thing as the natives termed it and sculled by moonlight to the Five Miles – Here turned in – 'done up' – regular bricks here and no mistake.

('Upware' visitors' book, quoted in
Arthur B. Gray, *Cambridge Revisited*, 1921)

Forthcoming events 6 March 1877:

Tuesday 6th	Cambridgeshire Hounds, 11 a.m. Paxton Hall; 7 miles from Huntingdon. Midland train at 8 a.m. to Huntingdon.
	Debate at the Union on Permissive Bill at 7 p.m. Opener W. R. Philips Trin. Hall.
Wednesday 7th	Trinity Foot Beagles meet Railway Crossing, Milton Rd.; 3 miles from Cambridge.
	Bicycle Meet. To Royston and back. 28 miles. Second and Third Division Races.
Thursday 8th	Herr Joachim presented with hon. degree in Senate House at 2 p.m.
	C.U.M.S. concert 8.15 p.m.
	Fitzwilliam Hounds. Washingley Hall, 4 miles from Holme station on G. N. line. Trains not convenient.

(*The Cambridge Tatler*, 6 March 1877)

Bicycling was very popular:

Whenas on wheels my Julia goes
Then, then methinks how sweetly shows
The piston-action of her toes

Next when I cast mine eyes and see
That brave vibration each way free
O how that waggling taketh me

(*Cambridge Review*, 3 December 1896)

[229]

26. Cricket on Parker's Piece, 1854

and riding, shooting and skating.

Henry Fawcett rode and skated despite his blindness:

It was very trying to ride with him or to see him riding, he was so reckless in his blindness. Two friends used to ride with him, one on each side, Black Morgan usually one of the two. He always wanted to shave the corners on the road, and to get into any large field for a wild gallop. My last skate from Cambridge to Ely was with him, a much longer way by ice than by road. He went very fast, those immensely long limbs going like the sails of a windmill. His gyp at Trinity Hall was a first-rate skater, and he went always in front of Fawcett, holding a stick behind him, the other end of which was in Fawcett's hand. At one point of our voyage Fawcett's skate caught in a bit of cat ice which the gyp had not seen, and he came down with a tremendous crash, hat, stick, spectacles, body, limbs, all going in different ways. The look on his face for the first moment or two was terrible; one could realise the sense of not knowing what would happen. Then he called out 'Anybody damaged?' and we went on again as usual. I had to get back to Cambridge by train, but he just turned and skated back.

(G. F. Browne, *Recollections of a Bishop*,
1915)

The severe frost still continues, there has been skating the whole way from Grantchester to Littleport . . . 7 Jan 1854
Skated from Waterbeach in 17 minutes. Splendid ice! 10 Feb 1855
15 Oct 1853   Fen full of Snipe, and very wet, 4 guns – 14 couple.
16 Feb 1856   Came for a day's Snipe shooting, but went home with but 2

couple: found fen very dry, ditto Sportsmen, returned to Cambridge after a capital lunch.

('Upware' visitors' book)

Brains versus games prowess presented problems:

Munro . . . dashed *The Times* with quite a bang on the floor and said, 'What do you think that fellow Verrall has done?' [A. W. Verrall was a distinguished lecturer in Classics.] I said I did not know. 'Well,' he said, 'he's ploughed Foley for entrance to the College [Foley was a boy who had made a century in the Eton and Harrow match], and how do you think Verrall translates?' Here he went off with a piece of Greek, and gave Verrall's translation. I tried to look as shocked as I could, and he went on, 'I don't know what this College is coming to, when a man who makes mistakes like these in a straightforward piece of translation is allowed to plough a boy like Foley.'

(J. J. Thomson, Recollections and Reflections, 1936)

Colleges were rude about each other and stories abound of inter-college exchanges, such as:

Trinity, about Magdalene:

that transpontine refuge for fallen undergraduates.

Magdalene, about Trinity:

that overgrown establishment opposite Mr. Matthew's shop.

From the beginning of the century, 'reading men' as opposed to 'non-reading men' walked for exercise:

C. A. Bristed in the 1840s:

The staple exercise is walking; between two and four all the roads in the neighborhood of Cambridge – that is to say within four miles of it – are covered with men taking their constitutionals. Longer walks, of twelve or fifteen miles, are frequently taken on Sundays or days succeeding an examination. The standard of a good walker, is to have gone, not once, but repeatedly, fifteen miles in three hours, without special training or being the worse for it next day. A number of my acquaintances professed to be able to do this.

(Five Years in an English University)

Leslie Stephen:

The one pursuit in which I am not contemptible is walking; and I still think with complacency of the hot day in which I did my fifty miles from Cambridge to London in twelve hours to attend a dinner of the Alpine Club. That admirable institution was just started at that time, chiefly by Cambridge men.

(Some Early Impressions)

About half-past one, or a little later, reading men shut up their books, took a very light lunch (often only bread and butter) and went out for some exercise . . . In winter we often got up a game of football on Parker's Piece. None of the colleges, as far as I remember, had 'grounds' of their own – but both undergraduates and dons took more walking exercise than is now customary. Charles Simeon is said to have recommended his freshmen to make sure every day that the third mile-stone from Cambridge was in place. We often followed his advice, or else did the round by Trumpington and Grantchester. On this pairs of men, both young and old, abounded, or could be seen on a wet afternoon pacing backwards and forwards in the shelter of the cloisters of Nevile's Court, Trinity.

(*Memories of a Long Life*)

Edward Henry Palmer, Reader in Arabic and a famous linguist:

It is recorded that once, as he was coming home to College, he happened to meet the Master, Dr. Bateson, who, casting his eye over the water-boots and flannels, stained with mud and weather, in which the learned Professor had encased himself, remarked, 'This is Eastern costume, I suppose'. 'No, Master; Eastern Counties costume.'

(J. W. Clark, *Old Friends at Cambridge and Elsewhere*, 1900)

The coming of the railway had brought changes:

The Act of 1844 which authorised the construction of the line to Cambridge had sections giving officers of the University free access at all reasonable times to the Company's station at Cambridge and empowering them to ask for information from the Railway Company's servants regarding any person on the station 'who', in the words of the Act, 'shall be a member of the University or suspected of being such' . . .

There was a curious prohibition in the Cambridge Railway Act which affected the travelling public generally. Under a penalty of a fine not exceeding £5 for each offence 'for the benefit of Addenbrooke's Hospital or other County Charity to be decided by the University', the Company was prohibited from taking up or setting down any passenger at the Cambridge railway station or at any place within 3 miles of the same between 10 a.m. and 5 p.m. on any Sunday.* Parliament, however, was considerate enough to enact that if by some unavoidable accident a train was late, passengers might alight or join the train during the prohibited hours.

* Soon after the opening of the line cheap day tickets were issued on Sundays to Cambridge (7 a.m. from Shoreditch). This drew a protest in 1851 from the Vice-Chancellor of the University. Excursions on Sundays were, he wrote, 'as distasteful to the University Authorities as they must be offensive to Almighty God and to all right-minded Christians'.

(Reginald B. Fellows, *Railways to Cambridge, Actual and Proposed*, 1976)

As, at dawn on the outside of the mail, we drew nigh to Cambridge, the nightingales made the Trumpington copses and roadside groves ring with their notes; nor were they to be silenced by the guard's horn or the lively rattle of the leaders' splinter-bars. No nightingales are now to be heard by the freshman or graduate in the Great Eastern Railway coaches. About the time I took my degree this astonishing line made its first essays, under the title of the Eastern Counties Railway. It became distinguished for its unpunctuality and shortcomings. My first journey on it was from its terminus at Broxbourne to London. I reached Broxbourne by coach, expecting a speedy finish to the journey. We had not, however, gone more than a few miles on the line before we slowed down, then stood still. After waiting some time, I got out of the carriage, to find the engine a hundred yards ahead, detached and unable to raise steam enough to move along alone. Then the men in charge of it descended, and pulling up the wooden fencing, tried that for fuel; but finding the palings of no service, and the sun being well up and the day mild, they sat with their legs over the rear of the tender, their faces towards the unfortunate passengers, and proceeded quietly to make a meal. I quite forget what happened next, but I have some idea that I walked on to London.

(Reminiscences)

Women became increasingly part of the scene.

Leslie Stephen in the early 1860s:

In my day we were a society of bachelors. I do not remember during my career to have spoken to a single woman at Cambridge except my bed-maker and the wives of one or two heads of houses . . . We were beginning to propose some modification of the absurd system of celibacy . . . yet proposals to alter it excited horror.

(Some Early Impressions)

Henry Sidgwick to Oscar Browning, 7 June 1871:

I am choosing a house for our young women – which is a difficult task, as genteel Cambridge is increasing rapidly in numbers owing to Enlargement of Professoriate, Marriage of Fellows, and Movement generally, which, here at least, is against celibacy. Female education is centering here. Miss Davies is collecting funds to build a college two miles and a half (or $\frac{3}{4}$) off. Thus we shall have two systems of Higher Education of Women going on side by side. However, we are accustomed in Cambridge to a complexity of systems, and there are plenty of fine old arguments to prove that it is a help rather than a hindrance. The work takes up my time rather, but is very entertaining. And I am growing fond of women, I like working with them.

(A Memoir)

But there were objections, not always so easily overcome.

1869
Soon after the College was opened I well remember travelling one day between Hitchin and London, and was scarcely seated in the train, when a clergyman in

the carriage said to two ladies 'Ha!. This is Hitchin, and that I believe is the house, where the College for Women is – that *infidel* place.' I remember the fire that flushed my face as I said 'Oh no! not infidel; why do you say that?' and then how I explained that the College for Women was founded on the same principles as the men's colleges of Cambridge, and did not their founders desire and provide for religious observance? I can recall the recoil with which the ladies eyed me, but the clergyman shook hands as he left the train, and said he was glad I could give such a good account of affairs.

(Edyth Lloyd, Anna Lloyd, 1837–1925.
A Memoir, 1928)

Girton and Newnham began in a small way, following different paths, till their colleges were built in 1873 and 1875:

Girton (1870)

Thou asks for a description of our days, so I will describe one as best I can. We are called about 7.15 and struggle up as soon as we can be disentangled from sleep, so as to be down to prayers at 8 in the library. After prayers breakfast follows in the dining-room without ceremony, everyone leaves the table as soon as they like. Some take a walk after breakfast for half an hour; I always study, generally in the library for the first hour as my room is one of the last in being prepared. From 12 to 3 pm lunch and walking goes on, in an irregular manner. Some study till nearly 2 pm, others lunch soon after 12. From 3 to 5.30 we have our lectures, and at 6 dinner. After dinner we generally have a talk, and then go up to our rooms. I generally make myself some tea about 8, and get an hour and a half or two hours' study before bed-time. Of course we have little varieties, evening calls on one another, and so on, and sometimes sit up too late.

(Anna Lloyd, A Memoir)

Newnham (1871)

The first time I saw Miss Clough was at the Higher Local Examination of 1871 ... In October 1871, Mary Kennedy, Ella Bulley, Edith Creak, Annie Migault, and I came to be with her at 74 Regent Street, and in the following term we were joined by Felicia Larner, and one or two others. We lived very much the life of a family: we studied together, we had our meals at one table, and in the evening we usually sat with Miss Clough in her sitting-room. We did our best to keep down household expenses: our food was very simple; we all, including Miss Clough, not only made our beds and dusted our rooms, but we helped to wash up after meals, and we did the domestic sewing in the evening.

During the first year at Regent Street there were certain discomforts to be put up with. We went twice a week to the town gymnasium, but otherwise walks were our only form of exercise. We watched the undergraduates playing games on Parker's Piece, and envied them, and no doubt we made up for want of outdoor exercise by being rather noisy in the house, especially at meals. I believe we were all hard-working and well-intentioned, but during that first year there was a good deal of friction between Miss Clough and some of us. I think we were almost entirely to blame.

(Mrs. Alfred Marshall, quoted in B. A.
Clough, A Memoir of Anne J. Clough, 1897)

They met with whimsical admiration:

AD CHLOEN, MA
(Fresh from her Cambridge examination)

Lady, very fair are you,
And your eyes are very blue,
    And your hose;
And your brow is like the snow,
And the various things you know
    Goodness knows.

And the rose-flush on your cheek,
And your algebra and Greek,
    Perfect are;
And that loving lustrous eye
Recognises in the sky
    Every star.

You have pouting piquant lips,
You can doubtless an eclipse
    Calculate;
But for your caerulean hue
I had certainly from you
    Met my fate.

(Mortimer Collins, 1871)

Gradually the frontiers of education for women advanced into the male strongholds:

1878

Hurrah for women's rights!!! – We have another triumph – Now you know the people of Christs College have allowed Natural Science students to attend the lectures for the men but Miss Clough must go too, that is one of the conditions. Well Mr. Oscar Browning has been lecturing on History to about 4 of our girls & also giving the same lectures to the men of Kings – so he asked the Provost if the girls might attend the men's lectures to save his time – The Provost called a college meeting & the result is that Kings has opened its arms to the females.

D. Ll. G. Jones (née Davies), in *A Newnham Anthology*, ed. A. Phillips, 1979)

Graces were passed in the Senate allowing women to take Tripos examinations (although not yet becoming members of the University):

24 February 1881   5 p.m.

Hurrah! we have won! We had 398 against 32 for the 1st Grace, a large majority for the 2nd, & the 3rd was not opposed at all! I must relate to you in order, so that you may have a correct idea. Miss Morrison & I went out and passed down the street leading past the Senate House by accident of course! But we met a number of students doing the same, wh. was strange. I counted every intelligent looking man as a friend. After a few perambulations we called on a lady, & missed the éclat of the great announcement. It was arranged as follows. Mrs.

Sidgwick's sister Lady Rayleigh was at the Senate House with her pony carriage & was to drive with the news at once. But some of the students had another plan. One was to get the news directly it was out, she then went to Clare Bridge, waved her handkerchief to another on King's Bridge, who signalled to another on horse back, at the back of King's. She then galopped here at once with a white hand-kerchief tied on the end of her riding whip. Whereupon two others hoisted a flag on our roof, the gong was sounded & every one clapped. For about an hour a crowd of students stood outside the gates, waiting for news about the 2 other graces. The man who brought it was a classical lecturer who had been specially injured by the Vice-Chancellor's speech. We clapped him violently, then when Mr. Sidgwick came in sight we clapped still more, & he not knowing the cause ran on into the house, but afterwards waved his hat violently & seemed too delighted to keep still. After that we came into the house & clapped Miss Clough. The men at Ridley got on the roof & surveyed us with amazement thro' eye glasses. I am told the opposition gave up all hope yesterday, & the Vice-Chancellor telegraphed to his men not to trouble. Some did not even care to go to the Senate House, they were so sure of losing, altho' only this morning one of their party predicted certain victory. I believe the scene in the Senate House was too amusing. It was so crowded many could not sit. So they reserved one little spot, & each sat down for a second, gave his vote & jumped up again. They have to vote sitting on a piece *of wood*! We heard the odious Vice-Chancellor had hired all the M.A. gowns, but the procters were all on our side so they must have secured some for our women. When women get the Degrees (for this is only the thin end of the wedge) it will be nothing to this. We all feel it is the great crisis in the history of women's colleges. (If this does not interest you I'll

27. A student at Newnham College, 1877

28. Professor Jebb in motion, 1895 (*Granta*)

never write to you no more! I think Miss Lizzie Tiddeman wd. like to know all about it, so would you shew her this letter. Many thanks for Mother's this morning. I am glad she is better.)

(E. A. Andrews, in *Newnham Anthology*, ed. Phillips)

EPIGRAM ON THE PASSING OF THE GRACES

'The first Grace for admitting women to the University Examinations was carried by a majority of 366 to 32.'

> The votes by which the ladies won
>   Were as a Leap Year's days:
> A month's brief tale would all but tell
>   The number of the Nays.
>
> Thus, as the sun in heaven, our cause
>   Is dear to men of sense:
> The adverse tide is little more
>   Than lunar influence,

(Professor R. C. Jebb, in *Newnham Anthology*, ed. Phillips)

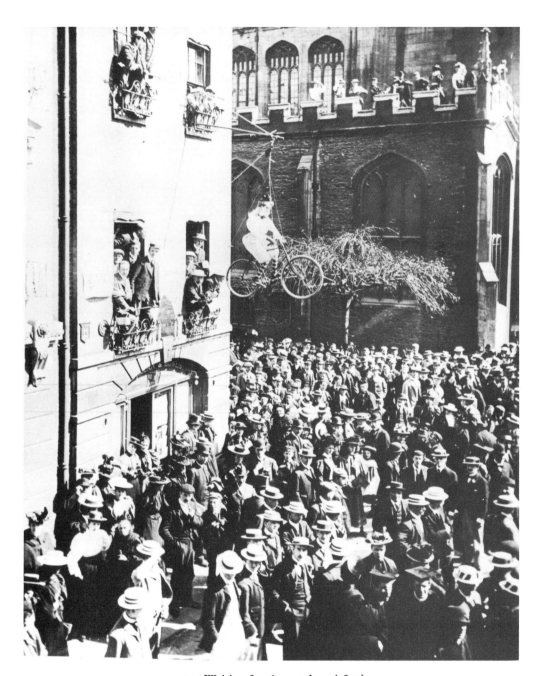

29. Waiting for the result ... (1897)

In 1887 Agnata Ramsey of Girton was the only candidate placed in the first class of Part I of the Classical Tripos. Three years later Philippa Fawcett in Part I of the Mathematics Tripos was placed 'above the Senior Wrangler':

The Senior Moderator, my old and tried friend Rouse Ball, came to me late on the night before the Mathematical Tripos list was to be read in the Senate House ... One of the women students was neither 'equal to' one of the men students nor 'between the two' of them. After a moment's thought I said, 'Do you mean one of them is "wooden spoon"?' 'No! It's the other end!' 'Then you will have to say, when you have read out the list of wranglers, – "Women. Above the Senior Wrangler"; and you won't get beyond the word "Above".'

I can never forget the shout that went up in the Senate House when that word 'Above' came out. I was in the gallery standing by Miss Clough and her Newnham students, and was the first person to shake hands with the daughter of my old friend Henry Fawcett.

(G. F. Browne, The Recollections of a Bishop)

An attempt to admit women to degrees in 1887 failed for various reasons:

1887.   If given the B.A., they must next have the M.A. and that would carry with it voting and perhaps a place in the Electoral Roll; a vote for the University Livings and all the rest. Even the B.A. degree would enable them to take 5 books at a time out of the University Library on a ticket countersigned by 'their tutor'. I am entirely opposed to the admission of women to 'privileges' of this character. And I honestly believe they are better off as they are.

(W. W. Skeat to Henry Sidgwick, quoted in
Rita McWilliams-Tullberg, Women at
Cambridge, 1975)

Other dons permitted themselves mild jokes about women. The effect of the
aesthetic movement was noted:

We were even brought at one time into momentary touch with the aesthetic movement, which would have stood no chance of effecting an entry into Cambridge while the old dons held the keys.

One got used to seeing limp and listless ladies mooning about, with a look of withered joy on their faces, and draped in loose-fitting robes of sickly green, and to hearing at dinner-parties the sort of language which du Maurier held up to ridicule in *Punch*.

I found Mrs. Fawcett laughing once, when I had called, at a remark which a lady visitor had just made to her. After gazing for some time, with clasped hands and a rapt expression at a row of porcelain plates above the drawing-room picture-rail, she exclaimed: 'O Mrs. Fawcett, how tender!' Newnham was more influenced than Girton by this passing fashion. I remember the difference between the two Colleges being debated at a dinner-party, when our irreverent, though reverend, host, who had been listening for some time with an amused expression, startled the company by blurting out, with more truth than elegance: 'The difference lies in a nutshell – Girton wears stays, Newnham doesn't.'

(T. Thornely, Cambridge Memories, 1936)

The latter decades of the century saw other innovations. In 1882 not only was
there a new College, Selwyn, but a Grace was passed allowing fellows to
marry:

Selwyn came into Cambridge amid an army of brides.

(Rev. A. L. Brown, Selwyn College, 1906)

The new statutes in 1882 gave permission for the marriage of fellows and that October term was marked by the arrival of many brides. The Master of Trinity Hall, dear old Ben Latham, told Mother he meant to have them to dine 'en masse, a perfect stream of white'. My Mother used to say that she thought Cambridge society became more ordinary, and that the wives whose husbands had had to make sacrifices to marry them were often women of marked ability.

> (Hester Mary Kempthorne (née Peile), daughter of the Master of Christ's, 'Notes on Cambridge', article in *Christ's College Magazine*, 1968)

The Senate had voted for the new College by 150 to 63. The Union motion, 'That this house disapproves of the foundation of Selwyn College' was only defeated by 12 votes in a house of 160.

'Living economically' was the keynote:

Economy in expenditure was promoted by the common meals in Hall, and by sumptuary regulations designed to restrict personal luxury. The College Dinner was of a simpler character than in other Colleges and the same dinner was served to the high table as to the undergraduates ... The College set a limit of £5 a term to the amount of personal expenditure on such luxuries as are eaten, drunk or smoked.

> (Brown, *Selwyn College*)

Then we were absolutely in the country. Cattle grazed and ruminated over Herschel Road and by the banks of the Binn Brook. The University Volunteers careered unrestricted, with an occasional interlude by the Polo Club, over a vast prairie now bisected by Cranmer Road, and Selwyn Gardens were literally what their present name denotes. On the other side the buildings of Ridley Hall were running us a close race, which they eventually won, for the finish, and Newnham College, then about half its present size, gazed at us from an as yet respectful distance.

'The Catholic Church' was built:

The present church of Our Lady and the English Martyrs was consecrated on October 8, 1890, on which occasion some serious misgivings arose in certain circles by the fact that the bells of Great St. Mary's ... pealed joyfully during that afternoon. Feelings were allayed, however, when enquiry revealed that the bells had been actually rung to signalize, as was then customary, the appointment of a new Professor.

> (E. A. B. Barnard, *A Seventeenth-Century Gentleman*, 1944)

In season and out of season, in term and out of term, there was coming and going and staying on:

Arthur Munby, poet, revisited Trinity in 1861:

Wednesday, 22 May ... Dined in Hall; walked up the lime avenue and along the backs, where crowds of gay people filled the grounds of King's; then up the parallelogram a little way, for auld lang syne; then back through the avenue, lingering a little on the bridge, while the boats shot under and the mellow afternoon light was on the river and the trees; and so to Joe's rooms at 5.30. The Ellises were there, invited to coffee, which had been set out in Henniker's rooms over-head: but the Prince of Wales, coming in from the flower show, had just gone upstairs, and finding the board spread, had expressed to Mary Ann his intention of staying to share what he supposed to be his friend's provisions. The faithful bedmaker, however, preferring her master to her prince, secretly removed the coffee pots & muffins, and sent for Henniker, who when he came was more distracted than even the Ellises, who were waiting for their meal in Joe's rooms below; for he could neither ask the Prince to stay & partake of what was not his, nor explain to him that he ought to go away. So the Prince stayed and Joe and his party waited and the bedmakers fretted outside: & thus I was obliged to leave them, after snatching a cup of coffee, and take the omnibus for the station ... So ends another visit to Cambridge; and the charm of it and the good of it who can tell? Who, indeed, can appreciate, even for himself, the results upon him of a pilgrimage - each time longer than the last - to the spot where his youth lies buried, and with it, all that was or is most loveable and memorable for him?

He came again in 1863:

Saturday, 4 April . . . to our Chapel at 6.30. It was, of course, a surplice night: and for the first time I wore my grandfather's M.A. hood, now mine, over my surplice.

It is a trivial matter, going to chapel thus clad, or walking through the streets and college grounds in one's Master's gown, but there is a powerful charm in the symbolism of the thing: it is a visible sign of membership, of being at home.

(D. Hudson, *Munby – Man of Two Worlds.*
The Life and Diaries of Arthur J. Munby
1828–1910, 1972)

The Prince and Princess of Wales visited in 1864:

Procession of boats
Trinity Hall boat, being 'the head of the river', was wreathed with flowers, and all the men wore flowers in their caps. Every other boat bore its distinguishing flag, and all displayed the national standard of Denmark . . .

At the grand ball 'given by the Master of Trinity (Rev. Dr. Whewell) under a marquee in Neville's [*sic*] Court' they stayed 5 hours. 'During the whole of that time, the Prince, who is an indefatigable dancer, never sat down, except at the supper table.'
(*Illustrated London News,* 11 June 1864)

Gwen Raverat on the Cam: 'unforgettable, unforgotten . . .'

I can remember the smell very well, for all the sewage went into the river, till the town was at last properly drained, when I was about ten years old (1895). There is a tale of Queen Victoria being shown over Trinity by the Master, Dr. Whewell, and saying, as she looked down over the bridge: 'What are all those pieces of paper floating down the river?' To which, with great presence of mind, he replied: 'Those, ma'am, are notices that bathing is forbidden.'

(*Period Piece,* 1952)

'Cambridge University Gazette', 11 November 1868:

We have much pleasure in announcing that her Majesty the Queen has contributed £100 towards the fund which is now being raised for the improvement of the river ... Her Majesty believes that in thus acting, she is only carrying into effect the wishes of the Prince Consort, the late Chancellor ... We are happy to learn that the Cam Purification Committee are not resting on their oars.

Henry Sidgwick complains:

1866: I hope to come to you on October 3 for a week – that is the day the University Library opens, and I want to get some books before the country clergy have gone off with them all ...

1869: We are wondering whether our usual concourse of May visitors will go on increasing, as it has the last few years; it seems that every show place gets every year more and more thronged, and it seems our destiny to turn into a show place. Learning will go elsewhere and we shall subside into cicerones. The typical Cambridge man will be the antiquarian personage who knows about the history of colleges, and is devoted to 'culture des ruines'.

(A Memoir)

Some visitors left awed impressions.

Of George Eliot F. W. H. Myers wrote:

I remember how, at Cambridge, I walked with her once in the Fellows' Garden of Trinity, on an evening of rainy May; and she, stirred somewhat beyond her wont, and taking as her text the three words which have been used so often as the inspiring trumpet-calls of men, – the words *God, Immortality, Duty,* – pronounced, with terrible earnestness, how inconceivable was the *first*, how unbelievable the *second*, and yet how peremptory and absolute the *third*. Never, perhaps, have sterner accents affirmed the sovereignty of impersonal and unrecompensing Law. I listened, and night fell; her grave, majestic countenance turned toward me like a Sibyl's in the gloom; it was as though she withdrew from my grasp, one by one, the two scrolls of promise, and left me the third scroll only, awful with inevitable fates. And when we stood at length and parted, amid that columnar circuit of the forest-trees, beneath the last twilight of starless skies, I seemed to be gazing, like Titus at Jerusalem, on vacant seats and empty halls, – on a sanctuary with no Presence to hallow it, and heaven left lonely of a God.

(Essays Modern, 1883)

Some found pleasing smells:

There is one thing that will strike you, especially if your visit is made during term time, and that is the powerful and rich odour arising from the college kitchen. As you pass through some screen, or passage from one court to another, it comes upon you with overpowering fulness, and raises in the mind bright visions of huge sirloins and savoury legs and haunches.

(Pictorial Guide to Cambridge, 1856)

Visitors' observations were often in character.

Robert Louis Stevenson:

Trinity   Autumn 1878

Here I am living like a fighting-cock and have not spoken to a real person for about sixty hours. Those who wait on me are not real. The man I know to be a myth, because I have seen him acting so often in the Palais Royal. He plays the Duke in *Tricochet et Cacolet*; I knew his nose at once. The part he plays here is very dull for him, but conscientious. As for the bedmaker, she's a dream, a kind of cheerful, innocent nightmare; I never saw so poor an imitation of humanity.

(To W. E. Henley in *Letters*, ed. Sidney Colvin, 1899)

Thomas Hardy (in King's College Chapel):

1879 – October

The reds and blues of the windows became of one indistinguishable black, the candles guttered in the most fantastic shapes I ever saw – and while the wicks burnt down those weird shapes changed form; so that you were fascinated into watching them, and wondering what shape those wisps of wax would take next, till they dropped off with a click during a silence. They were stalactites, plumes, laces; or rather they were surplices, – frayed shreds from those of bygone 'white-robed scholars', or from their shrouds – dropping bit by bit in a ghostly decay.

(Florence Emily Hardy, *Life*, 1928)

Henry James (also in 1879):

If I were called upon, however, to mention the prettiest corner of the world, I should heave a tender sigh and point the way to the garden of Trinity Hall. My companion, who was very competent to judge (but who spoke, indeed, with the partiality of a son of the house), declared, as he ushered me into it, that it was, to his mind, the most beautiful *small* garden in Europe. I freely accepted, and I promptly repeat, an affirmation so ingeniously conditioned. The little garden at Trinity Hall is narrow and crooked; it leans upon the river, from which a low parapet, all muffled in ivy, divides it; it has an ancient wall, adorned with a thousand matted creepers on one side, and on the other a group of extraordinary horse-chestnuts. These trees are of prodigious size; they occupy half the garden, and they are remarkable for the fact that their giant limbs strike down into the earth, take root again, and emulate, as they rise, the majesty of the parent tree. The manner in which this magnificent group of horse-chestnuts sprawls about over the grass, out into the middle of the lawn, is one of the most picturesque features of the garden of Trinity Hall.

(*Portraits of Places*, 1883)

Oscar Wilde in 1886:

His leave-taking was . . . characteristic of the man, though not altogether intentionally so. To the half-dozen of us who went down to the station to see him off and were clustered round his carriage window he kept up a stream of epigrams, timed to culminate at the moment of the train's departure. As an unkind chance would have it, however, the start was a false one and the train backed in again, his carriage once more opposite to the place on the platform where we were still standing. But the display was over, and not to be renewed. He promptly closed the window and remained absorbed in his paper until the real start was made.

(J. H. Badly, *Memories and Reflections*, 1955)

Caroline Slemmer (a bustling American view):

Cambridge, Oct. 16th, 1870

All these people here seem to me to lack something, backbone perhaps, which a business life gives (they despise business, and money, apparently). Jeanette is just like the rest: dreamy, poetical, imaginative, cultivated, but not robust, very intellectual, but lacking power, somehow. They all know a great deal more than I do, but I always feel as if I can tell them what to do.

but as Caroline Jebb she had a very happy Cambridge marriage:

Cambridge, April 5th, 1875

I wish you could find a cook who would be such a comfort to you as my Mrs. Bird is to me. I gave a dinner party on Thursday and left the preparation of most of the dinner to her, simply giving my orders, and everything was perfect. I got a girl in to help, paying her fifty cents, and I will tell you what Mrs. Bird had to do.

First, she made the rolls herself. (One is laid on each plate, you know, instead of bread. She makes excellent rolls.) Then she made white soup, she fried twelve fillets of sole, and made the lobster sauce to go with the fish. Next we had two entrées ordered from the college, which are handed around one at a time after the fish plates are changed. The first entrée was 'timballes de foie gras', and then, when this was eaten, and the plates changed, the second entrée, 'sweetbreads stewed with mushrooms and truffles', was passed. With these Mrs. Bird had nothing to do, which gave her breathing time to dish the main dinner. She roasted the leg of mutton, boiled the turkey, made its sauce of oysters, and cooked all the vegetables, potatoes, cauliflower and celery, which go with this course. When we were through with this, she sent up the roast duck with its sauce, and then her labours were ended. Wasn't that a great deal for her to do well, with only one assistant?

I hired two waiters to help Martin, and everything passed off delightfully. We had a plum pudding from College, and after that a Charlotte Russe, then cheese which always comes in after the puddings here, and then the table was cleared for dessert. All the wine glasses, decanters, etc., were taken off, the crumbs brushed away, and then new decanters put on, and dessert plates. The waiters then handed round one dish after another, of the dessert, after which we ladies arose and left the room to the gentlemen.

(Bobbitt, *With Dearest Love to All*)

A distinguished Fellow of Pembroke in my husband's time . . . was Professor Stokes, celebrated as the most brilliant mathematician and the most silent man in Cambridge. A young American niece of Lady Jebb when on a visit was told that at a dinner-party about to be given, she would be placed next to this learned professor. It was observed with surprise that they got on very well together and when she was congratulated on her success, she replied, 'Waal, I had been warned that it was difficult to make him talk, so I thought of a subject before-hand, and I asked him which he liked best, Euclid or Algebra' . . .

It was a joy to see Lady Jebb . . . in her elegant lightly-built victoria, a beautiful Victorian lady with long ostrich feathers swirling round her hat. The driver of the horse, Zoe, sat on a small dickey in front and received a poke from his mistress's parasol when she wished to give him any instructions. This usually resulted in an argument in which the coachman not infrequently had the last word. Another smart turn-out was Miss Waraker's high dog-cart driven by herself, with a diminutive footman, or 'tiger' behind, the wheels of pillar-box red . . . The most original turn-out was Mrs. Francis Darwin's governess-car drawn by two donkeys tandem. One of the donkeys was apt to stop dead and the only way to make him go was to rattle stones in a tin specially kept charged in the car for that purpose.

Mrs. Newall, wife of a professor, preferred to drive a pair of horses, and very beautiful they were, home-bred at Madingley Rise, sharing the paddocks with magnificent white turkeys. We had the honour of enjoying a feast provided by one of these handsome birds. The Professor was never reconciled to the motor-car, and to the end of his days drove into the town in a small closed carriage – like a brougham cut in half. Few of us could aspire to such glories. We travelled by the one-horse tram or a hired cab. Undergraduates occasionally ventured out with a dashing tandem, but this was a rare spectacle not encouraged by the authorities.

(F. M. Keynes, *Gathering Up the Threads*, 1950)

there were the river picnics. All summer, Sheep's Green and Coe Fen were pink with boys, as naked as God made them; for bathing drawers did not exist then; or, at least, not on Sheep's Green. You could see the pinkness, dancing about, quite plain from the end of our Big Island. Now to go Up River, the goal of all the best picnics, the boats had to go right by the bathing place, which lay on both sides of the narrow stream. These dangerous straits were taken in silence, and at full speed. The Gentlemen were set to the oars – in this context one always thinks of them as Gentlemen – and each Lady unfurled a parasol, and, like an ostrich, buried her head in it, and gazed earnestly into its silky depths, until the crisis was past, and the river was decent again.

(Raverat, *Period Piece*)

Even Autumn had its pleasures:

Sept. 7th 1880,
And now they have all gone cheerfully away to their own places, mostly of amusement. It really reminds me of the chapter in the Bible. One man must go

home to see his mother's maid married; another to Normandy, his people were so very dull and discontented, and so on. You would think they all, for their own sakes, would *prefer* to stay in Cambridge for September, grinding over their books, but that it behooved a man not to be too selfish.

And, indeed, to go away now is to lose something. The air and weather generally never are so nice in Cambridge as during this month. One could dance in delight getting out into these big solitary college gardens, with such a sky overhead, such clear sunshine, still trees and beautiful colours.

(Caroline Jebb to her mother, in Bobbitt,
With Dearest Love to All)

September 16, 1876

This is absolutely *saison morte* in Cambridge, but we have one or two friends near by a happy accident. In about a week most of them will have re-assembled, and be in preparation for the term's work. There is a prevailing theory that Cambridge is unhealthy in September, but I believe this to be due to an inversion of cause and effect not uncommon; it is said to be unhealthy because every one goes away then, and not *vice versa*.

(Henry Sidgwick, A Memoir)

CAVENDO TUTUS – SAFE BY BEING CAUTIOUS

The nineteenth century saw the growth and development of science.

Darwin's 'Origin of Species' had splintered some of the citadel walls of his university. Adam Sedgwick, at Trinity from 1804 and from 1818 professor of geology, wrote to Darwin:

Parts of it I admired greatly, parts I laughed at till my sides were almost sore; other parts I read with absolute sorrow, because I think them utterly false and grievously mischievous. You have utterly *deserted* – after a start in that tramroad of all physical truth – the true method of induction ... Many of your wide conclusions are based upon assumptions which can neither be proved nor disproved ... Passages in your book ... greatly shocked my moral taste. I think, in speculating an organic descent, you *over*-state the evidence of geology; and that you *under*-state it while you are talking of the broken links of your natural pedigree ... Lastly then, I greatly dislike the concluding chapter ...

And now to say a word about a son of a monkey and an old friend of yours. I am better, far better, than I was last year. I have been lecturing three days a week (formerly I gave six a week) without much fatigue, but I find, by the loss of activity and memory, and of all productive powers, that my bodily frame is sinking slowly towards the earth. But I have visions of the future ...

I have written in a hurry, and in a spirit of brotherly love. Therefore forgive any sentence you happen to dislike; and believe me, spite of our disagreement on some points of the deepest moral interest, your true-hearted old friend.

(J. W. Clark and T. M. Hughes, *Life and
Letters of A. Sedgwick*, 1890)

Degree time:
A problem paper in the Senate House (*Cambridge Scrapbook*, 1859)

It was not until 1874 that Cambridge had any proper laboratory:

As you walk down Pembroke Street you see some seven or eight acres to right and left of you, covered with buildings devoted to 'Science'. That is the grown, or rather the growing, tree: What was the seedling 60 years ago from which it has developed? I should say that it was a small table, such as two people might take their tea at; a table not in constant use, but brought into the Arts School three times a week during the May term. This will need some explanation. I am not speaking of the medical schools; and exception must be made of the Sedgwick Geological Museum, which already existed on the ground floor of the Cockerell Building in the University Library. But it is more than epigrammatically true of all the other modern departments. The performer at that table was Professor Stokes during his lectures on Physical Optics. He had the use of the room just for the purpose of his lectures. In 1856, when I attended, an assistant followed him with a heliostat, a prism, and one or two similar articles, which were placed on the table, and removed at the end of the lecture. Very likely he had more apparatus in his college rooms, but that was all we students knew of. It is possible that Miller, the professor of Mineralogy, and Henslow, of Botany, adopted similar devices; but I have some doubts as to this. Willis, the Jacksonian professor, had, I am told, a collection of mechanical models; but there was no museum in which to keep them.

(Venn, *Early Collegiate Life*)

William Cavendish, seventh Duke of Devonshire, was at Trinity and in 1829 was second wrangler and first Smith's prizeman. He gave his name and motto to the laboratory:

Holker Hall, Grange, Lancashire
My dear Vice-Chancellor,   October 10 1870
    I find ... that the buildings and apparatus required for this department of Science are estimated to cost £6,300. I am desirous to assist the University in

carrying this recommendation to effect, and shall accordingly be prepared to provide the funds required.

The first professor of experimental physics was James Clerk Maxwell of Peterhouse and Trinity. During the building of the Laboratory he wrote from Scotland:

Laboratory rising I hear, but I have no place to erect my chair, but move about like a cuckoo, depositing my notions in the Chemical Lecture-room 1st term; in the Botanical in Lent, and in Comparative Anatomy in Easter.

His inaugural lecture in 1871 set the tone:

It may possibly be true that in some of those fields of discovery which lie open to such rough observations as can be made without artificial methods, the great explorers of former times have appropriated most of what is valuable, and the gleanings which remain are to be sought after, rather for their abstruseness than for their intrinsic worth. But the history of science shows that even during that phase of her progress in which she devotes herself to improving the accuracy of the numerical measurement of quantities with which she has long been familiar, she is preparing the materials for the subjugation of new regions, which would have remained unknown if she had been contented with the rough methods of her early pioneers . . .

It will be a result worthy of the University if by the free and full discussion of the relative value of different scientific procedures, we succeed in forming a school of scientific criticism.

On the death of Maxwell in 1879 Lord Rayleigh was his reluctant successor. Senior wrangler in 1865 at Trinity, he had written several papers, the titles of some of which are as follows:

'On the invisibility of small objects in a bad light'
'On the theory of illumination in a fog'
'Sensitive flowers'
'The form of standing waves on the surface of running water'
'The soaring of birds'

(from J. G. Crowther, The Cavendish Laboratory, 1874–1974, 1974)

When Rayleigh retired in 1884 he was succeeded by J. J. Thomson, who was then only 27:

1890s:
The tea hour was in many ways the best time in the laboratory day. The tea itself had no special quality; the biscuits were unattractive in the extreme, and very dull; the conversation sparkled and scintillated, and as a social function tea was an outstanding success. There seemed to be no subject in which J.J. was not interested and well informed; current politics, current fiction, drama, university sport, all these came under review. The conversation was not usually about physics, at least not in its technical aspects, though it often turned on the

personalities or idiosyncrasies of scientific men in other countries, who were known personally to some of those present and by reputation to all. J.J. had something to say on nearly any subject that might turn up. He was a good raconteur, but also a good listener, and knew how to draw out even shy members of the company.

(R. J. S. Rayleigh, J. J. Thomson, 1942)

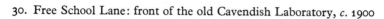

30. Free School Lane: front of the old Cavendish Laboratory, *c.* 1900

IONS MINE
(to the tune of Clementine)

In the dusty lab'ratory
'Mid the coils and wax and twine,
There the atoms in their glory,
Ionize and recombine.

Chorus Oh my darlings! Oh my darlings!
Oh my darling ions mine!
You are lost and gone for ever
When just once you recombine! *etc.*

(from G. P. Thomson, *J. J. Thomson and
the Cavendish*, 1964)

The year 1895 is one of the most important years in the history of the Cavendish
Laboratory, for then a regulation came into force by which graduates of other
universities were admitted to Cambridge as 'Research Students', and if after
two years residence at Cambridge they submitted to a Committee a thesis
containing an account of their researches, they were entitled to a Cambridge
degree (first M.A., later Ph.D.), provided the Committee declared it was 'of
distinction as a record of original research'.

(J. J. Thomson, *Recollections*)

*One of the first to come to Cambridge under this scheme was Ernest Rutherford,
who came from New Zealand in 1895. He was soon working on wireless waves.
Rutherford wrote frequent letters to Mary Newton, later to be his wife:*

29 Feb. 1896. When I left off last time I had just been out on the Common
trying to detect waves at long distance. The next day I tried and got an effect
from the Lab. to Townsend's diggings a distance of over half a mile through
solid stone houses all the way. The Professor is exceedingly interested in the
results, and I am at present very useful when he is writing to various scientific
pots as he can mention what his students are doing at the Lab. Some good
startling effects with waves suit him down to the ground. The morning after my
midnight excursion, Sir R. Ball came down to see how I got along. He called in
the other day and told me I could make use of the Observatory which is about
a mile out of town . . . it is a very good offer . . .

May 1896 Breakfast with McTaggart, Hegelian Philosopher and Fellow of
Trinity, but he gave me a very poor breakfast worse luck. His philosophy doesn't
count for much when brought face to face with two kidneys . . .

July 1896 I have been working pretty steadily with Professor J. J. Thomson
on the X-rays and find it pretty interesting . . . We are all supposed to go into
College if we come up for the long vacation.

Trinity College: 27 Aug. 1896 . . . I have been very busy today running over
my experiments for the British Association. Pye, the workshop man, has made
some things very nicely for me and I will be very well equipped for my apparatus . . .

11 Nov. 1896 ... On Saturday night the Science Club met in Mr. Shipley's rooms at Christ's College, which are reputed to be the finest in the University.
2 Dec. 1896 He (J.J.) is just 40 and looks quite young, small, rather straggling moustache, short, wears his hair (black) rather long, but has a very clever-looking face, and a very fine forehead and a most radiating smile, or grin as some call it when he is scoring off anyone ...
12 Dec. 1897 ... I have a great piece of news to tell you ... I went in for the Coutts Trotter Scholarship, and it has been awarded to me for two years at £250 a year, think of it – nearly enough to get married on.

(A. S. Eve, *Rutherford*, 1939)

In August 1898 he was appointed to the professorship of physics at McGill University in Montreal. He did not return to Cambridge until he was appointed Cavendish Professor in 1919 in place of 'J.J.' who became Master of Trinity.

Rutherford was now the 'character':

As I was standing in the drawing-room at Trinity, a *clergyman* came in. And I said to him: 'I'm Lord Rutherford.' And he said to me, 'I'm the Archbishop of York.' And I don't suppose either of us believed the other.

(Rutherford on himself, as reported by C. P. Snow, *Variety of Men*, 1967)

On the occasion of one of his discoveries, the writer said to him: 'You are a lucky man, Rutherford, always on the crest of the wave!' To which he laughingly replied, 'Well! I made the wave, didn't I?' and he added soberly, 'At least to some extent.'

(A. S. Eve and J. Chadwick in *Obituary Notices of Fellows of the Royal Society*, 1937)

I went to no more lectures, except to Rutherford, whom I could not resist. He would boom on, talking about all kinds of interesting things, occasionally producing gems like 'integral y. dx; dx is small, we will neglect this'. He talked so easily and informally, he knew it all in an instinctive, relaxed way and the answer always somehow came out right. As someone said: 'The α particles were his friends, he knew what they would do' (there was a story, which I have not verified, that in one of his early papers the mass of an α particle came out as 3.3 on which he commented: 'we take four as the nearest integer').

(Sir Edward Bullard in *Nature*, 30 August 1974)

One man complained to Rutherford that he was being starved of apparatus. 'Why,' said Rutherford, 'I could do research at the North Pole.'

(Crowther, *Cavendish Laboratory*)

Despite the active beginnings in engineering by Farish and others, the first professorship was not approved until 1875. Although it was agreed by 74 votes to 36, there was much opposition. Dr. Robert Phelps, Master of Sidney Sussex noted it:

with profound regret and humiliation . . . As I, of course, expected, the whole force of University Radicalism and the corps Professional were in favour of the Grace.

James Alfred Ewing said in his inaugural lecture:

I have to plead for nothing less than the inclusion of a complete School of Engineering in that new Cambridge which is fast springing up with the old.

(T. J. N. Hilken, *Engineering in Cambridge,*
1783–1965, 1967)

But it was not until 1894 that there were new buildings and a new tripos.

The twentieth century:
a sunny world

The glow of the last years of Queen Victoria's reign, the radiance of the Edwardian era and the still sunny world inherited by King George V, are all reflected in the memoirs, letters and diaries of those who were in Cambridge during that time, until the Great War in 1914.

Academic histories, like academic memoirs, have the curious effect of distancing and embalming the conditions they describe. Thus we are prone to view the whole academic past in the pale violet tints of Andrew Lang's or E. F. Benson's or Sir John Betjeman's anecdotage.

(J. A. W. Bennett, *Chaucer at Oxford and Cambridge,* 1974)

Others of that set have gone almost out of my mind and some of them out of the world. But still their forms appear in the golden mists of dawn and almost I catch their voices through talk of younger generations, heard under the same chapel walls and the same chestnut groves, on the same great lawns, under the same stars reflected in the same sluggish yet lovely stream that will hear perhaps for centuries yet the same voices at the same budding time of youth; unless – who knows? they fall silent even before the eternal silence closes upon me.

(Forster, *Goldsworthy Lowes Dickinson*)

31. The still sunny world – Clare Bridge. (From Walter M. Keesey, *Cambridge – A sketchbook*, 1913)

That gold and violet haze enveloped many recollections but what undeniably shines through the mist was a sense of pleasure and enjoyment and a kind of innocence.

George Santayana, in King's for a year in 1896, describes the chapel:

That which at once catches the eye is the vault. It is held up, lifted up, as if it could move, like a baldachino over a procession; it is woven of intricate fan traceries, undulating slightly, without sharp arches, or heavy pendants; the fans open like palm trees from the piers, and then merge their branches in a chain of diamonds and circles down the flat central part. It is regal elegance, rather than religious mystery, that spreads this canopy over us; yet never was perspective more magnetic or vault more alive. We are in the presence of something magical, something sublime.

(My Host the World, 1953)

Maurice Baring remembers:

In spite of having learnt nothing in an academic sense at Cambridge, I am glad I went there, and I think I learnt a good deal in other ways. I look back on it and I see the tall trees just coming out in the backs, behind King's College; a picnic in canoes on the Cam; bookshops, especially a dark, long bookshop in Trinity Street where a plaintive voice told one that Norman Gale would be sure to go up; little dinner-parties in my rooms in Trinity Street, the food arriving on a tray from the College kitchen where the cook made *crème brûlée* better than anyone in the world, and one night fireworks on the windowsill and the thin curtains ablaze; rehearsals for the A.D.C., and Mr. Clarkson making one up; long, idle mornings in Trinity and King's; literary discussions in rooms at Trinity; debates of the Decemviri in Carr-Bosanquet's room on the ground floor of the Great Court; summer afternoons in King's College gardens, and the light streaming through the gorgeous glass of the west window in King's Chapel, where, listening to the pealing anthem, I certainly never dreamed of taxing the royal Saint with vain expense; gossip at the Pitt Club in the mornings, crowds

32. An alfresco tea in Honeysuckle Walk: Girton College students, 1906

33. Trinity College bridge, 1890

of youths with well-brushed hair and straw hats telling stories in front of the fireplace; the Sunday-evening receptions in Oscar Browning's rooms.

At King's my great friends were X and A. A was the most original of all the undergraduates I knew. He was shy and fastidious beyond words. He could not endure being shaved at Cambridge, and used to go up to London twice a week for that purpose. *(The Puppet Show of Memory, 1922)*

Ralph Vaughan Williams:

The first year (1892) he had rooms at 17 Magdalene Street, then he moved to 2 Whewells Court, where he remained for the rest of his time at Cambridge . . He and Randolph (his name for Ralph Wedgwood) used to lunch together almost every day, and their usual meal was biscuits and jam. They planned to go right through an alphabet of biscuits, but the grocer supplied a seven-pound tin of Abernethys to start with and on that rock the plan foundered.

(V. Vaughan Williams, *Ralph Vaughan Williams*, 1964)

Edward Marsh:

What strikes me most when I look back on the life which I and my companions led at Cambridge, is an extraordinary innocence and simplicity . . . We lived with a high degree of plainness, entertaining one another at breakfast, generally on eggs which we had personally 'buttered'. *(A Number of People, 1939)*

There were other simplicities:

1901
In the 'New Building' there was a W.C. on each staircase, and in the Second

[255]

Court there were three closets over a running stream, separate from another closet for the dons downstream. As far as I can remember these were the only conveniences in the College.

(E. B. Haddon in *Christ's College Magazine*, 1968)

The W.C.'s in Christ's were always known as Fourth Court

1911

After civilised London, it came as a shock to find that running hot and cold water were unknown in Cambridge. All we had were a bowl on a stand and a shallow tin bath, kept under the bed. Manservants, or 'gyps' looked after us, and arrived before 7 a.m. Their first job was to drag out the tin saucer and pour a large can of cold water into it ...

(Rex Salisbury Woods, *Cambridge Doctor*, 1962)

and rules abounded.

1902

It is forbidden [for students] ... to resort to, or take part in, meetings for the purpose of pigeon-shooting; to take part in a steeple-chase; to ride in a horse race ... to drive tandems or four-in-hand carriages ... to drive in a dog-cart or vehicle on Sunday without the written permission of their tutor ... to use a boat on the river above Newnham unless they have sent to the Junior Proctor a certificate ... that they can swim easily and well one hundred yards.

1913–14

to keep and use motor cars, motor bicycles, or other motor vehicles ... unless a licence from a Junior Proctor ... has previously been obtained.

34. 'Progged', 1910

Academical dress:

1902

On Sundays cap and gown must be worn in the courts and grounds; but students going for a country walk may wear ordinary dress provided they do not pass through the streets.

(Students' Handbook to the University and Colleges of Cambridge, 1902 and 1913/14)

but did not seem to affect pleasure abounding:

Leonard Woolf:

Late at night in the May term, I like to remember, Lytton, Saxon, Thoby Stephen, Clive Bell, and I would sometimes walk through the Cloisters of Nevile's Court in Trinity and looking out through the bars at the end on to the willows and water of the Backs, ghostly in the moonlight, listen to the soaring song of innumerable nightingales. And sometimes as we walked back through the majestic Cloisters we chanted poetry. More often than not it would be Swinburne.

(Sowing, An Autobiography, 1960)

A. C. Benson describes a cycle ride:

The space between the towpath full of masses of cow-parsley: the river sapphire blue between the green banks – the huge fields running for miles to the right, with the long lines of dyke and lode; far away the blue tower of Ely, the brown roofs of Reach, and the low wolds of Newmarket. It was simply *enchanting*! . . . I declare that the *absolutely* flat country, golden with the buttercups, and the blue tree-clumps far away backed by hills, and over all the vast sky-perspective is *the* most beautiful thing of all.

(David Newsome, On the Edge of Paradise. A. C. Benson the Diarist, 1980)

and a day in the country (instead of going to King Edward VII's funeral):

The place is quiet; half the college has gone to the funeral. The garden is delicious, especially the great burst of speedwell, just where the path under the bastion turns up to the arbour . . .

I can forgive to-day its heat for being so golden-sweet, so summer-scented. In the afternoon we motored out to Harlton, through fragrant air, the fields golden with buttercups. Everything has come out with a wild rush of leaf and bloom. Here we left the car and struck up from Eversden by the old clunch-pit into the Mareway. The landscape deliciously hazy; the Mareway itself held the rain of yesterday in its oozy ruts, and we mainly walked in breezy fields to left and right, with lovely silent views of wide champaign country, and by the corners of secluded woods. Then down through Wimpole and along the great avenue . . .

The great house blinked down the vast avenue, and we walked among cowslips and meadow-grass. It is a holiday today, and the roads are full of tall-hatted rustics and girls in mourning, enjoying themselves with infinite solemnity.

(A. C. Benson. Diary, ed. P. Lubbock, 1926)

Jacob on the river:

Where they moored their boat the trees showered down so that their topmost leaves trailed in the ripples and the green wedge that lay in the water being made of leaves shifted in leaf-breadths as the real leaves shifted. Now there was a shiver of wind – instantly an edge of sky; and as Durrant ate cherries he dropped the stunted yellow cherries through the green wedge of leaves, their stalks twinkling as they wriggled in and out, and sometimes one half-bitten cherry would go down red into the green. The meadow was on a level with Jacob's eyes as he lay back; gilt with buttercups, but the grass did not run like the thin green water of the graveyard grass about to overflow the tombstones, but stood juicy and thick. Looking up, backwards, he saw the legs of children deep in the grass, and the legs of cows.

(V. Woolf, *Jacob's Room*, 1922)

Rickie begins another term:

As soon as term opened he returned to Cambridge, for which he longed passionately. The journey thither was now familiar to him, and he took pleasure in each landmark. The fair valley of Towin Water, the cutting into Hitchin where the train traverses the chalk, Baldock Church, Royston with its promise of downs, were nothing in themselves, but dear as stages in his pilgrimage towards the abode of peace. On the platform he met friends. They had all had pleasant vacations: it was a happy world. The atmosphere alters.

Cambridge, according to her custom, welcomed her sons with open drains. Pettycury was up, so was Trinity Street, and navvies peeped out of King's Parade. Here it was gas, there electric light, but everywhere something, and always a smell. It was also the day that the wheels fell off the station tram, and Rickie, who was naturally inside, was among the passengers who 'sustained no injury but a shock, and had as hearty a laugh over the mishap afterwards as any one'. . . . They waited for the other tram by the Roman Catholic Church, whose florid bulk was already receding into twilight. It is the first big building that the incoming visitor sees. 'Oh, here come the colleges!' cries the Protestant parent, and then learns that it was built by a Papist who made a fortune out of movable eyes for dolls. 'Built out of dolls' eyes to contain idols' – that, at all events, is the legend and the joke. It watches over the apostate city, taller by many a yard than anything within, and asserting, however wildly, that here is eternity, stability, and bubbles unbreakable upon a windless sea.

A costly hymn tune announced five o'clock, and in the distance the more lovable note of St. Mary's could be heard, speaking from the heart of the town. Then the tram arrived – the slow stuffy tram that plies every twenty minutes between the unknown and the market-place – and took them past the desecrated grounds of Downing, past Addenbrooke's Hospital, girt like any Venetian palace with a mantling canal, past the Fitz William, towering upon immense substructions like any Roman temple, right up to the gates of one's own college, which looked like nothing else in the world. The porters were glad to see them, but wished it had been a hansom.

(E. M. Forster, *The Longest Journey*, 1907)

The philosopher, G. E. Moore, came up to Trinity:

17 St. John's Street
9 October 1892

My lodgings are two small angular rooms, with two windows for the sitting-, one for the bed-room. They are in the same house with at least three other sets of rooms, I think, and are on the top-floor. A young man waits on me, though I have seen a woman, who asked me if I wanted tea last night. The other, who seemed more pleasant at first than now, though he is quiet and neat, told me that I must get my tea and sugar, but that they would be willing to supply bread and butter ('commons'), porridge at 2*d* the soup plate, and a large set of meat-dishes at 6*d* each; he said that very many 'young gentlemen' had these hot things for breakfast and merely bread and butter or jam for lunch. My washing will be fetched by the college-laundress on Mondays, quite independently of the Landlady;... As for lighting, I had to choose between gas and lamp; and I chose the latter, thinking it was better for my eyes. My fire seems to smoke badly with this S.W. wind; but I think I shall like my quarters very well. The sitting-room faces nearly due north, the bed-room N.E. Both are moderately decorated. In the former there is even a small-leaved begonia (Wiltoniensis), standing on an ornamental wicker-table.

(Paul Levy, *G. E. Moore and the Cambridge
Apostles*, 1979)

Rupert Brooke came up to King's in 1906:

Nov. 1906 ... If you come to Cambridge at the end of the month you will see a performance of the Eumenides, in which an aged and grey haired person called Rupert Brooke is wearily taking the part of the Herald. I put a long horn to my lips and pretend to blow and a villain in the orchestra simultaneously wantons on the cornet. It is very symbolic.

(Letter to St. John Lucas)

9 November 1906
The idea of my playing Hermes fell through, but they have given me the equally large part of the Herald. I stand in the middle of the stage and pretend to blow a trumpet, while somebody in the wings makes a sudden noise. The part is not difficult. The rehearsals are very amusing.

(To his mother)

The Orchard, Grantchester

July 1909
It is a lovely village on the river above Cambridge. I'm in a small house, a sort of cottage, with a dear plump weather-beaten kindly old lady in control. I have a perfectly glorious time, seeing nobody I know day after day. The room I have opens straight out onto a stone verandah covered with creepers, & a little old garden full of old-fashioned flowers and *crammed* with roses. I work at Shakespeare, read, write all day, & now and then wander in the woods or by the river.

The Old Vicarage

This is a deserted, lonely, dank, ruined, overgrown, gloomy, lovely house: with a garden to match.

(To Erica Cotterill)

GRANTCHESTER

Ah God! to see the branches stir
Across the moon at Grantchester!
To smell the thrilling-sweet and rotten
Unforgettable, unforgotten
River-smell, and hear the breeze
Sobbing in the little trees.
Say, do the elm-clumps greatly stand
Still guardians of that holy land?
The chestnuts shade, in reverend dream,
The yet unacademic stream?
Is dawn a secret shy and cold
Anadyomene, silver-gold?
And sunset still a golden sea
From Haslingfield to Madingley?
And after, ere the night is born,
Do hares come out about the corn?
Oh, is the water sweet and cool,
Gentle and brown, above the pool?
And laughs the immortal river still
Under the mill, under the mill?
Say, is there Beauty yet to find?
And Certainty? and Quiet kind?
Deep meadows yet, for to forget
The lies, and truths, and pain?... oh! yet
Stands the church clock at ten to three?
And is there honey still for tea?

19 July 1912
and the youth of Grantchester quote my local patriotic poetry to me as I ride by on a bicycle.

(To Maynard Keynes)

Less well-known:

My heart is sick for several things
Only to be found in King's...

I do recall those haunts with tears,
The Backs, the Chapel, and the Rears...

O Places of perpetual mire,
Localities of my desire,
O lovely, O remembered gloom

And froust of Chetwynd lecture-room . . .
O spots my memory is gilding,
O Jumbo Arch! O Wilkins Building! . . .

Haunts where I drank the whole damn night!
Place where I catted till the light!
Dear spot where I was taken short,
O Bodley's Court! O Bodley's Court!

(In a letter to C. F. Schofield written in
Toronto, July–August 1913)

(*Letters of Rupert Brooke*, ed. Geoffrey
Keynes, 1968)

Menus for occasions

Cambridge University Drag & Beagle Hunt, 11 March 1892

Mock Turtle
Clear Spring Soup

Salmon, Cardinal Sauce
Smelts, Hollandaise Sauce

Sirloins of Beef
Saddles of Mutton

Braised Fowls à la Milanaise
York Ham

Winchester Puddings
Rhubarb Tarts
Jellies

Gonville and Caius Bump Supper, Saturday, 24 February 1894

Croûtes de Caviare
Potage à la get-out-at-the-Pike-and-Eel
Blanchailles au Cam
Boudin de Foie Gras aux Truffes
Canard Sauvage à la Ditton Fen
Pouding à la Grassy
Croûtes d'Anchois

May Week   Cambridge 1893   A printed programme for guests

Arrive	4.0. p.m. Saturday, 10 June 1893
Saturday	Tea at Westfield
	'The Mixture' Theatre Royal
Sunday	Service in King's Chapel
	Anthem 'Hear My Prayer' Mendelssohn
	Tea and Sacred Music at No. 13
Monday	To the Races in 'The Hearse'
	Dinner at Hard's

35. King's Parade (1897): a pretty promenade. (From T. D. Atkinson and
J. W. Clark, *Cambridge Described and Illustrated*)

Tuesday	Lunch in Caius, Mr. E. A. Donaldson
	River-party to the Races, Mr. Barclay-Smith
	Third Trinity Ball in the Guildhall
Wednesday	Lunch at Hard's, Mrs. Butler
	Oratorio 'Judith' in King's Chapel
	First Trinity Ball in Trinity College
Thursday	Lunch at 'Westfield'
	Mrs. Butler, 'At Home' Westfield
	Photographic séance and general frivol.
	Masonic Ball in Guildhall
Friday	Water Picnic SS *Otter*
	'Way down upon the Swanee River'
Saturday	Tea at No. 13
	Canadian Canoedling

13 Market Street   Westfield
Cambridge   Little Shelford

(All from Cambridge University Library.
Presented by E. A. B. Barnard, MA, FSA,
St. Catharine's College)

There was mountaineering, of a sort, in Cambridge itself:

GREAT COURT. – Circuit; time, 1–2 hrs. This expedition, offering as it does
almost every variety of roof climbing difficulty, and hindered as it is by every
form of authoritative residence, has only once been accomplished. In its absolute

entirety the circuit has never been completed, the Great Gate forming as yet an unconquered barrier. Sections of it are generally taken in connection with other routes.

Our excursion takes us to the leads on the Lecture-room side of the Great Gate. Avoiding all temptation to stray over the tiles into the almost unexplored back regions of Trinity Street or the problems of I Court (Route D), the first point calling for attention, with the exception of ankle-wringing drain-holes (most difficult to avoid in the dark) is the corner turret (B).

Mutton-Hole Turret is often generously simplified by the College Authorities by means of a species of iron-spoked rope which is left hooked over the battlements. If this is absent, the turret affords excellent practice for 'the men in a tower' method of backing up, and has of course the customary loose pipe. At this corner it is easy again to cross by the lead gutter and join the I Court (Route D, Trinity Lane Corner) . . .

The Lodge. – A natural awe, combined with apparent difficulties, has done much to prevent this part of the circuit being often visited; in fact it is only known to have been crossed once.

(Winthrop Young, *Roof-Climber's Guide to Trinity*, 1899)

Bertrand Russell went for walks:

1890   On Sunday it was our custom to breakfast late and then spend the whole day till dinner walking. I got to know every road and footpath within ten miles of Cambridge, and many at much greater distances, in this way. In general I felt happy and comparatively calm, while at Cambridge, but on moonlight nights I used to career round the country in a state of temporary lunacy. The reason, of course, was sexual desire, though at the time I did not know this.

(*Autobiography, 1872–1967*, 1967–9)

There was a preoccupation with sport of every kind:

I was 'up' once at the time of the Oxford and Cambridge Sports and well do I remember the great crowd of undergraduates and dons . . . waiting at the Union for the telegram which would tell who had won the final event. Suddenly 'click, click' went the machine, and as the clerk came out with the message there was a wild rush to the board. A don who had torn his gown in the rush was bent over the paper, touching it with his spectacled eyes, and everyone was impatient. Suddenly the old don looked up and turned away in disgust saying, 'Bah, it's only from the House of Commons', and a shudder of disappointment went through the crowd.

In the afternoon gowns are at a premium . . . Men pour out of their rooms arm-in-arm, or cycling in the bright hued blazers and costumes of every branch of sport, from rowing to lacrosse. The calm slow river which seemed in the quietness of the morning like a canal in a garden is now alive with bright boats. The ear is greeted with pleasant sounds, the roll of the sliding-seats, the grating of the oars in the rowlocks as the men bend together over the stretchers, then the clean gripping of the water by eight blades and the boat is heard to leap strongly through the water. The green fields for miles around are tinted with ruddy boisterous life . . . As the light grows dimmer the young athletes, with glowing bodies all spattered with mud and rain, return to cosy rooms to scores of genial tea-parties enjoyed in an atmosphere sweet with smoke and fire-light.

(Article by S. B. Kitchen, in *Empire Review*, 1903)

One 'sport' was hoaxes.

The visit of the Sultan of Zanzibar:

We collected two friends from Cambridge, and another from Oxford, went to London, and got made up at a theatrical costumier's. From London we took train back to Cambridge, first sending off a telegram to the Mayor warning him to expect us. We signed the telegram 'Lucas' I remember, simply because someone said that high colonial officials always bore that name.

Anyhow, everything went off perfectly. We were met at the station by the Town Clerk and driven in a carriage to the Guildhall, where we were formally received by the Mayor. We then paid a royal visit to a charity bazaar which was going on there, Cole as the Sultan's uncle making enormous purchases at all the stalls, and then emerged into the town, where we were shown the principal colleges.

When all was over, the Town Clerk conducted us back to the station, and then arose the problem of escape . . . as soon as we reached the platform we lifted our skirts, fled through the crowds waiting for the train, jumped into hansoms and drove off. We just told the cabbies to drive for all they were worth, and directed them out into the country.

(Adrian Stephen, *The 'Dreadnought' Hoax*, 1936)

Even examinations were not always taken too seriously.

Rupert Brooke:

Guildhall (Cambridge)
10.30. 18 May 1909

Your tidings make even this grey place, in which I sit, bright. For I am a prisoner beneath the picture of the late Queen Victoria, in a room where a hundred and eight damned fools are writing Greek verses for the classical Trip. And I am writing an ode to spring and a letter to you. Also there is a bald invigilating don, asleep.

(*Letters*, ed. Geoffrey Keynes)

Bets on the tripos:

Bets and sweepstakes were not wholly unknown and Cambridge swarmed with men able to tell you the several years and places of all notable persons and of many obscure . . . In the town, Tripos Lists were as interesting as news from Newmarket or Epsom. On going to order my B.A. gown and hood, my tailor made me a bow, pointed to our list posted up in the shop, and said in a voice of triumph, 'We've got three in the first six, Sir.'

(Heitland, *After Many Years*)

31 January 1889

Myers once told me that he recovered in London a portmanteau containing a mass of papers (unlooked over) of the Moral Sciences Tripos, just half an hour before the man who had taken it by mistake was about to carry it off with a lot of others to the West of Ireland, where, as he told M, he 'might not have looked at it for weeks!' But this, I imagine, is the kind of hair-breadth escape that only happens to imaginative persons.

(Henry Sidgwick to H. G. Dakyns, from *A Memoir*)

Degree fees:

The fees were paid in golden sovereigns. Eight were dropped into a wooden bowl before one signed the book. The degrees were conferred in the order of the candidates in the Mathematical Tripos Part I ... The last man to pass the Tripos was known as the Wooden Spoon. His friends in the Gallery of the Senate House dangled over his head a large wooden spoon about six feet high held in position by ribbon of his College colour with his name and College painted on it. As soon as the Vice-Chancellor had conferred on him his B.A. degree, he produced a large pair of tailor's scissors from his coat pocket, cut the ribbons and put the spoon on his left shoulder. He then marched out of the Senate House to the applause of all the spectators.

(T. Knox-Shaw, *Sidney Sussex* [1905]. *Reminiscences*, 1972)

Undergraduates or students?

The technical University term at Cambridge for a student before he has taken his first degree is 'undergraduate'; the B.A. and M.A. members of the University

36. 'The world's workers' (an examiners' meeting, 1914)

are called 'graduates' ... It may be noted in passing that our undergraduates in speaking amongst themselves do *not* employ the term 'student' ... There are Scottish 'students' and Welsh 'students' and Irish 'students', but a young Englishman studying at Cambridge or Oxford generally uses the term 'man' ... 'a Cambridge man', 'a Trinity man', 'a third year man'.

(K. Breul, Students' Life and Work in the University, 1908)

In 1896 I went to Canada, with no expectation of return. But the College recalled me, and the day after I landed in England, in 1901, I met Sikes ... We greeted, spoke a few words, and then 'Excuse me', said Sikes, and turned to speak to a young man. He came back to me. 'Was that a student?' I asked simply. 'We don't use that word here', said Sikes austerely.

(T. R. Glover, Cambridge Retrospect, 1943)

Undergraduate conversation:

'The cow is there,' said Ansell, lighting a match and holding it out over the carpet. No one spoke. He waited until the end of the match fell off. Then he said again, 'She is there, the cow. There, now.'

'You have not proved it,' said a voice.

'I have proved it to myself.'

'I have proved to myself that she isn't,' said the voice. 'The cow is *not* there.' Ansell frowned and lit another match.

'She's there for me,' he declared. 'I don't care whether she's there for you or not. Whether I'm in Cambridge or Iceland or dead, the cow will be there.'

It was philosophy. They were discussing the existence of objects. Do they exist only when there is some one to look at them? Or have they a real existence of their own? It is all very interesting, but at the same time it is difficult. Hence the cow. She seemed to make things easier. She was so familiar, so solid, that surely the truths that she illustrated would in time become familiar and solid also. Is the cow there or not? This was better than deciding between objectivity and subjectivity. So at Oxford, just at the same time, one was asking, 'What do our rooms look like in the vac.?'

'Look here, Ansell. I'm there – in the meadow – the cow's there. Do you agree so far?'

'Well?'

'Well, if you go, the cow stops; but if I go, the cow goes. Then what will happen if you stop and I go?'

Several voices cried out that this was quibbling.

'I know it is,' said the speaker brightly, and silence descended again, while they tried honestly to think the matter out.

(E. M. Forster, The Longest Journey)

Leonard Woolf:

We were intellectuals, intellectuals with three genuine and, I think, profound passions: a passion for friendship, a passion for literature and music and a passion for what we called truth.

(*Sowing*)

Bertrand Russell:

The one habit of thought of real value that I acquired there was intellectual honesty. This virtue certainly existed not only among my friends, but among my teachers.

(*Autobiography*)

Lytton Strachey:

Cambridge, whose cloisters have ever been consecrated to poetry and common-sense.

(*Eminent Victorians*, 1918)

J. M. Keynes (as an undergraduate):

I've had a good look round the place and come to the conclusion that it's pretty inefficient.

(Quoted by C. R. Fay in *Essays on John MaynardKeynes*, ed. Milo Keynes, 1975)

G. M. Trevelyan (before coming up):

As far as I can make out the Cambridge people are intellectual but not serious.

(Mary Moorman, *G. M. Trevelyan. A Memoir*, 1980)

E. M. Forster:

The College, [King's] though small, was civilised, and proud of its civilisation. It was not sufficient glory to be a Blue there, nor an additional glory to get drunk ... The direction of the swim was determined a little by the genius of the place ... and a good deal by the tutors and resident Fellows, who treated with rare dexterity the products that came up yearly from the public schools. They taught the perky boy that he was not everything and the limp boy that he might be something. They even welcomed those boys who were neither limp nor perky, but odd – those boys who had never been to a public school at all, and such do not find a welcome everywhere. And they did everything with ease – one might almost say with nonchalance – so that the boys noticed nothing and received education, often for the first time in their lives.

(*The Longest Journey*)

Rose Macaulay on E. M. Forster:

There is a Way, a Truth, a Life: you may call it, he seems to tell us, Cambridge ... Cambridge is one of Mr. Forster's symbols for the saved state.

(*The Writings of E. M. Forster*, 1938)

Brothers of the Society of the Apostles:

It was a principle in discussion that there were to be no *taboos*, no limitations, nothing considered shocking, no barriers to absolute freedom of speculation. We discussed all manner of things, no doubt with a certain immaturity, but with a detachment and interest scarcely possible in later life. The meetings would generally end about one o'clock at night, and after that I would pace up and down the cloisters of Nevile's Court for hours with one or two other members. We took ourselves perhaps rather seriously, for we considered that the virtue of intellectual honesty was in our keeping. Undoubtedly, we achieved more of this than is common in the world, and I am inclined to think that the best intelligence of Cambridge has been notable in this respect.

(Bertrand Russell, *Autobiography*)

J. M. Keynes:

I went up to Cambridge at Michaelmas 1902, and Moore's Principia Ethica came out at the end of my first year . . . its effect on *us* . . . dominated, and perhaps still dominate (*sic*), everything else . . . This influence was not only overwhelming . . . it was exciting, exhilarating, the beginning of a renaissance, the opening of a new heaven on a new earth . . .

Nothing mattered except states of mind, our own and other people's of course, but chiefly our own. Those states of mind were not associated with action or achievement or with consequences . . . The appropriate subjects of passionate contemplation and communion were a beloved person, beauty and truth, and one's prime objects in life were love, the creation and enjoyment of aesthetic experience and the pursuit of knowledge . . . How did we know what states of mind were good? . . . We entirely repudiated a personal liability on us to obey general rules. We claimed the right to judge every individual case on its merits, and the wisdom, experience and self-control to do so successfully. This was a very important part of our faith, violently and aggressively held, and for the outer world it was our most obvious and dangerous characteristic . . . We were, that is to say, in the strict sense of the term, immoralists. The consequences of being found out had, of course, to be considered for what they were worth . . . Before heaven we claimed to be our own judge in our case . . . we repudiated all versions of the doctrine of original sin, of there being insane and irrational springs of wickedness in most men. We were not aware that civilisation was a thin and precarious crust erected by the personality and the will of a very few, and only maintained by rules and conventions skilfully put across and guilefully preserved. We had no respect for traditional wisdom or the restraints of custom . . .

I have said that this pseudo-rational view of human nature led to a thinness, a superficiality, not only of judgment, but also of feeling . . . And as the years wore on towards 1914, the thinness and superficiality, as well as the falsity, of our view of man's heart became, as it now seems to me, more obvious . . .

If therefore I altogether ignore our merits – our charm, our intelligence, our unworldliness, our affection – I can see us as water-spiders, gracefully skimming, as light and reasonable as air, the surface of the stream without any contact at all with the eddies and currents underneath. (*My Early Beliefs*, 1949)

Lytton Strachey (physically up at Cambridge only from 1900 to 1905, a frequent visitor thereafter, and spiritually always there):

1 February 1902

My dearest Mama – This is to say – before I am committed to oaths of secrecy – that I am now a Brother of the Society of Apostles - How I dare write the words I don't know! – I was apparently elected yesterday, and today the news was gently broken. The members – past and present – are sufficiently distinguished. Tennyson was one of the early ones. But I shall know more when I visit the Ark – or closet in which the documents of the Society are kept. It is a veritable Brotherhood – the chief point being personal friendship between the members. The sensation is a strange one. Angels are Apostles who have taken wings – viz. settled down to definite opinions – which they may do whenever they choose. I feel I shall never take wings. This has once occurred with the apparent result that the Ap. was eventually transported for life! Another person whom I don't know called Sheppard (King's) was elected at the same time as me. We meet each other tonight . . .

William Rothenstein describes him:

Lytton Strachey's look in those early days was very unlike his later appearance. Long, slender, with a receding chin, that gave a look of weakness to his face, with a thin, cracked voice, I thought him typical of the Cambridge intellectual. Dining one night with Isobel Fry, I recollect saying that poetry, usually regarded as a vague and high-falutin' art by many, was in fact the clearest expression of man's thoughts. Strachey replied acidly. Who, indeed, was I to talk of matters with which I was not concerned? And I thought that here was the cultured University man, who lies in wait, hoping one may say something foolish, or inaccurate, and then springs out to crush one, in high falsetto tones. But I was mistaken. Of course Lytton Strachey was much more than a cultured Cambridge man; he was to become a master of English prose.

Later Strachey wrote:

1908: . . . So far my successes among the younger generation have not been remarkable. Am I altogether passé? But I occasionally find myself shattered, and I *have* embarked on various intrigues. But it won't do, it'll none of it do. Beauty is a torment and a snare, and youth is cruel, cruel! Today I drove in a barouche to the races with a select assortment of undergraduates. Doesn't it sound romantic? But it was merely rather nice. Yesterday I drank champagne from 11 to 1, and discussed love and friendship, and the day before I went to the A.D.C. . . . and was bored – or amused? – I really can't make up my mind.

To Leonard Woolf:

After Cambridge, blank, blank, blank.

(Michael Holroyd, Lytton Strachey, 1968–8)

Two retrospective views of this group

Harold Nicolson:

17th January 1951 . . . I am reading Roy Harrod's book on Keynes which I find entrancing. Really that Cambridge set were more gifted than anything we have seen since. They make Balliol look like an old cart-horse.

(Diaries, ed. Nigel Nicholson,
1966–8)

Goronwy Rees:

At one end of the scale Strachey and his friends carried the banner of revolt but at the same time they were also pillars of the establishment . . . Cambridge had given them faith in the supreme power of reason, in the virtue of absolute intellectual and emotional honesty and of complete frankness in personal relations. Highly intelligent and highly sophisticated, they were also imbued with the innocence of an immense optimism . . . They also thought that nowhere were the values they believed in so completely realised as in Cambridge . . . Anything that came after Cambridge . . . could be nothing better than a come-down and their tasks – ruling an Empire, administering its finances, directing its education – were necessarily only a second-best . . .

They [Strachey and Keynes] established an intellectual and personal domination over their contemporaries at Cambridge which set the tone of undergraduate life for many years to come. It would probably be true to say that it lasted until the early '30s.

(Brief Encounters, 1974)

Three Kingsmen of the time were memorable figures

Oscar Browning:

He was a genius flawed by abysmal fatuity. No one had finer gifts than he: he could think on big lines, he could strike out great ideas, he had wit, he had the power of planning largely and constructively, he had courage and a high scorn of ridicule, it was impossible to come into contact with him without being conscious of great intellectual force. But it was impossible not to be aware that he was a buffoon.

(E. F. Benson, As We Were, 1930)

The claret he tasted – gratis – every day at luncheon, with a mutton chop, vegetables, and a pudding. His breakfast was no less copious; and before breakfast he had bread and butter in bed with his early tea, and a special bottle of ale at 3 a.m. for which he was awakened by an alarm clock. Afternoon tea, for him, required solid accompaniments, after hard daily tennis and a Turkish bath. It was he that introduced Turkish baths into Cambridge. Tea by no means took away his appetite for dinner in Hall: always a choice of thick or clear soup, then fish, a joint, a hot sweet, a cold sweet, and a savoury, washed down with champagne.

(George Santayana, My Host the World)

for many he must have opened doors to knowledge and led them for part of the way along the path.

'Oh, there you are, old man! How are you? Come and sit next me in Hall and tell me everything you've been doing!' This, at the beginning of a term. We are seated and I begin. 'Well, I went to France for about three weeks. I was in the south-east most of the time – at Digne and Sisteron...' O.B. sits drumming with his fingers on the table and gazing before him with a lack-lustre eye. When I have spoken for about a minute, he breaks in, 'Oh, did you really? How very interesting!' (pronounced 'veynsing'). 'Well, I – I –,' and for the rest of the meal there is a monologue.

(M. R. James, Eton and King's, 1926)

It was said that Tennyson, on a visit to Cambridge, had been entertained by the Fellows of King's, who came up one by one, mentioning their names. When O.B. came up and said, 'I'm Browning', Tennyson looked at him and said, 'You're not'.

(Bertrand Russell, Portraits from Memory, 1956)

Though he had clung tenaciously to Cambridge for many years, the moment he quitted it, it became for him a place where no gentleman would willingly live. I remember him coming up to me in the Athenaeum with that curious sidling motion of his big frame, taking my hand, and drawing me towards him as he was wont to do. 'You're wasted at Cambridge, old man. Go out into the world! Come to Bexhill.'

(A. C. Benson, Memories and Friends, 1924)

Walter Headlam:

Headlam, one of the finest of all interpreters of Greek thought and language, was a pure-bred scholar, descended from scholars. In 1902 he was thirty-seven years old and seemed to have only a frail contact with reality. Travelling was difficult because he could not take the right train... Letters were difficult, because he chose his stamps only for the beauty of the colours. But his rooms in Gibbs Buildings were open to everyone who cared to come, and anyone who could make their way through the piles of manuscripts and bills was sure to be listened to and taught. The pupils' work was usually lost and rapidly disappeared under the mass of papers, but Headlam sat 'balancing an ink-pot on one knee', as Shane Leslie described him, 'and scribbling words into Greek texts, missing since the Renaissance, with the other...'

(Penelope Fitzgerald, The Knox Brothers, 1977)

We went to a race meeting at Newmarket, and entirely bowled over with adoration for the splendour and the speed of the flying hooves and the rhythm of their galloping, he felt that he must instantly learn to ride: He ordered some elegant riding breeches and hired a horse, and we set out along the Backs. One of his feet slipped out of its stirrup, but in these first moments of poise upon a horse's back, he did not think it wise, in spite of advice and proffered assistance, to imperil his balance by recovering it, and in consequence, when his horse decided to walk into the shallow water of the Grantchester mill-pool and drink, he slipped gently out of the saddle and fell in. Then he thought he would like to go for a drive, as a less hazardous method of commerce with horses, and he asked a friend to come out for a spin with him. On arrival at the livery stables, a high dog-cart was made ready for them, and Walter Headlam asked his friend if he would do the driving. The friend very properly replied that he had never done such a thing in his life, and so he said, 'Nor have I', and was instructed that the reins went in the left hand, and the whip in the right. A little way out of Cambridge, in trying to turn a corner, he drove up a bank at the side of the road, and the dog-cart upset. As he flew out of it (still with the reins in his left hand) he was heard to observe, 'Damn: I shall never finish Herodas', and alighted unharmed in a hedge.

(E. F. Benson, As We Were)

J. E. Nixon:

The memory of Nixon is very kindly. It is also incredibly comic... His oratory was a little difficult to follow. Such words as 'laboratory' he was supposed to, be able to pronounce in one syllable, 'fish sauce' stood for official sources, 'hairpin' for high opinion, 'temmince' for ten minutes, and so on ...

The following incident is typical. Journeying forth on his tricycle one afternoon for air and exercise, he came to sad grief at the bottom of Madingley hill, was picked up and brought home and laid up for three weeks. When restored to health, he went forth again on the mended tricycle, accompanied by his friend George Chawner, to survey the scene of the disaster. 'It was just here,' he said, 'that it happened. I was merely doing like this . . .' His recollection was doubtless accurate. Over went the tricycle again and three weeks more in bed were the result.

(M. R. James, Eton and King's)

There are various apocryphal stories about heads of houses; Montagu Butler, Master of Trinity from 1886 to 1918, for instance:

Montagu Butler had been heard saying in a London bus, 'Master of Jesus, shall we alight?' and old Morgan replying, 'Master of Trinity, are you sure we have reached our destination?'

or:

After a meeting in London attended by several Heads of Colleges, some circumstance led him to take a bus to King's Cross, in the far corner of which he presently espied the grumpy old Master of Jesus. The conductor came round for his fare, and on his asking how much it was held up two fingers. 'Master of Jesus, Master of Jesus', Dr. Butler cooed across the bus, 'how shall I interpret this mystical gesture?' 'Master of Trinity, pay your tuppence like a man.'

(Marsh, A Number of People)

More likely is A. C. Benson's story about him as the guest of the Master of St. John's, saying:

in his sweetest tones: 'Dear Master of John's, *you* can enlighten me: with your marvellous memory you will have retained the name of that chivalrous and gentle guide who conducted us up the Schulthorn at Mürren – that model of courtesy and consideration – whose name I have often endeavoured to recall, but without success.' To which the M. of J. said very gruffly, 'I suppose you mean Arnold Küpfer.'

'That was the name!' cried the Master of Trinity in an ecstasy. 'That was the name; and I must endeavour to retain it in my memory. Thank you a thousand times, dear Master of John's, for recalling to me a name which brings back to me some of the best and sweetest days of my life – happy hours when guided by that chivalrous Arnold Küpfer we took the wings of the morning on the Alpine ridges.' He presently withdrew. Someone shortly after said to the Master of John's. 'Was Küpfer really so delightful a guide? I never even heard of him.'

'Neither have I', said the M. of J. gruffly, choked with food. 'I invented the name. I could not have Butler going on like that.'

(Newsome, *On the Edge of Paradise*)

Sidney Sussex:

Dr. Phelps was Master from 1843 to 1890 and he was a complete tyrant . . . Phelps, when he was aging, used to be taken round country lanes in his landau. He was passing through Willingham and was attracted by the village. He asked his companion its name. His companion replied, 'You should know, Master, because you are its rector.' He was Rector of Willingham from 1848 to 1890, but is only known to have taken two services there, both of them funerals, to which no doubt a fee was attached.

There used to be in the Fellows' Garden a quince tree near the classical gateway going into Jesus Lane. Charles Smith (Master, 1890–1916) did not like quinces in his apple tart and so, in September when there were no Fellows about, he used to go in and knock every quince off the tree.

(Knox-Shaw, *Reminiscences*)

There were other notable figures.

James McTaggart:

His tall portly form used to float into the lecture-room like a barrage-balloon, and he held his big, round baby's head with its benign expression and spectacles so much on one side that he generally drifted after it. This one-sided trend kept him walking along close to any wall that he encountered as he crossed the quads or even a room, and I can quite believe the story that he once floated up to the fountain in Trinity Great Court, and continued circling round it deep in thought until some kind passer-by detached him. He had many interests and achieved the feat of believing in immortality but not in God.

(Frances Partridge, *Memories*, 1981)

I was laughing at him for the way he spoilt Pushkin: 'Why', I said, 'I believe if there was only one cosy chair in the room you would give it to Pushkin and take the floor yourself.' 'Of course I would', he said, 'it would be only fair. I could think about the Absolute and I don't believe Pushkin can.'

(G. Lowes Dickinson, *McTaggart*, 1931)

Bertrand Russell:

My first experience of the place was in December 1889 when I was examined for entrance scholarships. I stayed in rooms in the New Court, and I was too shy to enquire the way to the lavatory, so that I walked every morning to the station before the examinations began. I saw the Backs through the gate of the New Court, but did not venture to go into them, feeling that they might be private...

For a long time I supposed that somewhere in the University there were really clever people whom I had not yet met, and whom I should at once recognise as my intellectual superiors, but during my second year, I discovered that I already knew all the cleverest people in the University. This was a disappointment to me...

One of my earliest memories of Crompton (Llewellyn Davies) is of meeting him in the darkest part of a winding College staircase and his suddenly quoting, without any previous word, the whole of 'Tyger, Tyger, burning bright'. I had never, till that moment, heard of Blake, and the poem affected me so much that I became dizzy and had to lean against the wall . . .

For two or three years, under [McTaggart's] influence, I was a Hegelian. I remember the exact moment during my fourth year when I became one. I had gone out to buy a tin of tobacco, and was going back with it along Trinity Lane, when suddenly I threw it up in the air and exclaimed: 'Great God in boots! – the ontological argument is sound!'

(*Autobiography*)

He is remembered by Edward Marsh on a walk:

In a disquisition on the capacity of mankind for misery he said he had never been so unhappy that he would not have been cheered, in an appreciable measure, by the sudden offer of a chocolate cream.

(*A Number of People*)

G. E. Moore:

George Moore . . . came to Trinity in my third year, and whipped us all up with an egg-whisk. He had the most discovering face I ever saw, with sharp little spectacled acetylene eyes that lit up the lowest bottom of Erebus, and a nose that looked ready to cut platinum.

(Marsh, *A Number of People*)

G. E. Moore was a perfect March Hare. His gown was always covered with chalk, his cap was in rags or missing, and his hair was a tangle which had never known the brush within man's memory. Its order and repose were not improved by an irascible habit of running his hand through it. He would go across town to his class, with no more formal footwear than his bedroom slippers, and the space between these and his trousers (which were several inches too short) was filled with wrinkled white socks.

(Norbert Wiener, *Ex-Prodigy. My Childhood and Youth*, 1953)

A. W. Verrall (classical scholar and in 1910 first Professor of English Literature):

In my day a crowd of undergraduates, some of them not reading Classics, used to converge on the Great Court of Trinity to attend Verrall's lectures, largely in the hope of hearing him declaim, or rather chant, the Forsaken Merman, or the Grammarian's Funeral, or whatever of his favourite English lyrics it might be ... In 1909, when I heard him, he was so crippled with arthritis that he had to be carried into the lecture-room as helpless as a joint of meat on a dish. Deposited on a table, his legs drawn under him like a fakir's, he demonstrated astonishingly how a mind could work independently of a body ... His voice had an uncommon range of pitch, as the substance of his talk had an uncommon range of reference ... He had a great wit, and the queer crowing laugh which his sallies ended enchanted his audience.

(E. M. W. Tillyard, *The Muse Unchained*, 1958)

Ronald Firbank:

I knew him in 1907 when I went to Cambridge and found him in my college, Trinity Hall ...

His clothes – although made by the best tailors – always looked a little foreign somehow – perhaps because he wore French ties from Doucet's and from Charvet's and always had his hair waved in 'artistic disorder', besides often wearing either a Chinese green jade ring, or one of those Egyptian blue earthenware ones. He was very anxious to remain slim at that time and used to starve himself, go out for runs in all weathers, etc. He looked so absurd in his running togs that I believe he was once ... mobbed by the rougher elements of the college.

(A. C. Landsberg, quoted in *Ronald Firbank, Memoirs and Critiques*, ed. Marvyn Horder, 1977)

Rupert Brooke, remembered, among other things, for his looks:

A herald made a pretty figure, spoilt by a glassy stare...(*see page 259*)

On one occasion I recollect that he came dressed in a coal-black flannel shirt, with a bright red tie and a suit of grey homespun. This carefully calculated costume did not convey any sense of affectation, though it undoubtedly threw up the fine colouring of his head into strong relief.

(A. C. Benson, *Diary*, ed. P. Lubbock)

YOUTH

A young Apollo, golden-haired,
  Stands dreaming on the verge of strife,
Magnificently unprepared
  For the long littleness of life.

(Frances Cornford, 1910)

Visiting or re-visiting Cambridge was always an experience.

A. C. Benson back at King's in 1901:

Monday, 5 August: . . . Then to Christ's: here the pool in the garden, with the old pavilion and busts, muffled in dark leaves, was simply enchanting; so too the fellows' building – white with black stains, seen beyond the winding thickets and velvety grass of the gardens . . .

Then went to Newnham. Found Aunt Nora [Mrs. Sidgwick] who slipped out to see me, like a graceful ghost or Prioress in her widow's dress, entertaining Sir R. Ball and three American Professoresses . . . We trailed all round the College and I liked it. The great garden at the back, the cool white hall, the ranges of corridors all like *The Princess* . . . She is herself like a porcelain shadow, with a pathetic eye and mouth. 'Professor Sidgwick' still painted on a door.

(David Newsome, Edwardian Excursions, 1981)

Raymond Asquith to H. H. Asquith, 3 June 1900:

On Tuesday I went over to Cambridge to speak at their Union. It is a detestable place to speak in, and the Cambridge orators are as repulsive a crew as I have ever seen: not one of them speaks English – I don't mean the idiom but the dialect: they all have the manner and accent of Welsh missionaries. Their secretary is a pure-bred Boer called Van Zijl but even he had a strong Glasgow accent. I dined and breakfasted with them, both gloomy meals. I sat next to Oscar Browning who is their treasurer: he had just entertained the King of Sweden and was quite unbearable.

(John Joliffe, Life and Letters of Raymond Asquith, 1980)

Edward Marsh to Rupert Brooke 1913:

15 June. Here I am at the old place again, but I miss the undergraduates who are all gone down. Arthur Benson dined here last night, and Jane Harrison this evening. I went to luncheon at Downing with my Da – all sere-ish yellowish leaves. I went to the Fitzwilliam! (it reflects great credit on Cockerell) and read a little in the backs. It all reminds me of a contemporary of mine called Arthur Paley who was blamed for not taking part in the life of the place and said, 'But what *does* one come to Cambridge for except *absolute* peace and quiet?'

(from Christopher Hassall's Edward Marsh, 1959)

Augustus John was commissioned to paint the portrait of Jane Harrison, Newnham classics don.

Jane Harrison, 15 August 1909:

He was perfect to sit to; he never fussed or posed me, but did me just as I lay on the chair where I have mostly lain for months. I look like a fine distinguished prize-fighter who has had a vision and collapsed under it . . . it seems to me beautiful but probably as usual I am wrong!

Maynard Keynes inaccurately reports from King's, 23 July 1909:

John is encamped with two wives and ten naked children . . . I saw him in the street today – an extraordinary spectacle for these parts . . .

and two days later, to Duncan Grant:

All the talk here is about John . . . Rupert seems to look after him and conveys him and Dorelia and Pyramus and David and the rest of them about the river . . . According to Rupert he spends most of his time in Cambridge public houses, and has had a drunken brawl in the streets smashing the face of his opponent.

The talk reverberated round the colleges to such an extent that special parties of Raverats, Verralls and the like would arrange expeditions to the field to catch a glimpse of them, watching Dorelia make a pair of Turkish trousers, or the children gnawing bones for their supper then falling asleep on straw round the camp fire – and other marvels. 'We cause a good deal of astonishment in this well-bred town', Augustus observed.

(Michael Holroyd, *Augustus John*, 1974–5)

John's own version:

I drove in every day to paint Miss Harrison at Newnham College. I portrayed the Greek scholar reclining on her couch while she smoked innumerable cigarettes and talked learnedly with Gilbert Murray.

Above her hung an early Wilson Steer. Murray used to visit our camp with Rupert Brooke. Both were charming, good-natured and playful with the children. Rupert Brooke had a blond, robust style of good looks, of which he was naturally not unconscious: a delightful fellow, I thought, but perhaps none the better for a too roseate environment. Except for a visit to James Strachey at King's, I saw nothing of University life. The atmosphere of those venerable halls, standing in such peaceful and dignified seclusion seemed to me likely to induce a state of languor and reverie, excluding both the rude shocks and the joyous revelations of the rough world without. A party of undergraduates boating past our camp one day were reported by D. to have permitted themselves observations, to which the subject of them replied in a style as forcible as it was unexpected. The young gentlemen were observed to row away in silent thought.

(Augustus John, *Chiaroscuro*, 1952)

Three undergraduate friends, Charles Sayle, Theodore Bartholomew and Geoffrey Keynes invited Henry James to stay in Sayle's rooms in Trumpington Street. He wrote approving the programme:

Reform Club   20 May 1909

My dear Charles Sayle,

You are all magnificent & I am dazzled, overwhelmed – deeply affected. I subscribe to everything, delight in the prospect of everything, give myself up to you to do with me whatever best suits your convenience – on which, indeed, through everything, I shall keep my eyes jealously & devoutly fixed. I shall have to tear myself from you on the Tuesday a.m. – & I exhibit the one invidious preference for Tea in one of your gardens (oh delirium!) over even the sight of your contending crews. But for the rest I am of each & all of you the grateful slave, & have gluttonously marked with rapturous accent the items of the list you have so kindly enclosed.

They took him to a concert, to King's, to lunch in Pembroke, to the Fitz-william Museum and to a play at the A.D.C.

Geoffrey Keynes writes:

A vivid memory remains of Henry James . . . pausing to look up at Erasmus's tower to exclaim, with hands raised in wonder, 'How intensely venerable!'

James wrote a PS to his thank-you letter to Charles Sayle:

Just a momentary drop to meaner things to say that I appear to have left in my room a sleeping-suit (blue & white pyjamas – jacket & trousers) which in the hurry of my departure & my eagerness to rejoin you a little in the garden before tearing myself away, I probably left folded away under my pillow. If your brave House Keeper (who evaded my look about for her at the last) will very kindly make of them such a little packet as may safely reach me here by parcels' post – she will greatly oblige yours again (and hers).

(Geoffrey Keynes, *Henry James in Cambridge*, 1967)

D. H. Lawrence's visit was not a success in the end. He writes to Bertrand Russell:

24 February 1915

I want to come on the 6th and stay to the 8th – but are the two nights too long? I don't want you to put up with my talk, when it is foolish, because you think perhaps it is passionate . . . My world is real, it is a true world, and it is a world I have in my measure understood. But no doubt you also have a true world, which I can't understand . . .

I hope I shall see Lowes Dickinson too.

2 March 1915

Also I feel frightfully important coming to Cambridge – quite momentous the occasion is to me. I don't want to be horribly impressed and intimidated, but am afraid I may be . . . Will you tell me if I need bring evening suit.

Dear Russell, It is true Cambridge made me very black and down. I cannot bear its smell of rottenness, marsh-stagnancy. I get a melancholic malaria. How can so sick people rise up? They must die first.

> (*The Letters of D. H. Lawrence*, vol. II, ed. George J. Zytaruk and James T. Boulton, 1982)

Towards the end of the nineteenth century and the beginning of the twentieth there were eddies of change in various university circles; sometimes these met with resisting obstacles.
Henry Sidgwick, in a flysheet circulated on 19 October 1891, backed the idea of dropping compulsory Greek, which had been favoured by a progressive party since the 1860s and had made no headway:

The question is frequently argued as though the University were being asked to take sides with Physical Science against Classics: and we are accordingly told with much emphasis that it is as important for an educated person to understand human history as to understand the laws of the physical world, and that the influence of Greece and Rome upon human history is unique and unparalleled, etc., etc. But all such comparisons are irrelevant to the present issue; since if the proposed Syndicate were to recommend the extremest change that the terms of its appointment allow, the predominance of classics over physical science in our educational system would still be indisputable. For students of physical science would still be required to devote a solid portion of their school time to the study of classics; while students of classics would still be allowed, as at present, to remain in absolute ignorance of physical science.

(*A Memoir*)

In 1906 it was proposed to set up a government commission to enquire into the working of the University. McTaggart writes:

I shrink with selfish horror from the idea of the loss of time a commission would be, and I should like the initiative to come from the University rather than from the State. But I am so radical academically that I think I should welcome most of the changes such a commission would probably make. I should anticipate: (1) Equality for women; (2) No compulsory Greek; (3) Some condition for the M.A.; (4) Teaching to be more University and less college; (5) Abolition of mere prize fellowships; (6) A poverty test for the money of scholarships; (7) Something done to heads of colleges. All these I should welcome.

(Dickinson, *McTaggart*)

A proposal for an English tripos had been made in 1880:

Is it too much to hope that among the readers of this *Review* there may be some few possessed of such a measure of enthusiasm for the magnificent literature that extends in almost unbroken continuity from Beowulf to the latest production of the Victorian age as may prompt them to use their best efforts to found an English School? Something has been done lately in this direction by the establishment of an Anglo-Saxon Professorship – if we may claim any merit to ourselves for merely accepting a gift from Oxford – but there is no examination in Anglo-Saxon to induce any number of students to attend the new Professor's lectures, though he is willing as he is able to teach. An examination in Anglo-Saxon alone would of course be far too restricted to be of much practical use; what is wanted is an English tripos as broad and comprehensive as the Classical tripos.

(*Cambridge Review*, 5 May 1880)

(*This was not to be implemented for about forty years.*)

'More like a cruel stepmother than an Alma Mater.'

(A. C. Haddon)

In spite of support from heads of houses, the University set its face against the setting up of a proper department of anthropology and a museum to house the treasures which A. C. Haddon, pioneer of field anthropology, brought back from Polynesia and elsewhere.

1900. I certainly have need for all my philosophy as I have had many disappointments in life and now have so much to discourage me. Unless I get something more at Cambridge [a lectureship at £50 a year] I must give up the struggle . . . give up Anthropology . . . and return to Dublin. If I could get £200 for five years, my wife and I are willing to chance it, I would throw up my Dublin post whatever it may be worth . . . devote myself to Anthropology and Cambridge, and risk what happens at the end of the period. But all this is visionary. Who cares for Anthropology? There's no money in it.

(A. H. Quiggin, *Haddon, The Head Hunter*, 1942)

In 1904 the department of anthropology launched a public appeal for funds for a museum:

No better centre than the University of Cambridge can be found for the study of anthropology or for the development of a museum of the best kind; many of her students are led for purposes of research, or in the discharge of professional duties, or for pleasure, to divers quarters of the globe, and not a few among these have enriched the museum with valuable collections. The opportunities for the study of primitive society, and for the formation of collections illustrative of its various phases, are rapidly vanishing before the advance of European civilisation. The funds of the university have been strained to their utmost of late years to keep even the older scientific departments abreast of the times.

(*Nature*, 18 August 1904)

On the other hand the Appointments Board set up by the University in 1899, reflected changing attitudes to employment and perhaps to the question of vocational training. Five years later its secretary writes:

Of late years the University of Cambridge has been compelled to provide among other objects for the scientific study of engineering and of agriculture, for the equipment of explorers to carry out the economic, scientific and geographical survey of the Empire, for the study of tropical diseases, and for the training of archaeologists to preserve at least some knowledge of the precious relics of the past history of mankind . . . Not a few of our students aspire to political life, while many have been in the past, more are in the present, captains and lieuten-ants of industry; and it has been found desirable to recognise in the new Cam-bridge honours school of Economics and Politics, the necessity of providing a special training for these students. Finally we must expect to make provision for an ever-growing class of undergraduates, qualifying for a degree which will assist them to fill scientific positions in our great industrial undertakings . . .

In the case of a particular college . . . we have during 1865–70 but 3.3 per cent of men devoting themselves to a commercial career or to the application of science to industry . . . Of the students matriculating in 1900 and 1901 no fewer than 21 per cent were destined for commerce, on either its administrative or technical side.

(H. A. Roberts, 'The Employment of the Graduate', *Empire Review*, VIII, 1904)

University politics were important, as always:

The most important branch of political activity is, of course, closely connected with *Jobs*. These fall into two classes, My Jobs and Your Jobs. My Jobs are public-spirited proposals, which happen (much to my regret) to involve the advancement of a personal friend, or (still more to my regret) of myself. Your Jobs are insidious intrigues for the advancement of yourself and your friends, speciously disguised as public-spirited proposals. The term Job is more com-monly applied to the second class. When you and I have, each of us, a Job on hand, we shall proceed to go on the Square.

Squaring can be carried on at lunch; but it is better that we should meet casually. The proper course to pursue is to walk, between 2 and 4 p.m., up and down the King's Parade, and more particularly that part of it which lies between the Colleges of Pembroke and Caius. When we have succeeded in meeting accidentally, it is etiquette to talk about indifferent matters for ten minutes and then part. After walking five paces in the opposite direction you should call me back, and begin with the words, 'Oh, by the way, if you should happen . . .' The nature of Your Job must then be vaguely indicated, without mentioning names; and it should be treated by both parties as a matter of very small importance. You should hint that I am a very influential person, and that the whole thing is a secret between us. Then we shall part as before, and I shall call you back and introduce the subject of My Job, in the same formula. By observing this pro-cedure we shall emphasise the fact that there is *no connection whatever* between my supporting your Job and your supporting mine. This absence of connection is the essential feature of Squaring.

Remember this: *the men who get things done are the men who walk up and down King's Parade, from 2 to 4, every day of their lives.* You can either join them, and become a powerful person; or you can join the great throng of those who spend all their time in preventing them from getting things done, and in the larger task of preventing one another from doing anything whatever. This is the Choice of Hercules, when Hercules takes to politics.

(F. M. Cornford, (*Microcosmographia Academica*, 1908)

The twentieth century:
wars, aftermaths and omens

The outbreak of the Great War in 1914 changed lives in Cambridge as elsewhere; sometimes the changes were idiosyncratic.

Rupert Brooke writes to Russell Loines, December 1914:

It's astonishing to see how the 'intellectuals' have taken on new jobs. Masefield drills hard in Hampstead and told me with some pride, a month ago, that he was a Corporal and *thought* he was going to be promoted to Sergeant soon. Cornford is no longer the best Greek Scholar in Cambridge. He recalled that he was a very good shot in his youth and is a Sergeant-Instructor of Musketry. I'm here. My brother is a 2nd lieutenant in the Post Office Rifles. He was one of three great friends at King's. The second is Intelligence Officer on H.M.S. *Vengeance*, Channel Patrol. The third is buried near Cambrai. Gilbert Murray and Walter Raleigh rise at six every day to line hedgerows in the dark and 'advance in rushes' across the Oxford meadows. Among the other officers in this Division are two young Asquiths, an Australian professional pianist who twice won the Diamond Sculls, a New Zealander who was fighting in Mexico and walked three hundred miles to the coast to get a boat when he heard of the war, a friend of mine, Denis Browne – Cambridge – who is one of the best young English musicians.

(*Letters*, ed. G. Keynes)

Arthur Cecil Pigou (Fellow of King's and Professor of Political Economy):

The war which broke out in 1914 was grievous to Pigou. It hurt his deepest instincts. During term-time he stayed in Cambridge ... since he thought it essential that the work of the University should be carried on ... But during practically every vacation he went to the front; at Christmas, 1914, and Easter and June, 1915, to the Friends' Ambulance Unit, commanded by Philip Noel-Baker, which was based on Dunkirk and worked at the front from Ypres to the north; in August 1915, and succeeding vacations until the end of the war, to the First British Ambulance Unit in Italy, commanded by George Trevelyan. Much of his work was very close to the firing line during big offensives.

(John Saltmarsh and L. P. Wilkinson,
A. C. Pigou. A Memoir, 1960)

The Heretics:

The present rumpus on the continent ... has caused the decease, or at any rate hibernation, of a large number of the various societies without which a normal Cambridge is hardly imaginable. But neither decease nor hibernation has over-taken 'The Heretics'; for though most of the Committee and a large number of members have swallowed their prejudices and joined the Church of England in order to be allowed to serve their King and Country, the attendance has, all along, been hardly perceptibly diminished – in fact, even prominent members of Newnham College have been obliged to seat themselves on the floor for lack of more adequate accommodation.

(C. K. Ogden in *The Cambridge Magazine*,
5 December 1914)

Even the familiar was different.

Sir Arthur Quiller-Couch, 'Q', Fellow of Jesus and later Professor of English Literature, recalls:

We came up in October to find the streets desolate indeed. The good soldiers who had swarmed in upon town and college in August . . . had all departed for France . . . already many of them slept in French earth. They had left a historical piece of plate to the high table; and some photographic groups in Stearn's window. A Head of House halted me before one of these groups and ticked off the cheerful resolute faces of those fallen, by the Marne or the Aisne, since he had entertained them a few weeks ago. In one row of a dozen West Yorks, he could find two survivors only . . .

In College one seldom met, never heard, an undergraduate. A few would gather to Hall, the most of them in their O.T.C. uniforms after a strenuous afternoon out by Madingley. The scholar read grace with an unwonted reverence. '*Sic Deus in nobis et nos maneamus in Illo*' – and we took our seats to a meal decently frugal . . . The Belgian refugees from their Universities had found harbour with us. On the King's and Clare Cricket Ground lines of hospital sheds were growing up . . . A notice-board at the entrance of Burrell's Walk advertised the 1st Eastern General Hospital, and on any afternoon you might see the Red Cross motor ambulances bringing in the wounded. A whole block of King's had been handed over to house the nurses. But here, as at the Research Hospital, the work had been so quietly and thoroughly organised that you had to go out of your way to find anything strange. For the rest, Cambridge life had merely been arrested . . .

We returned in January to a vastly different Cambridge. She had become a garrison town . . . the lines of artillery horses beside the Trumpington Road, Adams Road, Jesus ditch . . . the mud in which the poor brutes stand fetlock deep, each mournfully chewing his neighbour's head-rope . . . the mud on Midsummer Common, and worse mud on the road to the Rifle Butts . . . of Whewell's Buildings occupied by the Monmouths, who take it for an Elementary School, and . . . most wonderful spectacle of all – the crowds of Tommies navigating the Backs in Canadian canoes and other bounding shallops.

(*The Cambridge Mind: Ninety Years of 'The Cambridge Review' 1879–1969*, ed.
E. Homberger, W. Janeway and S. Schama, 1970)

Airship raids were a constant menace, and the eastern counties were specially exposed to them . . . some of the machines flew nearer to Cambridge, and the danger to King's Chapel was obvious and alarming. It was necessary to discontinue the lighting of all towns, for without this precaution any place might at any time be bombed during the dark hours. So Cambridge was wrapped in a medieval gloom for some three years, and men had to grope their way about the streets as best they could.

(Heitland, *After Many Years*)

What I chiefly remember from this period is accompanying mother to an endless succession of memorial services in college chapels or Cambridge churches. In a way, what distressed me most ... was the unashamed public grief of the fathers of the young men ... According to the standards of our family circle, tears were to be shed only by children. Very occasionally women perhaps might weep – but grown men never ... The sight of distinguished professors and famous men whom I had been brought up to regard with awe openly crying in church disturbed me profoundly.

(Barbara Wootton, *In a World I Never Made*, 1967)

I went up in 1915 and sat my Tripos in 1918, so the First World War is the inescapable background of all memories. The preponderance of women in the classrooms made the salutation of 'Gentlemen' more ridiculous than ever. The colleges housed soldiers doing courses, studying this and that, marching and counter-marching through the streets and the countryside. Working in the Library at Newnham you could hear them going by, singing the haunting songs of those years, which still have the power to twist the heart. 'There's a long, long trail awinding' always brings back that scene. Two war memories stand out. Coming out of the cool cavern of the Guildhall, where we were sitting the Tripos in June of 1918, into the blazing heat of the market place and falling upon the newsboys to get the early papers and know if Amiens still held out against the German advance: and standing breathless in the still sunlight of early morning to catch in the far distance the sound of the guns in France.

(Mary Woods, in *Newnham Anthology*, ed. Phillips)

On coming out of Hall (one night in January 1917) met the officious donkey McTaggart in a sort of military cap, prowling about. He said he was 'looking at our lights' as a special constable. This is the role which suits a pragmatical busybody like McT. to go about not really to safeguard the state, but to make himself unpleasantly felt. If he summons us, I will deliver my opinion freely about him, as a sneaking informer. This is what happens to the philosopher who wants to pose as a practical man.

(A. C. Benson, in Newsome, *On the Edge of Paradise*)

The Cambridge conscience worked in different ways. Goldsworthy Lowes Dickinson writes:

To me, the worse kind of disillusionment was that connected with universities and historians. Hardly a voice was raised from those places and persons to maintain the light of truth. Like the rest, moved by passion, by fear, by the need to be in the swim, those who should have been the leaders followed the crowd down the steep place. In a moment, as it were, I found myself isolated among my own people. When I say isolated, I do not mean in any sense persecuted. I suffered nothing in Cambridge except a complete want of sympathy. But I learned, once for all, that students, those whose business it would seem to be to keep the light of truth burning in a storm, are like other men, blindly patriotic, savagely violent, cowardly or false, when public opinion once begins to run strongly. The younger dons, and even the older ones, disappeared into war work. All discussion, all pursuit of truth ceased, as in a moment. To win the war or to hide safely among the winners, became the only preoccupation.

(Autobiography, ed. D. Proctor, 1973)

In 1916 Bertrand Russell was fined for issuing a 'seditious' leaflet.

The Trinity College Council met on 11 July 1916, when:

It was agreed unanimously that, since Mr. Russell has been convicted under the Defence of the Realm Act, and his conviction has been confirmed on appeal, he be removed from his lectureship in the College.

Soon afterwards a memorial was sent to the Council signed by 22 Fellows:

The undersigned Fellows of the College, whilst not proposing to take any action in the matter during the war, desire to place it on record that they are not satisfied with the action of the College in depriving Mr. Russell of his lectureship.

(G. H. Hardy, Bertrand Russell and Trinity, 1970)

Russell later wrote:

It was a blow to me during the War to find that, even at Cambridge, intellectual honesty had its limitations. Until then, wherever I lived, I felt that Cambridge was the only place on earth that I could regard as home.

(Autobiography)

After 2,162 members of the University had been killed and 2,902 wounded
(a third of those who served) came the Armistice:

Town and Gown went mad and everything became chaotic, with a bewildering mixture of joy for the end of the slaughter and grief for the countless ghosts of the lost generations, whose silent presence pervaded the clanging uproar. (Out of seventy undergraduates who came up to John's in 1913 only four returned to resume their interrupted University career, of whom two were my brother and my future husband. The fourth member of this sad little group died almost immediately in the flu epidemic.)

As one man we downed pens and books and rushed down town to mingle with the milling yelling crowds. The big bell of Great St. Mary's was tolling away, and there was a strong rumour that it was a Newnhamite who had climbed the tower and was pulling the bell-rope.

(Dora Lawe, in Newnham Anthology, ed.
Phillips)

Armistice Day. 11 o'clock on the 11th day of the 11th month, 1918. Pandemonium broke out in Cambridge. I spent some time climbing up the pinnacle in the middle of the market place . . . which has since been removed. I was sitting on

37. Newnham College, 1971

top of that and enjoying the scene when I heard a name. I came down to King's
Parade to see a crash of glass breaking. Ogden [C. K. Ogden, founder of Basic
English and pacifist editor of *The Cambridge Magazine*], by that time, was the
owner of three shops in Cambridge; one was a picture gallery, the other were
book stores. There he was, standing by the door of one of them, busy at a
peculiar trick. He used to take his glasses up to the top of his head and press the
corners of his eyes with his fingers. He could distort the lens slightly and get
better vision . . . so he believed. Partly because his hands were over his eyes and
mouth, nobody recognized him. I took my stand beside Ogden. Twenty or thirty
drunken medical students were sacking the shop. Pictures were coming out
through the plate glass in very dangerous fashion . . . Duncan Grant, Vanessa
Bell, Roger Fry . . . right out into the street; it was very lucky no one spotted
Ogden. He'd have been in the river. That night he came to call on me, to see if
I could help him in recognizing any of the rioters. And later, in the small hours,
we stood together on the little winding stair in 1, Free-School Lane and for the
first time we talked together – for three hours, outlining the whole of *Meaning of
Meaning*.

(I. A. Richards. Essays in his Honour, ed.
R. Brewer, 1973)

At Girton:

just after the First World War ended, a horde of undergraduates stormed out
from Cambridge, up the drive and under the archway and lit a bonfire in the
quad, yelling, 'Where are the women we have been fighting for ?' Hanging out
of every window and preparing to descend were, needless to say, the women in
question. Miss Jex Blake, like an Abbess, in her plain alpaca bodice and full long
skirt, followed by a retinue of senior dons, received the invaders at the doorway
under the arch, stood with clapsed hands before her and, with great dignity,
enquired: 'Gentlemen, to what do we owe the honour of this visit ?' Then she
invited them to a dance at the College on the following Saturday.

(Dora Russell, The Tamarisk Tree, 1975)

*At a Commemoration sermon in 1919, the Rev. H. F. Stewart, Dean of
Trinity, said:*

I take the War List and I run my fingers down it. Here is name after name which
I cannot read and which my elder hearers cannot hear without emotion – names
which are only names to you, the new College, but which to us, who knew the
men, bring up one after another pictures of honesty and manly beauty and goodness and zeal and vigour and intellectual promise. It is the flower of a generation,
the glory of Israel, the pick of England; and they died to save England and all
that England stands for.

(T. E. B. Howarth, Cambridge Between Two
Wars, 1978)

*Life began to flow again along the frozen or withered arteries.
In 1919 J. B. Priestley, after demobilization, came to Trinity Hall:*

The Cambridge I knew was crowded and turbulent. Men who had lately commanded brigades and battalions were wearing the short tattered gown and broken
mortar-boards of the undergraduate. Freshmen who had just left school, nice

pink lads, rubbed elbows with men who had just left Ypres and Scapa Flow . . .
College rooms were loud with argument until dawn . . . Porters reprimanded
their late commanding officers.

(Introduction to T. Thornely, Cambridge
Memories, 1936)

Chaperones at Newnham:

in my very first term the War ended . . . Amongst those who appeared were
some ex-Bedales boys, my brother Tom and a lot of naval officers on a course.
What was to be done about the antiquated rules which decreed that no female
undergraduate could visit a male one in his room, or entertain him in hers,
unless a married lady was present as a chaperone? It seems quite incredible now,
but so it was. For my part I was reduced to inventing an imaginary duenna called
Mrs. Kenyon, whose services I called on quite often. Of course Pernel Strachey
didn't believe in her; she must have been well acquainted with all the Cambridge
ladies, so I think it was mainly to tease me that she suddenly said to me one day,
when I was lunching at the high table: 'And what is this Mrs. Kenyon like? Do
you find her charming?' Goodness knows what nonsense I mumbled.

(Partridge, Memories)

Making amends

From the Minutes of the Council

28 November 1919

A letter signed by 27 Fellows asking that Mr. Russell be appointed to a lectureship was received and ordered to be circulated.

12 December 1919

(i) The Council had under consideration a letter signed by 28 Fellows and
supported by 5 other Fellows asking that Mr. Russell be invited to return to the
College as a lecturer and pointing out that such an invitation would involve no
imputation that the action taken during the war was not right in the circumstances. It was agreed that the letter be placed in the Report Book.

(ii) It was agreed that a lectureship in Logic and the Principles of Mathematics tenable for five years from 1 July 1920 be offered to Mr. Russell.

(Hardy, Bertrand Russell and Trinity)

Shadows remained:

When I look back on it, it seems to me that the Cambridge I knew was haunted
inescapably by the old war; it was always there in the background conditioning
the prevalent sensibility, with its preference for tragedy and bitter wit, its
rejection of cosy pretences and its refusal to accept any criterion of behaviour
except one: does your action cause suffering to another?

(John Lehmann, The Whispering Gallery,
1955)

Courses were held for the Navy and Army. Of the first engineering course for
naval officers in 1919, Kipling wrote:

Soft, blow soft on them, little East Wind! Be smooth for them, mighty stream!
Though the cams they use are not of your kind, and they bump, for choice,
   by steam.

Lightly dance with them, Newnham maid – but none too lightly believe.
They are hot from the 50-month blockade, and they carry their hearts on their sleeve.
Tenderly, Proctor, let them down, if they do not walk as they should;
For, by God, if they owe you half-a-crown, you owe them your four years food.

Michaelmas term entry of 1918 at Caius College

included Joseph Needham, a product of Sanderson's Oundle, biochemist and sinologist, who would one day hold the Chinese order of the Brilliant Star, and be Master of the College; A. B. Cobban, a great historian of France; R. Cove Smith, an outstanding rugby international, who became a celebrated paediatrician; Hamish Hamilton, the publisher, who stroked a British Olympic crew; two notable Olympic athletes in Harold Abrahams and H. B. Stallard, who became Hunterian Professor of the Royal College of Surgeons; a future star of the musical comedy stage, Claude Hulbert, and a notable radio producer, Eric Maschwitz; and G. F. Hopkinson, perhaps the most daring and original paratroop commander of the Second World War, dropped into the sea off Sicily and picked up by a boat commanded by a fellow member of the Caius First VIII.

(Howarth, *Cambridge Between Two Wars*)

It was still an old-fashioned life. A maid's view:

I was put on Bottom Old Corridor with 9 Students' Rooms and it came as rather a shock to think you had got 9 stoves and 9 rooms to do before breakfast and in those days there was no electric light, one did stoves and rooms by candle light which did seem very old fashioned. It meant being up by 5 o'clock every morning. Still everyone got up and one soon got used to it. One got all the Stoves done first then all the girls met in the Servants' Hall at 6 a.m. for Cocoa. Doing stoves by candle is all very well in a way but when you were raking the ashes out of the grate and by accident a cinder would fall on the candle and out it went you would then have to feel for your matches and sometimes if the Students had left their cups and saucers in the hearth they would be smashed too, you would often find yourself falling over chairs, tables, and humpties. The only alternative was taking the Paraffin Lamp which every Student was supplied with but that too had its disadvantage for if the Students left their windows open which they often did the draught would blow the chimney of the lamp off and smash it would be and you would be trying to pick the pieces of glass up without cutting yourself . . .

(G. Crane, *Girton Memories, 1919–48*, 1948)

The University still could not accept women with a good grace; there was a noticeably ambivalent attitude.

College notes, St. John's:

John's has been shaken to the core! One night last week a fresher attempted to bring a lady into hall. She was skilfully removed by the head waiter amidst sustained applause.
The Hockey people went down badly to Pemmer. But who cares? Are we not playing Newnham *at Newnham* – and afterwards tea.

(*Cambridge Magazine*, 22 November 1919)

A. C. Haddon (before the war):

He was discussing Sociology and, as happened so often when he was talking about his Torres Straits Islanders, had exceeded his hour. He was describing how in some islands the women, not the men, make the proposal of marriage, when the women students of Girton College, knowing that their cab would be waiting impatiently outside, unostentatiously slipped out at the back. The temptation was too great. He called out, 'No hurry, there won't be a boat for some weeks.'

But in 1925 there was a dinner in Christ's to celebrate his seventieth birthday:

Heated discussions, with agitated notes between chairmen and secretaries, were caused by the daring proposal that women subscribers to the Portrait Fund should be admitted to the Dinner. It was assumed by the Chairman that Mrs. Haddon and the two daughters should be permitted to view the proceedings in proper obscurity from the gallery, and to those familiar with Cambridge politics there was a piquancy in the suggestion that the profane innovation of women dining should be inaugurated with Ridgeway at the head of the table . . . it was no slight test of Ridgeway's affection for Haddon when he had to assent to the proposal made in accordance with the well-known wishes of the chief guest, that women should be admitted to the dinner on equal terms with men.

(Quiggin, *Haddon, The Head Hunter*)

There was a certain frivolity in the air:

Contrary to the current opinion, we Girton girls did not wear severe shirt blouses with formal ties, nor did we drag back our hair; we were most fashion-conscious, much given to saucy hats, designed to impress male colleagues at lectures, who would stamp their approval when any one of us entered looking especially glamorous.

(Dora Russell, *The Tamarisk Tree*)

All England had gone dancing mad and so had Cambridge. A University dance club called the Quinquaginta was formed, meeting weekly and admirably supplied with music by a jazz band of undergraduates. Dot and I were original members, and immodesty compels me to admit that we were among the stars, and our programmes filled up a week ahead. Lord Louis Mountbatten was one of the early members and I used to have a dance with him every week, though too shy to make much headway into friendship. But money for clothes was hard to come by . . .

The difficulty about this obsessional dancing life was that all we cared about in our partners was their technical ability – they must be first-rate performers – and such young men were often great bores to talk to. We finally got paired off with two good dancers with whom we invariably went to May Week Balls. We always behaved with impeccable decorum and chastity and our conversations were of the most superficial sort, but I believe my partner must have had a great deal more in him than I credited him with, as he ended up Lord Chief Justice, and Lord Parker of Waddington.

(Partridge, *Memories*)

Instead of favouring holy retreats at occasional weekends, or going to College chapel on Sunday evenings, we would ask for an exeat permit and be off to Heretics. This was not much favoured at the top level in Girton, but it was not forbidden. C. K. Ogden, who was the prime mover in the Heretics, was to become one of my real friends and a considerable influence in my life. He had a flat high up in Petty Cury, which he called Top Hole. It was here that the Heretics used to meet. I used to bicycle off there of a Sunday evening with a most agreeable feeling of defiance and liberation. If you joined the Society you were called upon to reject authority in matters of religion and belief, and to accept only conviction by reasonable argument. You could, if not certain of your position, become an associate, who merely believed in open discussion but had not entirely rejected authority.

(Dora Russell, *The Tamarisk Tree*)

and new tremors:

The preliminary wave of Labour unrest . . . has not left untouched even the backwaters of Cambridge, and it is significant that the Bedmakers are the first to present their demands in an audible and coherent form. It is true that the surrender of the University Press to organized Unionism was an event of greater significance to those who consider the solidarity movement as a whole . . . and the recent victory of the laboratory assistants will doubtless be a potent cause of heart-searching amongst academic financiers. But the demands of the Bed-makers are more romantic in their appeal to popular sentiment, and are stimu-lated as much by the decline in the volume of perquisites, which the passing of the gilded youth has brought in its train, as by the rise in the cost of living which all devout economists deplore.

   . . . the hours which one woman has worked for 18s 9d a week: 6.15 a.m. to 12.30 p.m.; 2.30 p.m. to 4.45 p.m.; 7 p.m. to 8.30 p.m.

(*Cambridge Magazine*, 19 April 1919)

as well as a resumption of old enjoyments and the discovery of new ones. 'The Family':

From the day I joined it . . . till I left Cambridge and automatically ceased to be a member, its meetings were things to look forward to . . . There was little formality; whist was played after dinner – Day, who was rather deaf, carrying on a moaning soliloquy of, 'Crazy? Crazy! Seventy years have I played and never a trump in my hand . . .' Day was critical of the menu. He always preserved it carefully and took it home; as early as opportunity offered he went to Norwich and discussed it in detail with his old friend Canon Heaviside . . . 'Two white meats together'. 'Needn't have had that second sweet . . . nobody touched it.' As he walked back from Magdalene one night with Whitting and me . . . I recall his saying in a loud crying voice: 'The soup wasn't what you expect from a College kitchen, and I *hate* mackerel.'

(James, *Eton and King's*)

Housman's wines for a 'Family' dinner in the twenties:

Meursault Goutte D'Or 1918
Oloroso
Steinberg Cabinet Auslese 1921
Pommery 1921
Romanée Conti 1921
Cockburn 1878
Latour 1920
Cognac Courvoisier 1869

(S. C. Roberts, *The Family*)

Rowing:

Among the great Cambridge figures was Steve Fairbairn, greatest of all rowing coaches, a massive, quiet personality whom one saw every afternoon on the towpath; the centre of fierce, almost religiously fierce controversy, through which he took his quiet way unperturbed, bringing his Jesus boats to the head of the river year after year. It was largely his influence that abolished the torture of fixed seats on which I first rowed, for orthodoxy thought them essential to the development of the ability to swing. Fairbairn's ideas were more liberal, and centred on the moving of the boat by the natural thrust of the thighs, the draw of the muscles in back and shoulder. At least his crews enjoyed their rowing . . . the river seemed to me then infinitely worth while. In the twenties the pre-war tradition, that the good name of a college largely rested on the performance of its boat club, still persisted in some measure . . .

The greatest joy of rowing . . . is the gradual apprehension of the meaning of rhythm, and the intermittent experiencing of it in its delighted perfection; intermittent only, because the power, as it were something external, which takes hold of a crew and welds them into a unity that seems so that they move mysteriously and without effort, the crew at one with boat and river, is not often achieved.

(T. R. Henn, *Five Arches*, 1980)

Bathing in the fens:

Happily the country round Cambridge, especially towards the north-east where the fens are, is wonderfully well provided with wild pools . . . One of these pools lies very difficult to find in what is practically a piece of untouched fen. It is surrounded with reeds whose stems are almost white, but bear at the top their long green blades which stream unanimously out in one direction if there is a little wind. If you lie flat on the bank of the diving-place and look along the pool, you see a picture of reeds in the best Chinese manner. Then if you dive in, you find the water absolutely clear and beautifully brown, contrasting marvellously with the brilliant blue of the surface, reflecting the sun. Or at midnight, on one of those few nights of the year when the air and water are warm enough, it is lovely to swim through the moon and stars glittering on the water . . . Growing all around the pool you get ragged robin, purple loosestrife, scabious, and what Scottish friends call mouse's pea. And there in some convenient place you may lie, reading and swimming alternately . . . meanwhile, wherever you look, the

38. Nightclimbing: Trinity library chimney (from Hederatus,
Cambridge Nightclimbing, 1970)

heart is rejoiced. In the distance, across the flat landscape, certain rows of poplars stand up, and an uninterrupted view of the whole sky can be had. There are those who pretend that no landscape has virtue unless it contains hills; to please them, everything must be at an angle to the horizontal, and flatness is dull. But others, of whom I am one, find constriction in hills and freedom in the plain . . . Market Hill . . . is quite hilly enough for me.

> (Joseph Needham, *History is on our Side*, 1946)

Oh how can I express my deep, my indurated, my passionate, my unforgettable, my *eternal* debt, to that flat, dull, monotonous, tedious, unpicturesque Cambridgeshire landscape. How those roads out of Cambridge come back to my mind now! Those absurd little eminences known as the Gog and Magog hills . . . those meadows towards Grantchester where there is that particular massive and wistful effect about the poplars and willows.

> (Powys, *Autobiography*)

Motor cars 1925:

> *There was a debate in the Senate House on whether undergraduates should be permitted to use cars before 12.30 a.m. and after 8.30 p.m. (10 p.m. in summer).*

Master of Sidney: It would be a grave restriction on the liberty, which only necessity would justify, if they were prevented from using their cars before 12.30. A good many of them lived a good distance from their laboratories and lecture-rooms and they saved a good deal of time in the morning by using their cars. . .

Mr. MacCurdy: . . . in actual practice, if he wished to go any distance under three miles from Cambridge it was quicker for him to take his bicycle . . .

Mr. Gardner Smith: . . . There could be no legitimate reason why a man should take his car out after dinner and take it into the country. There had been a serious accident on the Newmarket Road between 11 p.m. and midnight. It seemed to him that it was within the legitimate functions of the Proctors to prevent that kind of thing . . . it was common knowledge that such immorality as took place in Cambridge now took place entirely through the use of motors.

> (*Reporter*, 17 February 1925)

Drama (December 1922):

All the intellectuals in Cambridge turned up at the ADC for the Greek play. I saw Adrian Bishop, who looks like a decadent Roman Emperor, or a Spanish Oscar Wilde, Stewart Perowne, Dadie Rylands, miraculously blond, Denman, Hazlitt, Sebastian Sprott. Hunt was selling programmes. Lytton Strachey and Irene Vanbrugh had come up specially from London.

During the interval, the audience rushed to the club room to shout and smoke. Lytton Strachey peered at everyone through thick glasses, looking like an owl in daylight. He is immensely tall, and could be even twice his height if he were not bent as a sloppy asparagus. His huge hands fall to his sides, completely limp. His sugar-loaf beard is square and reddish, but the hair on his head is thick and dark, worn long in the fashion of an arty undergraduate. Topsy Lucas, Eton-cropped and draped in a Spanish shawl, held a reception in one corner. Irene Vanbrugh, I noticed, did not leave her seat. Apart from her scarlet and gold turban, there was nothing stagy about her. Without make-up, her complexion reminded me of crumbled dog biscuits.

ἕστηκα δ' ἔνθ' ἔπαισ' ἐπ' ἐξειργασμένοις

39. The Greek play, midway to its centenary, *The Oresteia*, 1933
(woodcut by Gwen Raverat)

We had something of an improvement in the second act. Arundell did splendidly; and the intensity of the tragedy sustained even poor Herbage, though his final exit was superbly ridiculous.

The play got terrific applause at the end. When we came out, the streets were filled with Rollses.

(Cecil Beaton, The Wandering Years, Diaries, 1961)

The General Strike of 1926 was 'rather a lark':

From 6 May the 'Gownsman' published a news sheet, 'Daily News', price 1d:

May 6 ... Everyone who wishes to help the Government should enrol at the Guildhall where they will be asked to state their qualifications etc. They should inform their tutor. The responsibility of the undergraduate ends there. This means that he should carry on his usual Academic work as calmly as possible. It should be understood that there is perfect co-operation between the Guildhall and the University ... Students are being placed in 13 grades according to the present necessity of their work. In grade 1 are students who have no immediate exams in prospect ... to the 13th, students in their 3rd year sitting the Tripos, who will naturally be the last to go. But this grading is by no means definite.

The stoppage of a passenger train outside Bishop Stortford caused considerable excitement yesterday, and foul play was suspected, but it turned out that the cause of the delay was the loss of the amateur engine-driver's felt hat.

May 10.   The emergency Tutorial Committee think it desirable that volunteers who are unfit for hard work and are therefore not formed into the present general gangs, should form themselves into

SPECIAL GANGS FOR LIGHT DUTY

. . . Each gang leader should register his name and those of his gang at Mr. Whetham's office in Pembroke College.

May Week:

'Miss Dobson', he went on, turning to Zuleika, 'we have an institution in Cambridge known as May Week. As many commentators have explained, it isn't exactly a week and it isn't in May, but it can be quite pleasant. Concerts, you know, and balls and boatraces and –'

'I know', said Zuleika quietly.

'Well, a sister-in-law of mine is bringing a few friends this year to be my guests. Couldn't I induce you to join us?'

Zuleika pondered. She had to confess to herself that the evening had been enjoyable, though she did not quite know why. To be admired and adored by men was nothing new to her; but Cambridge men gave no sign of wanting to lie down and die for her. Instead, they stood about and made harmless jokes. Zuleika still knew what she liked; and she was growing a little tired of innocent fun.

(S. C. Roberts, Zuleika in Cambridge, 1941)

The young:

I do feel that Cambridge in spring, with its young men, is very lovely. Last night (24 May 1927) I sat out in the College garden with three of them, till 10.30 – one of those rare English nights when one can do that. And I was delighted, as so often, by the candour, sensitiveness, and intelligence of these boys – a small minority, no doubt, in the whole mass of athletes and womanisers, but still very charming. It will pass quickly, of course – it's like the bloom in the cheek of youth.

(Lowes Dickinson, Autobiography, ed. Proctor)

King's Fellows' Garden:

In Fellows Gardens, May 4th, 1928:
Yesterday and today sunshine and lovely May weather. A great thunderstorm Wednesday cleared away the clouds at last. I have been sitting in the garden this morning browsing partly on Goethe, partly on Ryland's book, Words and Poetry, partly on the flowers – the cherries past their best, but scattering white snow on the grass, tulips yellow red and white, irises, bushes of pyrus japonica, all dazzling in the sun.

(Forster, Goldsworthy Lowes Dickinson)

A GLIMPSE

O grasses wet with dew, yellow fallen leaves,
Smooth-shadowed waters Milton loved, green banks,
Stone serious familiar colleges,
Arched bridges, rooks, and rain-leaved willow-trees,
For ever mine –
The figure of a scholar carrying back
Books to the library – absorbed, content,
Seeming as everlasting as the elms
Bark-wrinkled, puddled round their roots, the bells
And the far shouting in the foot-ball fields.

The same since I was born, the same to be
When all my children's children grow old men.

(Frances Cornford, Different Days, 1928)

TRINITY SUNDAY

As I walked in Petty Cury on Trinity Day,
   While the cuckoos in the fields did shout,
Right through the city stole the breath of the may,
   And the scarlet doctors all about

Lifted up their heads to snuff at the breeze,
   And forgot they were bound for Great St. Mary's
To listen to a sermon from the Master of Caius,
   And 'How balmy', they said, 'the air is!'

(Rose Macaulay, The Two Blind Countries,
1914)

There were two 'Bloomsbury' visitors.

Carrington to Lytton Strachey:

10 o'ck (February 13th, 1920)   In train to Oxford, approaching Bletchley

I am now in a slow crawling microbe moving towards Oxford. Yesterday morning was simply Milton in its fairness. Ralph [Partridge] loved your Cambridge, and confessed he found it more sympathetic than Oxford! I saw your Willow Tree by Kings Bridge and thought of you. He was full of appreciation over Trinity. It certainly looked at its very best with the willow pale green, and so new, and the sun shining cleanly on the pinkish stone library . . . I went in after seeing him off at the station and saw Sheppard. There were two young men there, [T. H.] Marshall and [Patrick] Blackett. The former looked rather intelligent and dominating . . . Sheppard is producing the White Devil on the 9th March . . . [He] was delighted because the Newnham Authorities have forbidden the young ladies to act in Webster, so that the female parts can now all be taken by young men! The young men I thought however, didn't show the same enthusiasm at the abolition.

(David Garnett, Carrington, 1970)

and Virginia Woolf:

Lunch in King's

the lunch on this occasion began with soles, sunk in a deep dish, over which the college cook had spread a counterpane of the whitest cream, save that it was branded here and there with brown spots like the spots on the flanks of a doe. After that came the partridges, but if this suggests a couple of bald, brown birds on a plate you are mistaken. The partridges, many and various, came with all their retinue of sauces and salads, the sharp and the sweet, each in its order; their potatoes, thin as coins but not so hard; their sprouts, foliated as rosebuds but more succulent. And no sooner had the roast and its retinue been done with than the silent serving-man, the Beadle himself perhaps in a milder manifestation, set before us, wreathed in napkins, a confection which rose all sugar from the waves. To call it pudding and so relate it to rice and tapioca would be an insult. Meanwhile the wine-glasses had flushed yellow and flushed crimson; had been emptied; had been filled. And thus by degrees was lit, half-way down the spine, which is the seat of the soul, not that hard little electric light which we call brilliance, as it pops in and out upon our lips, but the more profound, subtle and subterranean glow which is the rich yellow flame of rational intercourse. No need to hurry. No need to sparkle. No need to be anybody but oneself. We are all going to heaven and Vandyck is of the company . . .

Dinner in 'Fernham' (a woman's college)

Here was my soup. Dinner was being served in the great dining-hall. Far from being spring it was in fact an evening in October. Everybody was assembled in the big dining-room. Dinner was ready. Here was the soup. It was a plain gravy soup. There was nothing to stir the fancy in that. One could have seen through the transparent liquid any pattern that there might have been on the plate itself. But there was no pattern. The plate was plain. Next came beef with its attendant greens and potatoes – a homely trinity, suggesting the rumps of cattle in a muddy market, and sprouts curled and yellowed at the edge, and bargaining and cheapening, and women with string bags on Monday morning. There was no reason to complain of human nature's daily food, seeing that the supply was sufficient and coal-miners doubtless were sitting down to less. Prunes and custard followed. And if anyone complains that prunes, even when mitigated by custard, are an uncharitable vegetable (fruit they are not), stringy as a miser's heart and exuding a fluid such as might run in misers' veins who have denied themselves wine and warmth for eighty years and yet not given to the poor, he should reflect that there are people whose charity embraces even the prune. Biscuits and cheese came next, and here the water-jug was liberally passed round, for it is the nature of biscuits to be dry, and these were biscuits to the core. That was all. The meal was over. Everybody scraped their chairs back; the swing-doors swung violently to and fro; soon the hall was emptied of every sign of food and made ready no doubt for breakfast next morning. Down corridors and up staircases the youth of England went banging and singing.

(A Room of One's Own, 1929)

In 1919, by way of the Crimea and Greece, a flock of Nabokovs – three families in fact – fled from Russia to western Europe. It was arranged that my brother and I would go to the University of Cambridge . . . Living expenses were to be paid by a handful of jewels . . .

I still feel in my bones the bleakness of the morning walk up Trinity Lane to the Baths, as one shuffled along, exuding pallid puffs of breath, in a thin dressing-gown over one's pyjamas and with a cold, fat sponge-bag under one's arm . . . The usual attire of the average Cambridge undergraduate, whether athletic or leftish poet, struck a sturdy and dingy note: his shoes had thick rubber soles, his flannel trousers were dark grey, and the buttoned sweater, called a 'jumper', under his Norfolk jacket was a conservative brown . . .

Of the games I played at Cambridge, soccer has remained a wind-swept clearing in the middle of a rather muddled period. I was crazy about goal-keeping . . . Mists would gather. Now the game would be a vague bobbing of heads near the remote goal of St. John or Christ, or whatever college we were playing. The far, blurred sounds, a cry, a whistle, the thud of a kick, all that was perfectly unimportant and had no connection with me. I was less the keeper of a soccer goal than the keeper of a secret. As with folded arms I leant my back against the left goal-post, I enjoyed the luxury of closing my eyes, and thus I would listen to my heart knocking and feel the blind drizzle on my face and hear, in the distance, the broken sounds of the game, and think of myself as a fabulous exotic being in an English footballer's disguise, composing verse in a tongue nobody understood about a remote country nobody knew . . .

Such things as hot muffins and crumpets one had with one's tea after games or the newsboys' cockneyish cries of 'Piper, piper!' mingling with the bicycle bells in the darkening streets, seemed to me at the time more characteristic of Cambridge than they do now. I cannot help realizing that, aside from striking but transient customs, and deeper than ritual or rule, there did exist the residual something about Cambridge that many a solemn alumnus has tried to define. I see this basic property as the constant awareness one had of an untrammelled extension of time. Nothing one looked at was shut off in terms of time, every-thing was a natural opening into it, so that one's mind grew accustomed to work in a particularly pure and ample environment, and because, in terms of space, the narrow lane, the cloistered lawn, the dark archway hampered one physically, those ever-present time-vistas were, by contrast, especially welcome to the mind, just as a sea view from a window exhilarates one hugely, even though one does not care for sailing. I had no interest whatever in the history of the place, and was quite sure that Cambridge was in no way affecting my soul, although actually it was Cambridge that supplied not only the casual frame, but also the very colours and inner rhythms for my very special Russian thoughts. Environment, I suppose, does act upon a creature if there is in that creature already a certain responsive particle or strain (the English I had imbibed in my childhood). Of this I had my first inkling just before leaving Cambridge, during my last spring there, when I suddenly felt that something in me was as naturally in contact with my immediate surroundings as it was with my Russian past, and that this state of harmony had been reached at the very moment that the careful reconstruction of my artificial but beautifully exact Russian world had been at last completed. I think, one of the very few 'practical' actions I have ever been guilty of was to use part of that crystalline material to obtain an Honours degree.

(V. V. Nabokov, *Speak, Memory*, 1951)

What was Cambridge?

6 April 1930

Much though I hate Cambridge, and bitterly though I have suffered from it, I still respect it. I suppose that even without education, as I am, I am naturally of that narrow, ascetic, puritanical breed . . .

11 October 1930

Having been born within the Polar region of Cambridge, I tend by education not instinct to frigidify.

(Virginia Woolf, to Ethel Smyth, in *Letters*, vol. IV, ed. N. Nicolson, 1978)

I find Cambridge an asylum in more senses than one.

(Housman, quoted in Grant Richards, *Housman*, 1973)

At Oxford they [the undergraduates] walked as though the street belonged to them. At Cambridge they walked as though they didn't care to whom it belonged.

(Shane Leslie, *The Film of Memory*, 1938)

Not that it was always easy to live up to Cambridge standards . . . It was more difficult to be as exact in talk, and as severely accurate in making a reference or an allusion, as the genius of the place demanded. I remember that my wife once found herself discussing with her neighbour at a dinner-party whether it might be possible to found a society 'for the promotion of recklessness in conversation' . . . I have always loved a phrase which I learnt from an Oxford friend, 'a margin of imprecision' . . . If I have any criticism of Cambridge and the quality of Cambridge thought, it is that Cambridge as a place of thought is more precise than the skies above it, and less hazy and less suggestive than the far and pensive distances dimly revealed in its landscape.

(Ernest Barker, *Age and Youth*, 1953)

That voice? It reminded me of all the Stracheys I had ever known . . . It is my belief that the Bloomsbury voice was a product of the Strachey family and the Cambridge intellectuals combined, although the Cambridge strain had a special quality, being softer, more monotonous and less violently emphatic.

(Partridge, *Memories*)

Family connections:

The grandchildren and great-grandchildren of Charles Darwin have extended the intellectual affiliations of the family. Three of his second eldest son's children have played a part in this extension. The eldest, Sir Charles Darwin, F.R.S., Master of Christ's and director of the National Physical Laboratory, married a daughter of F. W. Pember, Warden of All Souls. The second, Mrs. Gwen Raverat, who was the wife of the French artist, Jacques Raverat, has two daughters, one of whom married Dr. Mark Pryor, zoologist and Fellow of Trinity . . .

The third and youngest daughter of Sir George Darwin became the wife of the surgeon and bibliographer, Sir Geoffrey Keynes.

Lord Keynes claimed to be the first son of the marriage of a Fellow of a college with a graduate of Newnham, and the year 1882 in which they married was the date when the university statutes were reformed to permit any Fellow of a college to marry. Their grandson, Dr. Richard Keynes, married the daughter of Lord Adrian, O.M., Nobel Prizeman and Master of Trinity.

Sir Horace Darwin's elder daughter, Ruth, became a civil servant and married a civil servant, Mr. Rees Thomas. His younger daughter married the Treasury official, Sir Alan Barlow, whose father was physician to three sovereigns and President of the Royal College of Physicians. Sir Alan's niece married Mr. Carl Winter, Fellow of Trinity and Director of the Fitzwilliam Museum. His son, Dr. Horace Barlow, Fellow of Trinity and then of King's, is related through his grandmother to the late Lord Farrer. Lord Farrer was brother-in-law to Sir Edward Bridges, the son of the Poet Laureate and Permanent Secretary to the Treasury, and to the historian, the Hon. Steven Runciman, Fellow of Trinity, whose mother obtained a first-class in the history Tripos of 1890.

Sir Francis Darwin was the father of Mr. Bernard Darwin, author and The Times correspondent, whose son, Mr. Robin Darwin, is principal of the Royal College of Art. Sir Francis was also the father, by his second wife, of the poet Frances Cornford, who married Professor Cornford, Fellow of Trinity. Their eldest son was John Cornford, the young Communist intellectual, who was killed in the Spanish civil war and whose son is a scholar of Trinity. Mrs. Cornford's mother was not only a Fellow of Newnham; she was also a cousin of Henry Sidgwick, the prototype of the new academic class. Sidgwick's grandfather was a Yorkshire cotton spinner, his father a clergyman and grammar school headmaster who was last Wrangler in 1829, and he himself was a Rugbeian who resigned his Fellowship of Trinity in 1869 on the grounds that he could no longer conscientiously sign the thirty-nine articles. Later, when professor of moral philosophy, he took the lead in promoting university reform and women's education. He married the sister of A. J. Balfour and thus became related to the physicist, Lord Rayleigh, F.R.S., who had married another sister, and to Professor F. M. and Gerald Balfour, Fellows of Trinity. Mrs. Sidgwick became Principal of Newnham. Sidgwick's brother Arthur was Second Classic, became a Fellow of Corpus, Oxford, and was the father of the partner in the publishing house of Sidgwick and Jackson. His cousin Alfred was a philosopher, his nephew Professor Arthur Carr Sidgwick a scientist. Sidgwick's youngest sister married her first cousin once-removed. This was E. W., later Archbishop, Benson who taught Sidgwick at Rugby and thus the trio of Benson brothers, A. C., E. F. and Father Hugh Benson were all Sidgwick's nephews.

The following Wedgwoods are cousins of the Darwins. Dr. Ralph Vaughan-Williams, O.M., whose maternal grand-parents were a Wedgwood and a Darwin; the novelist Arthur Wedgwood; Sir Ralph Wedgwood, railway director, and his daughter, the historian and literary editor of *Time and Tide*, Miss Veronica Wedgwood; Mrs. Irene Gosse, a Wedgwood through her mother and second wife (though the marriage was later dissolved) of Mr. Philip Gosse, son of Sir Edmund Gosse, critic and author of the brilliant description of a nonconformist childhood, *Father and Son*. Finally there were the children of the first Lord Wedgwood, who married the daughter of the judge Lord Bowen: his son the artist and second baron; his fourth daughter, the anthropologist the late Hon. Camilla Wedgwood; and his eldest daughter Helen, who married Mr. Michael Pease, the geneticist and son of E. H. R. Pease, the secretary and chronicler of the Fabian Society and grandfather of Mrs. Andrew Huxley.

> (Noel Annan, 'The Intellectual
> Aristocracy', in *Studies in Social History: a
> tribute to G. M. Trevelyan*, ed. J. H. Plumb,
> 1955)

A certain family likeness in Cambridge character preserved continuity.

W. H. Macaulay:

I like to think of an uncle who died a few years ago; he was Vice-Principal of King's, and the one I dedicated *They Were Defeated* to; he had been an agnostic (very noble in character) from his undergraduate days on; but when he was dying he said to his sister who had mentioned God and a future life, 'Well, there's nothing so rum it might not be true', which pleased me very much.

> (Rose Macaulay, *Letters to a Friend*, 1961)

Lowes Dickinson:

he believed in the imagination – believed in the sense that he was interpenetrated by it, and so was not personally mortified either by the victories or by the defeats of reason. 'Sidgwick was the Cambridge spirit at its best, and therefore with its limitations most clearly and tragically apparent', he writes to Mrs. Moor. 'He felt, as he said, that he was put like a soldier to hold just that position. I have the same intellectual position. Only I feel increasingly that *all* intellectual positions "hang in a void of nescience". And in the void and the dark strange wonderful things brush me. Well –'

> (Forster, *Goldsworthy Lowes Dickinson*)

Pernel Strachey:

The Principal of Peile Hall was Pernel Strachey, sister of Lytton. In my clearly remembered portrait of her she has the engaging appearance of a shy, faintly amused giraffe, and advances into the room with her arm folded round her tall, slender body, while her small intelligent face – tilted back (as if in reluctance) on her long neck – is almost obscured by the large round lenses of her spectacles, brilliant with reflected light. From this face emerged a small, precise voice, which manifested the peculiar dynamics of her family in miniature.

> (Partridge, *Memories*)

[She later became Principal of Newnham, where she was affectionately known as 'the Streak'.]

J. T. Sheppard (Provost of King's in 1933):

Many of those who came into residence he got to know sometimes by the simple method of stopping them in the court and saying, 'Who are you, dear boy?' One replied, 'I'm not your dear boy; I'm at Selwyn.'

(L. P. Wilkinson, *A Century of King's 1872–1972*, 1980)

A. E. Housman:

an extremely retiring bachelor of caustic wit, with drooping moustache and austere expression. His favourite afternoon walk took him past the Botanic Gardens, where he could be seen, clutching a walking stick and attired in a nondescript grey suit, elastic-sided boots, high stiff single collar, and close-fitting cap with a button top, like a schoolboy's . . . the nicest story about him concerns a feast in his honour when . . . he remarked: 'In this place, where Porson was once sober and Wordsworth once was drunk, here am I – a greater poet than Porson and a greater Classic than Wordsworth – betwixt and between.'

(Rex Salisbury Woods, *Cambridge Doctor*)

26 September 1931
Down to Cambridge with old Gaselee . . . We dress for dinner. Black tie. We assemble. A. E. Housman and a don disguised as a Shropshire Lad. We have 1789 Madeira and Haut Brion and tripe and oysters and grouse-pie and mushrooms. The firelight flits on the silver of the smaller combination room and there are red shades, highly inflammable, to each candle. Housman is dry, soft, shy, prickly, smooth, conventional, silent, feminine, fussy, pernickety, sensitive, tidy, greedy, and a touch of a toper. 'What is this, my dear Gaselee?' 'This is Estrella 1789.' 'A perfect wine.' Yet not eighteenth-century and still less 1890. A *bon bourgeois* who has seen more sensitive days. He does not talk much except about food. And at 10.30 he takes his leave.

(Harold Nicolson. *Diaries*, vol. I, ed. N. Nicolson)

Mansfield D. Forbes:

The most striking eccentric of the time, perhaps our only genuine one, was Mansfield Forbes of Clare. He was a bachelor, living in large and lovely rooms that looked out over the River, where he entertained with erratic munificence. On Sunday mornings there were breakfast parties of a dozen people; they started at nine a.m. and were apt to go on indefinitely. It was said – I was not there on that occasion – that he had scoured the country to collect seven red-haired curates as a sort of centrepiece to one of his breakfasts, and on another occasion a large number of guests all of whose names ended in – bottom or – botham, and left them to mutual introductions. He lectured, rather sporadically, for his health and energies were uncertain, on Blake, and I think the Pre-Raphaelites. A slight elfin figure, with a hint of a lisp; his spectacles always mended with sealing-wax or plaster and padded on the side-pieces with pipe-cleaners. His mind was erratic, brilliant, metaphysical in its habit of producing the most astounding and improbable illustrations to literature or architecture.

(Henn, *Five Arches*)

Historians, coming to Cambridge from all parts of the world, now sought out Coulton, not in order to pick his brains, but to bask in the sunshine of that scholarship and knowledge, which, like the sun, gives itself without stint. They knew that in his College rooms they would find, not only Coulton in his old dressing-gown, but also Coulton's intellect and Coulton's makeshift but nutritious meals, at their disposal . . .

These College rooms of Father's were from 1921 so very much his own that it is impossible to believe that they were ever inhabited by anyone else . . . Enormously inconvenient, like the rooms in most Cambridge colleges, they were heaven to him. Water had to be fetched from a medieval-looking fount on the stone landing; there was no heating save two coal fires, and fuel for these had to be lugged up sixty-three stone steps worn to a dip in the middle by generations of rushing feet. Draughts were everywhere terrific and had to be excluded by home-made draught resisters, generally in the form of sausage-shaped bags filled with sand, which caused all doors to open with a ghostly creaking sigh most unnerving to the timid newcomer. But these very inconveniences were dear to Father, giving as they did scope for his restless ingenuity . . . There were already two enormous desks, but neither could be moved near the fire, nor transported into the smaller room to catch the sun. So Father bought himself an old wooden washstand, small enough to be portable, and fitted that up as a writing desk. There was a large piece of cardboard attached to the right-hand side to shade his face from the fire's blaze; there was an Ovaltine tin full of pencils and crayons, easy to his hand; there was another tin full of fountain pens . . . And there was always – or nearly always – a cup of hot, tepid, or stone cold cocoa standing somewhere in the jumble and making rings all over the manuscripts . . .

The cocoa . . . had to be a special brew . . . In the first place, the stuff had to be specially ordered, and was stocked in Cambridge (for Coulton, and no one else that we ever heard of), by the complaisant Matthews; it came in the form of berries, or nibs, which had to be ground down on a special grinder, which in its turn had to be fixed to the kitchen table by special nuts, screws, clamps etc. Then, when the nibs were ground, they had to be measured out into a special saucepan – a singularly beautiful one, of brilliant blue enamel, but that was quite incidental – and boiled. The first boiling took four hours, and filled the house with steam and a smell; the second took longer, for the exhausted beans, when their first essences had been drained, took longer to yield up their sweetness to the water *en seconde noces*. The issue of both marriages was then combined, and allowed to cool on the larder floor in a special jug . . .

Some portion of it would be consumed at 201 [Chesterton Road], while he criticised the strength, flavour and quality of it; but the greater portion went down to College with him in special blue enamel flasks with smelly corks, one of which (full) or one (empty) could always be found at the bottom of the rucksack he bore on his back. Then at last the cocoa was heated up and drank, only a few yards from where it originated.

And this drinking was also become something of a ritual. Nib cocoa contains more fat – or more floating fat anyhow – than ordinary cocoa; and, though it was avowedly for this fat that Father bought the special beans, he always took elaborate care to remove it before he drank the liquid. Visitors to the College rooms may have been puzzled by several sheets of *Radio Times* or some such solid journal, scattered against the fender in the big room. When the time came for Father at last to put this draught of his into his system ... he tore up the newspaper into neat strips, and drew them carefully across the surface of his brew, collecting all the fat.

(Sarah Campion, Father, 1948)

Eric Milner-White (Dean of King's):

> Milner-White
> Looks well by candle-light;
> That's why
> We have our service High.

(Basileon)

(On Christmas Eve 1918 he initiated the service of nine lessons and carols. This was first broadcast in 1928.)

R. V. Laurence:

He was essentially a bachelor don and served as Tutor of Trinity for several years. 'These married fellows', he said to me once, 'don't understand what it means to live as a tutor in college, always exposed, week-days and Sundays alike, to pupils and their parents. D'you know, when I was Tutor, I often used to take the train to London, simply to have a little snooze at the club.'

(S. C. Roberts, Adventures with Authors, 1966)

Sir Arthur Shipley:

On degree day, candidates were led up to receive their degrees, each holding a finger of a college official called the praelector, who presented each candidate by name as he knelt, his hands raised in an attitude of prayer, before the vice-chancellor. The latter placed his hands outside those of the kneeling candidate and conferred the degree in Latin. When my uncle, Sir Arthur Shipley, was vice-chancellor, a candidate of the same surname was presented. Instead of 'auctoritate mihi commissa admitto te ad gradum baccaulaurei in artibus in nomine Patris et Filii et Spiritus Sancti', he was left wondering if he had really received a degree on hearing the rhythmical intonation of 'I didn't know there was another man in the university called Shipley, come to lunch with me tomorrow at Christ's Lodge at one-fifteen.'

(G. Evelyn Hutchinson, Kindly Fruits of the Earth, 1979)

G. D. Liveing:

Professor G. D. Liveing of St. John's, who lived to ninety-seven, until he collided with a woman cyclist on his way to Hall, was the yearly guest of honour at the Fellow's Dinner on his birthday, December 21. The Master always made a short speech. Somewhere about 1922 he reminded us how the Professor had witnessed the introduction of railways, electric telegraph, motors, aeroplanes, etc., etc.: a formidable list. He added, drily, 'and we hope he will live to see baths at St. John's'.

(G. C. Coulton, *Fourscore Years*, 1943)

A. C. Pigou:

In social life he assumed an elaborate persona, which he expected to be recognised as such, based on an exaggeration of his genuine proclivities. He was addicted to an extraordinary burlesque jargon, part Victorian, part home-made, which was often accompanied by an indefinable foreign accent. His sartorial insouciance, so well known in later life (the scarf picked up on the hills, the white gym-shoes with black laces), was already apparent in his youth. He would often start the day in flannels and a mackintosh ... For many years his only concession to sartorial elegance at the High Table was a double-breasted lounge jacket filched from a parcel of clothes which his aunt was sending to a Church Army shelter.

(Saltmarsh and Wilkinson, *A. C. Pigou*)

G. H. Hardy:

The chimes of 6 o'clock falling across Fenner's on a quiet, lovely May evening, he remarked, 'it's rather unfortunate that some of the happiest hours of my life should have been spent within sound of a Roman Catholic Church'.

He brought with him, even on a fine May afternoon what he called his 'anti-God battery'. This consisted of three or four sweaters, an umbrella belonging to his sister and a large envelope containing mathematical manuscripts such as a PhD dissertation, a paper which he was refereeing for the Royal Society, or some tripos answers. He would explain that God, believing that Hardy expected the weather to change and give him a chance to work, counter-suggestibly arranged that the sky should remain cloudless.

(C. P. Snow, *Variety of Men*)

David the bookseller:

The Quartier Latin, between King's Parade and Peas Hill, had not yet been demolished to make way for The Arts Theatre, and the *virtuosi* of the day would meet every Friday evening in the musty, gaslit interior of David's shop in St. Edward's Passage, to inspect the latest consignments from Bond Street and Chancery Lane.

What memories that Daumieresque setting revives! The present Librarian of the Foreign Office poking about in the indescribable chaos for the missing half of a broken-backed incunable; an abominable runner from the University Library scuttling like some kind of spider from one pile of books to another; the late Public Orator, goggling with pleasure at finding a volume of the Cambridge Platonists; Mr. Lytton Strachey piping for joy over a copy of Gibbon's Miscellaneous Works in contemporary russia; and, above all, David, himself, wrapped in an immense overcoat, the browned stub of a cigarette permanently attached to his lower lip, muttering softly to himself and croaking encouragement to timid undergraduates.

(John Hayward, article in the *Cambridge Review*, 2 December 1939)

[306]

There he stood on all days save Thursday and Saturday; always smoking but at your service; inscrutable with a subdolent smile which lit up with something like affection on the approach of some tried favourite among his clients ... On Saturdays, when the merry costers invaded the market, like some grave Tyrean trader he withdrew to the neighbouring eminance of Peas Hill, and there, among the fried fish stalls, undid his corded bales ... If you hesitated over a purchase or passed in too great a hurry to snap it up the odds were you would miss it for ever. It had been swept back overnight into his shop, in which to recover it was to search for a needle in a haystack. Legend even held that he disposed each day's surplus stock under the *hic jacets* of St. Edward's Churchyard.

(from the *Cambridge Review*, 27 November 1936)

Ludwig Wittgenstein, the eminent Austrian philosopher, was Professor of Philosophy from 1939 to 1947, having been at times both an undergraduate at Trinity and an 'advanced student':

Wittgenstein was always exhausted by his lectures. He was also revolted by them. He felt disgusted with what he had said and with himself. Often he would rush off to a cinema immediately after the class ended. As the members of the class began to move their chairs out of the room he might look imploringly at a friend and say in a low tone, 'Could you go to a flick?' On the way to the cinema Wittgenstein would buy a bun or cold pork pie and munch it while he watched the film. He insisted on sitting in the very first row of seats, so that the screen would occupy his entire field of vision, and his mind would be turned away from the thoughts of the lecture and his feelings of revulsion. Once he whispered to me 'This is like a shower bath!' His observation of the film was not relaxed or detached. He leaned tensely forward in his seat and rarely took his eyes off the screen. He hardly ever uttered comments on the episodes and did not like his companions to do so. He wished to become totally absorbed in the film no matter how trivial or artificial it was, in order to free his mind temporarily from the philosophical thoughts that tortured and exhausted him.

Wittgenstein used to call at my rooms frequently to get me to accompany him on walks. These were usually on Midsummer Common and beyond, along the river. He usually brought bread or sugar to feed the horses on the Common. A walk with Wittgenstein was very exhausting. Whatever we talked about, he turned his mind to it with great seriousness and intensity, and it was a formidable strain on me to keep up with his thoughts. He would walk in spurts, sometimes coming to a stop while he made some emphatic remark and looking into my eyes with his piercing gaze. Then he would walk rapidly for a few yards, then slow down, then speed up or come to a halt, and so on. And this uncertain ambulation was conjoined with the most exacting conversation! The freshness and depth of Wittgenstein's thinking, no matter what the topic, was highly demanding of his companion. His remarks were never *commonplace*.

(Norman Malcolm, *Wittgenstein, A Memoir*, 1958)

Lectures and supervisions are remembered.

'Q' (a kindly view of a vexing habit):

A little late by design ... Q would enter, rather too carefully dressed for Cambridge; and, nervously looking round at his mixed audience, would begin with his time-honoured 'Gentlemen' – his way of recognising that he was lecturing before a University which barbarously excluded women from full membership. Despite his nervousness, his discourse had nothing of the amateur about it. Every sentence had been weighed and fashioned with loving care; every passage chosen and marked for reading, as a singer may mark his score. Q never overloaded his lecture, but made every point tell and ... dismissed his audience with the belief that literature was an ennobling, beneficent, humane matter, and that its study was an adventure full of joy and excitement.

(Obituary by H. S. Bennett in the
Cambridge Review, 10 June 1944)

F. R. Leavis:

Leavis was a stimulating Tutor. He would arrive at the Tutorial dressed in an open shirt which shocked us to the depths of our conventional souls, his bald head brown with nature-culture; he would fling down the small common-or-garden sack which he carried slung over his shoulder, extract from it a battered copy of the Oxford Book of English Verse and launch himself into his attack on Quiller-Couch and all his works. Quiller-Couch along with Dowden and Bradley ... were soon lying in fragments on my floor. It was Donne and Ezra Pound, The Sacred Wood and Practical Criticism who reigned in their stead; I. A. Richards was the Evangelist and *Scrutiny* was to become our Epistles!

(T. C. Worsley, Flannelled Fool, 1967)

Reading an essay:

Now here I was gowned, seated uneasily on the edge of the chair, reading my first essay aloud to my history tutor, the dreaded Mr. Gorse. The subject of the essay was: 'Better England Free than England Sober'. I had finished it with some pride: it exactly suited my idea of Mr. Gorse's requirements – snappy, epigrammatic, a bit daring in its language, sprinkled with witticisms borrowed unacknowledged from Mr. Holmes. Only now, for some reason, all my effects seemed to have gone wrong: the verbal fireworks were damp; the epigrams weren't epigrams but platitudes, pompous, painfully naive, inept and priggish. It was positive misery to have to utter them. I writhed with embarrassment, coughed, made spoonerisms, gabbled through the worst bits with my face averted: 'Apart from this consideration, there is no doubt that our own liquor restrictions are demoralising ... The French café, with its refinement, its high social status and its atmosphere of harmless gaiety' (Phew) 'is as far removed from the English pub as the hotel is from the brothel ...'

'How do you know', snapped Mr. Gorse, 'how far an hotel is removed from a brothel? Very often it *is* a brothel. Go on.'

I grinned nervously, and faltered through to the end. The last paragraph was particularly heavy going, because Mr. Gorse had begun to drum with his fingers on the mantelpiece. 'Yes, yes ...' he kept muttering: 'Yes, yes ...' as though his impatience were increasing with every word. 'Well', he told me, when, at last, I had finished: 'I'll say this for you – it's not the work of an entirely uneducated fool.' He paused. I grinned hopelessly; regarding him like a poodle which is going to be kicked. 'Look here, Isherwood', he appealed to me abruptly, 'don't you yourself agree that it's all tripe?'

Alarming as it was, there was something very attractive about Mr. Gorse's manner; he was so fidgety, so impetuous, so direct. Pale and fair-haired, his handsome, aggressively intelligent face was like the edge of a very sharp tool.

(Christopher Isherwood, *Lions and Shadows*, 1938)

and a supervision 'plus' in the late thirties:

TRANSIT

O a little lonely in Cambridge that first Fall
of fogs & buying books & London on Thursdays for plays
& visiting Rylands in his posh room at King's
one late afternoon a week

He was kind to me stranded, & even to an evening party
he invited me, where Keynes & Auden
sat on the floor in the hubbub trading stories
out of their Oxbridge wealth of folk lore

(John Berryman in *Love and Fame*, 1970)

Examinations loomed large in everyone's consciousness:

The sky was fiercely blue all day; the air breathless, heavy. To walk into the town was to walk into a steam bath, where footsteps moved ever more languidly, and the dogs lay panting on the pavement, and the clocks seemed to collect themselves with a vast effort for their chiming.

This week there was nothing in your mind save the machine which obeyed you smoothly, turning out dates and biographies, contrasting, discussing, theorizing.

Judith walked in a dream among the pale examination faces that flowed to their doom. Already at nine o'clock the heat struck up from the streets, rolled downwards from the roofs. By midday it would be extremely unpleasant in Cambridge.

This was the great examination hall. Girls were filing in, each carrying a glass of water, and searching in a sort of panic for her place. Here was a white ticket labelled Earle, J. So Judith Earle really was expected, an integral part of this grotesque organized unreality. No hope now ...

The clock struck nine.

'You can begin now', said a thin voice from the dais.

There was an enormous sigh, a rustling of paper, then silence.

The questions had, nearly all, at first glance a familiar reassuring look. It was all right. Panic vanished, the mind assembled its energies coolly, precisely, the pen flew ...

Three hours. It was over. You could not remember what you had written; but you had never felt more firm and sure of mind. Three hours nearer to life.

(Rosamund Lehmann, *Dusty Answer*, 1927)

Of course in May Term one had to be very quiet for it was the Exam. Term and one often heard the door open if a Student was making a noise and someone would say 'Silence Hours Please'. At Tripos time the first years used to get up in the morning about 7 o'clock and make tea and take a cup to each Student in their subject who was taking Tripos. Sometimes we would give them a Horse Shoe cut out in Cardboard and covered with Silver Paper just for luck. There used to be crowds of Students and Dons to see them go off by bus at 8.30 a.m. and the last day Students of the same subject used to sit on the gate waiting for their return, then provide a very nice tea for them in one of their rooms. Sometimes the Cook would dish the Potatoes up in the shape of a horseshoe for we were in those days very interested in our Students, we used to be very proud if one of our's got a Wrangler or a First.

(Crane, *Girton Memories 1919–48*)

Housman was credited with being the second of the two examiners who heard the 'blithe new-comer' on a spring walk to Madingley:

First don. O cuckoo, shall I call thee bird,
          Or but a wandering voice?
Second don. State the alternative preferred,
          With reasons for your choice.

(Grant Richards, *Housman, 1897–1936*, 1973)

Professor H. M. Chadwick suggested a tripos question: what were the recreations in the Viking Age of (a) men and (b) women? which prompted A. B. Cook to enquire whether a candidate might earn full marks by answering: (a) women and (b) men.

(Howarth, *Cambridge Between Two Wars*)

Pleasures were taken seriously.

Rugger – after the Varsity match:

Donald at last got into a carriage with twenty-three others and had to stand for an hour and five minutes, including a halt of twenty minutes outside Waterloo. There were two schools of opinion in the carriage. One faction, consisting of eleven young men with bedraggled light-blue favours and one rather passionate urban dean, maintained warmly that Cambridge had won by two goals, two tries, and a penalty goal against two tries, or nineteen points to six. The rival group of partisans were handicapped by internal dissensions, for seven of them were positive that Cambridge had not scored at all, whereas they had definitely seen Oxford score three tries, convert one of them, and also score a dropped goal, thus winning by fifteen points to nil; while four of them knew for an incontrovertible fact that Oxford had scored, in addition, three penalty goals from penalties awarded, and rightly awarded, against Cambridge for dirty play in the scrums.

It was only because they were tightly wedged into the carriage and none of

[310]

them could move hand or foot that prevented, so it seemed to Donald, actual violence – certainly the urban dean's language was enough to justify manslaughter – and he was astonished when the controversy dissolved into hearty laughter and they all started chaffing the dean. The dean's powers of repartee were quite devastating.

But all doubts were settled when the train at last pulled in to Waterloo at 6.25, for the evening papers were being sold on the platforms with the authoritative statement that the match had been drawn – each side having scored one try, or three points each.

(A. G. Macdonell, England My England, 1933)

Cricket:

He [J. G. W. Davies] is always remembered as the man who bowled Bradman for a duck. It was on a fair May morning at Fenner's in 1934, and though the pitch was flawless as ever, Jack, in 'sneakers' as usual and with sleeves flying loose, was bowling his off-breaks round the wicket. The Don pushed forward, possibly playing for just a shade of turn, and the ball hit the off-stump. Such was the victim's reputation that the undergraduate crowd greeted the event with embarrassed silence, almost as though someone had committed some sudden gaffe in a cathedral. Don mounted the pavilion steps with a wry smile, saying, 'I reckon it must have slipped out of his hand.'

(E. W. Swanton, Follow On, 1977)

Acting:

1938 . . . at the Arts Theatre in Cambridge The Marlowe Society presented *King Lear* in its entirety. The tragedy could not have been more fully realised, or played with greater lucidity. The anonymous and impersonal actors seemed to be saturated not only in their own parts but in the whole play. The acting was vital: a good deal of natural vigour had been schooled out of existence – the effect of this was that there were no obvious accents, no tours de force. Thus, these performances did *King Lear* a rare service: they offered an unobstructed channel for the rush of the play. Too often, the natural and imperative rhythm has been tampered with; the scenes have been re-arranged – at Cambridge they were played in their written order, and in this order their power is cumulative.

(Elizabeth Bowen, in the New Statesman
and Nation)

Upstairs, downstairs.

Head porter of Pembroke:

Comber, a Fellow of the college . . . was chatting to Stoakley on the day following a Foundress' Feast.

'Well', he said, 'it was nice to see some old friends last night.'

'Yes', said Stoakley, 'and do you know, sir, that as Mr. — (naming an impecunious country vicar) was leaving, he put half-a-crown into my hand. Well, you know, sir, half-a-crown to him is like a sovereign to you or me.'

(Roberts, Adventures with Authors)

A porter of Clare:

a simple Porter (as of those days) interviewing a Korean graduate student who, on my advice, wanted to join Clare. His name was Pin Chuan Ho. 'What's your name?' asked the Porter. 'Ho', replied the student. 'Ho!' returned the Porter. 'Ho's not a name, it's a staircase.'

(Raymond Priestley (Fellow 1923–34), quoted in *Clare College Association Annual*, 1968)

There were more students from different backgrounds, coming to a Cambridge which might be thought to be changing:

Dazzled by the façade of Cambridge I did not perceive that it was the architecture of the Cavendish, not of King's or Trinity Great Court, or even of neo-Gothic Girton, that corresponded to the new standards of quantitative, scientific 'truth', to the Cambridge of the present. I did not realise that the new thought which inhabited the Gibbs Building, the Senate House, the Gothic and Renaissance courts and libraries, the Victorian avenues of elm and lime, was no longer that which had built them and which their forms continued to express and communicate . . .

Perhaps I would never have accepted such spurious truths of Cambridge rationalism had I not closed my heart; which could never have been deceived by the new doctrine that 'honesty' consisted in disregard of feeling (which was 'purely subjective') in ourselves and others: a quantitative, positivist honesty . . . Feeling is at a disadvantage when it argues its truth against that of cold reason. In the Cambridge of the 'twenties this was the more so because the scientific materialism generated in the prestigious Cavendish Laboratory and its encircling power-houses made reason itself serve the quantitative verifiable.

(Kathleen Raine, *The Land Unknown*, 1975)

Disciplines and faculties multiplied, and between 1919 and 1938 there were no fewer than thirty new professorships, eleven of them in science and mathematical subjects such as aeronautical engineering, mineralogy and petrology, biochemistry and animal pathology. In 1931 there was a professorship of experimental psychology and of industrial relations and in 1933 of Chinese language and history and, at last, anthropology.

It was a time of expansion and building.

The University Library

For many months, since its steel skeleton appeared on our horizon, awkward pauses at our tea-tables have been covered with polite skirmishes on the subject of the Library tower, whether it is, or is not, a Mistake. We have on Tuesday, as we toyed with bread and butter, condemned it as an eye-sore, on Friday, as we negotiated a meringue, declared that, whatever anyone may say, *we* think it is beautiful – in a way of its own of course but definitely beautiful; while on Sunday, in the intervals of saying, 'A very small slice please', and 'No, really, nothing more', we have agreed that it would be admirable in any place but this.

(M.P.S.W., 'The Tower', in the *Cambridge Review*, 6 June 1934)

The sight of such a building would effectually deter a student from paying it a visit. I do not know whether it is too late, or if we are irrevocably bound to this motor factory, or steam laundry, or whatever the model is; but if not, some physician ought to administer an emetic to the Buildings Syndicate.

(W. H. D. Rouse, letter to the Cambridge Review, 18 October 1929)

The books were removed with remarkable despatch in the Long Vacation of 1934, despite rumours that it would require a scenic railway along the Backs. At 4 p.m. on 31 May the last reader left and the following morning the task began of moving 1,142,000 books in 689 loads. The Library staff and a team of porters from Messrs. Eaden Lilley worked daily from 8 a.m. to 6 p.m. The job was completed in exactly eight weeks. Horse-drawn vans were used, since it was felt that the greater vehicular speed would have resulted in a congestion of filled boxes at one end and empty boxes at the other. The length of the building is 420 feet, the height of the tower 156 feet and it has 40 miles of shelves. It was and is a pleasant place to work, but Cambridge has never been fond of it as a piece of architecture.

(Howarth, Cambridge Between Two Wars)

It is a comforting thing to see hundreds of undergraduates, not only in the great reading room but also up and down the Library, in almost every stack and at almost every table; you feel that here is a library in use, and democracy in action . . . there is a magic in free access to the hundreds of rows of shelves.

(Ernest Barker, Age and Youth, 1953)

Queens' New Building

Is there some lacuna in Cambridge culture that leaves us blind to the visual arts ?

(E. A. Crutchley, in the Cambridge Review, 23 October 1936)

Scientists were at work everywhere.

Hamilton Hartridge, later a professor at St. Bartholomew's Hospital, London, was the first:

to make an adequate approach to the problem of the avoidance of objects by bats in flight. This was at King's in 1920, in his Gibbs' set E5. On fine summer evenings the bats would fly in and circle round the big room – sometimes more than 100 at once, he alleged. With a quorum of bats inside he closed the shutters. Fine silk threads were stretched across the room, one end fixed to the wall, the other to tension indicators in a box. The bats never collided, even when reversing the direction of their circling. They also avoided the threads; and if the door into the inner room was left six inches ajar they flew in there, but not if opened less. It made no difference whether the light was on or off. In a four-page article of admirable clarity describing the experiments (*Journal of Physiology* **54**, 54–7), which has been far too little regarded, he concluded: 'Their flight is directed (from obstacles) by a specialised sense of hearing, since the sound waves of short wave length they are known to emit are capable of casting shadows and forming sound-pictures.' Intensive experiments recently made in many laboratories have entirely confirmed Hartridge's view. He had anticipated sonar.

(Wilkinson, *A Century of Kingsmen*)

Another view of King's College Chapel:

King's College Chapel has a double roof. From the floor to the under surface of the inner roof, the beautiful fan vaulting which is the wonder of all architects, is just eighty feet. Above this stone roof is a space which varies in height from seven to ten feet, and this space opens to the outside by certain windows through which the pigeons gain access to their homes. It was in this inter-roof space and on an unused spiral staircase leading to it that the chief fauna were found. In the main they centre round the second vertebrate, the pigeon *Columba livia*, and consisted of animals and larvae that lived on or in the pigeon, or lived upon the unused mouldering food of the birds, or finally lived predaceously upon one another.

Only one species of mollusc was taken, a snail *Helix arbustorum*, of which a single living example and one empty shell were found in a dark corner of the roof space.

Spiders were, however, very plentiful, and were found in all parts, but they have not as yet been identified. Little pseudo-scorpions or false-scorpions, with their superficial resemblance to the real article, were found in numbers among the rubbish.

(Shipley, *Cambridge Cameos*)

J. B. S. Haldane, then reader in biochemistry, was active in his experiments on salt metabolism, which on occasions involved running round and round Market Hill, a flat area in the middle of the town, with a bottle to be filled for analysis in the subterranean men's room.

(Hutchinson, *Kindly Fruits of the Earth*)

As a young research student (in the 1920s) I wished to try out a radio circuit . . . by screwing some components to a 'bread board'. When I went to get a piece of wood for the purpose Lincoln (the head of the workshops), pointed to a pile of scrap wood in the corner and invited me to take a piece, but as I was leaving the room he ran after me and said, 'Here, Mr. Ratcliffe, do you really need mahogany?'

. . . there were signs of sophistication in the later 1930s. The presence of people like Kapitsa and Cockcroft, with experience as engineers, and the establishment of the Mond Laboratory, generously endowed, helped to start a trend that continued after the war . . .

There was, I think, a feeling that the best science was that done in the simplest way. In experimental work, as in mathematics, there was a 'style' and a result obtained with simple equipment was more elegant than one obtained with complicated apparatus . . . When Bullard [Sir Edward Bullard, FRS, of Clare] wished to compare the periods of two pendulums, one in Cambridge and one in Africa, he first considered transmitting the timing of one from the other by radio, but he ultimately adopted a neater arrangement by which both pendulums were timed against each other against the morse signals emitted by a high powered commercial transmitter.

(J. A. Ratcliffe, 'Physics in a University Laboratory', in *Proceedings of the Royal Society*, 342A, 1975)

Sir Alan Hodgkin, Nobel Laureate and Master of Trinity from 1978, recalls:

In those days [1934–5] laboratory life was rather informal, at any rate in Cambridge. I never worked for a Ph.D. and didn't have a research supervisor. You might easily start in a bare room and have to build most of your equipment yourself, apart from a few standard bits like smoked drums, Palmer stands and kymographs. This sounds depressing but it actually wasn't.

(Sir Alan Hodgkin in *The Pursuit of Nature. Informal Essays on the History of Physiology*, 1977)

The Cavendish had its own aura of romance and antiquity:

I arrived in the Cavendish in October 1927, as a raw research student from the antipodes, whom Rutherford had kindly admitted to what was then, by far, the greatest physical laboratory in the world . . . I entered a small office littered with books and papers, the desk cluttered in a manner which I had been taught at school indicated an untidy and inefficient mind. It was raining, and drops of water ran reluctantly down the grime covered glass of the uncurtained window.

I was received genially by a large, rather florid man, with thinning fair hair and a large moustache, who reminded me forcibly of the keeper of the general store and post office in a little village in the hills behind Adelaide where I had spent part of my childhood. Rutherford made me feel welcome and at ease at once.

As I left, two large young men strode from a room opposite, nearly colliding with the very diffident newcomer. With a charming smile, a handsome and impressive man said:

'I'm Blackett. This is Dymond. Who are you?'

These members of the Laboratory were clearly friendly. I told them of my instructions and my lack of knowledge of the geography of the Laboratory. They led me down the stairs to the open door of the large basement laboratory known as the Garage, and told me that I would find J.J.'s set-up in the far corner, and Aston in a room beyond. Reluctantly, I made my way towards the place where two men worked whom I regarded with the same awe as I did Rutherford, and whom I had never thought to meet in the flesh. Fortunately for me, neither J.J. nor Aston was in, so I was saved considerable embarrassment, but J.J.'s assistants, Everett and Morley, chatted with me for a while mostly about the pleasures of motor cycling. They were in attendance upon an amazing mass of glass tubing, taps and flasks, spread over two or three tables, and covered with dust. I had the impression that it had grown continuously since J.J. discovered the electron thirty years previously, each new experiment being added, and nothing ever removed or cleaned.

(Mark Oliphant, *Rutherford – Recollections of the Cambridge Days*, 1972)

It was a companionable world:

John Desmond Bernal (known as Sage) was the first lecturer in Structural Crystallography in 1927.

The Bernals settled at first in the country outside Cambridge at Hildersham. This led to the practice of Bernal and his students having lunch in the lab and talking together. Every day, one of the group would go along and buy fresh bread from Fitzbillies, fruit and cheese from the market, while another made coffee on the gas-ring in the corner of the bench. One day there was talk about anaerobic bacteria at the bottom of a lake in Russia and the origin of life, another, about Romanesque architecture in French villages, or Leonardo da Vinci's engines of war or about poetry or painting . . .

(Dorothy M. C. Hodgkin, 'Bernal' in *Biographical Memoirs of Fellows of the Royal Society*, 1980)

Bernal headed . . . a sub-department housed in a few ill-lit and dirty rooms on the ground floor of a stark, dilapidated grey brick building. These dingy quarters were turned into a fairy castle by Bernal's brilliance . . . Within a few weeks of arriving, I realized that Cambridge was where I wanted to spend my life.

(Max Perutz quoted in H. F. Judson's *The Eighth Day of Creation*, 1979)

There were continual excitements:

Living in Cambridge, one could not help picking up the human, as well as the intellectual, excitement in the air. Sir James Chadwick, grey faced after a fortnight of work with three hours' sleep a night, telling the Kapitsa Club how he had discovered the neutron; P. M. S. Blackett, the most handsome of men, not quite so authoritative as usual, because it seemed too good to be true, showing plates which demonstrated the existence of the positive electron; Sir John Cockcroft, normally about as much given to emotional display as the Duke of Wellington, skimming down King's Parade and saying to anyone whose face he recognized: 'We've split the atom! We've split the atom!'

(C. P. Snow, 'Rutherford and the Cavendish', in *The Baldwin Age*, ed. John Raymond, 1960)

William Lawrence Bragg became Cavendish Professor in 1938. In 1915 he was a 25-year-old Fellow of Trinity when he and his father received the Nobel Prize for work on X-rays and the structure of crystals – no-one younger than he has ever been a Nobel Laureate. (Three years later he was awarded a Military Cross when in the Army in France.)

He thought the purest pleasure in scientific life was to see the germ of an idea planted in a younger man's mind develop to an extent that could not have been foreseen, and to see him get recognition for his work.

When Bragg gained one of his insights, especially in optics and the properties of matter, he often worked out the details with lightning speed, producing neatly drawn sketches and a perfectly written description. This capacity reminded Perutz of Mozart's composing of the overture to the Marriage of Figaro in a single night.

(Crowther, The Cavendish Laboratory)

Max Perutz recalls:

One morning in March 1938, a friend walked past my window at the Cavendish and told me that Hitler had invaded Austria. There are certain events, like the death of a loved person, which you dread so much that you cannot contemplate their happening, even if all the evidence tells you that they will. The threat to Austria, which I loved, had not been uppermost in my mind when I decided to come to Britain; I came for scientific reasons, but I should have taken the threat more seriously. The invasion changed my status overnight, from a guest to a refugee. My father's money was soon exhausted, and as a foreigner I was not allowed to earn any, not even by College supervision. How was I to finish my studies?

... I waited from day to day, hoping that Bragg would come around to the Crystallographic Laboratory to find out what was going on there. After about six weeks I plucked up courage and called on him in Rutherford's Victorian office in Free School Lane. When I showed him my x-ray pictures of haemo-globin his face lit up. He realised at once the challenge of extending x-ray analysis to the giant molecules of the living cell, and obtained a grant from the Rockefeller Foundation to appoint me as his research assistant. Bragg's effective action saved my scientific career and enabled me to bring my parents to England, so that they escaped the holocaust.

(New Scientist, 31 January 1980)

Several eminent scientists from Germany and Austria found refuge at Cambridge. Two biochemists came through the good offices of Nobel Laureate, Albert Szent-Gyorgyi, who worked at Cambridge in the twenties.

Max Rudolf Lemberg:

1933 After a lecture of his at Heidelberg, Szent-Gyorgyi took me aside and brought me the invitation of my English friends to come back to Cambridge at once. [He went on to Australia later.]

(C. Rimington and C. H. Gray, 'Lemberg',
in Biographical Memoirs of Fellows of the
Royal Society, 1978)

Hans Krebs:

The Hague 12 April 1933

Dear Colleague ... I am sorry to hear you have personal difficulties in Germany. During the last few days I was in Cambridge where people have in mind helping you somehow. Of course I have encouraged them as much as possible and I hope that my words will have contributed a little toward the realization of the plans ...

With kind regards
Albert Szent-Gyorgyi

P.S. If you really would like to come to Cambridge it would be best if you wrote to Hopkins and told him you would be content with very modest opportunities. Senior posts are not available and perhaps he might be diffident to offer you a junior position.

Krebs writes:

ten weeks later I was installed in Cambridge.

(*Search and Discovery. A Tribute to A. Szent-Gyorgyi*, ed. Benjamin Kaminer, 1977)

The beginning of radar.

Cockcroft writes:

We [Cockcroft and Fowler, Rutherford's son-in-law] motored from Cambridge to Woodbridge across the heath country I was to know so well later. The mysterious towers of Bawdsey rose into the sky and we were admitted to the road through the woods which led to the fantastic nineteenth-century manor house used as headquarters of A.M.R.E. [Air Ministry Research Establishment]. There we met Watson-Watt, who produced for us the Child's Guide to R.D.F. [radio direction finding].

Bragg:

I went down with Cockcroft and Ratcliffe . . . What really helped to save a year, and thus enabled radar to play its part, was what subsequently took place. For it was arranged that physicists from the universities, really under the aegis of the Cavendish, should go to the various radar stations being built round the coast, and learn exactly how radar worked. This, in the period between Munich and the outbreak of war, brought the young academic scientists into radar and that was the thing that really mattered.

(Ronald W. Clark, *The Rise of the Boffins*, 1962)

By the mid-'thirties it was very rare to find a physicist under forty whose sympathies were not on the Left.

This process of political crystallization had begun years before when the leaders of the young radical scientists had already emerged: J. D. Bernal, Blackett, J. B. S. Haldane. All three were men of tough character and immense intellectual ability . . .

Before Rutherford's death, a number of the younger scientists were already preparing for the war. Blackett, as usual giving them the lead, had been getting himself used to military problems for some years before. He had been put on the Air Defence Council by Tizard, who wanted talent regardless of politics and who was a specially good judge of talent when it came his way. It was for such reasons – and because England had just gone through its greatest age of physics – that the English scientists were by and large more effective than those of any other country throughout the war with Hitler.

(Snow, 'Rutherford and the Cavendish')

At a time of economic depression, political disillusion and the rise of Nazism and Fascism, for some people, of whom a few have since become notorious, Cambridge was where they learned and taught Marxism:

Bernal, at Emmanuel:

7 November (1919)   It was all so clear, so compelling, so universal. How narrow my Irish patriotism seemed, how absurdly reactionary my military schemes . . . My universe was broken to bits.
and next day an ambiguous entry:
A turning point in my life. At last I have been shifted into the first eight and row three.

(Hodgkin, 'Bernal')

Kim Philby (Trinity):

One of my first acts on going up to Cambridge in 1929 was to join the Cambridge University Socialist Society (CUSS) . . . Through general reading, I became gradually aware that the Labour Party in Britain stood well apart from the mainstream of the Left as a world wide force. But the real turning-point in my thinking came with the demoralisation and rout of the Labour Party in 1931 . . . It was a slow and brain-racking process: my transition from a Socialist viewpoint to a Communist one took two years. It was not until my last term at Cambridge, in the summer of 1933, that I threw off my last doubts. I left the university with a degree and with the conviction that my life must be devoted to Communism.

There were the early Left-wing Associations in Cambridge. But I had never joined the Communist Party in England.

(My Silent War, 1968)

Burgess (Trinity) and Maclean (Trinity Hall). Statement made to the Press in Moscow on 11 February 1955:

At Cambridge we had both been Communists. We abandoned our political activities not because we in any way disagreed with the Marxist analysis of the situation in which we still both find ourselves, but because we thought, wrongly it is now clear to us, that in the public service we could do more to put these ideals into practical effect than elsewhere.

Burgess was a member of the Apostles, with their aura of secrecy:

I was unable to persuade Guy to tell me who his fellow-members were.

(Tom Driberg, Guy Burgess, 1956)

1937:   It was the fashion among the Apostles to be Radical, a fashion less political than literary and metaphysical . . . When politics were touched on by the Apostles it was in an amused and rather patronizing way. ''Twas a very pretty little revolution in Saxony', wrote Hallam in 1830, 'and a respectable one at Brunswick.' The dilettante tone has charm after the sweeping statements, the safe marble gestures, the self-importance of our own 'thirties – 'I stand with the People and Government of Spain.'

(Graham Greene, Collected Essays, 1969)

It was a time charged with excitement.

David Haden Guest (Trinity):

I well remember how David came into a meeting of the Cambridge 'Moral Science Club'... with a copy of Lenin's Materialism and Empirio-Criticism. He was bubbling over with excitement about it, and kept reading passages aloud, especially those parts which deal with a class basis of philosophy. Some of the students were rather shocked, others thought he had gone crazy, but he took no notice and kept reading out the passages just the same... I went straight home and read the book, and therefore decided to join the Communist Party.

(Maurice Cornforth, 'Reminiscences', in Carmel Haden Guest, *A Memoir*, 1939)

John Cornford (Trinity):

Looking back over political life in Cambridge one sees him everywhere – in a swirl of people and lights in Benet Street at the end of a torchlight procession; waiting on Parker's Piece with a body of followers ready to deal with an expected Fascist descent one summer when Mosley's vans were making frequent appearances; sitting in the middle of a hall at a Fascist meeting in an outlying village, like a captain amidst his troops of hecklers.

(Victor Kiernan, 'Recollections', *A Memoir*, ed. Pat Sloan, 1938)

Julian Bell (King's):

The anti-war demonstration, 11 November 1933:

His beaten-up Morris car, in which he had terrified his friends as he drove them along the roads of Cambridgeshire, he now attempted to transform into a military vehicle. 'I tried to use the Morris as an armoured car (stript of everything breakable)', he wrote to Quentin. The armour of the car was mattresses, and his navigator was Guy Burgess, a research student at Trinity. They entered the line of march, and as they moved slowly and conspicuously along, they were a tempting target for tomatoes, and got well pelted. But they made a couple of good charges at the enemy – 'hearties' again, attempting to break up the parade – before they were ordered out by the police. Julian merely changed his tactics, drove round through a circuitous route and rejoined the march towards its head. His letter to Quentin concludes: 'There was one good fight, which I missed, when they stole our banner and gave a man a concussion.' At that point the police had intervened again, using their batons.

(P. Stansky and W. Abrahams, *Journey to the Frontier: Julian Bell and John Cornford*, 1966)

Nevertheless good manners prevailed:

14 June 1932

Dear Guest,

Hearty congratulations on your First, which I am sure was well deserved, and which is particularly gratifying with so severe and fair an examiner as Moore. You can be perfectly sure that the First represents genuine good work and not mere good luck.

I suppose you will celebrate your success in the usual way by attacking the 'lackeys of the Bourgeoisie' and being locked up for it. When you are out again I hope to see you sometime.

(from Professor C. D. Broad, Trinity College, quoted in Carmel Haden Guest, *A Memoir*)

Cornford wrote to his College Tutor:

4 Oct. 1936

I am writing this letter to resign my scholarships, as by the time this reaches you I shall already be on the way to rejoin the unit of the Anti-Fascist Militia with which I have been fighting this summer. I am sorry I did not have time to discuss it personally.

I should like to take this opportunity of thanking you, and through you other Fellows of the College I have not had time to write to, for the tremendous personal kindness and interest you have always shown me, even though you must have looked with disfavour on many of my activities.

(*A Memoir*, ed. Sloan)

Polite civilisation sometimes seemed irrelevelant:

Cornford's first rooms were a double set which he shared with a friend over the gateway between Bishop's Hostel and New Court. There was one long room suitable to meetings, where he usually sat frowningly on the floor; it was furnished with an austerity that expressed the man, and was lit with naked electric bulbs.

(Kiernan, 'Recollections', in *A Memoir*, ed. Sloan)

David's room in Trinity absolutely bare except for a large bookcase, a piano, a picture of Lenin and the famous piece of very mouldy cheese on a shelf. The long political discussions, in which David showed great eloquence. Murmurs from the less strong-minded that they were very hungry and would like a pause for a meal. David's offer to share cheese which was refused . . .

and learning was tough going:

On arrival at Trinity for a study group meeting; David discovered playing the piano – the precise almost mechanical seventeenth-century music. His scornful attitude to the more emotional music of the nineteenth century. Appeared to be interested almost entirely in form.

Study classes on *Capital* for inquiring minds – chapter by chapter progression

[321]

through the book for 4 months ... We did not understand half that was said, but were stimulated to go on reading.

(M. T. Parker, 'Flashback Images', in Guest, *A Memoir*)

David Haden Guest, John Cornford and Julian Bell were all killed in the Spanish Civil War.

Not all left-wing sympathisers lived austerely, certainly not Julian Bell:

'Beagling and the Apostles'

1929 My first year at Cambridge, lived in lodgings, 12 St. Edward's Passage was a failure on the whole. I read history, supervised by John Clapham and did some work at it. I beagled seven days a fortnight all the winter.

The most important event of my Cambridge life was being elected to the Apostles; this happened to me in my second year, just after I had moved into college. The whole period was one of great expansion and a feeling of richness and possibilities in the world. I published my first poems in The Venture and Cambridge Poetry that autumn: I had a car, and my own rooms, furniture, pictures – all the amenities of Cambridge at its best. There was an extraordinary *douceur de vivre*, a combination of material wealth (part boom, part credit system) the general ease of college life, a certain relaxation of work, and a great many new friends. The core of this was the Apostles – my first meeting – – – was terrifically impressive – – I really felt I had reached the pinnacle of Cambridge intellectualism – – – Since then almost all my male friends have been drawn from the Society, and in general it has played a more important part in my life than any other institution.

(*Essays, Poems and Letters*, ed. Q. Bell, 1938)

On 9 December 1933 he wrote to the 'New Statesman':

In the Cambridge that I first knew, in 1929 and 1930, the central subject of ordinary intelligent conversation was poetry. As far as I can remember we hardly ever talked or thought about politics. For one thing, we almost all of us had implicit confidence in Maynard Keynes's rosy prophecies of continually increasing capitalist prosperity. Only the secondary problems, such as birth control, seemed to need the intervention of the intellectuals.

By the end of 1933, we have arrived at a situation in which almost the only subject of discussion is contemporary politics, and in which a very large majority of the more intelligent undergraduates are Communists, or almost Communists. As far as an interest in literature continues it has very largely changed its character, and become an ally of Communism under the influence of Mr. Auden's Oxford Group ...

But this is only one side of the picture. If Communism makes many of its converts among the 'emotionals', it appeals almost as strongly to minds a great deal harder. It is not so much that we are all Socialists now as that we are all Marxists now. The burning questions for us are questions of tactics and method, and of our own place in a Socialist State and a Socialist revolution.

But by no means all undergraduates were communist sympathisers:

Blunt is recorded as saying that in 1934–5 'almost all the intelligent and bright young undergraduates who had come up to Cambridge had suddenly become Marxists under the impact of Hitler's coming into power'.

This is arrogant rubbish. It is characteristic of communists and the extreme left to move soiely within the tiny circle to which they belong, only extending from time to time a tentacle like an octopus to ensnare some potential comrade who swims past their lair. Their numbers were really very small and by no means all of them were brilliant. True, they made up for this by making a lot of noise, suffering martyrdom by selling the *Daily Worker* outside the Mill Lane lecture-rooms and hissing when 'God Save the King' was played at the flicks. But such myopia on the part of Professor Blunt is barely credible. There were plenty of bright and intelligent undergraduates at other colleges who were not attracted by communism . . . Many clever undergraduates were conservatives, not in the sense of supporting Baldwin and Chamberlain, but as young men with an innate scepticism towards ideologies and rhetoric. Other intelligent students cultivated their gardens and gave up attending open meetings of discussion clubs where the communist clique bored those who attended with interminable speeches and points of order, much as their *gauchiste* successors in the late 1960s and 1970s did in the student unions.

(Noel Annan, *The Times Literary Supplement*, 7 December 1979)

One Kingsman, friend of many Apostles, went to great lengths to keep his own secrets:

in 1936, for the first time, Dilly [Alfred Dillwyn Knox] began to refuse his invitations to Founder's Feast. The reason was simple; the dinner was noted, even among Cambridge colleges, for its hospitality and its fine wines, and, in consequence, for the occasional indiscretions of the guests. These, to be sure, were heard by Kingsmen only, but the time had come when Dilly could not risk even the hint of a shadow of a reference to what he was doing . . . It was the business of the Foreign Office's Department of Communications to solve Enigma and, later, the Enigma Variations. [This was the beginning of the unravelling of German secret ciphers.]

(Penelope Fitzgerald, *The Knox Brothers*)

Pleasures were still 'hot i' the mouth' for some, but with a tiny cloud on the horizon:

The red roses and the lion *passant gardant* of Tudor England which made up the college crest, decorated the panelled walls . . . The food was very good (three courses for lunch, five for dinner); and the two bottles of hock . . . provided the easiest of all drinks to swallow. We were waited on hand and foot, as was everyone else. We played poker-dice for the wine, though discreetly; there must surely be some ancient statute which forbade scholars to resort to gaming at table. I sighed as I lost the final round; two bottles of hock, even 1926 Liebfraumilch, cost twelve shillings, and already, at the end of my third year, there stretched behind me and in front of me a vast series of such bills which would, within a month, all have to be confessed to my father.

It was nearly three o'clock by the time we had scooped up the last chalky crumbs of the Stilton, and drained the second glass of port, and decided that lunch was ended. Slightly overfed, definitely muzzy, well contented we made for the door . . . presently we were standing in the shadow of Great Gate, making up our minds what to do next.

'A flick . . . Who's for the flicks?'

. . .

'What I really mean', I said, 'is why can't things stay the same?'

'What things?'

'Oh, everything . . . I mean, all the stuff in the newspapers – strikes and hunger marches and the dole and unemployment. What's going wrong? It used not to be like this. It's only the last four years. It used to be like –' I waved my hand round the room, full of elegant Lucullans having a good time, 'well, like this.'

. . .

'People will actually have to work when they get to Cambridge. *If* they get to Cambridge.'

'What, *everybody*?'

'Yes, everybody.'
(Nicholas Monsarrat, Life is a Four Letter Word, 1967)

It was in the era before the Second World War . . . that we had those well-remembered cricket matches between the staff and the undergraduates in the Long Vacations . . . The undergraduates usually beat us, but there were several famous occasions when they had been too generous in their behaviour in the field. Quite a good proportion of the Fellows would look in during the progress of the game and take tea with us. This was served to us by the students. After the Match an excellent cold supper was served in Hall. In the palmy days Scotch Salmon and Cucumber would be the main course with real Mayonnaise Sauce (not the stuff which comes out of a bottle). There is just no substitute for a Mayonnaise Sauce made in a College Kitchen. Fruit Salad and Cream and a delicious Trifle would be served as Sweets. There was always plenty of Beer, Cider and Iced Lemon Squash to allay the thirst developed on the cricket field. This supper was also served to us by the students, and they would even do the washing-up afterwards while we retired to the Fellows' Garden for Bowls or a stroll and a smoke. As soon as it was dark we would have a rousing Smoking/Drinking Concert in the Large Lecture-room . . . a student would perform and then call upon one of us to render an item . . . Dr. F. H. A. Marshall (who was the lay dean and in charge of students in the Long Vacation) was Master of Ceremonies at these Concerts and an excellent one he made.
(W. L. Falkner, Bursar's Clerk, Christ's College Magazine, 1970)

The summers of 1938 and 1939 had a special flavour:

It was an odd summer which preceded Munich. Life went on at different levels. There was work, which assumed gigantic proportions before the days in May when one tremulously presented oneself at the Senate House or the Corn Exchange for the tripos examinations. Work was always at odds with love and pleasure; its shadow both darkened and heightened these activities. Whatever one was doing, drinking coffee in the Copper Kettle or tea at midnight in someone's rooms, taking a punt up the river or leaning out of a window sniffing the fragrance of early summer, one should instead have been working. The complications of courtship; the daydreams, the jealousies, the embuscades, the enfilades, the idled moments in Sidgwick Walk, the muffed kisses on the Fen bridges; were all underlined by the uneasiness of work waiting.

One would cycle down from college to buy Chelsea buns for tea, turn left up Queens' Lane, where the richer undergraduates seemed always to be revving up the engines of their little sports cars, past the forest of bicycles and tennis rackets, through into King's Parade, into that sweet discordance of chimes, bicycle bells, pianos played at open windows and young men calling, 'Peter', 'Michael' and 'John'; cupped voices shouted and Peter, Michael and John, gilded by youth and summer, leant, amused, indifferent or truculent, from their windows. Then one rounded the corner into the Market Place, past the flower and fruit stalls and the book stalls and the man selling shrimps from Harwich, and there on the Petty Cury corner would be the newspaper man, with the London evening papers and the 'Cambridge Daily News', and there, casually against their bicycles or the wall, their placards would be; and the bright world would waver and topple as one glanced at them: 'Hitler speaks again', 'Hitler's fresh demands', 'The Truth about Hitler's Tanks'. After that, it was hard to know which mattered least: work or love or pleasure.

(Helen Foley, *A Handful of Time*, 1961)

The Vice-Chancellor blows his whistle, and everything starts. The Term surges forth. The Spring Term, the May Term, the Summer Term. Call it what you wish – the best Term of all. The Term of Grantchester Meadows and the First and Third (Trinity's Boat Club). A grimy train trundles in from Bletchley bringing an assortment of popular-fronters and academics. An exotic 1939 Zephyr slides suavely up to Trinity Gate bringing a bit of Debrett's peerage and a quarter bottle of Bollinger Special Cuvée. Deanna (Durbin, an ingénue film star of great celebrity) is here thrilling the evening multitudes, and King's dons can see *Snow White* another dozen times this week. May Week gets nearer ... Mozart's *Idomeneo* fills the pentagonal Arts (Theatre), Cambridge is having another English première, producer Camille Prior sits in a box justly proud. The May Sunday excursions are crowded with purple lovelies. They walk down through King's and back through Trinity and the sun glows. A cape of pale Russian lynx. An off-shoulder dress of emerald tulle ... A world of lawns and punts, neckties and shirting-patterns, *crème brûlée* and paprika salad. The Vice-Chancellor blows his whistle. What a term it's going to be.

(Editorial of 'The Granta' quoted in Howarth, *Cambridge Between Two Wars*)

Memories of 1939 are often connected for me with the garden at Newnham. It was difficult to dig the air-raid shelters because of the wetness of the ground, and they could not be sunk deeper than three feet. There was also another hazard: during the digging of those outside Peile Hall, some ancient burials were found. Moved by a rather recent interest in archaeology, I went along to help, and spent most of Whitsunday removing the earth from the bones with a tablespoon. There were a number of burials; I particularly remember a grave where two adult skeletons lay inextricably mingled, and one where three – apparently man, woman and child – lay side by side. They were not straight, but lightly flexed; their bones had acquired a beautiful red-brown patina, and they looked wonderfully comfortable.

(M. Mann Phillips, in *Newnham Anthology*, ed. A. Phillips)

Fanny heard Mr. Chamberlain's voice as she stood on Garret Hostel Bridge; that voice, those words vibrated through the blue and plumy September air . . . it was Sunday and one could tell it even without church bells. Fanny leaned over the bridge and listened. Through the open windows of Trinity Hall came the modified boom of fate and then the wireless was switched off, there was silence, and for a minute no one on the bridge but Fanny. The first blown leaves rustled and the water sighed against the masonry.

She had prayed for war, but not under that name, under all the euphemisms of non-appeasement. It was odd that in the end it had come in that shape and announced in that voice, like the number of the next hymn. A punt came slowly down the river with a don's family riotously cheering their father's efforts at punting. She wondered whether she should tell them that we were at war with Germany.

(Foley, *A Handful of Time*)

on September 3rd, I stood in the garden early in the morning. It was a lovely autumn day, and I was more or less on duty, as the College had accepted a number of evacuees from London, mothers and children from Soho . . . a mistaken air-raid warning had sent them all into the shelters for the first time, and the garden which appeared empty was full of people. It was odd to stand there and hear the whisper of talk rising from the ground, as one might expect to hear leprechauns talking in an Irish hillside.

(Mann Phillips, in *Newnham Anthology*, ed. Phillips)

Preparations for the worst were being made:

To the Editor of the Cambridge Review

SIR, – Panel by panel the stained glass of King's College Chapel is daily borne away to a place of safety, where we trust it will survive the chances of war, to shine again in its former glory when peace is restored. The ancient problem inevitably recurs: by what happy chance has it survived so long . . .

That each Fellow, when the Civil War broke out, made himself responsible for one window, took it down with his own hands and removed it by a secret passage to the College manor-house at Grantchester – this seems to be no more than a picturesque invention of the romantic nineteenth century. For one thing, we have before our eyes at this moment a tangible demonstration of the time, labour and skill required in removing the windows; I leave it to you, Sir, to judge whether the Fellows of King's were ever equal to such a task. The only tangible piece of evidence which lends verisimilitude to the tale is the secret passage. The Grantchester end of it is still there. From the cellars of the manor house it runs down into the bowels of the earth; but no one knows where it ends. A fiddler, they say, once tried to find out. Playing his fiddle as he went, he descended the passage; by the sound of his fiddle the people of Grantchester followed his progress further and further into the fields, till the notes grew fainter and fainter and died away; and the fiddler was never seen again. An old survey of Grantchester marks a field by the name of Fiddler's Close, not far from the Grantchester end of the present footpath to Cambridge. Perhaps the name records the spot where the fiddler was last heard on earth.

In deference to tradition, Canon Milner-White and I visited Grantchester Manor House, just before war broke out, to see whether the secret passage would lead us to a suitable hiding-place for the windows; but it did not. However, we were more fortunate than the fiddler; for we returned.

(John Saltmarsh, *Cambridge Review*,
10 October 1939)

Members of the University Officers' Training Corps and University Air Squadron were of course called up immediately. Other young men left as they volunteered or their conscription numbers came up; and several dons volunteered for war work of various kinds:

There is one simple antidote at hand for those who wonder whether it was the Cambridge ethos or the cult of personal relations or the social disorders of the times that was the poison which the Cambridge spies swallowed . . . The very influences at Cambridge . . . created one intelligence agency which was the most successful of any nation during the war. It was staffed by loyal and dedicated men and women who, together with those who in London and in the field interpreted and made use of their intelligence material, maintained secrecy for over thirty years after the war. They were never penetrated by spies or betrayed their obligation not to reveal what they had been doing. What is more it must be admitted with trembling in the face of today's journalists that many of them were public schoolboys, some even from the upper classes. These were the cryptographers in Bletchley Park, deciphering Ultra. The station was largely staffed in the early years from Cambridge, and one at least of its most brilliant innovators was a homosexual.

(Annan, *The Times Literary Supplement*,
7 December 1979)

King's College   14 October 1939

The intelligentsia of the left were loudest in demanding that Nazi aggression should be resisted at all costs. When it comes to a showdown, scarce four weeks have passed before they remember that they are pacifists and write defeatist letters to your columns, leaving the defence of freedom and of civilisation to Colonel Blimp and the Old School Tie, for whom Three Cheers.

(Maynard Keynes to the *New Statesman*, from Wilkinson, *A Century of King's*)

There was a strange turn of events:

Woolwich and Sandhurst have both been closed on the outbreak of war, and some of those who had been intending to go there now wish to come to Cambridge. As neither of these institutions required a knowledge of Latin or Greek from their entrants it has been decided to allow such candidates to matriculate without having passed the Latin or Greek section of the Previous Examination or their equivalent. Thus for the first time there may be members of the University who have never studied a word of Latin in their lives.

(*Cambridge Review*, January 1940)

A. S. F. Gow, a don at Trinity, started a series of 'circular' letters to men of Trinity in the forces, whom he called his parishioners:

9 May 1940 ... Spring has been very lovely here. The crocuses indeed got so nipped and buffeted that they were below form and the editors, so far as I observed, prudently left their stock picture of our Avenue in its drawer, but the other spring flowers – daffodils, fritillaries, cowslips and so on – and the blossoms (including the wistaria in the Great Court) have been better than usual, and one has perhaps appreciated them the more for the current vileness of man. They came on with a rush owing to one or two warm days at the end of last month, and the only thing I have missed is the convoys of ducklings on the Backs. The ducks seems to have decided that the Upper River makes a better nursery.

(*Letters from Cambridge*, 1945)

Some activities went on regardless.

Union Debate, 7 November 1939:

That increased student participation in the control of their studies and life would be desirable.

For the motion 62 votes; against 32 votes.

Mr. Carr was dull except for saying that the University Library was a Phallic Emblem.

(*Cambridge Review*, 11 November 1939)

Blues:

It was agreed that no 'Blues' would be awarded, but a representative sweater with the initials of the club, a full band on the chest for clubs awarding the full Blue and a blue and white band for the half-Blues.

(Knox-Shaw, *Sidney Sussex: Reminiscences*)

The Pentacle Club (the only magical society entirely confined to members of the University) announces its annual entertainment of Magic at the A.D.C. Theatre on March 6, at 8.30 and on March 8, at 2.30 and 8.30. Amongst several new illusions, the Club is hoping to present a new and exclusive method of 'Sawing a Woman in Half'. The profits will, as usual, be devoted to the British Red Cross Society.

(*Cambridge Review*, 7 March 1941)

Cambridge housed countless strangers and exiles. Exile was sometimes unimaginable freedom:

The traveller who has left the Third Reich behind and walks for the first time through King's or Clare towards the University Library cannot help feeling both drunk at the taste of freedom and overwhelmed by the unbroken unity of medieval tradition and modern life.

(F. Hildebrand, *Melanchthon: Alien or Ally?*, 1946)

for some, ghostly:

And is there honey still for tea? Returning to Cambridge after a long absence, an obscure graduate, recognised as a B.A. only by the Hellenic Travel Society, I can find no one to answer this question for me. In the once familiar haunts, I see only strange faces. There is a new generation of porters at the gates, and I look in vain for the nod of recognition beneath the inherited bowler. Cambridge does not notice the return of her once prodigal sons and it is, therefore, with the feelings of an intruder that I creep through the narrow streets and try to penetrate unnoticed into the courts where I once made merry with future pro-consuls and civil servants, stockbrokers and journalists, headmasters and bankers, mothers-of-five and divorcées. That the honey which sweetened my dead past still exists somewhere in Cambridge, I do not doubt. But I do not expect to discover where and in what form it is to be found. A ghost, after all, can hardly complain if he is not invited to the feast. In any case, no ghost retains his sense of taste after he has – the expression is apt – gone down.

(John Hayward in *Cambridge Review*, 2 December 1939)

for some, a state of mind:

From that North – still literal, though already metaphorical also – I came in 1940 to Cambridge, on scholarships and exhibitions that I had won through fierce competition. It had been for too many years the pinpointed objective of my own and my parents' ambitions; it was impossible that Cambridge, or any other place, should have lived up to the hopes that we had placed on it. And to this day I cannot tell how much of the rancorous unhappiness which I often feel when I am in Cambridge harks back to the predictable and inevitable disappointment that it was to me thirty-six years ago . . . Some time in that span of years I arrived at the diagnosis which I adhere to still: that the Cantabrigian ethos – is it Cromwellian? I persuade myself with some gratification that it is – leaves no margin for *caprice*, for that free-running, freely associating, arbitrary and gratuitous play of mind out of which, not exclusively but necessarily, art-works arise . . .

Undoubtedly when, in my second term, I was supervised by Joan Bennett in her house at Church Rate Corner in Newnham, the somewhat self-applauding 'stringency' of the Cambridge ethos, and its disputatiousness, were very much to my taste; I felt secure and at home with these modes or fashions of intellectual life. But outside of my studies, Cambridge in 1940 seemed to be peopled or at any rate dominated by exquisites from King's or swells from Trinity.

(Donald Davie, in *My Cambridge*,
ed. Ronald Hayman, 1977)

Some refugees suffered a second indignity:

Walter Wallich, who after the war was thirty years with the BBC, was rescued from Germany in 1933 and sent to Bradfield College from where he won a scholarship to King's:

By now he identified himself totally with this country and was on the verge of being naturalized and completing a Ph.D. thesis when, following Dunkirk, he was suddenly interned in the Isle of Man and then transported to a camp in northern Canada. There, in 1941, he was recognized by Alec Paterson, the most humane of all our Prison Commissioners, who had known him as a boy. He was returned to Britain to enlist in the Pioneer Corps. On his first evening back in this country he revisited his old digs in Cambridge to collect the papers he had been working on (for his Ph. D.) – to be assured by his kindly landlady that he need not worry, she had burnt them all the night he had been taken away by the police, just in case.

(Obituary in *The Times*, 7 May 1981)

The real war came:

1940   The Easter Term came to an end with an abruptness probably unparalleled since the sixteenth century when the studies of the place were liable to interruption from intermittent visitations of the plague . . .

The King of the Belgians had ordered his army to surrender; the Dunkirk evacuation was in progress; the German High Command was boasting that the Allied armies were 'annihilated'. It was undesirable, for military reasons, that the undergraduate population should remain in Cambridge any longer than was necessary . . . There was a very natural run on the butteries, and the atmosphere of Cambridge streets that evening (31st May) was reminiscent of nothing so much as the Duchess of Richmond's ball on the eve of Waterloo. By Tuesday the Colleges were virtually empty except for their non-academic residents, and patient dons, wrestling with examination papers.

(Editorial in the *Cambridge Review*,
11 October 1940)

Words in the wind:

University Sermon preached in Great St. Mary's Church, 9th June, by the Rev. E. S. Abbott, MA, Jesus College, Warden of the Scholae Cancellari, Lincoln.

'Shall not the day of the Lord be darkness and not light? even very dark and no brightness in it?', Amos v. 20.

'This is your hour and the hour of darkness', Luke xxii. 53.

(University sermon, reprinted in the
Cambridge Review, 11 October 1940)

29.9.40 ... In Trinity the approach to the Great Gate is obstructed with cement-mixers and piles of gravel because we are constructing a new A.R. shelter under the cycle-shed, meaning, when circs. permit, to remove the unsightly shanty and shelter the cycles underground. Otherwise you would notice only that the sandbag defences of the Porters' Lodge and of the Hall cellar, which were becoming sadly dishevelled, have now been neatly encased in concrete; and whereas it was previously believed that they would withstand high explosives, it now seems improbable that they can be removed without them. King's, who have been gradually taking the stained glass out of their Chapel at a cost of £75 per window, have desisted, leaving only four out of twenty-six windows, the rest being partly glass but mostly boarding. I suppose they were wise though I sometimes wonder what they will do with the windows if the Chapel is demolished.

(*Letters from Cambridge*)

Soon after I had moved to London, a bomb (small, thank Heaven!) landed on the front doorstep of our Cambridge house. Diana just managed to get her head under the bedclothes as the window blew in. She then proceeded to put out an incendiary bomb which had come through the roof; in the words of the Austrian refugee we had taken in, 'Voss Mrs Crutchley running up and down stairs with baskets of vatter'. Repairers moved in quickly, and we let the house 'for the duration', while Diana joined the ranks of the Air Force. Her first posting on being commissioned was back in Cambridge, where she was lodged with her unit in Selwyn College. The Fellows still in residence were delighted to have her breakfasting with them in hall and to get a chance of supplementing their own cereal with her unwanted cooked dish, but the time had not come when a woman could dine at high table, so in the evening she ate alone in the gallery.

(Brooke Crutchley, *To Be A Printer*, 1980)
(*Cambridge Review*)

Brooke Crutchley also tells the story of a bachelor don of Trinity who had been invited by a Cambridge hostess to dinner on the following day. 'I regret', he replied, 'that the commitments of a Fellow of Trinity do not admit of the impromptu.'

Extract from diary of an RAF pilot. (He was killed ten days later.)

8 November 1940
Very much refreshed by being amongst my old surroundings, so redolent of peace and peaceful occupations – and the kindness of friends of the old time, so much softer than the hard high friendliness of man to man under the shadow of 'morale'. I obtained pleasure from the touch of the ugly old walls, even striking my hand against their rough sides to convince myself of their reality; the contrast all the sharper since by rights I should be 'en mission' at this time.

(*Cambridge Review*)

Harold Nicholson:

23 January 1941
We have taken Tobruk. I go down to Cambridge. I go to see Sir Will Spens, Master of Corpus and Regional Commissioner. He feels that it would be

dangerous to be complacent about the public morale . . . I go round to Trinity, and there to my surprise I find Gerry Wellesley and Anthony Powell. I sit next to the Vice-Master. The lights in hall are shaded but the portraits are still lit up and the undergraduates in their grey flannel bags are still there. Afterwards we adjourn for port and coffee to the Combination Room. I sit next to George Trevelyan, the Master. I look round upon the mahogany and silver, upon the Madeira and port, upon the old butler with his stately efficiency. 'It is much the same', I say to him. 'Civilisation', he replies, 'is always recognisable.' I then walk back with Gerry to the hotel.

(Harold Nicolson, *Diaries*, vol. II, ed. N. Nicolson)

2 May 1941

Sir, I should be most grateful if you could find a corner in the Review for the following:

'Would the Cambridge Don who bought from Blackwell's the only remaining copies of Rousselot's La Philosophie au Moyen Age very kindly loan or sell one to a fellow member of the University, now a lonely soldier in Ulster?'

Yours faithfully,

(*Cambridge Review*)

Gow:

1.6.41   You would have been surprised if you had walked through the College one radiant Sunday afternoon last month. You would have found by the Bridge the College fire-pump and an enormous Dennis engine supplying water . . . you would not have been less surprised to find me, one night shortly after this practice, rolling hoses in Nevile's Ct at 11 p.m. To tell you the truth I was surprised at this myself for I do not count rolling hoses part of a Warden's duties and I lent a feeble hand and foot only because the Fire Party, with Triposes staring them in the face, were backward with corvées of that sort. Less unusual, though perhaps as surprising to you, would be to find me in the small hours perched (commonly with company) on the ridge of the Library roof. The explanation would be that if, when I am not on duty, I am roused by explosions in what seems indecent proximity, or by other untoward sounds, I am apt to go the rounds and, if the night is fine, to ascend one of the local summits to brood on the prospect, somewhat (but only somewhat) like stout Cortez upon a peak in Darien. I do not much enjoy these exercises, and the Library roof is a hard, cold, seat for the arthritic, but in moonlight Cambridge is very lovely from aloft, and one night in particular when, under a full moon, the sky was patterned with exhaust-trails and searchlights, I should have been sorry to miss. I think, however, of patenting some form of pyjama trousers, which can be guaranteed not to come down when their occupant is halfway up a ladder. Mine have so far withstood the demands made upon them, but they add to my anxieties.

Trinity and St. John's had one day a joint gas exercise.

(*Letters from Cambridge*)

After lunch we did some warwork. I discovered one could think about Uniform Convergence while washing 400 spoons, or while fixing coloured rags on to camouflage netting. But as we raced while pulling up onions, concentration on simple properties of Quadrics was all that would fit well! When we did roof drill to be ready for incendiary bombs, I did no Maths *at all* in case I got involved in experimental projectiles . . .

While we studied we assembled transmitters for paratroopers, or fixed rubber sleeves over the turned-back outer covers of wires, keeping to a colour code. We used as a tool little pieces of glass tubing drawn to a point (in place of expensive three-pointed scissors), and this brilliant idea of Miss Chrystal's set people at Pye's factory wondering how it could happen that a specialist in Hebrew and Theology could have such *practical* brilliance.

(A. C. Dillon, in *Newnham Anthology*,
ed. Phillips)

The stream that flows by many a college wall
Was sung by Cambridge poets, great and small.
Old Milton, several centuries ago,
Described it, 'reverend' Camus, 'footing slow';
Byron immortalized its banks and sedges,
Tennyson 'lazy lilies' on its edges,
Coleridge wrote verses to it, and a score
Of lesser poets added to the store.
The days of poetry are overpast,
To degradation has it come at last.
New notices proclaim in every quarter
The poets' Cam is merely 'Static Water'.

(A. H. Quiggin, *Cambridge Review*,
13 June 1942)

Gow:

20.9.42   . . . You would notice a large but not unsightly tank of static water on the grass at the east-end of King's Chapel (and on one occasion you might have noticed punts and canoes laboriously transferred to it by some local humorist) and some unsightly but not dishonourable scars on the east front of Whewell's Ct. By poking about you might find some other wounds in that neighbourhood, and since both the B.B.C. and the papers, daily and illustrated, have disclosed that the Union was set on fire and glass in Whewell's Ct. broken, I believe it will not be indiscreet to say that all our windows on Sidney St. perished but that they were our only casualties.

(Letters from Cambridge)

1944.   The event of the week has been the Marlowe Society *King Lear* . . . it moved me more than any performance of the play that I've seen. Most of the cast are only so-so, except for the supreme merit (nowadays) of universal audibility; but there were three remarkable performances: Dadie Rylands himself, who I think is the best Lear I ever saw, especially in the last part of the play, from his flower-wreathed appearance at Dover to the end: Donald Beves, the King's don, was excellent as Gloucester; and a King's undergraduate, Frank Duncan, was a most admirable Edgar.

(Edward Marsh, *Ambrosia and Small Beer*,
1964)

40. George Rylands as Othello, Donald Beves as Iago, 1943

Later in 1944 there were happenings that could not be written about:

10 June – four days after Normandy landings

Dear Master,

You will undoubtedly be glad to hear that the operations we studied in your College have been carried out according to plan . . . I hope that some day I might be able to explain to you fully how the plans laid in Trinity helped to mould the course of history. We have a stiffish fight coming.

Gerald Bucknall

(G. M. Trevelyan, *Autobiography*, 1949)

Lt. General Bucknall also wrote to St. John's:

On 28 March 'Exercise Conqueror' based on a beautifully constructed model of Normandy and its beaches, began. I think the main model study room was at St. John's . . .

A Fellow of St. John's, J. S. Boys Smith, recalls:

My only personal recollection is of a meeting of the College Council at which the Master, Mr. Benians, sought the consent of the Council to the use of the Combination Room for an undisclosed purpose of national importance. The consent was quickly given. Questions were not asked. And there were no Minutes.

('The Combination Room and "D" Day',
The Eagle, LXII, June 1968)

VE Day:

We remember the bells of Great St. Mary in full peal; . . . the Mayor addressing a vast crowd on Market Hill – a close-packed crowd which filled every corner of the market-place and overflowed into Rose Crescent and on to the roofs . . . later on some scores of servicemen and civilians who danced for the whole of the hottest hour of a hot afternoon . . . To have been on the balcony then is to have had an unforgettable experience . . . One was face to face with a representative section of the common people of England . . . One remembered what the common people had suffered; one remembered the men of the Cambridgeshire Regiment – the sons, husbands and brothers of this attentive crowd on Market Hill – who were still in prison camps in the East; and one remembered those men, of both Town and Gown, who had loved Cambridge and its beautiful ways, who had so often crossed Market Hill on their way to shops and offices, to lectures, to Hall, or to the river, and will never come back from the war to cross it again. Quorum animis proprietur Deus.

(Editorial in the *Cambridge Review*,
12 May 1945)

Gow:

June 1945 . . . The war-time visitors, though not to my knowledge responsible for any loss of life, have done far more damage to College property than the bombs . . . From the start we had R.A.F. Initial Training Wings . . . These had their headquarters in Jesus and occupied the requisitioned parts of eight other

[335]

41. Cambridge, 1983

colleges ... Queens' housed the Bart.'s medical school, Christ's the London School of Oriental Studies; Peterhouse, King's, and St. Catharine's portions of London University. King's had also an R.A.F. transport unit which parked its lorries, omnibuses, and what-nots under the trees in the Backs and has left scarce a blade of grass behind it. Caius, Corpus, Trinity, and Sidney had Civil Servants ... various colleges have put up Dominion, Colonial and U.S.A. troops sent here for a weekly educational course.

(Letters from Cambridge)

A. S. F. Gow himself:

It was typical of him that when as tutor he felt apprehensive at signing permits for pupils to have flying lessons at Marshall's Flying School, he reassured himself by spending a month of the vacation taking the course personally, and 'did not dislike it' – a characteristic understatement.

(Obituary by Walter Hamilton, in the *Cambridge Review*, 5 May 1978)

Casualties:

The pre-war members of the Cambridge University Air Squadron had paid a heavy toll with 128 of their number killed in action. There were four V.Cs, at least 17 D.S.Os and 70 Distinguished Flying Crosses.

(*Cambridge University Air Squadron. A History 1925–75*, official publication, 1976)

In most of the colleges there are rolls of honour for those who died in the Second World War alongside those of the First World War. The visitor who cares to count would find, for instance, 60 names in a small college like Peterhouse, 115 in Christ's, 116 in Queens', 149 in Pembroke, and in Trinity, one of the largest colleges, the figure is 389.

The modern University

Plus ça change ...

When the war ended, the returning warriors came up in crowds, as freshmen or to complete their broken courses, while the full tale of Fellows was again complete. Never had Trinity, never had Cambridge, been so full of strong and splendid life, though the College shared to the full the austerities and stringencies of the country at large. Such was the condition of things when on June 3, 1947, we celebrated the Fourth Centenary of our Foundation by Henry VIII, under royal auspices and on a perfect summer day; when George VI and Queen Elizabeth drove across the Great Court up to the Lodge in their open motor car, as Victoria and Prince Albert had driven in their horsed carriage a hundred years before, and when the twelve trumpeters on the roof of the Great Gate proclaimed their entry, it was clear to all the world that England and Trinity had survived the war.

(G. M. Trevelyan, *Autobiography*)

Some were more tentative in their approach:

I almost didn't go to Cambridge. My headmaster thought I should, and I thought I should, but my father wasn't sure. I wasn't bright enough to get a college scholarship and my father wasn't poor enough for me to apply for a state scholarship. So while I did National Service there was the possibility that I might not actually get there: it was in any case dreadfully distant, an escape from the drudgery of the army into the bright and tranquil life of the mind. I wrote a poem addressed to Cambridge. 'Shall I ever rest on your learned lawns?' I enquired. That was my image of it, a lot of serene young men sitting around on the Backs reading serious books.

So when, during a first roll-call of freshmen in Great Hall at Trinity, a student answered his name with 'Here Sergeant', and I joined the general titter, it was from relief.

(Thom Gunn, in *My Cambridge*, ed. Hayman)

Supervisor to undergraduate: Don't let your wife rule your life. I object to that back-seat essay-writing.

(*Pem*, 1946)

People from big cities who go to Cambridge realize what it is like to live in the country. Each Cambridge winter day began with the river smell, mixed with the scent of damp leaves and, as often as not, bonfire smoke, hanging in the tall bedrooms, windows ritually open. Then a quick run to the outside lavatory. It was the time when running water and gas fires were gradually coming in; coal was still rationed to a sack a term...

'Any more for Jesus?' the porters at the station cried, evangelically, as they loaded taxi after taxi, mine bound for Queens', with my heavy borrowed suitcase. My sister's old college trunk was waiting in the Lodge, together with a bicycle borrowed from a cousin, and I found myself surrounded by public schoolboys a head taller than I, talking in loud, self-assured voices...

I knew nobody at Cambridge. I was, I believe, the second boy from my school to go to Cambridge, a university known only to the geography master, and I had picked my college with a pin in the Hither Green branch of the Metropolitan Borough of Lewisham's libraries.

(John Vaizey, in *My Cambridge*, ed. Hayman)

'Why did you apply to Trinity?' I asked one applicant from a northern grammar school whom I had invited to come for an interview. 'I wrote to Downing' he replied 'and got no reply. So one evening Dad and I sat down and wrote to all the Colleges. You were the first to reply.' [This was before UCCA.]

(J. S. Morrison, *Cambridge Magazine*, no. 6, 1980)

There were some changes:

The Grace admitting women to membership was voted on 6 December 1947...

At the last moment we were informed that it would be possible for some of us to attend in the Gallery of the Senate House to see 'the fatal cap-lifting by the Proctor'. Six of us were there ... Some Graces of minor importance were taken first, and as the word 'Placet' promptly followed the reading of the Grace, the Proctors lifted their caps. Then our Grace was read: 'That the recommendations of the Syndicate ... appointed to consider the status of Women in the University be approved.' A long pause followed during which we held our breath. Someone *might* – though no one thought he would – say 'Non Placet' at this last moment. But if any opponent was present he said no word. The pause ended. The word 'Placet' was pronounced. The caps were lifted and replaced. A slight tremor passed over the assembly, like a wind over a cornfield, and the thing was over. In future our visits to the Senate House for the passing of Graces would be as of right and duty. The six hurried back to College where there was a small impromptu celebration.

(Myra Curtis, in McWilliams-Tullberg, *Women at Cambridge*)

1952

Our gowns were of a different cut from the men's ... Nevertheless we were proud of them. But any hope that they would make us fully accepted members of the University was vain ... A single morning in Mill Lane, negotiating a male-muscled crowd wielding masculine bikes, sitting on a man-sized bench and listening to a male orator playing for effects and riding the gusts of male laughter is neatly designed to remind a girl of her female, and therefore subject condition.

(Alison Ravetz, *Cambridge Review*, 24 February 1962)

1949–50

Until further notice the wearing of the academical cap is not required, but no other headdress may be worn with a gown (except that women may wear hoods or scarves with gowns in bad weather or in the evening).

(*The Students' Handbook to the University and Colleges of Cambridge*)

1954

When the Michaelmas term starts in October, Girton and Newnham will at last have been joined by Cambridge's long-awaited Third Foundation for Women ... For its first years 'New Hall' will have a temporary existence in 'the Hermitage' ... almost in Newnham, but in 1960 all will be moved to 'the Orchard' in Huntingdon Road, half way to Girton. 'The Orchard', a long, dark, ivy-covered Victorian house built by Sir Horace Darwin ... has been presented as the new college's permanent home by his daughters...Most of the men's colleges are helping financially ... but the current story is that one college – variously identified – put itself down ... in deep contempt for five guineas.

(*The Sunday Times*, 7 February 1954)

What evidence is there that over and above the undergraduates now accommodated in Girton and Newnham there is any substantial number of young women ready and able to profit from a Cambridge Tripos course?

('Senator' writing an editorial in the
Cambridge Review, 29 November 1952)

1949–50 (repeated as late as 1966–7):

Smoking while wearing academic dress is a breach of discipline as is the wearing of blazers (other than plain dark blue or black blazers) with academic dress except on the way to or from a dinner at which blazers are worn with evening dress.

(*Students' Handbook*)

The University's worst fears about the financial prospect for the next quinquennium have proved to be unjustified. Although it is not yet known what proportion of the new grant will come to Cambridge, it does not seem rash to hope that we shall be spared the worst of the crippling retrenchments that were recently prophesied. The Boat Race will not be the only event of the vacation that we shall anxiously wait and see.

(editorial, *Cambridge Review*, 8 March 1952)

1948.
Among the 'air-lift' commodities destined for Berlin are, unless accidents intervene, a play of Shakespeare's, *Measure for Measure*, and Webster's *The White Devil*. They will be escorted and presented by members of The Marlowe Society of Cambridge, which means that they will be well-spoken, simply staged, and 'put across' with no nonsense. That, nowadays, is the Cambridge tradition: the Marlowe men do not have 'fun' with the classics. They let the author say his piece and they do not distract the attention by irrelevant costumes or curious notions of new business . . .

Gillian Webb, now turned professional, continues to tackle the big roles of the classics with firmness, good sense, and no pretences . . . Noel Annan did well in the pink (Cardinal's), Ross Lewis got through long and difficult parts with skill, and Richard Baker's Lucio had the right impudence of wit.

(Ivor Brown, in *The Observer*)

I often think that young men who are in danger of being flashy should go to Cambridge, and those who are in danger of being dull should go to Oxford: too often the opposite principle is adopted.

(Trevelyan, *Autobiography*)

29 January 1956
Cambridge, wet, cold, abstract, formal as it is, is an excellent place to write, read and work.

(Sylvia Plath to her mother, in *Letters Home*, 1975)

Cambridge's main contribution to the tone of intellectual life has been a ruthless, forthright intellectual honesty, of which the Puritan revolution is the exemplar. Not for them any soft Carolinian ways. I think that this intellectual ruthlessness has appalling effects on the manners and emotions, but excellent results on the intellectual morals of the Cambridge young . . . I would have been a nicer but a wobblier man if I had gone elsewhere. It is the wobblies who get on.

(John Vaizey, in *My Cambridge*, ed. Hayman)

27 March 1955 . . . watching Boat Race . . . damn those filthy Cambridge people, they always cheat.

(Harold Nicolson, *Diaries*, vol. III, ed. N. Nicolson)

There is a story about when Abba Eban, one time foreign secretary of Israel, was congratulated on his Oxford accent, he said, ' Sir I would have you know that I went to Cambridge – but in public life you must expect to be smeared.'

Academic life continued to inspire and excite. There was growth in many faculties and especially in science and engineering. Between 1944 and 1950 new professorships were founded in electrical engineering, chemical engineering, applied thermodynamics and veterinary clinical studies.

Biochemistry:

At Bryanston School and St. John's College, Cambridge, I was probably above average but not an outstanding scholar . . . I decided to study science and, on arrival at Cambridge, became extremely excited and interested in biochemistry when I first heard about it, principally through Ernest Baldwin and also other members of the relatively young and enthusiastic Biochemistry Department that had been founded by F. G. Hopkins. It seemed to me that here was a way to really understand living matter and to develop a more scientific basis to many medical problems.

After taking my B.A. degree in 1939 I remained at the University for a further year to take an advanced course in Biochemistry, and surprised myself and my teachers by obtaining a first class examination result. I was a conscientious objector during the war and was allowed to study for a Ph.D. degree, which I did in the Biochemistry Department with A. Neuberger, on lysine metabolism and a more practical problem concerning the nitrogen of potatoes. It was Neuberger who first taught me how to do research, both technically and as a way of life, and I owe much to him. In 1943 A. C. Chibnall succeeded F. G. Hopkins as Professor of Biochemistry at Cambridge and I joined his research group working on proteins and, in particular, insulin. This was an especially exciting time in protein chemistry. New fractionation techniques had been developed, particularly by A. J. P. Martin and his colleagues, and there seemed to be a real possibility of determining the exact chemical structure of these fundamental components of living matter. I succeeded in developing new methods for amino acid sequencing and used them to deduce the complete sequence of insulin, for which I was awarded the Nobel Prize for Chemistry in 1958.

(Frederick Sanger, autobiographical note in *Les Prix Nobel*, 1980)

Molecular biology:

Bragg's period of office in Cambridge coincides with the decline of the Cavendish Laboratory as the world's leading centre of atomic physics. This was an inevitable consequence of the war and the transformation of atomic physics to 'Big Science', to which the tradition and structure of Cambridge University were ill-adapted. Rather than fight a rearguard action, Bragg decided to back two new applications of physics in which the Cavendish was again to lead the world.

One of these, the build-up of molecular biology, took place gradually after the war . . .

(Max Perutz, article in *Acta Crystallographica*, March 1970)

How did it happen that so many talented people joined us? Kendrew's interest in protein crystallography had been aroused by Bernal whom he met in the Far East during the war. One day in 1948 an eccentric German mathematician came to inquire whether I would accept a friend of his as a Ph.D. student. I wondered what diffident character needed such a strange ambassador to pave his way when Francis Crick entered and put us all in high spirits with his laughter . . . A year later Hugh Huxley joined Kendrew as a research assistant. What Kendrew, Crick and Huxley had in common was experience of science applied to war, which made them think harder than the average graduate about their future research and realise that the greatest promise of physics and chemistry lay in their application to the understanding of life.

In 1950 a strange head with a crewcut and bulging eyes popped through my door and asked me without so much as saying Hullo, 'Can I come and work here?' I said 'Yes' because I guessed that this must be Jim Watson whom Salvador Luria had recommended to Kendrew.

(Max Perutz, *New Scientist*, 31 January 1980)

Jim Watson continues the story:

We then went for a walk to look over possible digs for the coming year. When Max realised that I had come directly to the lab from the station and had not yet seen any of the colleges, he altered our course to take me through King's, along the backs, and through to the Great Court of Trinity. I had never seen such beautiful buildings in all my life, and any hesitation I might have had about leaving my safe life as a biologist vanished.

The following morning I went back to the Cavendish, since Max wanted me to meet Sir Lawrence Bragg. When Max telephoned upstairs that I was here, Sir Lawrence came down from his office, let me say a few words, and then retired for a private conversation with Max. A few minutes later they emerged to allow Bragg to give me his formal permission to work under his direction. The performance was uncompromisingly British . . . The thought never occurred to me that later on I would have contact with this apparent curiosity out of the past . . . I assumed he must be in effective retirement and would never care about genes.

(Jim Watson, *The Double Helix*, 1968)

42. Watson and Crick with the Double Helix, 1953

He [Francis Crick] came to Cambridge only in 1947, aged thirty-one. His college, as a research student, was Gonville and Caius . . . Crick never lived in college. He worked for the Medical Research Council, never the University; he never taught, nor supervised research students. 'But I must point out that I never felt in any way excluded from the *scientific* life of Cambridge', Crick said . . . After the Nobel Prize, he was granted dining rights by one and another of the colleges. When, in 1960, Churchill College was opened, a new foundation in modern buildings west of the river, Crick was elected a Fellow – and when thirty thousand pounds were given to the college for the purpose of building a chapel, Crick protested that a chapel was an offensive anachronism, and quit.

(Judson, *The Eighth Day of Creation*)

1953

During his first free moment back in the Cavendish he [Bragg] slipped away from his office for a direct view. Immediately he caught on to the complementary relation between the two chains and saw how the equivalence of adenine with thymine and guanine with cytosine was a logical consequence of the regular repeating shape of the sugar-phosphate backbone . . .

Todd made his official visit later in the week, coming over from the chemical laboratory with several younger colleagues. Francis' quick verbal tour through the structure and its implications lost none of its zest for having been given several times each day for the past week. The pitch of his excitement was rising each day, and generally, whenever Jerry [Donohue] or I heard the voice of Francis shepherding in some new faces, we left our office until the new converts were let out and some traces of orderly work could resume. Todd was a different matter, for I wanted to hear him tell Bragg that we had correctly followed his advice on the chemistry of the sugar-phosphate backbone. Todd also went along with the keto configurations, saying that his organic-chemist friends had drawn enol groups for purely arbitrary reasons. Then he went off, after congratulating me and Francis.

(*The Double Helix*)

[Lord Todd, O.M., Professor of Organic Chemistry 1944, Nobel Prize for Chemistry 1957, Master of Christ's College 1963-78.]

Francis Crick and Jim Watson (with Maurice Wilkins of London University) won the Nobel Prize for the solution of the structure of deoxyribonucleic acid (DNA). Later, in 1962, Max Perutz and John Kendrew, both of Peterhouse, were awarded the Nobel Prize for solving the structure of globular proteins.

Radioastronomy (this was the second application of physics backed by Bragg after the war):

During the war, Martin Ryle, a young Cambridge physicist working on radar, had become interested in radar operators' reports of signals from the sun and the galaxy. Joining J. A. Ratcliffe, a lecturer in physics who studied the ionosphere, Ryle constructed the first radio-telescope from ex-War Department components. Bragg realised the promise of Ryle's early attempts at detecting radio signals from outer space; besides, the location of these signals intrigued him as a problem in optics. When, some years later, Ryle and Ratcliffe decided to set up a large radio-telescope near Cambridge, Bragg warmly supported their approach to industry which resulted in the endowment of the Mullard Radio Observatory. In time this led to the discovery of quasars and pulsars and the mapping of radio sources in the most distant parts of the Universe.

(Max Perutz, in *Acta Crystallographica*, March 1970)

The Cambridge School of Economics flourished as it had done before the war under the influence of Keynes:

I was at Cambridge for nearly ten years . . . It is a town of haunting beauty, where one has been happier than anywhere else, and unhappier than anywhere else. It was there . . . that I learnt what intellectual excitement was. In my time, economics was a great faculty . . . not perhaps as great as microbiology was about to become, or as physics and economics had been in the 1930s, but still eminent enough to command the view, to dominate the horizon, of the undergraduate. I remember once walking along the Backs, trying to explain to a friend . . . just how exciting some aspect of Mrs. Robinson's capital theory was; the euphoria was immense, and, alas, incommunicable. Though I have long since forgotten the point that excited me, I retain the sense which I had at that moment – an aesthetic sense, it seems – of the supremacy of truth, and of remorseless logic, which should be pursued at any cost. Perhaps all that remains of this in my middle age is my manner – usually described as 'provocative'. Like other Cambridge men, and perhaps this is why so few of them become Prime Ministers, I am perennially surprised at the hostility that friendly frankness brings.

(John Vaizey, 'Education and Government
Policy', in *Proceedings of the Royal
Institution of Great Britain*, vol. 45, 1972)

13 May 1953   I spent a lovely, quietest weekend at King's College, Cambridge. Richard Kahn is Keynes's successor as Bursar and he and his friends seem to be carrying on the true Bloomsbury tradition, with its stress on quiet personal relationships. He took immense trouble to organize my weekend and to make me feel at ease. The nicest part of it was a long Sunday walk with him and Joan Robinson, the economist. Apparently they walk every Sunday and sometimes the Kaldor children and other children come on horseback or bicycles to the lunch place. It all reminded me of Virginia Woolf's To The Lighthouse. How roughly Cambridge guests must feel they are treated in Oxford, where life is public affairs, not private affairs . . .

The Kahn – Kaldor – Robinson set are all keen Socialists but somehow they are detached from practical politics. On the other hand, they curiously succeed in giving one the impression that they care about what one's doing, and mind, which is a nice consoling pillow on which to lay one's head.

(*Backbench Diaries of Richard Crossman*,
ed. Janet Morgan, 1981)

In other subjects too, lectures had their fascinations.

John Raven, lecturer in classics in the early fifties:

Although John read his lectures, they sounded new minted for the moment every time. He had the particular gift of being able to write in a way that corresponded exactly to how he spoke . . . The exactness of his delivery reflected long and hard thought about precisely what he wanted to say – and about how he wanted to say it. His notes are full of underlinings, single, double, hachured and zigzag, of

CAPITAL LETTERS, of braces and brackets indicating phrasing. They are not so much lecture notes, as a musical score.

(Geoffrey Lloyd, 'Classics in Cambridge', in *John Raven by his friends*, ed. John Lipscomb and R. W. David, 1981)

Professor John Wisdom, although he denies that occasionally during his philosophy lectures he left his horse tied to a lamp-post, must have given 'racy' lectures, judging by this:

We shall have to reject much, indeed most, of what the common herd unthinkingly accept as real knowledge, most of what we ourselves in unthinking moments have taken to be real knowledge. To begin with, we shall have to recognise that we never really know what is still in the future, much less what would happen if this or that were to come about, or what would have happened if things had been otherwise. For when a man says 'I know he'd have won if Richards had ridden him' we know that the most he really knows is that the horse turned round as the tapes went up and thereby lost some three or four lengths, that he nevertheless was beaten by no more than half a length, and that horses seldom or never turn round at the gate when Gordon Richards is riding. Does such knowledge absolutely guarantee what would have happened in this case? Certainly not. No one knows what would have happened. Maybe *this* horse would have turned round in spite of Gordon's subtlest persuasions. Maybe this horse would not have exerted himself if he had not been left behind at the start. Maybe if he hadn't got left he'd have got bumped or jumped the path across the course, or anything of too many things. Nor is it otherwise with cars. With horses it's obvious that there are a thousand accidents and follies that may 'upset your calculations', with horses it's notorious that 'you never can tell', that 'one never knows'. What's not so obvious is that this is fatal to all knowledge.

(John Wisdom, *Other Minds*, 1952)

In 1959 C. P. Snow gave the Rede Lecture. His subject was, 'The Two Cultures and the Scientific Revolution'; in it he expressed concern at the polarisation of knowledge, instancing the difficulties of communication at high table nowadays between scientists and non-scientists:

But I believe the pole of total incomprehension of science radiates its influence on all the rest. The total incomprehension gives, much more pervasively than we realise, living in it, an unscientific flavour to the whole 'traditional' culture, and that unscientific flavour is often, much more than we admit, on the point of turning anti-scientific. The feelings of one pole become the anti-feelings of the other ... The polarisation is sheer loss to us all. To us as people, and to our society.
(*Rede Lecture*, 1959)

In explaining the non-communication between these two 'cultures' Snow later claimed, as a scientist and a novelist, to have a foot in both camps. This was too much for Leavis, a practised demolisher of literary reputations:

Snow is in fact portentously ignorant ... intellectually as undistinguished as it is possible to be ... The Two Cultures exhibits an utter lack of intellectual distinction and an embarrassing vulgarity of style ...

[346]

Snow is, of course, a – no, I can't say that; he isn't; Snow thinks of himself as a novelist. He can't be said to know what a novel is. The nonentity is apparent on every page of his fiction.

Leavis could also be positive and constructive but enjoyed his enmities:

Like Snow, I look to the university. Unlike Snow, I am concerned to make it really a university, something (that is) more than a collocation of specialist departments – to make it a centre of human consciousness: perception, knowledge, judgment and responsibility. And perhaps I have sufficiently indicated on what lines I would justify my seeing the centre of a university as a vital English School. I mustn't say more now about what I mean by that. I will only say that the academic is the enemy and that the academic *can* be beaten, as we who ran *Scrutiny* for twenty years proved. We were, and knew we were, Cambridge – the essential Cambridge, in spite of Cambridge: that gives you the spirit of what I have in mind. Snow gets on with what he calls 'the traditional culture' better than I do.

(F. R. Leavis, Nor Shall My Sword, 1972)

THE RINGING GROOVES OF CHANGE

To give a contemporary picture it is necessary to produce a collage made up mostly of magazine and newspaper articles, excerpts from journals and official publications: history in its raw state, unmellowed by recollection in memoirs and letters. The years since 1960 brought change at an accelerated rate. The collage therefore reflects the changes in approach advocated by the 1962 Bridges Report, identifying as it did the needs brought about by the breakaway from colleges (more lecturers than fellows, more research students, more laboratories and their personnel). It reflects the growth of student consciousness and its sense of a need for participation and power, its final liberation from a filial regard for college authorities no longer in loco parentis (for were not the parents themselves being forced into abdication?). The most startling change of all has been the introduction, from possibly mixed motives, of 'co-residence' (the neutral officialese word itself containing overtones which would be incomprehensible to our forebears) into all but two or three colleges.

What it also reflects is that in spite of, or perhaps because of, such change, intellectual rigours still prevail; disciplines and undergraduates proliferate; research changes views of knowledge and sometimes of the world. Nobel Laureates abound, with more prizes won by Trinity College than by France, more by the Medical Research Laboratory at New Addenbrookes Hospital than by any other scientific institution in the world.

The sixties came in like a lamb and went out like a lion.

Two views:

The autumn air comes cold off the water, the everlasting river-smell gets into the nostrils, and on the homeward spell against the stream the receding reach between the willows spreads like a dusty rippling road towards the trees and the church and the little farms of Ditton. The day is dying in the high sky over the flats. There are winking lights along the railway. The roofs of Cambridge across Midsummer Common hold a dim promise of tea and toast by the fire in the small hours before hall. You may feel desperately tired, but even your weariness is sweetened by the blessed sense of achievement. The coach on his bicycle, pedalling slowly beside you on the tow-path, has said that you will probably make a Lent eight if you come out five afternoons a week for the next six months ...

Lesser men, back from the fields, know no such ecstasy, for they have been playing the game they learned at school. Out on the college grounds beside Barton Road, Grange Road or Long Road, they have been punting footballs or clashing hockey-sticks. 'How're the blisters?' they enquire, smiling when you lower yourself gingerly into a chair.

(R. J. White, *Cambridge Life*, 1960)

I suppose Mr. White's Cambridge exists. But so do Todd's chemistry, Hodgkin working on nerve fibre, Ryle on the Barton Road, the prodigies in the Molecular Biology Unit, and the marvellous prose of the Regius Professor of History ... The language of modern literary criticism (which was used by witnesses for the defence and which set Lawrence's book free) is largely the product of Cambridge minds; and why do research students come from all over the world here to study economics? ... Cambridge is more than a jolly seminary. Some undergraduates love learning and are inspired by teachers, whose works they read or experiments they follow, whose controversies and clashes in the world outside Cambridge they observe and judge ... young men here have been singing madrigals, playing instruments or acting plays in College Halls for far longer than they have been running up and down the touchline and towpath.

(Noel Annan, review in the *Cambridge Review*, 26 November 1960)

Changing roles:

Will Colleges continue to provide the tutor and supervisor (in which case the College is likely to remain the focus of loyalty for the undergraduate)? Or will supervisors and perhaps even tutors become based on laboratory or department or faculty office (in which case the College might deteriorate into a mere place of residence)? ... Will scientists, some of whom are already unwilling to undertake the chores of College teaching and administration, lose interest in Colleges, and leave the Fellowships to be filled by non-scientists? Upon the answers to these and similar questions depends the future of the Cambridge system. Many of us believe this system to be the most effective instrument for educating and civilising young men ever devised in Europe.

(Eric Ashby, Master of Clare, in *Clare College Association Annual*, 1961 – he is forecasting effect of Bridges Report)

THOUGHTS ON RE-READING BELLOC'S FAMOUS LINES ON DONS

Remote and ineffectual Don,
Where have you gone, where have you gone?
Don in scarlet, Don in tails,
Don advertising Daily Mails,
Don in Office, Don in power,

Don talking on Woman's Hour,
Don knocking up a constitution,
Don with ideas on prostitution,
Don who is permanently plussed,
Don floating an Investment Trust,
Don judging jive at barbecue,
Don dressing down the E.T.U.,
Don architecturally brash,
Don not afraid to have a bash,
Don with Bentley, Don with Rolls,
Don organizing Gallup Polls,
Don back from Russia, off to Rome,
Don on the Third, the Light, the Home,
Don recently ennobled Peer,
Don Minister, Don Brigadier,
Don brassy, Don belligerent,
Don tipping off for ten per cent,
Don christian-naming with the Stars,
Don talking aloud in public bars,
Remote and ineffectual Don,
Where have you gone, where have you gone?

(A. N. L. Munby in J. Ziman and J. Rose,
Camford Observed, 1964)

Robert Rossshire is not, as he himself hastens to point out, the Master of his College ... He is one of those who in recent years have helped to create the national image of the New Don.

After distinguished war-service with the XIXth Lancets (learning to manage men) and brief but no less brilliant periods in Whitehall, Washington and Wall Street (learning paper-work), Rossshire returned to Cambridge.

Even as a junior Fellow he instinctively understood that what his College needed was a new profile ... The changes Rossshire then planned were not confined to administrative and architectural matters (as Cambridge reforms too often are): 'It's *ab*solutely no good stopping at the lavatories' is a characteristically forthright policy-making slogan he coined at that time ...

Rossshire's major contribution to the life of the University has not come through work in his own subject (important as that has been). His real contribution are his reforms.

Within two months of his nomination to the (amalgamated) offices of Bursar and Tutor, the national press was able to report that '9.45 a.m. instead of the traditional 7.30 has now been fixed as the beginning of the bedmakers' working day at St. Bevin's'. As expected, before very long several Cambridge Colleges followed suit. Equally original – *and* controversial – was his proposal that the post of Proctor should, whenever possible, be filled by a fifth- or sixth-year undergraduate. Next, due to his initiative, an experimental course in Academic Politics was started in the College for the benefit of younger Fellows.

But undoubtedly the most far-reaching of all has been his reform of the

Fellowship of his College. It was his idea to see represented under the ample roof of St. Bevin's as many major aspects of our national life as possible – to achieve 'a clean breakthrough of University education into society'. Thus an eminent printer, a trade-unionist, primary school-master (C-stream), station-master, TV-director, grocer's assistant, journalist and taxidermist have all been given staff-fellowships. True, the full implications of this bold reform have as yet to be felt. But this much is obvious already: as a result of widening its scholastic basis, St. Bevin's has escaped the danger of becoming a stagnant academic backwater.

('Cambridge Collotypes IV', Cambridge Review, 3 March 1962)

The great difference I observe when I visit Cambridge nowadays is that, compared with my own time there, they are all – dons and undergraduates alike – on the run, and, as is the way with fugitives, tend to discard more than they need to make a getaway. Whereas in my time poor boys like myself were induced to copy the others – their clothes, their ways, their speech – now it is the other way round. The upper-class boys copy the poor ones, decking themselves out in a weird kind of proletarian fancy dress, and speaking in an accent which sounds like a badly rehearsed number in a satire show. They are social descenders, who display, in reverse, all the absurdities, and more, of social climbers.

(Malcolm Muggeridge, Chronicles of Wasted Time. 1 The Green Stick, 1972)

Playing parts:

It is said that, in his heyday as Tutor, Sir Kenneth Pickthorn used to warn undergraduates of two activities as being inordinately wasteful of time and energy – a taste for amateur dramatics and a virtuous attachment.

(Corpus Christi College Association Letter, 1966)

Nevertheless the contemporary theatre owes much to university dramatic societies:

He [Ian McKellen] did a lot of acting at school, though he went up to read English at Cambridge with no real ambition to become a professional actor. McKellen's interview with his tutor, Brigadier Henn, a Yeats scholar and theatre enthusiast, turned into his first and most successful audition. Asked by Henn to perform a little something, McKellen stood on a chair and almost blasted him out of his study with 'Once More Unto the Breach Dear Friends.' He was awarded an Exhibition.

At Cambridge, he says, he suddenly met a crowd of people as dotty about the theatre as himself. Among his contemporaries were Trevor Nunn, actors Derek Jacobi, Corin Redgrave, Clive Swift, directors Richard Cotterill and Toby Robertson, playwright Simon Gray, critic Michael Billington, John Tydeman, now deputy head of drama at BBC radio, Clive Perry, who runs Birmingham Rep, and David Brierley, now General Manager of the Royal Shakespeare Company.

Preceding this astonishing Cambridge generation of the early 1960s were John

Barton and Peter Hall, who had just taken his degree at McKellen's college, St. Catharine's.

The formative influence on them all was George Rylands, then a don at King's and the mainstay of the Marlowe Society, of which McKellen became president. It was Rylands, he says, who instilled in him, and in everyone else, the most scrupulous attention to the classic texts, transforming their understanding.

(John Heilpern, in *The Times*, 9 June 1981)

A nest of sharp-beaked birds.

The break up of 'establishment' attitudes in the late fifties and sixties was mirrored in a new wave of undergraduate satirical reviews which nurtured talents later to be responsible for 'Beyond the Fringe', 'That Was The Week That Was', 'Monty Python's Flying Circus', and so on.

Jonathan Miller:

The smart thing in Cambridge in the early fifties was to be queer – rather wittily queer: and therefore people feigned queerness as a way of escaping, or seeming to escape, from the austerity.

I was a privileged young man with a decent Public School education and nothing to complain about, and therefore I wasn't angry or annoyed. I was slightly *nettled* by things, but that was because I was amused by them rather than really outraged.

On 'The Granta':

In the years that I was at Cambridge it was taken over by Mark Boxer – later he did the 'Life and Times in N.W.1' cartoons in The Times with Alan Bennett, and he started the Sunday Times colour magazine – he started the whole business of really sharp, satirical, graphically aware lay-outs and designs in Granta – he got sent down for publishing a blasphemous poem. A lot of people who wrote for, and edited, Granta knew the theatre, Amateur Dramatic Club, Footlights people, so you have to take account of what people wrote in journals in Cambridge in the fifties. [Jonathan Miller was made an honorary fellow of his college, St. John's, in 1982.]

The next generation, in the sixties:

John Cleese:

They'd all said at Clifton 'You'd better go into the Footlights' – so when I went to Cambridge I went to this Guildhall where each society used to have its little stall to advertise its 'wares'. I went up to the Footlights stall – I said, 'I'm interested in joining', and they said, 'Well, what do you do? Do you sing?' Well, my jaw hit the floor – I think I was the only one in the history of my school who was not *allowed* to sing, I was so bad – I had to do extra Greek – and I said, 'Well, no'; and they said, 'Oh, well, do you dance?' – well, of course, if there's anything I'm worse at than singing, it's dancing. So I said, 'No', and they said, 'Well, what do you do?', and I said, 'I make people laugh' – and I blushed the colour of a beetroot, and ran – literally. And if it hadn't been for a very close friend of mine called Alan Hutchinson, who happened to have been at school with the treasurer of the Footlights, I don't know that I'd have ever got in.

(Roger Wilmut, *From Fringe to Flying Circus*, 1980)

The late sixties and early seventies were a time of world-wide student unrest and Cambridge did not escape:

There is beginning (it still has a long way to go) a movement of discontent among undergraduates ... It takes many forms: agitation against the rule requiring students to wear gowns after dark; complaint against the closing of college gates at night; resentment about the need to call on your tutor to get an exeat; pressure to include undergraduates on the college council; demand for courts of appeal against disciplinary measures.

(Eric Ashby, *Clare College Association Annual*, 1966)

As students we do not think it to our ultimate advantage to be considered as a privileged class to some degree exempt from the Law ... The authorities have tended to favour 'traditional' forms of rowdyism – Rugger Club exploits, Poppy Day hooliganism etc ... Offenders at political demonstrations, and those accused of sexual misbehaviour, have sometimes been treated much more harshly ... The question arises as to what sort of offence is committed by the undergraduate who has intercourse in his rooms. The only *regulation* which is broken is the one concerning visiting hours and we therefore recommend that this should be the only factor considered when the case is being judged. In matters of sex, the traditional Cambridge policy of lack of definition has come to seem quite inadequate; the colleges and the University must thoroughly re-examine their attitudes to this problem.

(*Student Representative Council, Report 3: Discipline*, 1963/64/65)

13 February 1970, on the back page of the 'Shilling Paper' (the journal of the Socialist Society):

GREEK FASCISTS HOLD A PROPAGANDA PARTY
ALL INVITED
7.30 PM FRIDAY 13TH
GARDEN HOUSE HOTEL

Cut out this poster, put it on a banner, and bring it to the Demo.

The party was the culmination of a Greek Week, sponsored by the Greek Tourist Office. The 'Shilling Paper' wrote:

apathy tonight will be a silent confirmation of the Junta's success in quieting international rejection of their regime and of the tourist agencies' success in misinforming Cambridge people of the situation in Greece.

About 350 students obeyed the call, of whom six were arrested by the police and a week later faced comparatively minor charges in the Magistrate's Court. But meanwhile the proctors were asked to give further names to the police and the upshot was that at the end of June at the Colchester Assizes, fifteen students faced the additional serious charges of riotous assembly and causing £2,000 worth of damage:

P.C.: I saw something lying on the sill of a broken hotel window. It appeared to me at the time to be a firework. This object was spurting out flame. The curtains were close and I had an idea they might catch light. I flicked it out of the way . . .

Det.Sgt.: Police helmets were being kicked around the garden of the hotel by demonstrators . . . in addition to hurling stones from the rockery of the hotel demonstrators were throwing things which gave off a bright flame. They were causing considerable panic . . .

Managing director of hotel: I and a hotel worker turned on a hose from an upstairs window to try to stop the demonstrators getting through the hotel doors . . .

Senior Proctor: It caused considerable resentment.

Univ. Motor Proctor: A certain amount of water came out on to the demonstrators. I would not say it was for more than a minute and there was a very small amount of water – it was more like water for watering the garden than quelling demonstrators . . .

Undergraduate A: There was no violence until a fire hose was turned on to the crowd from a window . . . The purpose of the demonstration was to indicate the position of those who wished to object to the holding of functions in Cambridge which could be interpreted as propaganda or publicity stunts of governments of which one strongly objected . . . I think there has been a serious exaggeration of the extent of the whole thing. There wasn't continuous breaking of windows. There weren't continually stones flying through the air . . . There was no one particular cheer leader. When someone thought of a slogan, they would shout it out, and if people approved they would repeat it . . .

Deputy Proctor: I saw a man throwing something. I went up to try to ask him if he was a member of the university. But I was hindered from getting to him by a group of a dozen or so young men. They didn't push me, but they stood in the way and attempted to engage me in conversation . . . I was standing in the terrace just behind, or with a row of policemen. I believe it was a brick or half-brick which struck me. I had five stitches put into my wound . . .

Undergraduate B: I heard cries of alarm. I ran forward to see what was happening and I stood on a low wall at the back of the terrace. The police line, which had been standing against the hotel, had broken and police were moving forward as individuals with truncheons . . . I noticed a stick lying on the ground and I picked it up. I wanted to use it to try to stop the front of the crowd being pushed forward into the police . . .

Undergraduate C: The police were pushing us backwards. I remember one of the policemen had his fist under my throat. I was a bit afraid I would be throttled and I moved the fist away quite gently. Then I saw three or four

[353]

policemen. They pointed at me. Then they rushed forward and took hold of me and took me inside the hotel.

Undergraduate D: I was swept into the hotel when the demonstrators surged forward. I fell over inside the hotel and I remember knocking over a table with glasses. I did not intend to knock it over . . . As I was being placed under arrest a woman came up to me and threw a drink in my face and yelled at me. Then a man – I think who was accompanying her – seized my glasses . . .

Undergraduate E: (accused of breaking a window) It was an involuntary act while off balance . . .

Proctor: One of the accused . . . urged the demonstrators to charge the (police) dogs. I told him not to be so bloody daft . . . (He agreed that during the protest some of the students had chatted to the police on the philosophy of the protest.)

P.C.: (identifying a student) In my opinion it was him, bearing in mind he had much longer hair and was of a scruffier appearance . . .

Fellow A: I went to take part in a peaceful demonstration against what I thought was the political exploitation of people in Cambridge . . .

Fellow B: There was some scuffling but I couldn't say that I saw a single act of violence.

(statements taken from The Times, The Daily Telegraph, and the Cambridge Evening News)

Eight of the students were found guilty and were given sentences ranging from 18 months to 9 months, with two sent to Borstal. The judge said the sentences would have been heavier were it not for the 'evil influence of some senior members of the university', some of whom he had seen as witnesses. This provoked an immediate letter to 'The Times' by five professors:

Each of us is well acquainted with the individual or individuals concerned in his own Faculty and strongly resent the Judge's insinuations, which we believe to be unfounded.

Later in the year the Cambridge Students' Union published a pamphlet giving their view of the affair:

What actually happened:

The intention was to picket arriving guests and listen to Marcus Dragoumis, an exiled Greek Deputy of one of the centre-left parties. A loudspeaker had been set up in a room overlooking the hotel for Dragoumis' speech . . . somebody cut the power . . . and in the freezing cold, demonstrators became restless. They began to move round to the back of the hotel . . . There were no police in the garden at all. If the demonstrators had been intent on their 'riot' this would have been the golden opportunity, for it was 20 minutes before any police arrived. However, in that time nothing more violent occurred than the chanting of slogans and the sound of people drumming on the dining room windows with their hands . . . The guests had not yet moved to the dining room. The focus of the action switched to the french windows leading to the bar, and here the first trouble occurred. Police opened the french windows from the inside to clear the immediate area and demonstrators at the back of the crowd pushed forward. The result was pressure at the front and scuffles. Someone in the hotel pointed a hose out of a first floor window drenching the demonstrators. It was very cold – some

10 degrees below freezing – and there was angry reaction as ice and stones were thrown at the window . . . A proctor was cut on the forehead, two policemen were concussed, and demonstrators were hurt. But the violence was short-lived.

In statu pupillari:

The student is required by statute (Grace 6 and 7. 3 December 1969): '. . . to pay due respect and obedience to the Vice-Chancellor, Proctors and Pro-proctors, and all who are in authority in the university'. They are required to give their names and the colleges to which they belong if asked by the Proctors, Pro-proctors, or anyone in authority. The disastrous results of what looks on paper to be an innocuous if faintly irritating regulation were shown only too clearly at the Garden House demonstration where students obeying this rule then found that their names had been passed on to the police.

> (Cambridge Students' Union, *The Cambridge Greek Affair*)

Alongside reports of the trial in the 'Cambridge Evening News':

STUDENTS SIGN ON FOR NIGHT VIGILS WITH OLD FOLK

and:

PRINCE CHARLES, B.A.

Days in the life of . . .

Sunday, 16th November 1970
Social Action Discussion 1.00 p.m. Emmanuel
Pembroke Debating – 8.00 Old Library 'Trade Union Reform must be left to the Unions'.
Labour Club 'Chemical and Biological Warfare' Tam Dalyell M.P. 8.15 Union
SOC Marxism Seminar, 'Development of Capitalism (3) Dynamics of Class' 3.00–6.00 Christ's
Madame Binh Breakfast – New Hall J.C.R. 11.00 a.m. Discussion 'Women's Liberation'

Wednesday, 19th November
Progressive Music Stereo Disco in King's 8.00
Military States – 2. Spain . . . plus a speaker from the Spanish Workers Defence Committee 8.15 King's
Cambridge Slant Group (Aquinas Society) 'The Importance of Ideology' Fisher House 8.15
C.U. Visual Art Society Bridget Riley Architecture School 8.30

> (*The Shilling Paper*)

4.25 p.m.   Learn at Porters' Lodge that (a) Master has returned from Paraguay; (b) undergraduate Y has recovered from desperate illness and is now on river with First Boat; (c) Dr. E wishes to know why the four thousand copies of Research Fellowship documents have not yet reached him; (d) undergraduate K has again assaulted landlady's husband. Telephone secretary, admitting 'nothing at this end' and hear that during my absence Headmaster of St. Jude's furious at inability to tell me in person that Head of School 'did not do himself justice in the examination'. Sir Humphrey Topsoil-Sandclay had called to ask why his son, a late developer, had not been admitted. While negotiating puddle en route for Fellows' Building am again thrust into bushes by undergraduate X (an early developer). Am told by passing Fellow that I have desecrated '*prunus subhirtella-var. autumnalis*'. On expressing surprise, am told that this means 'slightly hairy winter cherry'. Feel abashed.

4.45   Short conference with College Librarian, Garden Steward, Keeper of the Plate and Guardian of the Mulberries on pupil H, who wishes to change from Option O (iii) b. 2 to Option O (iii) b. 3, the last day for such notification having been yesterday and why did I not guess it in advance?

5.30   In attempting to circumnavigate *al fresco* conference of Radical Left (undergraduates M and N) trip over cobblestones. Steadying myself, am asked by Professorial Fellow if I have recovered from Peterhouse guest-night. Recall that undergraduate M recently broke window of building where Commonwealth Prime Minister was speaking. Ask him, amiably, to what passage in the speech he objected. He did not know, being outside the building at the time. Ask him name of Prime Minister. He does not know. Wonder if I have become a Fascist hyena.

(S. Gorley Putt, 'A Day in the Life of a Privileged Intellectual', *Christ's College Magazine*, May 1970)

One cause of unrest was expressed in a demand for greater participation in the running of the University, particularly as far as discipline was concerned. Many members of Regent House supported this view:

Grace 4 of 3 December 1969
The one issue in dispute is the proposal that junior members of the University should be eligible to fill up to two of the five places on the new Court of Discipline, which is to be a court of appeal from the Proctors for minor offences and a court of first instance for major offenders. Junior members already serve on the Courts of Discipline of some twenty other Universities in the United Kingdom. To object . . . is to imply that Cambridge undergraduates are in some way less responsible than those of other Universities.

The Grace was approved by 375 to 197 on 5 and 6 February 1970

(*University Reporter*)

On 3 February 1972 there was a sit-in in the Old Schools. The High Steward, Lord Devlin, conducted an enquiry and made a report.

The students had given in a leaflet their reasons for the occupation.

EDUCATION V. EXAMS

Three weeks ago, after discussions spanning 3 years, with dozens of student reps., scores of committees, a myriad of sub-committees and overwhelming student pressure, the Economics Faculty Board agreed to a set of proposals for reforming the Economics course which went some way towards meeting the students' demands. Last week, after grave deliberations lasting less than ten minutes, the University General Board vetoed everything out of hand. Not only were 3 years of effort and compromise totally wasted but students' feelings were treated with a studied, almost malicious, contempt.

The occupiers had problems, as the report shows:

There are no toilet facilities attached to the East Room. Its inhabitants used the public lavatories on Market Hill. This easement was interfered with by the counter-demonstrators, who allowed one-way traffic only, permitting no return. Three delegates were elected to negotiate with the Vice-Chancellor.

The students were allowed to use the Combination Room and the lavatories below, in return for accepting responsibility for any damage. They marched out on 5 February.

Lord Devlin's recommendations:

(1) a forum, such as the Senate Discussion, in which the student case can be publicly heard and debated,
(2) a student relations officer to defuse explosive situations and to sustain momentum in the detailed application of reforms agreed in principle,
(3) the publication of a 'Junior Reporter' to keep students informed about University affairs . . .
I think it necessary for the Proctors to retain all their powers of enforcement of the Disciplinary Regulations, subject to clarification of the so-called 'blanket' power given by Regulation 1(*a*). I think that they should be regarded as administrative officers only and I recommend the removal of the vestiges of their *in loco parentis* or judicial power.

(*Cambridge University Reporter*, special no. 12, 14 February 1973)

One undergraduate's comment:

The one unquestionable concrete achievement of the sit-in was obtaining the right to piss.

May 1978   After a rapid and abundant blossoming, student representation on Governing Bodies and Faculty Boards has lost its glamour and students are now just as likely as Dons to find that they have pressing engagements elsewhere and to find that they have too few candidates for the representation jobs.

(C. K. Phillips, in *Christ's College Magazine*)

The University still thought of itself as Alma Mater:

1965
The Council have given very careful consideration to the small but very difficult class of case which arises from 'nervous breakdowns' resulting from or aggravated by the imminence of a Tripos and without any physical cause sufficient to

account for the symptoms in question. They have consulted both a number of Cambridge physicians with large undergraduate practices, and two eminent London consultants, one a neurologist and the other a psychiatrist.

(Students' Handbook)

1970–1

While up at Cambridge a student may meet academic, social or personal problems. The collegiate structure of the University and the relationships between students and their Tutors, Director of Studies, Supervisors, Chaplains and other senior members usually provide a way for these problems to be overcome. However, sometimes problems arise when further counselling is required . . . When any of these professional services are consulted, whether with the Tutor's knowledge or not, there is no reference back to the Tutor, or parents, without the express permission of the student for such contact to be made.

(chapter on 'Residence and Discipline',
issued separately from Student's Handbook,
1967)

1970–1

Contraception: professional advice on any aspect of sexual behaviour, including contraception, can be obtained from general practitioners. Advice can also be obtained from . . .

1975–6

Those suffering accidents necessitating dental treatment should attend without delay. If a front tooth is dislocated and can be found, wrap it in a clean, damp cloth and report at once to a dental officer; if one reports early enough there is the possibility of reimplanting the tooth.

(University of Cambridge – Information and
Regulations)

All of a sudden, things were not the same:

In 1970 the Governing Body of Clare . . . met twice to consider the repeal of Statute 21(4) which read, 'No woman shall be admitted a member of the College either on the Foundation or otherwise.' A change in statute requires a majority of two-thirds present and voting. On both occasions the majority in favour of repeal comfortably exceeded this ratio.

(Clare College Association Annual)

In 1972 Churchill, Clare and King's Colleges became 'co-residential' and they
were followed, at various rates of urgency, by most of the other colleges.

The J.C.R. has had yet another quiet year, its tranquillity most brightly and colourfully broken by a demo – to emphasise the failure of the College to implement co-residence. [They accepted women in 1979.]

(St. Catharine's Newsletter, 1974)

1977.   We admit about 90 each year; and our firm policy is to admit those who we consider will best flourish at the College, with no preconceived ideas about their distribution by sex or subject to be read.   (Sidney Sussex Annual, 1977)

[358]

1980 (the year they accepted 98 men and 38 women).

For a College founded '. . . to LAUD and HONNEURE of SEXE FEMENINE' Queens' must have seemed remiss for the last 532 years.

(*Queens' Magazine*, 1980)

In 1975 Dame Rosemary Murray, Principal of New Hall, became the first woman Vice-Chancellor.

In 1979 Dr. Marie Axton, of Newnham College, became the first woman Proctor.

The consumer view: students began to issue their own guide books.

1973

Corpus Christi: Corpus Christi is the smallest college, and everyone knows everyone else. The atmosphere is rather introspective, and people outside tend not to know Corpus men . . . The food is quite good, and exotic dishes are often tried . . . Academic standards, measured in conventional terms, are very high . . . Gate hours are not strict but guest hours remain at 2 a.m. This can have considerable effect as it is very difficult to climb in or out.

King's: is a unique community . . . In progressive but constructive fashion, the college has discarded some of the more pointless traditions (such as guest rules, formal hall every night, the wearing of gowns) while retaining the sense of history deriving from an environment of ancient and beautiful buildings. It was in character for King's to become one of the first mixed colleges . . . King's is widely known as *the* left-wing college.

Churchill: The modern architecture is characterised by rather harsh right-angles, but the facilities are luxurious (it is after all the national monument to Sir Winston) . . . The college's recent founding has led to a 'liberal' administration. Churchill is one of the three co-residential colleges, and the rules are not severe. Gate and guest hour regulations have been abolished after intensive pressure from students, who are generally highly politically involved . . . Perhaps because newness breeds insecurity, the College places considerable emphasis on good exam results (if you don't pass you're sent down). Academic potential is stressed in the admissions policy, and therefore the proportion of public school entrants is much lower than in the rest of Cambridge, and equivalent to the norm for a provincial university.

1980

Girton: If you enjoy cycling, you would do very well to consider coming to Girton . . . The quality and variety of food has a reputation throughout the University for excellence . . . The atmosphere in college can loosely be described as friendly and relaxed.

Magdalene: is a small, relaxed college which has managed to marry the traditional with the modern in such a way as to create a splendidly idiosyncratic life and atmosphere. Spurned as the last bastion of conservatism by fresh-faced politicians from other colleges who find it difficult to accept that indifference to student politics can simply be indifference, since to them it must be Conservatism. The supposed characteristics of 'Mag. Man' are legendary within the University . . . This rare species is in essence rich and thick, and if asked to make the choice between having a Mistress or a Beagle would have to think about it . . . The reality, of course, is somewhat different as all types of people, from widely differing backgrounds come here.

Women: Don't imagine that all the colleges are going co-residential out of concern to give equal educational opportunities to women; in some colleges the major impulse is the class-lists – women do better than men in the Tripos . . . It's hardly a welcoming thought to be regarded as tripos statistic from the outset.

Other colleges have treated the impending arrival of women as though it were an invasion by aliens bearing no resemblance to the current residents. One college proposes building a separate laundry for the women because they thought the women would be affronted by the sight of men's clothing being washed. However, in the majority of cases, the change has been made calmly.

There is a great deal of myth based on the subject of interviews . . . hence some rather apocryphal stories: one prospective Cambridge undergraduate found his interviewer buried beneath his newspaper, smoking a pipe, for many minutes apparently unaware that anyone had entered the room; 'Entertain me', he eventually muttered. The candidate casually drew out a lighter and set fire to his newspaper – and won a scholarship.

(A Prospectus for Students)

Undergraduate views:

Avoid joining the Communist Party, at least until after you've been accepted. Dons still remember, with pain, the Cambridge of three or four years ago when sit-ins and demonstrations were regular features of the term. Politics is probably your only problem area – the less you have, the better.

(Prospectus for Students, 1976)

Conservative:

(In reply to a pamphlet decrying examinations):

It was also interesting to find exams as such blamed for the stress which turns otherwise completely normal and stable people into screaming psychotics. Obviously, the imminence of exams produces stress: so does the imminence of essays, practicals, job interviews, the practice of any profession, trade or employment, and . . . would you really want to be on an operating table, being treated by a surgeon, who had never been asked in a rigorous manner to demonstrate what he knew, because it might upset him?

(Cambridge University Conservative Association Newsletter, 8 June 1973)

Labour:

1977
As a student, you will have the right to vote in Cambridge, both in national and

local elections . . . In my opinion, the level of involvement of most students in the local community is disappointingly low. When canvassing in colleges during the County Council election last May, I found that the majority of students that I spoke to were completely unaware of local issues. This ignorance is understandable when one considers the circumstances of a typical student's life in Cambridge. The colleges (apart of course from the Tech.) protect him from the need to organise his life by cooking his meals, arranging social facilities and even employing someone to make his bed! Of course, this approach can help you concentrate on your academic work, but it is also claustrophobic and restricting. I suggest that you face reality and discover the world outside the lecture room and college bar – most people find the experience rewarding . . . Well, do your cleaner a favour, anyway, by making your own bed.

1975/6
Déjeuners divers sur l'herbe:
Other meetings.

Mondays.	Anti-discrimination Lunch Chetwynd Room, King's 1.00 p.m.
	Amnesty Lunch, Christ's New J.C.R. 1.00 p.m.
Wednesdays	Broad Left Lunch Trinity O.C.R. 1.00 p.m.
	Survival Lunch, Kennedy Room, Union Society 1.00 p.m.
Thursdays	Programmatic Lunch, Trinity O.C.R. 1.00 p.m.
Fridays	Grants and Anti-Cuts Lunch, Trinity O.C.R. 1.00 p.m.
	Third World First Lunch, Christ's New J.C.R. 1.00 p.m.

Tuesday 9 March 2.00 p.m. Picket of University Library for Library Syndicate meeting on possibility of re-opening the U.L. in the evenings.

> *(Cambridge Organisation of Labour Students Handbooks)*

6 March 1982
Last week we urged all students to demonstrate against cuts, but we have never urged anyone to organise a sit-in at Lady Mitchell Hall . . . Those who took such action do the students' case against the cuts nothing but harm. Occupying a University building, when the University is the victim, not the perpetrator, of the cuts, seems highly inappropriate.

> *(Stop Press, the undergraduate journal)*

Conservation areas:

1.

'Evening, Arthur,' said Skullion condescendingly.

'Evening,' said Arthur.

'Going off home?' Skullion enquired.

'Got something for you,' Arthur told him, leaning confidentially over the counter.

Skullion looked up. Arthur's attendance at High Table was a source of much of his information about the College. He rose and came over to the counter. 'Oh, ah,' he said.

'They're in a tizzwhizz tonight,' Arthur said. 'Proper tizzwhizz.'

'Go on,' said Skullion encouragingly.

'Bursar came into dinner all flushed and flummoxy and the Dean's got them high spots on his cheeks he gets when his gander's up and the Tutor don't eat his soup. Not like him to turn up his soup,' Arthur said. Skullion grunted his agreement. 'So I know something's up.' Arthur paused for effect. 'Know what it is?' he asked.

Skullion shook his head. 'No. What is it?' he said.

Arthur smiled. 'Master's called a College Council for tomorrow. The Bursar said it wasn't convenient and the Master said to call it just the same and they don't like it. They don't like it at all. Put them off their dinner it did, the new Master acting all uppity like that, telling them what to do just when they thought they'd got him where they wanted him. Bursar said he'd told the Master they hadn't got the money for all the changes he has in mind and the Master seemed to have taken it, but then he rings the Bursar up and tells him to call the meeting.'

'Can't call a College Council all of a sudden,' Skullion said, 'Council meets on the first Thursday of every month.'

'That's what the Dean said and the Tutor. But the Master wouldn't have it. Got to be tomorrow. Bursar rang him up and said Dean and Tutor wouldn't attend like they'd told him and Master said that was all right by him but that the meeting would be tomorrow whether they were there or not.' Arthur shook his head mournfully over the Master's wilfulness. 'It ain't right all this telling people what to do.'

Skullion scowled at him. 'The Master come to dinner?' he asked.

'No,' said Arthur, 'he don't stir from the Lodge. Just telephones his orders to the Bursar.' He glanced significantly at the switchboard in the corner. Skullion nodded pensively.

'So he's going ahead with his changes,' he said at last.

2.

Skullion went back into the Porter's Lodge.

'Going to supper,' he told the under-porter and trudged across the Court to the kitchen. He went down the stone stairs to the kitchen where the Chef had laid a table for two in his pantry. It was hot and Skullion took off his coat before sitting down.

'Snowing again they tell me,' said the Chef taking his seat.

Skullion waited until a young waiter with a gaping mouth had brought the dishes before saying anything.

'Dean's gone to see the General,' he said finally.

'Has he now?' said the Chef, helping himself to the remains of the poached salmon.

'Council meeting this afternoon,' Skullion continued.

'So I heard.'

Skullion shook his head.

'You aren't going to like this,' he said. 'The Master's changes aren't going to suit your book, I can tell you.'

'Never supposed they would, Mr. Skullion.'

'Worse than I expected, Chef, much worse.' Skullion took a mouthful of Ockfener Herrenberg 1964 before going on.

'Self-service in Hall,' he said mournfully.

The Chef put down his knife and fork. 'Never,' he growled.

'It's true. Self-service in Hall.'

'Over my dead body,' said the Chef. 'Over my bloody dead body.'

'Women in College too.'

'What? Living in College?'

'That's it. Living in College.'

'That's unnatural, Mr. Skullion. Unnatural.'

'You don't have to tell me that, Chef. You don't have to tell me. Unnatural and immoral. It isn't right, Chef, it's downright wicked.'

'And self-service in Hall,' the Chef muttered. 'What's the world coming to ...'

(Tom Sharpe, Porterhouse Blue, 1974)

Benefactions of all kinds, some of dimensions undreamt of by the early founders, have continued to be made to the University and to the colleges. Some of the benefactors are remembered only at the annual Founders' Days, where their gifts are meticulously catalogued and their donors remembered in prayer, some by the names of professorships, buildings, even colleges. The recent past has been one of refurbishing and modernising, of demolitions which to some have seemed wanton, and of new buildings, some praised, some condemned:

1966 Improvements are being made in the provision of lavatory and washing facilities on various staircases: the college takes the view that some abatement of the rigours of life is not a sign of decadence ... Elsewhere work is proceeding to strengthen the floor of the Parker Library, to eliminate the dry rot unhappily discovered to be rampant on I staircase (this has at last enabled I.6 to be re-decorated and for the traditional chocolate mousse colour on its walls to be replaced or at any rate concealed).

(Corpus Christi College Association Letter)

1971 St. Catharine's cafeteria system introduced.

(St. Catharine's Newsletter)

1972 We have continued with the programme of putting bathrooms into staircases with the result that there are now only three staircases without them.

(Peterhouse Magazine)

1973 ... at the risk of wallowing in Betjemanesque nostalgia, I can't help recalling the malodorous delights of Falcon Yard ... the rickety stairs and smoky warrens of the Footlights and Cruising Club where wonky pianos and flat jokes seemed less awful in the claustrophobic gloom ...

The jewel in this tarnished diadem was, no one may deny, the immortal Lion. The Lion was more than a pub or a hotel. It was a kind of marmoreal edifice, a sarcophagus of past Cambridge.

(S.M.S., Christ's College Magazine)

21 September 1975 The new Lion's Yard shopping centre has turned out to be as bad as opponents of the scheme many years ago predicted it would be ... Where there was a picturesque townscape, narrow winding alleys, there is now a lumbering, crudely trendy composition of standard architectural units; the slow curve of the south side of Petty Cury is replaced by a crass façade on two straight lines.

(Cambridge Review)

43. St. John's: the Cripps Building, 1981

St. John's

Cripps Building, 1963–7 by Powell & Moya, is a masterpiece . . . The building is of reinforced concrete, faced with Portland stone, and has bronze windows. It is four storeys high and has in addition a number of penthouses. One approaches it in studied meanness through the middle of New Court. The surprise is supreme. The building as first seen forms a turfed court with the dreary back of New Court. The E side is half open to the river. The Building only projects that far and turns E to meet the river with its thin end, just enough to make an explicit statement, not enough to prevail over New Court, the Bridge of Sighs, and Lutyens behind the weeping willows at Magdalene . . . The broken line of this long ribbon of a building is masterly. It is brought home with great intensity by the covered promenade which runs all along, mostly with inhabited space one side, but once – in a strategic position – open to both sides . . .

The Court between the new building and the School of Pythagoras is the second great surprise. Wandering along W from the court N of New Court one has no idea of this other court, or indeed of the building continuing beyond the SW–NE range. In the link between the two parts the Bin Brook is bridged, and here, close enough to the Common Room, is a pool, ready for the mooring of punts.   (Nikolaus Pevsner, *Cambridgeshire*, 1970)

Faculty of Arts, Sidgwick Avenue

The three sides of the long court, with premises for Medieval and Modern Languages, Slavonic Studies, Phonetics, and the Faculty Library, are Portland-

44. The History Faculty, Sidgwick Avenue, 1980

stone-faced on a recessed concrete cloister, mostly open to both sides. The grey concrete cloister has piquant white saucer-domes. The two upper storeys have systems of fenestration equally piquant – and there is the rub. However much most of the windows in position and size correspond to the function and importance of the room (and this is in any case not true of all of them), the visual effect is wilful or perhaps only playful, or one might be permitted to call it witty. This is what must have maddened the architect of the Faculty of History, who, through the gap between these three ranges and the longer wholly detached W range, seems to be shouting rude words at the Arts Faculty. Don't think, he seems to imply, you can play with architecture ... Perhaps, if Sir Hugh Casson had not been so playful, James Stirling might not have been so rude. People in the last ten years have spoken about anti-art. Here – and only here at Cambridge – is anti-architecture.

(Pevsner, *Cambridgeshire*)

Kettle's Yard

Kettle's Yard is a house and it is situated in Cambridge and is part of the University there. It might be called a museum, for there are a great many pictures there and much sculpture; but there are also a lot of pebbles ... There are shells too ... I am constantly amazed by the beauty of form and space, the glitter of light on surfaces, almost the music of such a composition as this ...

In 1957 it was four little deserted slum houses with an alleyway running

45. Interior of Kettle's Yard, 1982, the extension

between them. They were scooped out and turned into one house and the alley-way was bridged . . . as the cottages became a place, we began to invite people in. They came, cautiously, one at a time – perhaps two, but as the years swept by more people came . . . By this time we had to build an extension, designed by Sir Leslie Martin, and I quickly furnished it . . . Kettle's Yard is unlike a museum, for suddenly you find yourself looking at a Ben Nicholson or a Henry Moore in a bedroom or bathroom . . . There is a great deal of sculpture around the house by that great French artist Henry Gaudier-Brzeska. [The house was presented to the University in 1966.]

(Jim Ede, *Kettle's Yard*, 1974)

Robinson College has been granted diplomatic recognition by the University Library, in the form of a box of its own for its members' tickets. All that is required for the University to follow the Librarian's forward looking gesture is for the College to acquire a student or two. Meanwhile the scene of devastation of Herschel Road is clearly visible from the Library tower, if not from the roof of King's College Chapel.

(*Cambridge Review*, 28 January 1977)

THE ARK*

Our city was once a real country town . . . Something of the country, indeed,

[* The Museum of Classical Archaeology (now moved to the Sidgwick Avenue site).]

46. Robinson College, 1982

reached up to every college along the Backs. But here, by the Mill, was the perfect transition. One's studies over, one could slip down Little St. Mary's Lane, choose a punt and a pleasant companion, and glide past an old creeper-covered inn to a green world seemingly hundreds of miles away. I would tingle at the shock of sunlight after the darkness of libraries – and all not five minutes from the Ark! Yet how brightly Cambridge welcomed the returning truant! The meadow of buttercups, the friendly line of little cottages (ill replaced by the gaunt and pretentious Centre) and even the steeple of the Congregational Church – a very professional piece of architecture, if the truth be told – all 'composed' a vista of memorable brightness and beauty . . .

What do we see today? An assortment of buildings which, for individual ugliness and mutual incongruity, would be unworthy of modern North Oxford or even the North Circular Road: in the middle, a permanent pit, complete with hoardings and rusty base metal, on the site of the old creeper-covered inn: and the blank back wall of the Ark, a granary wall of uncertain date, the only object on which the eye can rest for a moment of pleasure . . .

When that overwrought student was sentenced for throwing his pebble at the Garden House, the Judge and the Press dilated with characteristic stateliness upon the wickedness of subversives and the decadence of our 'youth'. But I must confess that, surveying this corner of Cambridge and the tragedies of its recent history, I find the offence of the 'Garden House Rioters' and even its occasion, a protest against the Greek colonels, sinks into littleness and meanness

[367]

compared with the colossal guilt of all the Boards, Committees, Bursars, Benefactors and Building Tycoons, who found our paradise, and left it a nightmare –
who expelled Nature with a fork and made sure that she could never return.

(Hugh Plommer, *Cambridge Review*,
20 October 1978)

*Among the new buildings were new laboratories: there were the new chemical
laboratories in Lensfield Road in 1956, the MRC Laboratory of Molecular
Biology in the New Addenbrookes complex in 1962 and the New Cavendish in
1973, built in west Cambridge near the Institute of Theoretical Astronomy and
the Department of Geodesy and Geophysics. The University was spreading
out to the periphery of Cambridge.*

In 1971 a 5-km radio telescope was built:

With the advent of electronic computers new concepts in radio telescope design
became feasible and in Cambridge we adopted a synthesis principle ... The
essential feature of the synthesis method is the use of a number of small radio
telescopes, connected together in interferometric pairs, to simulate precisely the
action of a giant radio telescope covering the same area as that over which the
small dishes can be moved ... Under Sir Martin Ryle's inspired leadership and
skilful design, the method has been a brilliant success, and after some initial
scepticism beyond these shores it is now widely accepted in all major radio
observatories of the world. It was Dr. Beeching's closure of the railway line
between Cambridge and Oxford that provided us with a suitable site on which to
construct the most sophisticated of our synthesis telescopes – the 5-km telescope,
and with this we had our first really clear indications of the structure of radio
galaxies.

(Anthony Hewish, 'Radio Galaxies', in
Proceedings of the Royal Institution, vol. 53,
1981)

*In 1975 Ryle, together with Professor Hewish, was awarded the Nobel Prize.
To mark the award the Mayor, Jack Warren, arranged a reception in honour
of Cambridge's fifteen Nobel Laureates in residence. In 1980 one of these
Laureates, Frederick Sanger, received a second Nobel Prize, the only man to
have achieved this:*

In 1962 I moved to their newly built Laboratory of Molecular Biology in Cambridge, together with M. F. Perutz's unit from the Cavendish Laboratory, which
included F. H. C. Crick, J. C. Kendrew, H. E. Huxley and A. Klug. In this
atmosphere I became interested in nucleic acids. Although at the time it seemed
to be a major change from proteins to nucleic acids, the concern with the basic
principle of 'sequencing' remained the same ... This work has not been done
single-handed and it owes much to the excellent collaborators I have had. Many
of these have been students and postdoctoral fellows spending a few years in the
laboratory and bringing their experience and ideas with them.

(Sanger, autobiographical note in *Les Prix
Nobel*)

47. Radio telescopes, 1981

Among other important developments have been the setting up in 1975 of a School of Clinical Medicine on the New Addenbrookes site. The British Antarctic Survey has moved to Cambridge, conveniently near the Scott Polar Research Institute which has done important work in techniques such as radio-echo sounding and the understanding of the internal structure, flow and stability beneath the ice sheet.

Of great local interest is the Science Park to the North of Cambridge:

(in the late 60s) a University Committee with Sir Nevill Mott (then Cavendish Professor of Experimental Physics) [Nobel Prize winner 1982] as Chairman, recommended a moderate expansion of science-based industry in close proximity to the City, to take maximum advantage of the concentration here of scientific expertise, equipment and libraries and to increase feed-back of all kinds from such industry into the Cambridge science complex. Trinity College was impressed with the importance of the idea because it had a long tradition of science and technology from Newton onwards. Trinity men were involved in helping to start several of the major local science-based companies ... The Cambridge Science Park is at Milton Road, because Trinity had a 140 acre block of land there, most of which they or their predecessors had owned since 1443 ...

The first occupier was Laser Scan, created by physicists here at the Cavendish. The essence of all their machines is that a laser light beam linked to a computer scans to and fro across a photograph on a plan or a map, picks up the information there contained . . . stores it in the computer, and can there analyse it.

(John Bradfield, 'The Cambridge Science Park', in the *Magazine of the Cambridge University Industrial Society*, 1980)

It is science in all its aspects which makes headlines for Cambridge, although most people have heard of the Faculty of Economics if only because of the, frequently gloomy, six-monthly prognostications by the 'Cambridge Economists'. Only now and again do other faculties receive a mention in the national press:

Let Dons delight to bark and bite:

Dons dispute as children squabble, to test out and develop their muscles. If the English Faculty at Cambridge is in uproar, as yesterday's meeting of bewildered students suggests, that is not in itself matter for censure, nor should outsiders let themselves be unduly diverted over the tumult which may surround the germination of a new idea. Much more reason for concern if Cambridge showed signs of slumbering asleep in port, like late tempestuous Bentley in *The Dunciad*. But it cannot be denied that the ruffling of gowns at the English Faculty has all the ingredients of a first-rate academic spectacle, with resignations, censure motions, political jibes and malicious whispers in full flight – with its own distinctive shibboleth of 'structuralism' – and even with some genuine issues concerning the teaching of English half-lost in the furore . . . Structuralism is a red herring, though one that is fun to chew on. Peering beneath the rhetoric at the structures, we may guess that much of the force of the dispute comes from a sense of insecurity and discontent in the faculty generally. There are also signs of personal friction.

(*The Times*, 24 January 1981)

A flourish of frivolity:

Graffiti:

Exams kill by degrees
Are your finals the end or are your ends the finals?
Are you dead or just revising?

Cats:

The College is well known in the back alleys of Cambridge as a five star Rest and Recuperation Centre for the embattled cats of the city. Not so many years ago the editor was the proud patron (cats would surely disdain any right to be 'owned') of a ginger puss who mated noisily with the virile black Tom then living off immoral gleanings from the College Kitchens. Before they eloped to the great world beyond the Drummer Street Bus Station she bore him a massive litter of seven one evening in the undergraduates reading room during Top of the Pops – the only occasion when a student has actually fainted to the strains of Mick Jagger.

(S.M.S. in *Christ's College Magazine*, May 1972)

[370]

Mallards:

1972   This year a mallard with a proper sense of place and occasion nested in April and May under the mulberry tree in the Master's garden. She was escorted with her ten ducklings at the appropriate time by a mixed cohort of Fellows and undergraduates, via Free School Lane and Botolph Lane, across Trumpington Street and down Mill Lane to the water beyond the weir where a launch was successfully completed.

(Corpus Christi College Association Letter)

Real ale:

A Guide to the Beers, Bars and Pubs of Cambridge

For the new arrival in Cambridge, a wide selection of beers are on offer. In addition to the familiar Watney, Whitbread and Bass Charrington, you will find your College bar and local pubs serving Greene King, Tolly Cobbold and, if you're lucky, Charles Wells, Adnams, Ruddles and Sam Smiths too. This could be your first introduction to 'Real Ale', a valuable part of your Cambridge curriculum.

(Cambridge Organisation of Labour Students Handbook, 1977)

Going up:

St. John's Chapel . . . is almost as high as King's, but is aesthetically more philistine. Rising from a cluster of buildings, it is basically a large square tower, with four corner pinnacles. The whole effect is singularly unattractive. But it would be wrong to judge the climb by analysing the architectural form of the building. The beauty of the chapel lies essentially in its climbing. It is a climber's building and a climber's climb . . .

King's College Porter's Lodge . . . A strenuous climb, particularly on the hands, in an exciting position. Few people have been known to finish it without arousing some interest from below.

(Hederatus, *Cambridge Nightclimbing*, 1970)

Going down:

The Editor of last year's Journal referred . . . to 'Cambridge's crippling distance from any major caving area' . . . The gargantuan creative and self-expressive urges of 20 to 30 dedicated cavers are, for 85% of the term, left without a resurgence. The result is a dangerous and potentially destructive flood . . . the more introverted members of the Club have tended to become quiet and listless – rather like the pool formed at the entrance to swildons when the stream backs up – calm but dangerous. These tragic creatures can be seen drifting aimlessly from manhole-cover to sewage-pipe swinging a couple of well-polished krabs on the end of a bright yellow waistlength . . .

A select surveying party was next sent to the H.Q. of Cambridge caving – the Jesus Coll. Bar where a couple of enticing holes had been noticed at roof-level, at the top of three parallel pillars. This time an attempt was made to free-climb up to them, and a sporting back-and-foot brought Jont to the orifices. Unfortunately a short squeeze led straight back into the main passage and the other aperture proved to be an identical oxbow . . .

[371]

'I 3' staircase of Downing College's Kenney Court proved disappointingly trivial . . . the Grecian pillars of the Pitt Club in Jesus Lane proved rather more of a challenge, and, to date, only six people have succeeded. They widen towards the top and the classic route involves keeping one foot on the ground all the time. The right-hand side is slightly wider than the left and the bus-queue is usually very amused.

> (J. Leach, 'Getting Tight in Cambridge', in *Cambridge Underground, the Journal of the Cambridge University Caving Club,* 1972)

In 1982 most universities, Cambridge included, were talking about 'cuts':

Three headlines in 'Stop Press' (the undergraduate journal):

MUSEUM TO CLOSE?
FITZWILLIAM MUSEUM UNDER PRESSURE

WELFARE SLASHED
AXE POISED OVER STUDENT FACILITIES

MORE DONS HEAD FOR THE DOLE QUEUE
NEW REDUNDANCY THREAT FOR DONS

Prince Philip was installed as Chancellor of the University in June 1977. An Esquire Bedell recalls:

As his first procession left the Old Schools to parade round the Senate House Yard to the Senate House – no Chancellor! He had popped off to inspect the butter-measure part of the insignia of the Junior Proctor carried by his Constable. And as the procession emerged from the Senate House after the ceremony in the pouring rain, he said to the Bedells, indicating his gold-braided gown, – 'I hope this thing doesn't rust.'

> (Philip Sinker, 'The Esquire Bedells', in *Cambridge,* magazine of the Cambridge Society, no. 8, 1981)

Colleges, foundations and societies which have been given 'approved' status by the University since 1596

Downing College	1800
Girton College[a]	1873
Newnham College[b]	1875
Selwyn College	1882
New Hall	1954
Churchill College	1960
Darwin College (graduates only)	1964
Lucy Cavendish College	1965
Fitzwilliam College[c]	1966
Clare Hall (graduates only)	1966
Hughes Hall (graduates only)	1968
Wolfson College[d] (graduates only)	1973
St. Edmund's House (graduates only)	1975
Homerton College[e]	1977
Robinson College	1977

There are also the following theological colleges:

Ridley Hall	1877
Westcott House	1881
Wesley House	1921
Westminster College and the Cheshunt College Foundation[f]	1967

[a] Previously at Hitchin, 1869.
[b] First students at 74 Regent Street, Cambridge in 1871.
[c] Previously Fitzwilliam House, founded 1869.
[d] Originally University College, founded 1965.
[e] Founded 1695, moved to Cambridge in 1894; a college of education.
[f] Westminster College was founded in 1844 and moved to Cambridge in 1899. Cheshunt College was founded in 1768 and moved to Cambridge in 1905. The two colleges amalgamated in 1967.

Undergraduate numbers by subject

	1980–81				1981–82			
	Men	Women	Total	%	Men	Women	Total	%
Archaeology and Anthropology	97	97	194	2.0	95	90	185	1.9
Architecture	96	35	131	1.4	88	31	119	1.2
Anglo-Saxon, Norse, and Celtic	17	25	42	0.4	14	16	30	0.3
Chemical Engineering	90	4	94	1.0	94	12	106	1.1
Classics	177	96	273	2.9	166	108	274	2.8
Computer Science	89	12	101	1.1	104	12	116	1.2
Economics	380	85	465	4.9	384	86	470	4.8
Education	21	221	242	2.5	32	217	249	2.6
Engineering	739	54	793	8.3	746	55	801	8.2
English	392	297	689	7.3	358	334	692	7.1
Electrical Sciences	50	2	52	0.6	57	1	58	0.6
Geography	191	114	305	3.2	177	123	300	3.1
History of Art	38	19	57	0.6	30	33	63	0.6
History	489	198	687	7.2	492	224	716	7.4
Land Economy	78	21	99	1.0	67	28	95	1.0
Law	558	210	768	8.1	578	224	802	8.3
Mathematics	656	107	763	8.0	677	99	776	8.0
Medicine	540	274	814	8.5	535	286	821	8.5
Modern and Medieval Languages	284	281	565	5.9	261	320	581	6.0
Music	86	36	122	1.3	88	39	127	1.3
Natural Sciences	1,219	390	1,609	16.9	1,254	402	1,656	17.1
Oriental Studies	32	26	58	0.6	28	27	55	0.6
Philosophy	75	18	93	1.0	66	18	84	0.9
Production Engineering	29	3	32	0.3	42	7	49	0.5
Social and Political Sciences	50	30	80	0.8	46	35	81	0.8
Theology and Religious Studies	87	33	120	1.3	80	30	110	1.1
Veterinary Medicine	179	93	272	2.9	178	113	291	3.0
Totals	6,739	2,781	9,520	100.0	6,737	2,970	9,707	100.0

(*Cambridge University Reporter*, 20 August 198)

Acknowledgements

The editors and publisher gratefully acknowledge permission to reproduce copyright material from the following in this book:

N. Annan: *TLS* review of A. Boyle's *The Climate of Treason* (7 December 1979). Reprinted by permission of *The Times Literary Supplement*.

John Aubrey: *Lives of Eminent Persons*, ed. Anthony Powell. Reprinted by permission of Cresset Press.

Ernest Barker: *Age and Youth*. Reprinted by permission of Oxford University Press..

Cecil Beaton: *Diaries 1922–39. The Wandering Years*. Reprinted by permission of Weidenfeld & Nicolson Ltd and the author's Literary Executor.

Quentin Bell (ed.): *Julian Bell. Essays, Poems and Letters*. Reprinted by permission of the author's literary estate and the Hogarth Press.

Daphne Bennett: *King Without a Crown*. Reprinted by permission of Daphne Bennett.

J. Berryman: '*Transit*'. *Love and Fame*. Reprinted by permission of Farrar, Strauss & Giroux Inc. and Faber & Faber Ltd.

Rupert Brooke: *Letters*, ed. Sir Geoffrey Keynes. Reprinted by permission of Faber & Faber Ltd.

The Cambridge Review have given permission to quote from: N. Annan (26 November 1960); H. S. Bennett (10 June 1944); Cambridge Collotypes IV (3 March 1962); Quiller Couch (27 November 1936); Hugh Plommer (20 October 1978); John Hayward (2 December 1939); Alison Ravetz (24 February 1962); John Saltmarsh (14 October 1939).

Sarah Campion: *Father*. Reprinted by permission of Michael Joseph Ltd.

G. Crane: *Girton Memories 1919–48*. Reprinted by permission of the Mistress and Fellows of Girton College.

Richard Crossman: *Diaries*. Reprinted by permission of Hamish Hamilton Ltd.

Brooke Crutchley: *To Be a Printer*. Reprinted by permission of The Bodley Head Ltd.

H. C. Darby: *Medieval Cambridgeshire*. Reprinted by permission of the Oleander Press.

J. S. Diekhoff: *Milton on Himself*. Reprinted by permission of Oxford University Press.

W. L. Falkner, 'Bursar's Clerk'. Reprinted by permission of the Master, Fellows and Scholars of Christ's College.

R. Fellows: *Railways to Cambridge*. Reprinted by permission of the Oleander Press.

P. Fitzgerald: *The Knox Brothers*. Reprinted by permission of Macmillan, London and Basingstoke.

F. Partridge: *Memories*. Reprinted by permission of Anthony Sheil Associates Ltd and Victor Gollancz Ltd.

Max Perutz in *Acta Crystallographica* (March 1970). Reprinted by permission of the author.

Max Perutz: 'Origins of Molecular Biology' (31 January 1980). Reprinted by permission of the *New Scientist*.

N. Pevsner: *Cambridgeshire*. Reprinted by permission of Penguin Books Ltd.

J. H. Plumb (ed.): *Studies in Social History*. Reprinted by permission of the Longman Group Ltd.

K. Raine: *The Land Unknown*. Reprinted by permission of Hamish Hamilton Ltd.

G. Rees: *Brief Encounters*. Reprinted by permission of the author's literary estate and Chatto and Windus Ltd.

I. A. Richards: *Essays in His Honour*. Reprinted by permission of Oxford University Press.

Bertrand Russell: *Portraits from Memory* and *The Autobiography*. Reprinted by permission of Allen & Unwin Publishers Ltd.

George Santayana: *My Host the World*. Reprinted by permission of Cresset Press.

T. Sharpe: *Porterhouse Blue*. Reprinted by permission of Martin Secker & Warburg Ltd.

C. P. Snow: 'Rutherford and the Cavendish'. Reprinted by permission of Methuen London.

C. P. Snow: *Variety of Men*. Reprinted by permission of Curtis Brown Group Ltd and Macmillan, London and Basingstoke.

E. W. Swanton: *Follow On*. Reprinted by permission of William Collins Sons & Co. Ltd and John Farquharson Ltd.

G. M. Trevelyan: *Autobiography*. Reprinted by permission of the Longman Group Ltd.

R. Wilmut: *From Fringe to Flying Circus*. Reprinted by permission of Associated Book Publishers Ltd.

Virginia Woolf: *Jacob's Room, The Letters, 1929–31* (vol. IV), and *A Room of One's Own*. Leonard Woolf: *Sowing*. Reprinted by permission of the author's literary estate the Hogarth Press, and Harcourt Brace Jovanovich Inc.

Index of writers and major characters

(The index does not include the names of historians, biographers etc. where they are quoting diaries, memoirs or letters: these are included under the names of the original writers.)

Le Keux, John, 188
Lemberg, Max Rudolf, 317
Leslie, Shane, 271, 300
Lever, Thomas, 33, 40–1
Liveing, G. D., 305–6
Lloyd, Anna, 233–4
Lloyd, Geoffrey, 345–6
Lloyd, Sir Nathaniel, 151
Lort, William, 167
Lowe, Robert, 102–3
Lucas, F. L., 164–5
Lydgate, John, 1
Lytton, Edward G. E. L., Bulwer-Lytton, 1st Baron, 171, 202–3

Maberley, F. H., 177–8
Macalister, A., 136
Macaulay, Thomas Babington, 1st Baron 42, 175–6, 185–8, 202–3
Macaulay, Rose, 267, 297, 302
Macaulay, W. H., 302
McCarthy, Justin, 214
Macdonnell, A. G., 311
McKellen, Ian, 350–1
Maclean, Donald, 319
McTaggart, James, 250, 273–4, 279, 284
Mair, John, 31
Malcolm, Norman, 307
Manchester, 2nd Earl of, 88
Mansel, Lort, Bp., 165, 168,
Margaret, the Lady, see Beaufort
Marlowe, Christopher, 52–3, 59
Marsh, Edward, 255, 272, 274, 276
Marshall, Mrs. Alfred, 234
Mary Tudor, Queen, 40–2
Masters, R., 105
Mather, Cotton, 74
Maurice, F. D., 199
Maxwell, James Clerk, 248
Mede, Joseph, 64–5, 71, 74–5, 81–2
Mere, John, 43–4
Merivale, Dean, 174
Mildmay, Sir Walter, 49
Miller, Edmund, 127
Miller, Jonathan, 351
Milner-White, E., 305, 327
Milnes, Richard Monckton, see Houghton
Milton, John, 62, 68–9, 78–9, 181, 187
Monk, J. H., 124, 126, 129, 131, 150
Monmouth, Duke of, 104
Monsarrat, Nicholas, 323–4
Moore, G. E., 259, 274–5
More, Henry, 73
Morell, Thomas, 147
Morrison, J. S., 338
Moses, Serjeant, 115
Mount Charles, Lord, 173
Muggeridge, Malcolm, 350
Munby, Arthur, 240–1

Munby, A. N. L., 348–9
Myers, F. W. H., 212–13, 242

Nabokov, V. V., 299–300
Nashe, Thomas, 34, 50–2
Needham, Joseph, 289, 292–4
Neville, Thomas, 81
Newcastle, Thomas Pelham Holles, Duke of, 149, 152–3
Newton, Alfred, 214
Newton, Humphrey, 122
Newton, Sir Isaac, 121–3, 125, 128, 135, 137, 180–1
Newton, Alderman Samuel, 92, 103, 105–6
Nichols, John, 131, 151–2
Nicholson, 'Maps', 191–3
Nicolson, Harold, 270, 303, 331–2, 341
Nix, Richard, Bp., 39
Nixon, J. E., 272
Norris, Gerald, 226
North, Dr. John, 98, 101, 118
North, Roger, 96, 101, 118
Northumberland, John Dudley, Duke of 40–1
Nowell, Dr. Laurence, 18

Oates, Titus, 99
Ogden, C. K., 282–3, 287, 291
Oley, Rev. Barnaby, 84, 112, 118–19
Oliphant, Mark, 315
Oughtred, William, 64, 99

Paley, William, 142
Palmer, E. H., 232
Parker, Matthew, Abp., 20–1, 46
Parker, M. T., 321–2
Parr, Queen Katherine, 20
Partridge, Frances, 273, 288, 290, 300, 302
Paston, Lady Katherine, 66–7
Peacham, Henry, 32, 67
Peachell, J., 95, 104–5, 109
Peacock, George, 209
Peel, Sir Robert, 196
Pell, Albert, 215, 220, 233
Pembroke, Countess of, 16
Pepys, Samuel, 107–9
Perne, Andrew, 27, 40, 44, 52
Perutz, Max, 316–17, 342
Pevsner, Nikolaus, 364–5
Phelps, Dr. Robert, 252, 273
Philby, Kim, 319
Philips, Ambrose, 63, 71
Phillips, C. K., 357
Phillips, M. Mann, 326
Pigou, A. C., 282, 306
Plath, Sylvia, 340
Plommer, Hugh, 366–8